The Battle for Kyiv

The Battle for Kyiv

The Fight for Ukraine's Capital

Christopher A Lawrence
The Dupuy Institute

FRONTLINE BOOKS

First published in Great Britain in 2023 by
Frontline Books
An imprint of Pen & Sword Books Limited
Yorkshire – Philadelphia

ISBN 978 1 39904 848 4

A CIP catalogue record for this book is
available from the British Library

Typeset by Mac Style
Printed in the UK by CPI Group (UK) Ltd, Croydon, CR0 4YY.

Pen & Sword Books Limited incorporates the imprints of After
the Battle, Atlas, Archaeology, Aviation, Discovery, Family History,
Fiction, History, Maritime, Military, Military Classics, Politics,
Select, Transport, True Crime, Air World, Frontline Publishing, Leo
Cooper, Remember When, Seaforth Publishing, The Praetorian Press,
Wharncliffe Local History, Wharncliffe Transport, Wharncliffe True
Crime and White Owl.

For a complete list of Pen & Sword titles please contact

PEN & SWORD BOOKS LIMITED
47 Church Street, Barnsley, South Yorkshire, S70 2AS, England
E-mail: enquiries@pen-and-sword.co.uk
Website: www.pen-and-sword.co.uk
or
PEN AND SWORD BOOKS
1950 Lawrence Rd, Havertown, PA 19083, USA
E-mail: uspen-and-sword@casematepublishers.com
Website: www.penandswordbooks.com

Nicholas Krawciw was born on 28 November 1935 in Lvov, then part of Poland. His father was a journalist, poet and editor who was active in promoting Ukrainian nationalism. His mother was a teacher. In September 1939, the Soviet Union occupied Lvov as part of the pact made between Joseph Stalin of the Soviet Union and Adolf Hitler, the Chancellor of Germany. Before the Soviet Army took over this area, his father fled to German-held Krakow, Poland as he knew he was a marked man. The Soviet Union had already arrested and executed his sister and cousin while they were touring in the Soviet Union as part of a musical company.[1] The rest of family was held up because young Nicholas became seriously ill with flu. Therefore, he, along with his mother and his younger sister, remained behind for the time being. His father then arranged for them to be transported at night across the Sian River into German-occupied Poland. As they were rowing across the river, Soviet border guards intercepted the group and young Nicholas came under machinegun fire. He was already on the opposite shore, but as he said, "he froze under fire." His family pulled him to safety.

The family was reunited in Czechoslovakia, but they were again separated as both his father and mother were drafted into labor under the German "Third Reich." The family was reunited in Berlin in 1941 but their kitchen was destroyed in 1943 during an American daytime bombing of the city. They were in the bomb shelter at the time. To get out from underneath the Allied bombings, his mother volunteered the family to work as farm laborers, even though they were not farmers, but educated urbanites. They ended up in Bavaria in March 1944, but without their father, who remained behind in Berlin.

The German farmer, when he realized that Nicolas's mother was a teacher, instead insisted that she spend her time educating her two young children and did not employ the family as field hands. Nicholas was home schooled in Bavaria over the next year, sheltered by this German family. In 1945, the United States Army liberated the area, but not before Nicholas had come under American artillery fire during their approach. The family was reunited with his father after the war in the fall of 1945. He had spent months migrating across war-torn Germany to join them.

Living in refugee camps after the war, Nicholas Krawciw become involved in a boy scout troop run by Americans, which ended up defining the rest of his life. In 1949, Nicholas Krawciw and his family emigrated to the United States. They then started their American life in Philadelphia. Enamored with the militaries which had already machinegunned, bombed and shelled him, Nicholas Krawciw spent his high school years at Bordentown Military Institute in Trenton, New Jersey, graduating as the salutatorian. His education was paid for by a school loan that took him over a decade to pay back. He then attended the U.S. Military Academy at West Point. He was second in command in the West Point Class of 1959.

Nicholas Krawciw made his career in the United States Army, serving two tours in Vietnam in 1962–3 and 1968–9. He was seriously wounded in 1963.[2] During his time convalescing, he became the co-inventor of composite spaced armored produced by Aero Jet General Corporation that was used for most of the pilot seats of the Cobra and UH-1 (Huey) series of helicopters. He was awarded the Silver Star thrice (Silver Star with two oak leaf clusters).

From 1972–4 he served with United Nations Truce Supervision Organization (UNTSO) in and around Israel. He was the senior United Nations representative present at the start of the Yom Kippur or Ramadan War (the 1973 Arab-Israeli War). In 1974, he commanded a battalion in Germany right next to the village he had previously lived in, and finally rose to be commander of 3rd Infantry Division in Germany in the early 1980s, defending the area of Bavaria that he grew up in. Having risen to a Major General in the U.S. Army, he was forced to retire for medical reasons on 1 July 1990.

Nicholas Krawciw then served as an advisor and consultant to the U.S. Department of Defense (DOD) for Ukrainian affairs. He also took over as President and Chairman of the Board of *The Dupuy Institute* in 1995, working primarily as a part-time volunteer until 2015. He also served as the Secretary of Defense's Senior Military Representative to Ukraine from 1997 until around 2010 as part of the Partnership for Peace program. His involvement in that effort ended shortly after Victor Yanukovych's election in 2010.

Finally retiring, Nicholas Krawciw passed away on 29 September 2021 at Fort Belvoir, Virginia. He was 85 years old.[3]

Contents

Acknowledgements

U nlike many of our past projects, this was primarily a solo effort. I do want to personally acknowledge those people who discussed the situation in Ukraine with me and helped me better develop this book. Sasho Todorov has been particularly helpful and energetic. Help was also provided by my son William A. Lawrence, Dr. Richard W. Harrison, Jay Karamales, Stefan Korshak, and WarMapper at @War_Mapper.

Maps and Charts

Preface

On 5 December 2021 my son Sasha, born and raised in America but half-Russian, texted me asking about what is going on with Russia and Ukraine. He had been keeping up with the news better than I had, as I was buried trying to finish up a book about a First World War German ace. This prompted my first post about a potential Russian-Ukrainian War to my blog that same day called "Russian Invasions." The blog was pretty sleepy at that point and it was only the second blog post I had made that month. The previous blog post had been about Eddie Rickenbacker's race at Narragansett Park Speedway on 18 September 1915, just to show where my focus was at the time.

But, the subject grabbed my interest, and so I blogged about it again on 28 December. Then on 22 January 2022, things had heated up enough that I did a blog post called "So Is Russia going to actually attack Ukraine?" I did not think at that time that it was likely and stated so. I was still rather incredulous the following month with blog posts such as "So, what is everyone about to go to war over?" on 5 February, and then from 7 February, I started blogging almost every day about the war. This would continue until I had done more than a hundred blog posts on the war. It was then that I started thinking that if I had already written several hundreds of thousands of words about the subject, then maybe I should write a book about it. I sent that suggestion off to a British publisher I knew, represented by the author John Grehan, and he responded right away with "Absolutely, get cracking on a book on the Ukraine war."

Now, I am not **the** expert on the Ukrainian War. I have not spent the last few years wandering around Ukraine and Russia examining their armies. I do not have an extensive collection of friends in the Russian or Ukrainian armies, or the U.S. or UK intelligence services who are keeping me up-to-date with the latest information. What I do bring to the table is a basic understanding of conventional warfare drawn from decades of experience working for the U.S. Army, Trevor Dupuy and *The Dupuy Institute*; and an actual demonstrated track record for predicting losses, durations and results of operations in Bosnia, Iraq and Afghanistan (see my book *America's Modern Wars*), and some knowledge and understanding of the environment (see my various books on the *Battle of Kursk*). What I discovered as I was blogging was that my discussions were meaningful enough that other people were following what I was talking about. Our sleepy little "hobby blog" multiplied ten-fold as it appears that we actually did have something to say. Is it meaningful enough to stand alone in a book? That is for the reader to determine.

When I wrote my first book on the Battle of Kursk, I started with an exhaustive collection of unit records from both sides – the engaged German and Soviet units. I had a Russian research team, translators, and several people helping me. It was a research effort that involved a dozen people working over the course of two years. When I finally sat down to write my first Kursk book, I knew that I had as good or better material as anyone, and even if I did not fully understand what had happened, nobody else had a clearer picture. This made me brave enough to discuss in depth each of the hundreds of actions that made up that battle.

For this book, I have none of that. I do not have access to hardly any unit records, I do not have access to any participants (112 German and Russian veterans were interviewed for my book on the Kursk battle), I do not have access to any other accounts or memoirs, I do not have staff, I do not have translators, I do not have any of the crutches that allowed me to move forward confidently with my books on the Battle of Kursk. All I had was the newspaper accounts, Ukrainian and Russian general staff statements, reporter interviews, YouTube videos, and all the other noise that gets published in the middle of an on-going war. So, should I write something now based upon all this public domain "ash and trash" material, or wait twenty years for someone to write a proper book on the subject? There is some value in having something done now, even if we know it is far from complete, and far from properly researched. The results are in your hand.

Chapter 1

The History of an Independent Ukraine

The name Russia comes from the word "Rus." The Rus were mostly Swedish Norse who settled large areas of Russia and Ukraine over a thousand years ago. The primary occupants of these areas were various eastern Slavic tribes. Starting in the eighth century, the Norse migrated south down the river routes between the Baltic and Black Seas. Also known as the Varangians (the Byzantine name), they established a number of trading posts and major settlements among the native Slavic peoples along those routes. Among the cities they founded or over which they established themselves as the rulers of were Novgorod (first mentioned in chronicles in 859), Vladimir (first mentioned 990), Rostov (founded 862), Smolensk (first mentioned 863), Chernigov (first mention 907, transliterated as Chernihiv from Ukrainian) and Kiev (transliterated as Kyiv from Ukrainian).

According to legend Kiev was established in 482 by the local Slavic Eastern Polans tribe. The Eastern Polans were the eastern Slavic tribe that occupied the area around what became Kiev. They spoke the Old East Slavic language, which eventually branched into modern Russian, Ukrainian, Belarussian and Rusyns (sometimes considered a dialect of Ukrainian). Little is known of this early history as they were not literate, and the establishment of Kiev in 482 is debatable. The Rus state was clearly established by 879 with its capital at Novgorod. It was ruled by the Varangian Rurik dynasty, founded in 862 by Rurik in Novgorod. In 882, Oleg of Novgorod (845?–912) conquered Kiev, and moved their capital there. It would remain the capital of the Kievan Rus until 1240. During the Rus golden age from 980–1054 (the rules of Vladimir the Great and his son Yaroslav the Wise), the Orthodox Catholic Church teachings were accepted from Byzantium with Vladimir converting to Christianity in 988 and marrying a Byzantine princess. Their legal code, the Russkaya Pravda, was written during this time in East Slavic. By 1054, the Kievan Rus dynasty controlled the area from the Arctic circle, past the Gulf of Finland (where St. Petersburg lies today) down to Kiev and down to Crimea. Also, by this point in time, the rulers of "Rus" had switched from speaking old Norse to speaking Slavic, the language of their subjects. The first use of the word "Rus" or "Russia" to describe this area was well before AD 1000, with the Eastern Polans last mentioned in chronicles in 944, replaced by the name Rus.

Kievan Rus was in decline over the next two centuries, with other powers controlled by Varangian and Slavic rulers developed in such places as Vladimir-Suzdal, Novgorod, Galicia-Volhynia and, of course, the Grand Duchy of Moscow. Moscow first appears in historical records in 1147 and was part of the Principality of Vladimir-Suzdal. Then the Mongol Invasion occurred in 1237 and the various Russian states were not united. Moscow was burned down in 1238 by the Mongols and they sacked Kiev in 1240. Most of the Rus principalities were forced to become tithe-paying dependencies of the Mongols. Between 1241 and 1362 the Princes of Kiev, still part of the Rurik dynasty, accept the overlordship of the Mongols and Tatars, known as the Golden Horde.

In 1362 the Grand Duke of Lithuania, Algirdas, defeated a Golden Horde army and from 1362 to 1569 Kiev became part of the Grand Duchy of Lithuania. It was ruled by Lithuanian princes. From 1569 to 1793, the Kiev Voivodeship was officially part of the Kingdom of Poland.

The intervening centuries saw the rise of the Grand Duchy of Moscow which expanded its control over the areas around northern Russia. In 1667, as a result of the Truce of Andrusovo, Smolensk, Severia and Chernigov were ceded to the Tsardom of Russia, and Kiev was ceded to them for two years. In fact, Moscow-based Tsardom remained in control of Kiev and this was acknowledged as such in 1686. Kiev's autonomy was abolished by Catherine the Great in 1775.

From this point, until 1917, Ukraine was part of the new Russian state ruled from Moscow or St. Petersburg (which was founded in 1703). This state expanded to become the massive Russian Empire that reached its peak in 1914, just before the start of the First World War (1914–18). The Russian Empire controlled all the areas of modern-day Russia, the majority of modern-day Ukraine, parts of Belarus, Crimea and Sevastopol, all of Siberia, large parts of Central Asia, large parts of the Caucasus, the Baltic states, Finland and Poland. At the time, 1914, the Russian Empire was one of the four largest economic and military powers of the world (behind the U.S. but perhaps equivalent to the UK and Germany). Its fall from grace after 1914 is a long, tangled, violent and depressing story, that appears to be continuing to this day.

Ukraine is best discussed as six separate areas. First are the lands centered around Kiev, the capital of the Rurik dynasty until 882 to 1240 or 1362, and subsequently the capital of the state of Ukraine. To the west was the Ukrainian or Ruthanian areas that centered around Lvov (transliterated as Lviv in Ukrainian) and the Eastern Carpathian mountains (the area where Rusyns is spoken). This area of "western Ukrainian" has a different and separate history from Kiev, often being part of Poland while the Carpathian mountain areas were controlled by the Austrian Hapsburg monarchy from 1772–1918.

The third area was the Donbas, in eastern Ukraine, centered around the cities of Lugansk (transliterated as Luhansk in Ukrainian) and Donetsk. The definition of what makes up the Donbas varies depending on who is discussing it (and what their political agenda is), but this area was always mixed Russian and Ukrainian. It is where the two populations lived intertwined and often spoke Russian, instead of Ukrainian. During the 1600s and 1700s, it was a sparsely populated area between the nominally Ukrainian Zaporizhian Cossack Host and the Don Cossacks. It was primarily under control of the Ukrainian Cossack Hetmanate and the Turkic Crimean Khanate until the middle of the 1700s, when the Russian Empire started conquering the area. As Tsarist Russia expanded into these areas during the 1700s, they called it "New Russia," a term that has re-surfaced today.[1] The Zaporizhian Host came under control of the Russian Empire around 1734, and was crushed as an autonomous host in 1775. Lugansk was established in 1795 when the British industrialist Charles Gascoigne founded a metal factory near a Zaporizhian Cossack settlement. Donetsk was established in 1869 by Welsh businessman John Hughes as a worker's settlement for his steel plant and coal mines. Nikita Khrushchev (1894–1971), the head of the Soviet Union that gave Crimea to Ukraine, grew up in this town. So too did Victor Yanukovych, the President of Ukraine from 2010 until his disposition in 2014. According to the Russian Imperial Census of 1897, "Little Russians" (Ukrainians) made up 52.4% of the population of Donbas while ethnic Russians made up 28.7%.

Kharkov's history is different than the Donbas (Kharkov is transliterated as Kharkiv from Ukrainian). It was founded in 1654 by the Russian Empire and was primarily settled by local Cossacks and Russians. This was the area referred to as Sloboda Ukraine (roughly Tax Free Borderlands). It is the second most populous city in Ukraine, after Kiev.

The fifth area is Crimea, which had a very separate and distinct history up through the 1700s. It was part of the Ottoman Empire and populated by a majority of Turkish people until the Crimea Khanate was annexed by the Russian Empire in 1783.

Finally, there is the southwest corner of Ukraine, centered around the Black Sea port of Odessa (transliterated as Odesa in Ukrainian). It has an independent history as a Greek settlement dating back to the sixth century BC, ended up under control of the Khanate of Crimea, was ceded to the Grand Duchy of Lithuania, and then came under Ottoman (Turkish) control after 1529. It was taken by Russia in 1789. The City of Odessa was founded in 1794 by the German-born Russian Empress Catherine the Great, and was a free port, not part of any surrounding governance. For most of the 1800s Odessa and its surrounding areas were ruled by a governor directly answerable to the Tsar. In 1897 the Odeessky Uyezd had a population of 610,042 of which 37.4% of the residents spoke Russian as their native language, 22.0% spoke Yiddish, 21.9% spoke Ukrainian and 10.3% spoke German. It was the fourth largest city in the Russian Empire, after Moscow, St. Petersburg and Warsaw. Odessa became part of the Kherson governorate. It is now the third most populous city in Ukraine.

By 1600 the Ukrainian language was a distinct and different dialect from Russian. It was mutually intelligible, which causes many people to consider it a dialect, but there were enough differences that some people considered it is separate language, sometimes referred to as Ruthenian. Whether it is a dialect or its own language also seems to depend on what people's political agenda is. Both the Russian Empire and the Soviet Union considered it a dialect, and starting around 1800 the Russian Empire suppressed the language. This continued under the Soviet Union. When Ukraine declared itself independent in 1991, it became the official language of the country, even though a significant percentage of the population also spoke Russian. Still, in the Russian Empire census of 1897 there were 22 million Ukrainian speakers among the Empire's 126 million people. The founder of modern Ukrainian literature is the poet and writer Taras Shevchenko (1814–61) from central Ukraine.

So, as of 1240, there was a distinct and separate nation of Ukraine centered around Kiev. The Russian Empire did not come into existence until 1721, with its capital in Moscow. In 1667 Ukraine was taken and became part of the Grand Duchy of Moscow, which became the Russian Empire. Although their history had already been intertwined, up until that point they were distinctly different entities with different histories. One significant difference was that Moscow mostly followed the teachings of the Russian Orthodox Church. This church was originally founded and based in Kiev. Due to Kiev losing its position in the Rus world, the church was moved to Vladimir in 1299 and then to Moscow in 1325. The church originally reported to the Patriarch of Constantinople, but this tie to the Catholic churches was lost when Constantinople was taken by the Ottoman Turks in 1453. The Russian Orthodox Church declared itself independent from any higher earthly authority in 1448. From that point forward, although still a "Catholic" church, it was effectively independent of both of the Eastern Orthodox Church and, of course, the Roman Catholic Church.

Ukrainian Christians, on the other hand, are divided primarily between the Orthodox Church of Ukraine, which still reports to the Ottoman restored

Ecumenical Patriarch of Constantinople and the Ukrainian Orthodox Church, which reports to the Patriarch in Moscow. There are several other smaller orthodox churches in Ukraine, including the Ruthenian Greek Catholic Church that is in full communion with the Roman Catholic Church.

So, there were similar, but distinctly different religious traditions between the Ukrainians and the Russians. Even today, among the 71 percent of Ukrainians who considered themselves Christians as of 2018/2019, 13 percent of the Ukrainian Orthodox Christians are part of the Ukrainian Orthodox Church (Moscow Patriarchate) in contrast to 29 percent that are part of the Orthodox Church of Ukraine (Kyiv Patriarchate).[2]

While Kiev and other parts of Ukraine became a part of the Russian Empire (Tsardom of Russa) in 1667, Crimea was still seperate. Western Ukraine, centered around Lvov, was part of Poland, and Odessa was part of the Ottoman Empire. The Rusyn areas around the Carpathian Mountains were part of the Austrian Empire.

Crimea was taken by conquest by the Russian Empire in 1783. It was taken directly under control of the Russia Empire and was not part of Ukraine. The area of Odessa was taken in 1789 and the port of Odessa was founded in 1794. The area around Lvov had not come under Russian control until 1914, during military operations against the Austro-Hungarian Empire during the First World War. The town was retaken by the Austro-Hungarians in the middle of the following year. In late 1918 it briefly became the capital of the Bolshevik-inspired Western Ukrainian People's Republic. It then became part of Poland. All the parts that make up modern Ukraine were never under control of the Russian Empire and did not come under control of the Soviet Union until 1939.

The Russian Empire entered the First World War in 1914 and quickly found its military struggling against some of its many opponents. The areas around Lvov (also known as Lemberg) were part of the Austro-Hungarian Empire. They were briefly occupied by the Russian Empire and then retaken in mid-1915 by the Austrian Army. The Russian front stabilized in 1916 with a Germany in control of Poland and Lithuania. At this point, Russia was at war with Germany, Austria-Hungary, the Ottoman Empire (Turkey) and Bulgaria.

In 1917, the Russian monarchy was overthrown with a revolution that started on 8 March of the new calendar (called the February Revolution because they were using an older calendar) and a new state and provisional government was formed. During this period of political turmoil, the Russian Army began to collapse. In November 1917 (called the October Revolution)

Northeastern Europe, 1914 and the Eastern Front, March 1916.

the new Russian provisional government was overthrown by the radical Bolsheviks, led by Vladimir Lenin (1870–1924). The German advance into Ukraine was still limited at this point. A ceasefire was declared with the new Bolshevik government on 15 December 1917.

The Central Rada in Kiev adopted the proposal for Ukrainian autonomy (but not independence) on 23 June 1917, which was recognized by the Russian Provisional Government. The Bolshevik October Revolution was extended to Kiev and after the Bolshevik revolt in Kiev was suppressed by the local government, the Central Rada declared the Ukrainian People's Republic on 20 November 1917 and condemned the Bolshevik revolution. The hundred or so Bolsheviks in the Central Rada decamped to Kharkov and declared as a counter-state, the Bolshevik-led Ukrainian People's Republic of Soviets, on 25 December 1917. It was supported by the Bolshevik-led Red Army. Meanwhile an Odessa Soviet Republic was formed on 30 January 1918 from the Kherson and Bessarabia governates of the old Russian Empire. These two Bolshevik governments would them be joined to form the Ukrainian Soviet

Republic in March 1918. The Ukrainian People's Republic in Kiev then declared itself independent on 22 January 1918. It was also at this time that Finland declared itself independent on 6 December 1917, an independence that has stood until today.

In early 1918 the eastern parts of Ukraine were already under control of the Red Army, protecting the Bolshevik government in Kharkov and with control over the Donbas. This advancing Red Army was supported by a Bolshevik-led revolt in Kiev on 29 January 1918. While the revolt was put down, in the face of the larger advancing Red Army, the forces supporting the Ukrainian People's Republic withdrew from the city and Kiev was taken by the Bolsheviks on 9 February 1918. That same day the defeated Ukrainian government signed the Treaty of Brest-Litovsk and began receiving aid from German and Austro-Hungarian troops. Supporting the Ukrainian military commander, journalist Symon Petlyura (1879–1926), this combined force of Germans, Austrians and Ukrainians retook Kiev on 1 March. On 28 April, Germany dissolved the Central Rada and installed the Government of Hetman Pavlo Skoropadsky (1873–1945). Petlyura was arrested. The combined armies continued to expand Ukrainian control, taking the "Left Bank" of Ukraine (including Kharkov), Crimea and the Donbas.

Meanwhile, the ceasefire between the Central Powers and Russia had collapsed and the German Army now was advancing against the Russian capital of Petrograd (St. Petersburg) and through Ukraine. This forced Russia to sign the humiliating Treaty of Brest-Litovsk on 3 March 1918, which created an independent Ukraine, Estonia, Latvia, Lithuania, Poland and Finland. The Russian Empire had been reduced in the west to mostly just Russia. Russia was forced to sign a peace treaty with Ukraine on 12 June. At this point, the new Ukraine included the areas around Kiev, Odessa, Kharkov, the Donbas and Crimea. The westernmost areas of Ukraine were still under control of the Austro-Hungarian Empire or the newly created state of Poland.

In November 1918, the newly formed Directorate of Ukraine, a committee of the Ukrainian People's Republic, overthrew the government of Hetman Pavlo Skoropadsky. As Germany had signed an armistice to end the First World War effective 11 November 1918, they remained neutral in this little civil war. This new Ukrainian government, led by the released Petlyura, continued warring with Bolsheviks in eastern Ukraine even though there was nominally a peace agreement. The Ukrainian People's Republic also continued to exist, although now in exile and no longer in Kharkov. In the meantime, the German Army, which had been supporting an independent Ukraine, went home.

On 3 January 1919, an advancing Red Army took Kharkov. On 6 January, the Ukrainian Socialist Soviet Republic was declared, although it was initially

EASTERN EUROPE, 1914

OPERATIONS DURING 1918

located in Kursk. On 7 January 1919, the Red Army invaded Ukraine in full force. Chernigov was taken on 12 January, Poltava on 20 January and Kiev on 5 February. Petlyura's Ukrainian forces retreated to the center of eastern Ukraine and started a counteroffensive, taking back Kherson on 2 March, Mykolaiv on 12 March and Odessa on 6 April. The Ukrainians briefly entered Kiev on 7 May but were pushed out by Soviet troops commanded by Semyon Budyonnyii (1883–1973), who would later rise to fame as one of only two marshals of the Soviet Army at the start of the Second World War[3] and one of only five men awarded hero of the Soviet Union three times.[4] In the summer of 1919 the White Army forces of Anton Denikin advanced north against the Red Army, taking Kiev at the end of the August. This Tsarist-influenced White Army also refused to recognize Ukrainian independence. They were driven back by fall of 1919, but fortunes worsened for the Ukrainian nationalists, as the Poles had signed an armistice with the Soviet Union on 12 October (they had been at war with Soviet Russia since 14 February 1919). On 21 October, the Ukrainian Army retreated into Polish-controlled Galicia and were disarmed and placed in internment camps. At this point, Ukraine was under Bolshevik control.

The Russo-Ukrainian War was reignited in November 1921 with a two battalion-sized expeditionary force raiding into Ukraine. There were also a couple of independent republics created by revolts inside of Soviet-held Ukraine: the Medvyn Republic and Kholodny Yar Republic. These Ukrainian revolutions were both exterminated before the end of 1922.

On 30 December 1922, the Ukrainian Soviet Socialist Republic become one of the founding members of the Union of Soviet Socialist Republics (USSR), a state that would survive until Christmas Day 1991. The Ukrainian People's Republic government, led by Symon Petlyura, went into exile and he was assassinated in Paris in 1926. Some guerilla activity and other resistance continued until the 1930s.

The independent Kiev-based Ukraine would fight for its existence for three years, controlling Kiev for only about a year. During its existence, it was supported by the German Army and was both allied and fought with the various counter-revolutionary "White Russian" or anti-communist forces that were in the area. In particular they were opposed to the forces of Anton Denikin and allied with the forces Nestor Makhno.[5] Then in late 1919 they were allied with the independent Poland (which included Lvov) which had been at war with Soviet Russia since February 1919. There was considerable violence across Ukraine and all sides participated in anti-Jewish pogroms and depredations to some degree. Petlyura's forces nominally did the most, with the Bolsheviks much less so.[6]

At the end of the Russian Civil War (1917–22) Ukraine was under control of the Bolshevik-led Soviet Union while Lvov and surrounding areas remained a part of Poland. The Ukrainian and Rusyn areas of Galicia ended up as part of Poland. Poland, Finland, Lithuania, Latvia and Estonia, all part of the old Russian Empire, were free and independent countries, but four of these five states would lose their independence in 1939–40.

The next big shift in borders came in 1939, when German leader Adolf Hitler and the Russian leader Joseph Stalin decided to split Poland between them. Large parts, but not all, of the areas of Western Ukrainians now came under Russian control. Although the Second World War started because of Hitler's invasion of Poland, the Soviet Union was allowed at the end of the war to keep all the territory of Poland that they took in 1939. Part of that territory ended up being added to the province and future state of Belarus and part of that territory, including Lvov, ended up being added to the province and future state of Ukraine. Furthermore, both Ukraine and Belarus were given their own seats in the General Assembly of the newly formed United Nations in October 1945 and were officially separate and independent countries in that august body, even though the reality under the Soviet Union was very different. It was also at the end of the Second World War that the old German capital of Prussia, Konigsburg, was handed over to Russia and it remains a geographically isolated province of Russia called Kaliningrad, named after the Russian-born Soviet-era Bolshevik Revolutionary and politician Mikhail Kalinin (1875–1946). At the end of the Second World War, the territory of Carpathian Ruthenia was taken from Czechoslovakia and added to Ukraine so that the Soviet Union would have a direct overland connection to its occupied client state of Hungary.

An independent Ukrainian government was declared in Lvov on 30 June 1941, eight days after the start of the German invasion of the Soviet Union, by the Organization of Ukrainian Nationalists (OUN) faction led by Stepan Bandera (1909–59). Its government was arrested shortly thereafter by the Germans. The OUN, through its armed force the Ukrainian Insurgent Army (UPA), continued to push for Ukrainian independence during the war, primarily fighting against the Soviet Army. Kiev was conquered by the Soviet First Ukrainian Front commanded by General Nikolai Vatutin in November 1943. Stepan Bandera was released by the Germans in September 1944 and returned to Ukraine to fight against the Soviet Army. One of their signature accomplishments during this period was the mortal wounding of General Nikolai Vatutin in an ambush in western Ukraine in February 1944 (he died in Kiev in April). He is buried in downtown Kiev near the Ukrainian parliament.

A large number of Ukrainians wanted independence from the Soviet Union, in part because of the heavy repression and starving that killed millions during the Soviet famine of 1930–3, called the Holodomor. This was then followed by widespread purges in 1936–9. Nikita Khrushchev was the head of Communist Party in Ukraine from 1938 to 1949. Tens of thousands of Ukrainians joined the German Army during the Second World War and tens of thousands more of them began fighting against the advancing Soviet Armies as they swept across Ukraine in 1943–4.[7] The independent Ukrainian fighters were nominally led by Stepan Bandera, and they became an active guerilla movement that continued fighting against the Soviet Union until the early 1950s, and resurfaced briefly again during the invasion of Hungary in 1956 by the Soviet Union. It was a large insurgency, that resulted in the deaths of over 100,000 people, which is which is as bloody as the current the current war in Ukraine.

The Ukrainians continued their fight against the Soviet Union even after the end of the Second World War. This bloody quixotic insurgency was doomed to failure, but not before causing considerable losses. The Soviet Union lost over 15,000 troops killed and missing.[8] It is reported by General Volkogonov that in March 1946 the Soviet Union claimed 8,360 partisans killed or captured.[9] Overall, Ukrainian losses were much higher.[10]

Stepan Bandara was assassinated by cyanide gas in 1959 in Munich, Germany. This was carried out by the Soviet Union, as had been almost certainly been the case previously with Symon Petlyura. The names Petlyura and Bandera were added to the lists of people honored as patriots by many Ukrainians and considered traitors in the Soviet-era histories. Soviet propaganda at this time condemned Bandera and the UPA as fascist collaborators. Their names are also called out in some most recent Russian propaganda efforts.

The last shift in the Ukrainian border came in 1954, when the leader of the Soviet Union, Nikita Khrushchev, transferred Crimea to the province of Ukraine. This was a minor administrative adjustment at the time, of no particular significance until thirty-seven years later when Ukraine became independent. A Russian major naval base was located in Sevastopol, the largest city on the Crimean Peninsula.

Between 8 and 26 December 1991 the Soviet Union was dissolved. This started with a meeting between the leader of Russia, Boris Yeltsin (1931–2007), the leader of Ukraine, Leonid Kravchuk (1934–2022), and the leader of Belarus, Stanislav Shushkevich (1934–2022). At that point, each of these provinces became independent self-governing nations. They already had seats in the UN. Mikhail Gorbachev, the head of the Soviet Union, resigned on 25 December and on 26 December the Supreme Soviet of the Soviet Union voted the Soviet Union out of existence.

So, depending on what and how you wish to count it, Ukraine (Kiev) was the capital of the Kiev Rus for 358 years. It was a tithe-paying part of the Golden Horde for 122 years. It was part of Lithuania for 207 years, it was part of Poland for 98 years, it was part of the Russian Empire for 250 years, it was briefly independent for 1 to 3 years, it was part of the Soviet Union for around 71 years, and has been independent for 31 years since December 1991. Since 1917, it has been independent for roughly 34 years of the last 105 years. For the last 105 years, western Ukraine (Lvov) has been part of Poland for 22 years, part of Ukraine for 31 years, occupied by Germany for 3 years and part of the Soviet Union for 49 years (as part of the province of Ukraine). The Donbas has been part of the province of Ukraine since at least 1734, or 288 years. Crimea has been part of the Russian Empire since 1783. Since 1954, it has been part of Ukraine, 37 years as part of the Soviet Union and 23 years as part of an independent Ukraine. Since 2014, it has been part of Russia.

This all matters, because various people argue that it matters, and some justify wars based upon their arguments.

To quote from the President of Russia's speech given on 21 February 2022, days before he effectively initiated a war with Ukraine:[11]

> My address concerns the events in Ukraine.... The situation in Donbas has reached a critical, acute stage ... I would like to emphasize again that Ukraine is not just a neighboring country for us. It is an inalienable part of our own history, culture and spiritual space ... since time immemorial, the people living in the southwest of what has historically been Russian land have called themselves Russians and Orthodox Christians. This was the case before the 17th century, when a portion of this territory rejoined the Russian state, and after ... So, I will start with the fact that modern Ukraine was entirely created by Russia. Or, to be more precise, by Bolshevik, Communist Russia. This process started practically right after the 1917 revolution, and Lenin and his associates did it in a way that was extremely harsh on Russia – by separating, severing what is historically Russian land. Nobody asked the millions of people living there what they thought, of course. Then, both before and after the Great Patriotic War [Second World War], Stalin incorporated in the USSR and transferred to Ukraine some lands that previously belonged to Poland, Romania and Hungary. In the process, he gave Poland part of what was traditionally German land as compensation, and in 1954, Khrushchev took Crimea away from Russia for some reason and also gave it to Ukraine. In effect, this is how the territory of modern Ukraine was formed.... When it comes to the historical destiny of Russia and its

peoples, Lenin's principles of state development were not just a mistake; they were worse than a mistake, as the saying goes. This became patently clear after the dissolution of the Soviet Union in 1991. Of course, we cannot change past events, but we must at least admit them openly and honestly, without any reservations or politicking. Personally, I can add that no political factors, however impressive or profitable they may seem at any given moment, can or may be used as the fundamental principles of statehood … It is a historical fact! Actually, as I have already said, Soviet Ukraine is the result of the Bolsheviks' policy and can be rightfully called Vladimir Lenin's Ukraine [Lenin died in 1924]. He was its creator and architect. This is fully and comprehensively corroborated by archival documents, including Lenin's harsh instructions regarding Donbas, which was actually shoved into Ukraine. And today the "grateful progeny" has overturned monuments to Lenin in Ukraine. They call it decommunization. You want decommunization? Very well, this suits us just fine. But there is no need to stop halfway. We are ready to show what real decommunizations would mean for Ukraine.

This last sentence looks like an unveiled threat, vice a history lesson. But, to continue his speech:

Going back to history, I would like to repeat that the Soviet Union was established in place of the former Russian Empire in 1922 … In reality, the union republics did not have any sovereign rights, none at all. The practical result was the creation of a tightly centralized and absolutely unitary state. In fact, what Stalin fully implemented was not Lenin's but his own principles of government.

Chapter 2

The Orange Revolution, EuroMaidan and the First War

Ukraine became independent on either 24 August, 1 or 8 or 25 or 26 December 1991 with the dissolution of the Soviet Union.[1] The 24 August 1991 date is now celebrated as Ukrainian Independence Day. It has since been governed as an independent democratic nation with a democratically elected president and legislative body, although this has not been without issues.

The first president of Ukraine was Leonid Kravchuk (1934–2022). He was the Chairman of the Supreme Soviet before the fall of the Soviet Union, becoming acting president on 24 August 1991 and was elected the first president of Ukraine on 1 December 1991 with 61.6% of the vote. He officially took office as the president of an independent Ukraine on 5 December 1991. An independence referendum was also held on 1 December that saw 92% of the voters supporting succession from the Soviet Union. He ran for a second term in 1994 but was defeated by his former prime minister, Leonid Kuchma (b. 1938), because of the problems of a stagnant economy and rampant graft and corruption. Leonid Kuchma served the constitutionally limited two terms as president from 19 July 1994 to 23 January 2005.

During this time, Ukraine established a definite Western-leaning orientation, having formally established relations with the defensive alliance NATO (North Atlantic Treaty Organization) in 1992 when Ukraine joined the North Atlantic Cooperation Council. In February 1994 Ukraine became the first former Soviet Union country to become part of NATO's Partnership for Peace program. This was all done under the first president, Leonid Kravchuk. Meanwhile, in May 1992 the Supreme Soviet of Russia, which was not abolished until October 1993, declared that the Soviet government's 1954 grant of Crimea to Ukraine was an illegal act. This would set the stage for the conflict in 2014.

The second president, Leonid Kuchma, on 5 December 1994 signed, along with the leaders of the U.S. (William Clinton), UK (John Major) and Russia (Boris Yeltsin), the Budapest Memorandum of Security Assurances that eliminated nuclear weapons from Ukraine. This memorandum stated that it would "respect the independence and sovereignty and the existing borders of Ukraine," "refrain from the threat or use of force against the territorial integrity or political independence of Ukraine," and "refrain from economic coercion designed to subordinate to their own interest the exercise by Ukraine of the rights inherent in its sovereignty and thus to secure advantage of any kind."[2] Between 1993 and 1996, Ukraine gave up its nuclear weapons. This included 176 ICBMs, primarily Soviet SS-24 and SS-18 intercontinental ballistic missiles, and nearly 2,000 nuclear warheads and weapons. At the time, this was the third largest nuclear arsenal in the world. The memorandum contained no mechanism for enforcement in case a party violated these "security assurances," which Russia would later do in spades.

NATO-Ukrainian relations progressed unevenly for the rest of the 1990s. At the NATO enlargement summit of November 2002, the NATO-Ukrainian commission adopted the NATO-Ukrainian Action Plan and President Kuchma declared that Ukraine wanted to join NATO. Ukraine also deployed troops to Iraq in 2003, which remained there through 2005 and then was converted to a much smaller peacekeeping mission. The Ukrainian deployment in Iraq was, at its peak, over 1,700 troops. During that time, they suffered 18 dead. Still Kuchma wavered on his desire to join NATO, issuing a decree on 15 July 2004 that joining NATO was no longer their goal, although they wanted to deepen relations with both NATO and the EU.

In 2004, the first major leadership crisis occurred. This was the election campaign between a coalition of factions, led by the Western-leaning Viktor Yushchenko against the Russian-leaning Viktor Yanukovych and his Party of Regions. There clearly was some underhanded and perhaps outside interference in the election. On 5 September 2004, at a private dinner, Viktor Yushchenko was poisoned with a dioxin and his face was disfigured with chloracne as a result. It has still not been confirmed whether this poisoning was locally planned and developed or whether the Russian government was directly involved in it. Still Victor Yushchenko, with his Western-leading agenda, lead the first round of voting on 31 October with 40% of the vote, while Viktor Yanukovych had 39% of the vote. The second round of voting on 21 November gave Yanukovych 49.5% while Yushchenko only had 46.6%.

This voting was rife with reports of heavily manipulated voting in the Donbas regions. In Donetsk Oblast (province) turnout in the second round was 98.5%, over 40% more than in the first round and in some districts turnout exceeded 100%. This was obvious evidence of fraudulent voting and immediately resulted in extensive protests in the Kyiv and in western Ukraine, starting on the eve of the election and followed by massive protests the next day. This became known as the Orange Revolution where there were an estimated 500,000 protesters in Kyiv, many wearing or carrying orange, the color of Yushchenko's campaign coalition. It was the first of the "color revolutions" that became a periodic event in various states of the former Soviet Union. The ruling city councils of Lviv and Kyiv and several other cities refused to recognize the results. The protests continued for days, sometime drawing more than a million demonstrators. On 3 December, the Supreme Court of Ukraine declared the results to be invalid and another ballot was held on 26 December 2004. Yushchenko won that election with 52% of the vote compared with 44% for Yanukovych.

Yanukovych conceded defeat on 31 December and resigned as Ukraine's prime minister. Viktor Yushchenko was inaugurated at Ukraine's third president on 23 January, with coalition partner Yulia Tymoshenko as prime minister. This was the second of four major tests of Ukrainian statehood and independence. In the first statement of intent, they voted with 92% of the vote on 1 December 1992 to become an independent country. Now in November–December 2004, the Ukrainian people showed that they were willing to stand up for a free and fair election and to ensure that a Western-leaning leader would lead this country in the future. It also showed the division in the country where the western and central parts of Ukraine were willing to stand up for a Western-oriented government, while many of the eastern parts of Ukraine favored a Russian-leaning leader and party. It is a lesson that had to be repeated two more times, in 2013 and in 2022

Viktor Yushchenko was a strong supporter of NATO membership and in a 21 April 2005 meeting, the initial steps were taken towards Ukraine's entry into NATO. Both the president of Ukraine and of the United States publicly supported Ukrainian entry into NATO. Viktor Yushchenko made it clear that his goal was full membership in NATO and the EU. In 2006, the members of NATO announced they were ready to support Ukraine's entry into NATO.

In 2006, Viktor Yanukovych and his Party of Regions obtained 32% of the vote in the parliamentary elections, while Yulia Tymoshenko's party received 22% and Viktor Yushchenko's party received only 14%. This made the Party of Regions the strongest party in the parliament. In December 2004 the Ukrainian constitution had been revised to share more power between the president and the prime minister. A new coalition government was formed with Viktor Yanukovych as the prime minister and supported by some members of Yushchenko's Our Ukraine Party. By the end of the year, all members of Yushchenko's Our Ukraine Party were removed from the parliamentary run government.

This change in governance halted all progress towards joining NATO. The parliament was then dissolved a year and half later by Yushchenko and new elections were held. The results were similar, with the Party of Regions obtaining 34% of the vote, Tymoshenko getting 31% and Yushchnenko's Our Ukraine block again receiving only 14%. A new coalition government was formed, this time with Yulia Tymoshenko as prime minister, thanks to a coalition between her party and Yushchenko's party.

In January 2008, Yushchenko and Tymoshenko sent a letter requesting to join NATO. Meanwhile, the parliamentary opposition, led by Yanokovych, tried to force a referendum on joining NATO, clearly intending to derail the process. They also blocked any functioning of parliament from 25 January to 4 March to protest joining NATO. In April 2008, Putin spoke out against Ukraine joining NATO and attended the NATO summit in Bucharest. At the NATO summit in April 2008 it was decided that NATO would not yet offer membership to Ukraine or Georgia. Croatia and Albania were invited to join the alliance. The United States, under President George W. Bush, supported Ukraine joining NATO but France and Germany were hesitant. It appeared that by the year's end, the U.S. administration had also backed off pushing for membership and no action was also taken at the December 2008 summit. The Partnership for Peace program continued with Ukraine but NATO membership was deferred. These April/December 2008 decisions are still being questioned to this day.

For Ukraine to become a member of NATO takes more than just a vote at a conference. An accession protocol would have to be signed and then each of the twenty-six NATO members at that time would have to approve (ratify) Ukrainian membership in NATO, usually involving a vote in their legislative bodies or senates and being signed off by their heads of states. This can take some time, sometimes months, usually more than a year, as demonstrated in the past.[3] On 14 February 2010, the leader of the main opposition party in Ukraine that was opposed to NATO membership won the presidential election. This was only around twenty-one months after the NATO April 2008 meeting. His Party of Regions had been the largest party of the Rada (their legislative body) since 2006, and held 39% of the seats. It is doubtful that Ukrainian membership in NATO would have been approved before early 2010 and after the election of Yanukovych in 2010, it is unlikely that this request to join NATO would have continued moving forward. One does wonder how Ukraine would have been an effective partner in NATO when they elected the Russian-leaning Viktor Yanukovych as president in early 2010.

It was also at this time, on 22 July 2008, that a stabilization and association-type agreement was signed between Ukraine and the EU. In August 2008, a brief twelve-day war broke out between Russia and Georgia as a result of Georgia's actions in Ossetia.

In the 2010 Ukrainian presidential election, there were still three major parties lead by the same three squabbling candidates, two representing a tilt to the West and one representing a tilt towards Russia. This time, Victor Yanukovych collected 35% of the vote in the first round, Yulia Tymoshenko gaining 25% and the sitting president Viktor Yushchenko only receiving 5.5%. The second round of voting catapulted Yanukovych into the presidency with 49% and Tymoshenko with 45.5%. Tymoshenko would challenge these results, but to no avail and would refuse to recognize Yanukovych as legitimately elected and boycotted his inauguration. Still, the exit polls indicated that Yanukovych was the winner and international observers, including over 700 from the EU, reported no evidence of significant electoral fraud.

It is useful to look at the split of vote by regions in 2010, as this forms the landscape for the upcoming war.

Yanukovych took office on 25 February 2010 and on 4 March, Yulia Tymoshenko resigned as prime minister after losing a vote of confidence. Mykola Azarov of the Party of Regions was appointed as the new prime minister. Initially, Yanukovych continued the Partnership for Peace program but clearly stated in March that Ukraine would remain a European, non-aligned state. On 3 June 2010, the Ukrainian parliament passed a bill written by Yanukovych

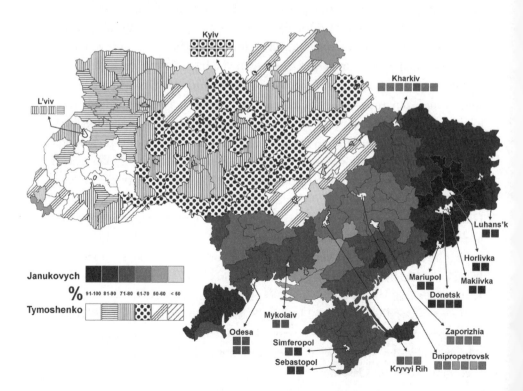

excluding Ukrainian membership in any military bloc. Therefore, cooperation with NATO continued, but there was now no plan to actually join NATO.

Meanwhile, Yushchenko, as one of his final acts as president, on 22 January rehabilitated Stepan Bandera and awarded him the title of Hero of Ukraine. This award was officially annulled in January 2011. Yulia Tymoshenko became the main parliamentary opposition to Yanukovych's government. On 12 May 2010, the Ukrainian prosecutor's office re-opened a closed 2004 criminal case, she was charged in another case on 20 December 2010, charged in a third case on 27 January 2011, a fourth case was opened on 10 April 2011 after the previous two cases had been dismissed, and a trial begun on 24 June 2011, and a new criminal investigation was started in July 2011. She was found guilty on 11 October 2011 of abuse of power and sentenced to seven years in prison and fined $188 million. Additional cases were prosecuted against her once she was in prison. Her jailing received international attention and condemnation. Other political opponents in Ukraine were also being investigated and charged, including former president Leonid Kuchma, who was still active in politics and had endorsed Yanukovych in 2010.

Meanwhile, Yanukovych scaled back participation in the Partnership for Peace program. On 21 April 2010, Russian President Dmitriy Medvedev and Yanukovych signed a treaty extending the Russian lease on naval facilities in Sevastopol for twenty-five years beyond 2017, with a five-year renewal option. This was in exchange for a multi-year 30% discount in natural gas contract from Russia. The move generated considerable resentment among Western-leaning Ukrainians and resulted in egg-throwing and a smoke bomb being released during the parliament sessions that ratified this agreement. The government of Yushchenko had previously declared that the lease would not be extended and that the Russian fleet would have to leave Sevastopol by 2017.

Still, Yanukoych continued movement towards Ukraine joining the EU. On 30 March 2012, the EU Association Agreement was initialed but not ratified, as there was considerable tension between Yanukovych and the EU leaders over the detention of Yulia Tymoshenko, which they considered to be politically motivated. EU leaders stated that these treaties could not be ratified until Ukraine addressed concerns over the "stark deterioration of democracy and the rule of law." So, at this point, association with the EU was in limbo and would remain so for the rest of 2012.

There are some that say that NATO's big mistake was to not include Ukraine into NATO in 2008. This opinion has been recently expressed by the current president of Ukraine, Volodymyr Zelenskyy. Yet, in 2010 Ukraine legitimately elected a leader who was clearly not interested is further developing their relationship in NATO. Therefore, it is not clear, in light of Ukraine's own electoral politics, how joining NATO in 2008 would have worked and how it would have been maintained. The subsequent failure of Yanukovych to join the EU is an object lesson as to the readiness of Ukraine to be a part of NATO. Added to that, Yanukovych reduced Ukrainian Armed Forces spending. In 2007, the Ukrainian defense budget was 10.6 billion UAH (Ukrainian hryvnia). It then dropped in the two subsequent years until growing again until 2012 when it was at 16.4 billion. It then dropped the next two years to 15.3 and 15.1 billion respectively.[4] Ukrainian GDP in 2013 was 190.5 billion, the highest it has been since independence. This put defense spending at about 8% of the nation's Gross Domestic Product, which is significant.

In the 28 October 2012 Ukrainian parliamentary election, Yanukovych's Party of Regions won 30% of the vote compare with 25.5% by imprisoned Yulia Tymoshenko's Fatherland Party. This election also saw the rise of new UDAR party led by international heavy weight boxer Vitali Klitschko with 14% of the vote and the rise of the far-right party Svoboda, which won 10.5% of the vote. Clearly these three opposition parties, which made up at least half the electorate, were not in line with Yanukovych's more Russian-leaning policies. These three opposition parties did not recognize the election results and challenged them in court and the EU reported irregularities in the election. It was clear at this point that Yanukovych was leading a minority government with the majority of the electorate opposed to him and his Russian-leaning policies.

On 1 January 2010, the Eurasian Customs Union for Belarus, Kazakhstan and Russia was established. This idea was expanded in 2011 to form a Eurasian Economic Union by 2015. In early 2013, they had begun discussion with Ukraine about them becoming a member of this developing Eurasian Economic Union. In February 2013, the Ukrainian ambassador to the EU rejected any preconditions for signing the association agreement with the EU but on 22 February, the Ukrainian parliament voted that it would ensure the EU recommendations were implemented. On 25 February, the President of the European Commission made it clear that Ukraine could not be a member of a Eurasian Economic Union and associated with the EU. Yanukovych, in response to EU concerns, pardoned and released the former Minister of Internal Affairs, Yuriy Lutsenko, from prison on 7 April 2013. He then took a number of other steps in response to EU concerns over democratic reforms, selective justice and corruption. It finally appeared that the EU association agreement was on track to be signed on 29 November at the EU summit in Lithuania, with the Ukrainian parliament expected to pass the remaining bills necessary for signing the agreement on 21 November.

On 21 November, the Ukrainian parliament failed to pass any of the six motions what would have allowed the imprisoned Yulia Tymoshenko to receive medical treatment abroad. The Ukrainian government suspended preparations for signing the association agreement, and instead proposed the creation of a three-way trade commission between Ukraine, the EU and Russia. In response, large protests were held in Kyiv starting that same day, organized by the opposition parties. On 26 November, the Ukrainian government admitted that Russia had asked Ukraine to delay signing the agreement with the EU. Yanukovych did attend the EU summit on 29 November, but the association agreement was not signed. Yanukovych insisted that additional financial compensation had to be provided to account for their loss of trade with Russia and again recommended trilateral talks. These ideas were rejected by the EU. On the other hand, in mid-December Russia did offer to provide $15 billion in aid to Ukraine with Russia providing $3 to $5 billion up front.[5]

Meanwhile, what came to be known as the Euromaidan or Maidan Uprising started on 21 November 2013 in the central square of Kyiv, Maidan Nezalezhnosti (Independence Square). It was provoked by the sudden decision that day by the Ukrainian government not to sign the EU-Ukraine Association Agreement and its drift towards Russia and its Eurasian Economic Union. The protest quickly expanded to call for the resignation of the President Viktor Yanukovych and the government of Prime Minister Mykola Azarov. While initially these large protests were peaceful, on 30 November the Ukrainian police violently dispersed the crowds.[6] The protesters reoccupied the square the following day. This time they erected a protest camp in the middle of Maidan Square, occupied by thousands of protesters day and night, even though winter was coming.

On 11 December, the police conducted a night assault on the camp in Maidan Square. Thousands of police attempted to drive tens of thousands of protestors out of the area. The Maidan activists were reinforced by other protesters during the night and the police failed in the face of the protesters' tenacity. This unsuccessful attempt by the government only further empowered the protesters.

In January the protests further expanded, even though it was the height of winter, culminating in deadly clashes on Hrushevsky Street between 19 and 22 January. On 19 January, over 200,000 protesters were marching on Hrushevsky Street in central Kyiv. It was their ninth large, Sunday mass protest in a row. It turned violent as the day continued, and there were sympathetic protests in other towns to block the movement of police and troops to support the government in Kyiv. Violent protests conducted by thousands continued over the next three days. On 22 January, the violence resulted in the deaths of four protesters, three by gunfire and one due to the police use of water cannons on protesters in freezing weather. Over a thousand protesters were injured. An uneasy truce was agreed between the protesters and the government in the days after.

The popular uprising reached its peak between 18 and 23 February in what is called the Revolution of Dignity or the Euro-Maidan Revolution. On the morning of 18 February, some 20,000 protesters advanced on the Ukrainian parliament, but were blocked by police. It became very violent, with the police using tear gas and flash and stun grenades and firing rubber bullets. As the day continued, some police started firing live ammunition, including the use of snipers to pick off protesters. As the fighting spread across central Kyiv, the Lviv Oblast declared itself independent from the central government. By the end of the day, at least twenty people were dead. By 20 February, at least seventy-seven people had been killed in the clashes. On 21 February, Yanukovych signed a compromise agreement with the opposition leaders, but protests continued in central Kyiv with the protesters taking control of all government buildings. A bill was introduced in parliament to remove Yanukovych and that afternoon, Yanukovych left for Kharkiv. The following day the 450-seat parliament voted 328–0 to remove Yanukovych from office and new presidential elections were scheduled for 25 May. Laws were passed that allowed for the release of Yulia Tymoshenko, who traveled from prison that day and addressed a crowd of more than 100,000 people from her wheelchair in Maidan Square. On 24 February, a warrant was issued for Yanukovych's arrest and on 25 February, the Interior Ministry special police, the Berkut, was dissolved. A new government, headed by Arseniy Yatsenyuk, was formed on 27 February. Losses due to the unrest were at least 108 protesters killed and over 1,100 wounded. In addition, the police suffered 13 killed and 272 injured.

Yanukovych had been unable to dislodge these protesters except by force and this was tried with negative results. It only seemed to increase the degree and virulence of the opposition to him. Yanukovych then adopted the unusual strategy of firing on the protestors with snipers. These snipers were never identified, but may have been from Russia. It was clear that the majority of Ukrainians were never going to accede to joining the Eurasian Economic Union instead of the EU and, apparently, they were willing to die over this. The situation could not have been clearer, and it was to Viktor Yanukovych who, on 21 February, gave up trying to resist and abandoned his opulent residence in Kyiv. He went to Kharkiv and then fled to Russia, never to return to Ukraine. The Ukrainian crowds toured his opulent residence in Kyiv, which clearly demonstrated the extent of graft and corruption in that government, although this was not a problem unique to this particular Ukrainian government. In general, international organizations had been hesitant to nuzzle up to Ukraine because of the perception of widespread corruption. This was an issue that would continue to haunt Ukrainian international efforts.

Russia declared the overthrow of the Yanukovych government illegal, which is technically correct, but entirely irrelevant. It was the third popular revolt by the people of Ukraine to determine their own leadership, their own path and their independence from Russia.

Unfortunately, violence began spreading in other parts of Ukraine. There was still support for the Party of Regions in the pro-Russian parts. On 22 February, the newly formed Congress of the Southern and Eastern Regions held a meeting in Kharkiv that was attended by Yanukovych. They insisted on taking responsibility for protecting the constitutional order in eastern and southern Ukraine. The following day clashes erupted in Kharkiv between thousands of pro- and anti-government protesters. The pro-Russian protesters stood guard over the statue of Vladimir Lenin in the center of the city. Lenin was the leader who established the multi-national Soviet Union in 1922. This monument was not removed until 28 September 2014, when a crowd of thousands of protesters demolished it.

On 1 March, thousands of people marched in Kharkiv, Donetsk, Luhansk, Melitopol. Mariupol, Odesa, Yevpatoria (in Crimea), Simferopol (in Crimea) and Kerch (in Crimea) to protest against the new government. On 1 March, Yanukovych made a request in writing to the president of Russia, Vladimir Putin, to send military forces "to establish legitimacy, peace, law and order, stability and defending the people of Ukraine." That same day, Putin received authorization from the Russian parliament to deploy troops to Ukraine. Russia had already mobilized forces in Crimea and Sevastopol.

On the night of 22/23 February, the Russian president convened an all-night meeting to discuss the situation in Ukraine. He claims he ended the meeting with the statement that "we much start working on returning Crimea to Russia."[7] The Crimean prime minister recognized the new provisional government in Kyiv. Pro-Russian protests occurred in Sevastopol, Simferopol and Kerch on 23 February, as did rallies to support the new provisional government. Some of these protests on both sides numbered in the thousands. Demonstrations continued for several days, until armed Russian forces, wearing their green uniforms but not any insignia, began seizing the government buildings on 27 February. These forces became known as the infamous "little green men" as Russia initially refused to acknowledge that they were their troops. A closed and only partially attended session of the Crimean parliament replaced the prime minister with a man that had only won 4% of the vote in the last election. Russian forces also secured all routes into Crimea. By 2 March, Russia had taken compete control of Sevastopol and Crimea.

On 11 March, the Supreme Council of Crimea and the Sevastopol City Council declared independence from Ukraine, held a referendum on 16 March with 95.5% voting to secede from Ukraine and join Russia, with a voter turnout of 83%. About 60% of the residents of Crimea were ethnic Russians. On 18 March, the Republic of Crimea and the federal city of Sevastopol were officially annexed by Russia. On 26 March, the last Ukrainian military facilities and Navy ships were taken by Russia. A total of around six people were killed in the seizure of Crimea. Putin would admit in April that the "little green men" were indeed Russian forces. This was an organized armed seizure and annexation of a neighboring territory by Russia for which they received considerable international condemnation.

In the eastern city of Donetsk, on 1 March, a crowd of 10,000–15,000 demonstrators gathered for a rally in support of the disbanded Berkut police force and to demand a referendum on the separation of the Donbas from Ukraine. Protests continued off and on during March resulting in two or three deaths. On 7 April, a protest by 1,000–2,000 protesters in Donetsk resulted in them taking control of the local government. They declared the "Donetsk People's Republic" that same day. A referendum was held on 11 May and 89% of the voters voted to proclaim the Donetsk People's Republic. There is no reason to believe that this was a fair or legitimate referendum. Their control did not extend much beyond the city of Donetsk and did not include the Donetsk airport.

On 5 March, in Luhansk, a crowd proclaimed a new "People's Governor" and on 9 March they stormed the government building in Luhansk and forced the incumbent governor to resign. Further protests and violence continued into April, as they fought over control of government buildings, with demonstrators again seizing buildings in Luhansk at the same time as the protestors in Donetsk. They proposed declaring a Luhansk Parliamentary Republic on 8 April, but this did not happen. By 12 April, the government had regained control of the seized government buildings with the help of the local police.

Several thousand protestors again gathered on 21 April. On 27 April, the protestors declared the Lugansk People's Republic and, on 29 April, they again seized the municipal building of Luhansk and began to spread their control to the villages in the province. By 10 May, they had expanded their control to take over about half of the Luhansk Province. They also held a referendum on 11 May and 96% of the voters favored self-rule with voter turnout at 81%. There is also no reason to believe that this was a fair of legitimate referendum.

Odesa, a city on the Black Sea, also witnessed significant unrest. The local government there was made up of members of the Party of Regions. In January and February there were anti-government demonstrations, and after the government was overthrown in Kyiv, from 1 March, there were pro-Russian demonstrations numbering thousands of people and counterdemonstrations. On 2 May, multiple clashes between pro-Maidan and anti-Maidan groups resulted in the deaths of six people. Anti-Maidan activists retreated to Trade Union House in the city center. The building was set on fire and forty-two people inside died.

The real prize was Kharkiv, which was the second largest city in Ukraine. The protest related to Euromaidan had been relatively small, in the hundreds. On 6 April 2014, a group of pro-Russian protesters seized the regional state administration and declared the Kharkov People's Republic. This was put down in less than two days by Ukrainian forces. On 13 April, more pro-Russian protesters temporarily took up residence in the regional state administration building. Violent clashes that day led to dozens of injuries. The mayor of the city, Hennadiy Kernes, stood with the government. He was a member of the Party of Regions but had previously supported the Orange Revolution. On 28 April, he was shot by a sniper while out bicycling (or hiking). Although sustaining a life-threatening wound, he continued as mayor, serving until December 2020 when he died in Germany from complications from COVID-19 at the age of 61.

On 21 March, the Ukrainian government lead by Yatsenyuk signed the EU-Ukraine Association Agreement.

Russia had gone from a position of lining up Ukraine to join the Eurasian Economic Union and abandoning the attempt to join the EU and NATO to a position where the Ukrainian leadership they favored had left Ukraine in disgrace and their influence in the country had now collapsed. They had seized and annexed Crimea and Sevastopol by 18 March. In what appeared to be Russian-orchestrated operations, people in the cities of Donetsk and Luhansk declared themselves independent of the interim Ukrainian government, raised forces, and declared themselves as two independent states, the Lugansk People's Republic (LPR), established on 27 April 2014, and Donetsk People's Republics (DPR), established on 7 April 2014. They both held independence referendums on 11 May 2014. This now dumped Ukraine into a civil war, with two areas of eastern Ukraine opposed to the rest of the state.

From that point, what developed was a low-level extended war, primarily fighting over control of Luhansk and Donetsk provinces. The rebels controlled about half of each province and were using their newly raised armies to try to take the rest of each province. Meanwhile, bits and pieces of the Ukrainian Army were deployed to the front to hold their progress back. The Ukrainian Army under Yanokovych was at its nadir. The Army only consisted of 49,000 poorly equipped ground troops.[8] This was certainly not enough to defend against any significant aggression. It clear that the Yanukovych government had left Ukraine extremely vulnerable.

Between the seizure and annexation of Crimea and Sevastopol, supporting a continued war in Ukraine and the later shooting down of Malaysian Flight MH-17, the reputation of the Russian government led by Vladimir Putin had taken a massive hit internationally. And these were far from the only incidents that had happened that damaged their international reputation.[9]

Yanukoych departed Ukraine for Russia on 24 February 2014. He has never returned and remains in Russian under a temporary asylum certificate. He still maintains he was illegally removed as president of Ukraine. His youngest of two sons died by drowning in Lake Baikal in Siberia on 20 March 2015 when driving his minivan on the ice. He was buried in Crimea. Yanukovych was divorced in 2016 and his wife moved to Crimea. He was reportedly in Minsk in 2022 at the start of the Russo-Ukrainian War in 2022, allegedly to be reinstalled as the president of Ukraine after Russia seized Kyiv.

On 3 August 2015, the former prime minister of Ukraine under Yanukovych, Mykola Azarov, announced the creation of the Ukraine Salvation Committee. This government in exile has had no influence on events but still makes pronouncements. Both him, his former president and other members of his government are on Interpol arrest lists and are unable to leave Russia.

The War Begins

On 12 April, pro-Russian groups seized the cities of Slovyansk and Kramatorsk and surrounding areas. These two cities were part of the Donetsk Province and had a census estimated population in 2021 of 106,972 and 150,084 respectively. Ukraine sent armored forces towards Slovyansk and Kramatorsk to retake them, but they were stopped before reaching there. Ukraine did retake Kramatorsk airfield. A handful of people were killed and wounded in these and related operations. On 2 May, a Ukrainian attack towards Slovyansk was repelled with a handful of losses. The new Ukrainian government acknowledged the loss of two helicopters in these operations. Another Ukrainian helicopter was confirmed lost on 5 May.[10]

In the south, on 6 May, pro-Russian militia fought for control of Mariupol. This effort involved scores of pro-Russian forces and resulted in a handful of casualties. The Ukrainian forces were driven out of the city by 9 May, although the Ukrainian Army remained deployed just outside of the city. It appeared that some of the local police had joined with the separatists. Mariupol was a large city with an estimated population of 431,859 in 2021. The city's steel workers conducted their own independent protests and then set up patrols in the city on 15 May, taking over major parts of the downtown area and pushing the separatists out of those areas. This led to control of the city being split between the steelworkers and the separatists. As military operations, these incidents around Slovyansk, Kramatorsk and Mariupol were relatively small and resulted in limited bloodshed. It was more like scattered bouts of political violence than anything that looked like organized warfare.

By the second half of May, it was clear that the separatists were establishing two distinct independent people's republics centered around the cities of Luhansk and Donetsk. They had armed volunteers, some from Russia, and were equipped with a panoply of modern weapons of war. On 22 May, a separatist attack on a Ukrainian checkpoint at the village of Volnovakha (population 21,441 in 2021) in the Donetsk Oblast (province) resulted in 16 Ukrainian soldiers killed and 30 wounded. Two soldiers later died of their wounds.[11] The separatists lost at least one person. This was the first large exchange of this war.[12]

Having already taken Slovyansk and Kramatorsk and split control over Mariupol, in late May, the advancing pro-Russian forces also seized Severodonetsk and Lysychansk. This was done with forces that did not exceed a thousand men. By the end of May, the DPR and LPR each held most of Donetsk and Luhansk provinces respectively.

The first major battle in the new war was created as they expanded their reach beyond the cities to take the surrounding countryside. While the Donetsk insurgents held the government buildings in Donetsk City, the Donetsk airport remained under Ukrainian government control. On 26 May, a separatist attack on Donetsk airport resulted in the first major fight of this war, known as the First Battle of the Donetsk Airport. On the morning of 26 May, pro-Russian fighters captured the terminal buildings of the airport and demanded that Ukrainian forces in the area withdraw. Their strength has been estimated at 200.[13] The Ukrainians struck back at 1300 with paratroopers supported by Ukrainian air strikes provided by Mig-29s and Su-25s jets, and Mi-24 attack helicopters.[14] By the evening, the Ukrainian government attack had pushed the Donetsk forces out, although they did conduct counterattacks later. Sporadic fighting and firing continued for the next couple days, although the Ukrainian Army maintained control of the airport. The death toll from this fight appears to have been at least 33 or 34 insurgents killed, at least 43 insurgents wounded and 2 civilians were killed.[15] The Ukrainian government authorities claimed they suffered no losses. Heavy separatist losses were also taken due to a friendly fire incident. A significant number of the casualties were Russian nationals.[16]

On 25 May 2014, a new presidential election was held in Ukraine. This had originally been scheduled for 29 March 2015, but the incumbent president was now residing permanently in Russia. Petro Poroshenko, a wealthy Ukrainian businessman famous for owning chocolate factories, won with almost 55% of the vote. The newly freed Yulia Tymoshenko placed second with almost 15% of the vote. There were nineteen other candidates. Among them were two far-right or neo-fascist candidates, the leader of the Svoboda Party winning 1.16% of the vote while the leader of the Right Sector party won 0.7% of the vote. The candidate from Yanukovych's Party of Regions obtained 3.03% of the vote. Fourteen candidates were rejected by the Central Election Commission for not meeting their qualifications, including one named Darth Vader; but the election in general was fairly conducted. Voter turnout was over 60% in the regions under government control. Needless to say, pro-Russian candidates were under-represented with the pro-Russian-leaning areas of Sevastopol and Crimea now annexed and the Donetsk and Luhansk provinces in open armed revolt. There were also twenty-seven mayoral elections held. Vitali Klitschko of UDAR endorsed Poroshenko for president and instead ran and won the office of the mayor of Kyiv, a position he still held in 2022 when the next war started. Poroshenko assumed the office of the president on 7 June, replacing the disgraced and absent Yanukovych. His inaugural address stressed the unity of Ukraine and stated that Ukraine would not give up Crimea.

Meanwhile, the underfunded and partially gutted Ukrainian Army began raising more units, including allied militia, and started pushing back against these pro-Russian incursions. In response, the separatists started receiving more and heavier arms, primarily from Russia. On 11 June, three T-64 tanks were reported to be supporting the separatists in Donetsk and their use was confirmed two days later.[17] More tanks would show up in separatist hands later. Ukraine would reclaim Mariupol on 13 June, which was not seriously contested. They captured at least thirty prisoners. On 19 June the biggest battle of the war developed, the Battle of Yampil near Lyman and Slovyansk. It involved forces numbering in the thousands and included tanks, armored vehicles and air strikes. This two-day battle resulted in a Ukrainian victory, at a cost of at least fourteen Ukrainian soldiers and at least two separatists.[18] The Ukrainians re-occupied Yampil (population 1,944) and secured Lyman (population 20,469).

The month of June also developed into a fight for control of the borders, with multiple clashes on border outposts in Luhansk and Donetsk provinces with separatist forces and Russian forces. In many cases, the Russian forces were conducting low-level operations across the border into Ukraine, including supporting artillery shelling. In an attempt to negotiate a settlement with the Donbas region, Poroshenko unilaterally declared a week-long ceasefire on 20 June. It was effectively ignored by the separatists and the war continued. Poroshenko did complete the signing of the association agreement with the EU on 27 June.[19] In early July the fighting for the areas about Luhansk and Donetsk continued. The Luhansk airport was claimed on 1 July by the separatists but the Ukrainians still held the Donetsk airfield. Donetsk airfield had been seriously contested on 26 May.

The Russian Artillery Strike that Spooked the U.S. Army[20]

In the second week of July 2014, elements of four brigades of the Ukrainian Army ground forces were assembling near the village of Zelenopillya, near highway E50/M03 leading north to the city of Luhansk, Ukraine.[21] Zelenopillya was a small village less than 6 miles (9km) from the Russian border. They were deploying along the border with Russia as part of an operation to cut the lines of supply to paramilitary forces of the separatist Lugansk People's Republic.

The government of Ukrainian President Petro Poroshenko had declared a unilateral ceasefire in late June. Ukrainian forces resumed the offensive at the beginning of July and fighting broke out around the Luhansk International Airport on 9 July.

At about 0430 on the morning of 11 July, a column of battalions from the Ukrainian 24th and 72nd Mechanized Brigades and 79th Air Mobile Brigade was struck with an intense artillery barrage near Zelenopillya.[22] The attack lasted only 3 minutes or so, but imagery posted online of the alleged aftermath reported a scene of devastation and scores of burned-out vehicles. Ukraine's Defense Ministry admitted to 19 killed and 93 wounded in the attack, though other sources claimed up to 36 fatalities. No figures were released on the number of vehicles lost, but a survivor reported on social media that a battalion of 79th Air Mobile Brigade had been almost entirely destroyed.

The Ukrainians quickly identified the perpetrators as "terrorists" using short-range BM-21 Grad multiple launch rocket systems (MLRS) firing across the border from Russian territory, which was only 9km from Zelenopillya.[23] Independent analyses by various open-source intelligence groups amassed persuasive circumstantial evidence supporting these allegations.[24]

On 16 July, the U.S. government instituted a round of additional sanctions against Russia, including Russian arms manufacturers and leaders and

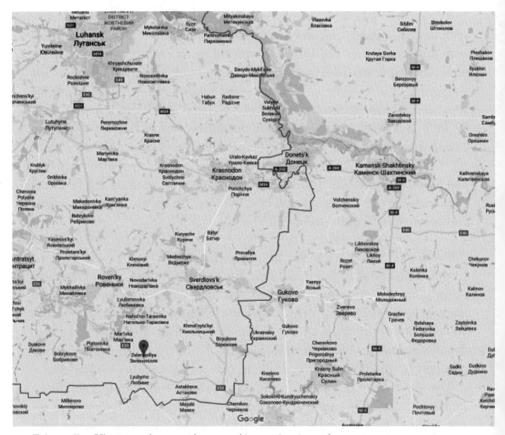

Zelenopillya, Ukraine and surrounding area. (*Source, Google maps*)

governments of the separatist Donetsk People's Republic and Lugansk People's Republic.[25]

Western military analysts took notice of the Zelenopillya attack and similar strikes on Ukrainian forces through the summer of 2014. To quote the influential retired U.S. Major General Robert Scales, "I couldn't help imagining a U.S. armored battalion subjected to a similar fire strike, I realized then that Ukraine had become Russia's means for showcasing what might happen if we ever fought a firepower-intensive battle against it. 'You know guys,' I mused in the moment, 'this is the first time since the beginning of the Cold War that an American war-fighting function has been bested by a foreign military.'"[26]

What caught their attention was the use of drones by the separatists and their Russian enablers to target Ukrainian forces in near-real time.[27] The Ukrainians had spotted separatist drones as early as May, but their number and sophistication increased significantly in July, as Russian-made models were also identified.

Analysts also noted that the Zelenopillya rocket strike incorporated a Dual Purpose Improved Conventional Munition (DPICM) mix of air-dropped mines, top-down anti-tank submunitions, and thermobaric fuel/air explosives to achieve a devastating effect. They surmised the munitions were delivered by Tornado-G 122mm MLRS, an upgraded version of the BM-21 introduced into the Russian Army in 2011.[28]

The sophistication and effectiveness of the attack, in combination with other technological advances in Russian armaments, and new tactics demonstrated in the conflict with Ukraine, prompted the U.S. Army Capabilities Integration Center, then led by Lieutenant General H.R. McMaster, to initiate the Russian New Generation Warfare Study to look at how these advances might influence future warfare.[29] The advent of new long-range precision strike capabilities, high-quality air defense systems, maritime anti-access weapons, information operations and cyber warfare, combined with the adoption of anti-access/area denial (A2/AD) strategies by potential adversaries led into the technologically rooted Third Offset Strategy and development of the Army and U.S. Marine Corps' new Multi-Domain Battle concepts.[30]

One does wonder if this widely discussed account of effective Russian use of drones and artillery in 2014 influenced the U.S. view of Russian capabilities to the point that they overrated the Russian Army and underrated the Ukrainian Army capabilities in 2022.[31] It does appear that in February 2022, U.S. intelligence and the U.S. DOD had a distorted picture of the relative capabilities of these two armies, and this distorted analysis was being fed to decision-makers at the highest level.

The Ukrainian Advance Continues

Meanwhile, the Ukrainian ground forces were developing from elements of a real army in addition to some highly motivated militia units. The Ukrainian regular forces were significantly supplemented by volunteer battalions like the Donbas, Azov and Dnipro battalions. These were significant independently raised militia units, with the Azov Battalion becoming infamous for their neo-fascist connections. But, they were opposed by a recently organized separatist militia, leaving the Ukrainian forces at an advantage. As such, they began to advance again the separatist positions.

Attacking Slovyansk, Kramatorsk, Severodonetsk and Lysychansk, they re-took Slovyansk and Kramatorsk on 5 July. The separatists withdrew from Slovyansk when threatened with surrounding. The Ukrainian Army continued advancing, taking Siversk on about 10 July. On 22 July, Ukrainian forces entered Severodonetsk and fighting continued the next day. The Ukrainians advanced into Lysychansk on 24 July after it was abandoned by most of the separatists. Ukraine secured the city by 25 July 2014. This was now developing into a significant conventional advance that the world seemed mostly oblivious too.

The separatist forces defending Slovyansk, Kramatorsk, Severodonetsk and Lysychansk were mostly under command of the Muscovite Colonel Igor Girkin (b. 27 December 1970), also known as Igor Strelkov.[32] Previously he had commanded at the Battle of Yampil. The situation in both Donetsk and Luhansk was getting perilous as the Ukrainian Army was closing in on both cities in early August. At this point, three-fourths of the territory once held by the separatists was back in Ukrainian hands. On 27 July, U.S. satellite photos were showing extensive use of Russian artillery on Ukrainian positions over the last week. They were fired from Russia. This cross-border firing would continue.

Operations continued into August with the Ukrainians now advancing between and splitting the territories held by the LPR from the DPR. On 5 August, Ukrainian forces pushed into the Petrovskyi district of Donetsk. By 9 August, Igor Girkin was claiming that Donetsk was "completely encircled." On 7 August, the Ukrainian Army advanced to the area around Ilovaisk, a town with a population of 15,447 to the east of Donetsk, halfway between Donetsk and the Russia border.

Aid and direct support from Russia was widespread and open, although Russia continued to deny it. Ukraine had advanced on Luhansk and Donetsk and held Mariupol, which was now the temporary Ukrainian administrative center for the Donetsk Oblast. It looked like the Russian attempt at "hybrid warfare" was indeed failing in the face of the Ukrainian Army advance. The government of the Donetsk People's Republic was being replaced: with the prime minister and former president resigning on 7 August and the commander Igor Girkin resigning on 14 August. On 14 August, Russia entered the Donbas in force with at least two-dozen armored personnel carriers. The president of Ukraine claimed that Ukrainian artillery destroyed a significant portion of the armored column, while Russia claimed the convoy did not exist. Neither was correct. These new Russian forces shifted the balance of power on the front, with the new prime minister of the DPR claiming that his forces now included 1,200 Russian-trained combatants.

Now, this appears a case where the Russian attempt at the much-heralded "hybrid warfare" was indeed failing in the face of a conventional army. The only response was the insertion of their own conventional army to counterbalance the Ukrainian Army. The militias and temporary forces were being pushed off the field of battle and it was now time for the big boys (trained conventional forces) to enter the fray.

As of 18 August, the Ukrainian Army had advanced into Luhansk city. At this point, if there was not a Russian intervention, then the LPR and DPR would have been overrun over the next few weeks. They were not significant enough to hold on their own. Instead, the Ukrainian forces around Luhansk and Donetsk began to receive push-back from the Russian reinforced insurgents. Russia continued sending in forces and by 24 August, the balance and the direction of the war had shifted back in favor of the separatists. Russian "little green men," uniformed soldiers without insignia, were now being seen in the Donbas. Around 25 August, ten of these "little green men" were captured. They were Russian paratroopers.

Meanwhile, the Ukrainian forces attempted to enter the town of Ilovaisk on 18 August. Rebuffed, they were able to storm the town on the night of 18–19 August led by the militia's Donbas Battalion. They also deployed the Dnipro and Azov battalions for these operations. During the subsequent days, fighting stubbornly continued in parts of the town, although it was clear that the majority of the town was controlled by Ukraine. On 24 August, regular Russian Army troops appeared, including BMD-2s and two days later T-72B3 tanks. This had now turned into a fight against Russian regulars. The town of Ilovaisk was encircled by Russian and DPR forces from 24–26 August. Two reinforcing Ukrainian columns were halted by Russian engagements on 27 and 28 August. Effectively at this point, the Ukrainian forces of up to 2,000 men in Ilovaisk were besieged.

On the 29th, the Ukrainians negotiated a withdrawal corridor. Two Ukrainian columns, of 1,000 and 600 men in strength, then withdrew from Ilovaisk. But as they withdrew, they were attacked with considerable losses. They had completed their withdrawal by 31 August while the Russians and DPR forces entered the town and were able to fully secure it by 2 September. Losses from this large, confused operation included more than 500 Ukrainian soldiers taken prisoner according to a Ukrainian official.[33] Some 17 Russian soldiers were captured during the fighting.[34] The official number of Ukrainian dead was given as 366, and may have been over 400 counting missing and unidentified individuals.[35] There were also 36 civilians killed and a third of the town was destroyed.[36]

On the Russian border near Mariupol, on 27 August DPR separatists supported by the Russian Army forces captured Novoazovsk, some 28 miles (45km) east of Mariupol. This assault and supporting columns consisted of armored vehicles, many of the vehicles marked with white circles or triangles. This was effectively a third front opened up in this war. It was a pretty naked invasion of Ukraine by Russia, with the forces not really disguised as separatists. These forces then pushed towards Mariupol, coming to within 10 miles (16km) before a Ukrainian counteroffensive pushed the separatist forces back.[37]

At this point, it appears that Russia was now conducting a second invasion of Ukraine so as to ensure that the collapsing DPR and LPR would survive. On 1 September, Luhansk airport was taken by the separatists. Throughout the process, Russian and Ukrainian delegations were still meeting in Minsk, trying to hammer out a permanent ceasefire. On 5 September, a ceasefire agreement, called the Minsk Protocol, was signed between Russia and Ukraine, the Swiss head of the OSCE (Organization for Security and Cooperation in Europe) and the representatives of the LPR and DPR. The whole negotiation effort was overseen by the leaders of France and Germany. The agreement failed to completely stop the fighting, leading to a Minsk II agreement early the following year. The active campaigning by both sides had now ended and the fighting subsided, but minor skirmishes would continue along the lines for the months to come. The OSCE monitors, put in place by the agreements, were able to document many of these violations. A follow-up agreement had to be signed on 19 September 2014 as the fighting continued.

Half of Luhansk and Donetsk provinces were in separatist hands and they had established local governments to rule them. The other half of the two provinces remained in Ukrainian hands, including the cities of Severodonetsk, Lysychansk, Slovyansk, Kramatorsk and Mariupol. These would all become contended for in 2022. In the case of Mariupol, multiple defensive lines were constructed to the east of city, manned by a number of Army and National Guard troops and supported by artillery. The border areas between Luhansk and Donetsk connecting back to Russia had been seized. The contentious Luhansk International Airport ended up in separatist hands, but had been closed since 11 June 2014. The Donetsk Sergei Prokofiev International Airport has also been shut down since 26 May 2014 and was still in Ukrainian hands. This left both the Lugansk People's Republic and the Donetsk People's Republic without a major civilian airport in their "country." Added to that, Sevastopol and Crimea had been annexed by Russia and were well occupied by Russian Army and Navy forces. According to President Poroshenko, in September the Armed Forces of Ukraine had lost between 60% and 65% of their deployed equipment during the war.[38]

Despite the Minsk Protocol, on 28 September the separatists attempted to retake the Donetsk airport. There has been ongoing skirmishing there since May, and the airport's position just to the north of Donetsk kept the Ukrainian Army within artillery range of the city. These more violent clashes on 28 September resulted in nine Ukrainian soldiers dead and twenty-seven wounded.[39] Repeated shelling over the next couple days resulted in the deaths of ten civilians in Donetsk.[40] On 2 October, the DPR forces began to advance on the airport, taking the old terminal building on the 3rd. Fighting continued through 28 October, with control of the airport remaining split between Ukraine and DPR. Losses were noticeable, probably in excess of 200 killed total.[41] The Ukrainian Army maintained control of the airport for the rest of 2014. This fighting continued even though a ceasefire was officially in place thanks to the Minsk Protocols. On 8 October, the UN OHCHR (Office of the High Commissioner for Human Rights) noted that from mid-April to 6 October, at least 3,660 people were killed and 8,756 were wounded in eastern Ukraine. They noted that at least 331 people had been killed since the ceasefire has started a little over a month ago (from 6 September to 6 October).[42]

The DPR made another attempt to seize control of the Donetsk airport on 9 October, but to no avail, and fighting and shelling again intensified in mid-October. Fighting there then stalemated but did not quite end.

Ukraine had consisted of twenty-four provinces and the special areas of Sevastopol and Crimea. It has lost those two special areas and half of two of its twenty-four provinces. The rest of the country, though, was now united and was beginning to rebuild itself back into a functioning democracy.

The military campaign season ended with another election, this time for the parliament. Elections were held on 26 October and the voting was obviously heavily slanted towards pro-Ukrainian and pro-Western-leaning parties. The People's Front, led by Arseniy Yatsenyuk, received a little over 22% of the vote while President Poroshenko's party received a little less than 22% of the vote. The pro-Russian Opposition Bloc received less than 10% of the vote. The Party of Regions did not participate in this election (but was not outlawed). Many members had migrated to the Opposition Bloc. With Sevastopol, Crimea and large parts of Donetsk and Luhansk provinces no longer participating in Ukrainian elections, the voting had now been realigned and pro-Russian parties were marginalized in the political scene. Yulia Tymoshenko's party received less than 6%. The far-right parties of Svoboda and Right Sector accounted for less than 7% of the vote together. Voter turnout was only 52%. The new parliament was seated on 27 November 2014. On 2 December, Yatsenyuk was again made prime minister.

Skirmishing and minor battles continued in the Donbas until the end of the year. Fighting continued at Donetsk airport and extended back to the nearby village of Pisky, a mile and half (2km) to the northwest of the airport. This village was the supply conduit for the Ukrainian defenders at the airport. This extended fight was referred to as "Little Stalingrad" in honor of the Soviet defense of Stalingrad in late 1942.[43]

It was reported in early December that at least 1,000 people had died fighting in the Donbas since the Minsk Protocol had been signed.[44] The Ukrainian and separatist forces agreed to a "Day of Silence" on 9 December and fighting died down for the rest of the year.

The Ukrainian Air Force in 2014

The Ukrainian armed forces were making use of airpower and had already lost four helicopters due to small arms fire.[45] Anti-aircraft efforts by the separatist forces also had some success, claiming two Mi-24 helicopters on 26 May (not confirmed) in the fight for Donetsk airport.[46] The Russian separatists then took down a Mi-8 helicopter near Kramatorsk on 29 May with the loss of fourteen Ukrainians, including a general officer. Sadly, the first death of civilians by an airstrike occurred on 2 June when eight people were killed and over twenty wounded in Luhansk by strikes by a Ukrainian Su-25 and a Su-27.[47]

On 6 June, separatist militias near Slovyansk shot down a Ukrainian propeller-driven An-30 surveillance plane using two shoulder-launched missiles. Five crew members were killed and two missing (and presumed dead). And on 14 June, the separatists took down an Il-76 transport plane as it approached the Donetsk airport, killing the nine crewmembers and forty troops on board. On 24 June, another Ukrainian Mi-8 was shot down near Slovyansk using a MANPADS (Man Portable Air Defense System such as a Soviet SA-7), killing all nine people on board. On 2 July, they damaged a Su-24 near Slovyansk using MANPADS. On 14 July, a Ukrainian An-26 transport aircraft (identified as 19 blue) was shot down by a surface-to-air missile (SAM) over eastern Ukraine while flying at 21,300ft (6,500m). This height was towards the maximum capability of a MANPADS, making it look more likely a Russian-operated SAM was involved. Two crew were killed, two captured by separatists and four rescued by the Ukrainians. The first air battle of the war occurred on 16 June, when a Russian Su-27 shot down a Ukrainian Su-25 over eastern Ukraine. The skies over eastern Ukraine has truly become dangerous.[48]

It appears that Russia moved up significant anti-aircraft assets near the border with Ukraine, and some of those crossed over into Ukraine to support the DPR and LPR separatist forces. This would lead to disaster when, on 17 July 2014, Malaysian Airlines Flight MH-17 was shot down over Donetsk Oblast at an altitude of 33,000ft (10,000m). This was almost certainly done by a missile fired from a self-propelled Buk M-1 manned by Russian volunteers.[49]

Airline companies had become used to a Europe where airliners could safely fly without fear, even though the war was now months old. It had simply not occurred to the majority of the commercial airline industry that they needed to avoid Ukrainian airspace at that time. They learned that mistake at the cost of 298 lives. This tragic event further undermined Putin's international standing. Among the dead were 193 people from the Netherlands, where Putin's eldest daughter lived at the time. She soon moved back to Russia and the Dutch Safety Board took the lead in investigating the shooting down. Arrest warrants for three Russians, including Igor Girkin, and a Ukrainian were issued by the Dutch government in 2019 and they were all tried *in absentia*. On 17 November 2022, Igor Girkin, another Russian, and the Ukrainian, were convicted *in absentia* and given life sentences, while one of the Russians was acquitted.[50]

On 23 July, two Ukrainian Su-25s were hit by missiles at an altitude of 17,000ft (5,200m) in the area where MH-17 crashed. According to Ukraine, on 7 August, pro-Russian separatist forces shot down a Ukrainian Mig-29 with a Buk SAM missile in Donetsk Oblast. The pilot managed to eject to safety but was captured.[51]

At a conference in London in November 2014 the Ukrainians provided a report of their air operations. As of mid-November 2014, they claimed to have flown 740 sorties with jet combat aircraft, Su-24s, Su-25s, Su-27s and Mig-29s. Their total aerial losses during the war were 22 aircraft, 9 combat, 3 transport aircraft and 10 helicopters: 1 Su-24, 6 Su-25s, 2 Mig-29s, 1 An-26, 1 An-30, 1 Il-76, 5 Mi-8/17s and 5 Mi-24s. A Mig-29 was shot down in air-to-air combat by a Russian Mig-29. The An-26 was shot down by a Buk missile a few days before Flight MH-17 was shot down.[52] For the jet aircraft this equates to 1.2% losses per sortie.

Losses for 2014
The total losses for the Maidan revolt (21 November 2013 – 23 February 2014) is given as 121 killed.[53] There were an additional 52 people killed in the political violence from late February to early May.[54] In the armed fighting in Ukraine from mid-April 2014 to 31 May 2016, the OHCHR (Office of the United Nations High Commissioner of Human Rights) estimated that at least 9,404 people were killed, which includes up to 2,000 civilians and an additional 298 civilians killed in the crash of Malaysia Airlines flight MH-17.[55] Most of these were lost in the Donbas region. The vast majority of these deaths probably occurred in 2014. The UN estimates to 85 to 90 percent of the civilian deaths were as a result of the shelling of populated areas with mortars, cannons, howitzers, tanks and multiple launch rocket systems. Of the

298 non-Ukrainian civilians killed when flight MH-17 was shot down, 193 were Dutch.[56]

The War in 2015

The war quietened down in the last couple of months of 2014. In 2015, right after New Year's Day, the number of violent incidents in the Donbas started to rise, mostly around the Donetsk International Airport. On 15 January, the new terminal building at the airport was recaptured by DPR separatists. It was clear that the Minsk Protocols had now completely broken down and the LPR and DPR leaders refused to attend new talks. The Ukrainian Army counterattacked at Donetsk airport on the weekend of 17–18 January and retook most of the airport. The Russians then appeared to reinforce the DPR forces and they ended up reclaiming parts of the new terminal leaving Ukrainian troops trapped on the second floor. The fighting at Donetsk airport was finally resolved between 19 and 21 January when the Russians reinforced their offensive with a reported 600 men, supported by tanks and artillery and pushed the final Ukrainian forces out of airport on 21 January.[57] When the fighting was done, at least thirty-seven Ukrainian troops were dead. The airport was clearly wrestled from Ukraine by 21 January. This was a fight that went for almost four months, from 28 September 2014–21 January 2015.

The fighting expanded along the "control line" in Donetsk and Luhansk provinces and down to Mariupol. France and Germany again tied to institute a ceasefire while the United States proposed sending armaments to Ukraine. The next and final major fight of this war erupted at the town of Debaltseve on 14 January. Debaltseve had an estimated population of 24,316 in 2021. It was on the road that went northwest to Artemivsk then to Slovyansk. Debaltseve had come under separatist control in April 2014 but was reclaimed by the Ukrainian Army on 29 July 2014. It was well defended with thousands of Ukrainian troops in the area. In mid-January, the separatist and Russian forces began heavily shelling the area and on 22 January DPR forces initiated attacks on the positions around Debaltseve. This appears to have been the follow-up operation to one at Donetsk airport. As the town was surrounded on three sides, this developed into a disadvantageous fight for the Ukrainians. Still, multiple separatist attacks towards the town were repelled over the next few days. The situation then worsened for the Ukrainians on 1 and 2 February as the separatist forces pushed closer to the town, almost isolating it. A ceasefire was agreed on 3 February and a humanitarian corridor was established on 6 February to allow civilians to escape. The separatists then renewed the offensive on 7 February. They claimed to have isolated Debaltseve on 9

February with the seizure of the village of Lohvynove and it is clear that the highway to Artemivsk was now cut. Heavy fighting continued up through the 15 February even though a new peace agreement was in the works.

A new Minsk Protocol was agreed to on 12 February, and this was supposed to bring about a ceasefire on 15 February. The DPR leader stated that the ceasefire did not apply to Debaltseve and continued offensive operations. They pushed into the town on 17 February. On the early morning of 18 February, the two thousand or so of Ukrainian forces based in Debaltseve withdrew across country toward Artemivsk, some 50km away. This withdrawal in the dark was plagued with coordination issues and soon came under heavy fire as the sun rose. The separatists were able to take control of Debaltseve on 18 February 2015 at 1500 EET (Eastern European Time, UTC +2 hours). The separatist forces took the remaining parts of Debaltseve by 20 February 2015. That was the last major operation of this current round of fighting, although skirmishing continued into March. Ukrainian losses in the fight are reported as 136 killed and 331 injured.[58] Hundreds of Ukrainian forces were captured and about 2,000 escaped in a poorly organized withdrawal. The failure to hold Debaltseve and the poorly conducted withdrawal from it embarrassed the government of Ukrainian President Pyotr Poroshenko. It was the second such botched withdrawal, reminiscent of the withdrawal from Ilovaisk.

The rest of the year was relatively quiet, although fighting flared up when the DPR launched at attack on Marinka on 3 June. Donetsk itself was hit with an anti-war protest of about 500 people on 15 June. They were objecting to the continued civilian casualties, caused in part by DPR forces locating artillery and other military sites near civilian areas. Skirmishing also continued through June and July, but no territorial changes occurred. The UN High Commissioner for Human Rights reported for this time that 165 civilians were killed and 410 were injured in eastern Ukraine from 16 February–16 August 2015.[59] Finally, the Ukrainian government, the DPR and the LPR agreed to a halt all fighting as of 1 September, in time for the start of the school year. This ceasefire held.

This war was broken into five phases.[60] First was the Spring Offensive from April–June 2014, which was the initial separatist occupation of the Donbas, using local proxy forces, a manufactured insurgency and foreign volunteers.[61] By the end of June, the separatists were starting to lose this war with the Ukrainian Army on the advance. The Ukrainian Army also had the advantage of airpower, which the LPR and DPR did not have. This became the Ukrainian Summer Offensive which started around 5 July and continued until around 20 August. The third phase was the Russian Summer Counter-

Offensive which started on about 11 July 2014 at Zelenopillya and continued to around 5 September 2014, really picking up steam around 24 August. This was when the Russian Army, initially as "little green men," directly intervened and this became a state-on-state fight for control of the Donbas vice a proxy war. The Russian attempt at hybrid warfare using proxy forces had failed and they were forced to directly intervene. This also included bringing in anti-air assets, which took out a number of Ukrainian aircraft and Malaysia Flight MH-17. The second phase ended with the Minsk agreement.

The fourth phase of this war is the Winter Offensive, which started from 29 September 2014 with the Second Battle of Donetsk Airport and ended on 20 February at the Battle of Debaltseve. This phase was ended by Minsk II

after only relatively minor exchanges of territory, primarily Donetsk airport and Debaltseve. The final phase ran from February 2015–February 2022 and covers the end period of static war or trench warfare. One could argue the original war started on 12 April 2014 and ended almost ten months later on 20 February 2015. This war ended with a 280-mile (450km) front running between the separatist and Russian forces and the Ukrainian Army.

The Stalemate War and Multiple Ceasefires in 2016–20

With the war stalemated and a ceasefire in place, 2016 was a quiet year, although not without some skirmishing. There were no major territorial changes this year. A new ceasefire was negotiated on 1 September 2016, and this one was more effective. The fighting finally almost completely stopped. Ukrainian losses in 2016 were 211 killed in combat. According to the UN OSCE, 83 civilians were killed and 205 were injured in the Donbas in 2016.[62] The war had settled to a stalemate across the front with only occasional fighting. The Ukrainian Army was slowly rebuilding itself in the face of this organized resistance and was reported by Ukraine in 2016 to have been 169,0000 in strength.

The new year brought new conflict in 2017, where fighting starting around the village of Avdiivka on 29 January 2017. A new ceasefire was agreed to on 20 February, although skirmishing continued. The year would continue with a series a skirmishes and ceasefires, although no significant ground ever changed hand. The year ended with a prisoner exchange on 27 December 2017 that traded 73 Ukrainian soldiers for over 200 separatists.

The pattern of 2018 was similar to 2017, with continued skirmishing, repeated ceasefires and repeated violations of the ceasefires. By the end of December 2018, the twenty-second ceasefire of the war had been agreed to. The same patten would continue in 2019 as they maintained the lines without exchange of territory, but were never quite at peace.

Meanwhile, elections continued in Ukraine with presidential elections held on 31 March (first round) and 21 April (second round) and parliamentary elections held on 21 July 2019. In the first round political newcomer Volodymyr Zelenskyy won 30% of the vote compared with only 16% for the incumbent Petro Poroshenko. These two candidates advanced to the second round, where Zelenskyy dominated, winning 73% of the vote against a sitting president. Voter turn-out from both rounds was 62–3%. The parliamentary elections of three months later were a similar sweep, with Zelenskyy's newly formed centrist Servant of the People Party winning 43% of the vote and taking 254 out of 450 seats in the Rada, more than enough for a majority. The party was only officially registered on 31 March 2018 and a little more than a year later took over half the seats in the Duma.

Thirteen other parties won seats along with thirty-seven independent ministers. Poroshenko's party won 8%, as did Yulia Tymoshenko's party. The pro-Russian, Eurosceptic OPZZh Party, which stands for "Opposition Platform-For Life," won 13% of the vote, making them the second largest party in the parliament. The other pro-Russian Opposition Bloc Party took only 3% of the vote. It clearly showed that 20% or so of the Ukrainian electorate in areas controlled by Ukraine remained favorable to Russia, even after five years of warfare. The far-right wing Svoboda Party won only 2% of the vote and placed one representative in parliament. The next parliamentary elections are scheduled for not later than October 2024 and the next presidential elections are scheduled for the spring of 2024.

In late 2019 the peace arrangements were developing in a positive direction. As part of this improving diplomatic climate, the Ukrainian Army withdrew from the town of Zolote on 29 October and Petrovske in November. It was agreed that all remaining prisoners of war would be exchanged by the end of 2019.

In March 2020 the fighting along the front did increase, with some nineteen civilians killed in that month. The coronavirus outbreak was also arriving, giving the governments a new issue to deal with. The twenty-ninth ceasefire came into effect on 27 July 2020 and this one actually held for a while. There were no combat losses in the Ukrainian Army until 6 September, when a soldier was killed by shelling. From 27 July 2020–7 November 2020, only three Ukrainian soldiers were killed. A total of fifty Ukrainian soldiers had died in 2020.[63]

Escalation in 2021

Shelling and skirmishing increased in the first part of 2021, there having been effectively six months of peace since the twenty-ninth ceasefire. In the first three months of 2021, twenty-five Ukrainian soldiers were killed.[64] It was also claimed that Russia was moving troops and equipment into the Donbas. In early April, the Russians conducted military drills in the area of Crimea and the Donbas, using by their own admission over 50 Battalion Tactical Groups (BTGs) consisting of over 15,000 soldiers.[65] Actual Russian armed strength in the area was much greater than that.[66] This was clearly an effort to put political pressure on Ukraine during the increased fighting. This was the largest Russian build-up since 2014. Meanwhile, on 9 April, Ukraine flew the first operational Turkish-made Bayraktar TB2 military drones over the Donbas.[67]

The build-up started with an announcement on 21 February 2021 that 3,000 Russian paratroopers would be deployed to the border for large-scale exercises. These forces were then supplemented with additional forces as a war of words developed between Ukraine and Russia over Crimea and other issues. These new deployments were estimated to be somewhere in the range of 40,000–60,000 Russian troops by mid-April and rose to a total of around 83,000 troops, with 41,000 on Ukraine's eastern border and 42,000 in the Crimean Peninsula.[68] This raised concerns over a possible invasion. The troops were partially withdrawn in June 2021, cooling down the international environment. But, this was a process that would repeat itself later in the year. It may have actually been training and preparation for what actually occurred less than a year later.

The Donetsk People's Republic, which has been surprisingly systematic in its reporting, claims that from 1 January–3 November 2021, sixty-five of its DPR servicemen and 6 civilians had died.[69] According to Russian claims, in late October, Ukraine regained control of the village of Staromarivka (population 305 in the 2001 census) in the neutral zone near Mariupol.[70] It was here in late October that Ukraine made the first use of the Turkish-made Bayraktar drone against DPR forces.

The stage was now set for the next phase of the wars with Ukraine. Some date the current war in Ukraine from 20 February 2014, giving the current war a length of over eight years.[71] This date is based upon an event related to Crimea and it is debatable why this date of 20 February is used to mark the start of anything. The seizure of Crimea did not generate any fighting, as the Ukrainian units there withdrew or surrendered in the face of overwhelming firepower. While there was clearly Russian support for the unrest and political violence in the Donbas at the same time, it did not break out into open combat engagements until around 12 April 2014 at Slovyansk and Kramatorsk. This first "war" is probably best dated from 12 April 2014–28 October 2014, giving it a duration of over almost 7 months (around 200 days).

It is clear that a de facto ceasefire had come into place by 28 October 2014, although it was violated over two-dozen times. From 2016–early 2022, the front remained static, even though there was continued shelling and skirmishing. From 27 July 2020–6 September 2020, there were no casualties in the Ukrainian Army. There appears to have been one war starting around 12 April 2014 and continuing to the end of October 2014. There was then an uneasy phase of skirmishing and artillery shelling that ran from January 2015–1 September 2015 when the effective first ceasefire came in. There were multiple violations and skirmishes in the subsequent years, ending with another phase of skirmishing and artillery shelling that ran from March 2020–27 July 2020 when the second effective ceasefire came in (and the twenty-ninth ceasefire overall). There was then a final phase of skirmishing and artillery shelling that ran from the start of 2021–23 February 2022. Then the Russo-Ukrainian War would start with a Russian invasion of Ukraine on 24 February 2022.

Populations

As of 1 February 2022, the estimated population of Ukraine was 41,130,432, excluding Crimea.[72] The population of Crimea is given as 2,416,856 for 1 January 2021 from Russian sources. This includes Sevastopol.[73] This is a significant decline from the 2001 Ukrainian census, when the population was 48,457,102. The Ukrainian population peaked in 1993 with over 52 million people (52,244,100) and has been in decline since. The 2021 Gross Domestic Product (GDP) was estimated at $198 billion. This equates to a per capita income of $4,830.

In contrast, the population of Russia is given as 145,478,097 including Crimea (and Sevastopol) as of 1 January 2022. Its GDP was estimated at $1,819 billion as of April 2022. This equates to a per capita income of $12,575.

The population of Donetsk Province is given as 4,056,405 in February 2022 and for Luhansk as 2,101,653. Probably more than half of these populations are under control of the DPR and LPR respectively.

Chapter 3

Build-up to the Second War

For many in the West, this war came out of the blue. In November 2021, news about any conflict between Russia and Ukraine was simply not in the news. In October 2021, Russia began again building up troops along the border, similar to what they had done in March and April. The first major publication in the West about this accumulation of troops was in the Washington Post, 30 October 2021.[1] This build-up was noted by Ukrainian President Zelenskyy on 13 November 2021, when he announced that Russia had massed around 100,000 troops near their borders. At that time, the American assessment was lower at 70,000 troops. Four Russian armies were now assembled near the border, 20th and Eight Guards Army which were already in the area, and the newly deployed 41st Army from Novosibirsk and the legendary 1st Guards Tank Army, normally deployed around Moscow.

By early December the Russians were reported to have gathered 175,000 troops on the border and 10 days of supply.

Now, 175,000 troops is a large, scary number. On the other hand, the reported strength of the Ukrainian Army in 2016 was 169,000, with the Ukrainian Armed Forces having a total of 255,000 active personnel.[2] So, it did not look like overwhelming force was being presented on the part of Russia.

Furthermore, ten days of supply is not a lot to bring with an army if they were going to prosecute a war. Most wars last longer than ten days, and many a whole lot longer than that. Ukraine is a large country and Kyiv is far away from the Russia border. As I noted at the time, "It does not look like Russia is planning on marching to Kyiv, especially with 10 days of supply. They are probably not even considering creating a land bridge to Crimea."[3]

I then trolled through the options of why they had assembled such a force what they might be considering. They were:

1. Help the local governments in rebellion take the rest of Donetsk and Lugansk.
2. Replace the local governments in Donetsk and Lugansk with their own governance (possibly in anticipation of formally annexing these two areas).
3. Make violent border demonstrations.
4. Or the build-up may be the message (most likely option).

The "build-up may be the message" I considered the most likely option. A little sword rattling for the sake of arguing a position related gas or oil prices, contracts, water for Crimea, or a host of other issues in the complex love-hate relationship that now existed between Ukraine and Russia. While 175,000 men and ten days of supplies was enough to be concerning, in my limited knowledge of the situation, it was not enough to actually successfully invade and conquer Ukraine.

One of the stated reasons for the build-up was over the issue of Ukraine joining NATO. Ukraine was in the Partnership for Peace program (as was Russia) and had been since 1994 (as had Russia). Their joining of NATO was seriously discussed in 2008, but was rejected at that time. Ukrainian relations with NATO declined from 2010–13 under the Yanukovych administration and he cut the Army down to only 49,000 troops. After Yanukovych had been chased out of the country, discussions with NATO were revitalized in 2014 and the size of the Ukrainian Army had more than tripled by the end of 2016.[4] There was no question at this point that Ukraine was very interested in joining NATO. On the other hand, NATO was still very hesitant about committing to defending Ukraine.

NATO added the former Warsaw Pact states of Czechia, Hungary and Poland to the defense alliance in 1999. They added Slovakia, Slovenia, Romania, Bulgaria, Lithuania, Latvia and Estonia to the defense alliance in 2004. That addition of the three former Soviet Baltic states resulted in NATO and Russia adding to a common shared border. This gave NATO an additional border of 207 miles (333km) with Russia.

This was not the first time Russia and NATO had shared a border. They have had a common border of 122 miles (196km) with founding member Norway since 1949. There has also been a common border with the isolated city-province of Kaliningrad with Poland since 1999 of 130 miles (210km) and since 2004 an additional border with Lithuania of 141 miles (227km). The NATO alliance, through Turkey, shared a border with the Soviet Union from 1952 to 1991. It was some 329 miles (529km) in length. Turkey still shares a border with partnership of peace program member Georgia of 157 miles (252km).

The Estonian border at Narva is only 84 miles (135km) away from the downtown of Russia's second city and former Tsarist capital of St. Petersburg (population 5,351,935 according to a 2018 estimate). This was a significant and potentially problematic addition to the NATO alliance, but was done at a time when Russia was not in a good position to strongly object, nor did they at this time. But NATO has shared a border with Russia and the Soviet Union since 1949.

But, NATO was not in any hurry to add Ukraine to the defense alliance. There were a multitude of problems with Ukraine. First, they were still in the middle of war with the Ukrainian separatists and Crimea and Sevastopol were occupied by Russia. Joining a defensive alliance while in a war with two separatist rebellions occurring and them still in a major territorial dispute with Russia created all kinds of complications. Does that mean that the day Ukraine joins NATO the defensive alliance is at war with the DPR or LPR or Russia? Obviously, the NATO alliance has no such interest in those entanglements.

The other major issues were related to governance and corruption. Ukraine's government and business life were extremely corrupt. The Transparency International Corruption Perceptions index as of 2021 ranked Ukraine at 122 out of 180 countries with a score of 32 out of 100. This was the pattern with many of these Eastern European countries. Ukraine has a Global Corruption Barometer of 23%, which is the percentage of public service users paid a bribe in the previous twelve months.[5] Belarus was ranked 82 out of 180 countries with a score of 41 out of 100 and a Global Corruption Barometer of 15%, Kazakhstan was ranked 102 with a score of 37 and 17% respectively, Georgia did much better, ranked 45 with a score of 55 and 4% while Russia itself was ranked lower than Ukraine or the rest of these other countries with a rank of 136, score of 27 and barometer of 27%. The former Commonwealth of Independent States (CIS) all tended to be riddled with corruption and unwarranted influence on the government by businesses. In contrast, NATO countries performed far better, for example, Germany was ranked 10 on the scale with a score of 80 and a barometer of 3%. Even the new NATO allies received higher scores, such as Poland which was ranked 42 with a score of 56 and Global Corruption Barometer of 10%. The three former members of the Soviet Union, Lithuania, Latvia and Estonia, were ranked 34, 36 and 13 respectively. One of the lowest ranking NATO countries in 2021 was Bulgaria, with a ranking of 78 (and score of only 42 and barometer of 19%).[6] Ukraine, and all of the former CIS countries, did worse than that. Clearly there was still much work to be done before Ukraine was ready to join the Western European community as defined by NATO and the EU.

Now, oddly enough for such a corrupt country, it has remained democratic since its independence in 1991. They elected presidents in 1991, 1994, 1999, 2004 (twice), 2010, 2014 and 2019. All but one of those elections were fundamentally free and fair. Also of significance, in three of these seven elections the incumbent lost the election (and in one other case the incumbent was thrown out of office by popular protests before his term ended). To date, no incumbent president has ever lost an election in Russia.

The first 2004 election in Ukraine suffered from wide-ranging voter fraud by Victor Yanukovych and the Party of Regions, but results of this election were the subject of the public protests that became the Orange Revolution, and then the election results were dismissed by the Ukrainian Supreme Court. The election was re-held. This second election was fair and free and Yanukovych did not win. But Yanukovych was fairly elected to be president of the country in 2010 and was thrown out of power by a popular revolt in 2013. The next election in 2014 was also free and fair, although significant parts of the Russian-leaning electorate were not represented because of the seizure of Crimea and Sevastopol and the creation of the DPR and LPR. There is no question that Ukraine is a functioning democracy, but that was not so clear in 2008 when it was previously being considered for membership in NATO. Yanukovych's fraudulent election and the Orange Revolution had occurred only four years earlier and his Party of Regions still held the most seats in parliament, obtaining 34% of the vote in 2007. It was only two years later that the pro-Russian Victor Yanukovych was elected president of the country. He then reduced his defense budget, shrunk the miliary to almost nothing, had his primary political opponent Yulia Tymoshenko arrested and jailed, further massively corrupting an already struggling government, and then decided to join the Eurasian Union against the wishes of the electorate.

But, I gather, Russia really did not want Ukraine to join NATO and now was making an issue of it. It is debatable why this suddenly became a significant problem as it was clearly not on the near-term horizon. NATO had shared a common border with Russia since 1949 and had moved the border to less than a hundred miles from St. Petersburg in 2004. This had not been a major source of friction in the intervening eighteen years. Now suddenly the potential that Ukraine would some day join NATO became the single most important issue in Eastern Europe, even though they had been heading in that direction since 1994.

In fact, the build-up at the border may have made the opposite point, showing the world that there really was a physical threat to Ukraine from Russia. These build-ups certainly reinforced Ukraine's desire to join NATO and put the issue back front and center with the existing thirty NATO members. Invading Donetsk or Luhansk or the rest of Ukraine would certainly work further against that goal. So, if the purpose was to dissuade Ukraine from joining NATO, they appeared to be doing just the opposite.

Of course, the real question is not whether Ukraine wants to join NATO, I gather that is a given. The real question is whether NATO was willing to take on the responsibility of defending Ukraine, especially with two provinces in open revolt and two entities (Crimea and Sevastopol) annexed by Russia. Up until February 2022, I gather the large majority of NATO members favored Ukraine as a NATO member, but no one was currently standing up and encouraging this. Ukrainian's NATO membership appeared to be in limbo, which I gather that is what Russia preferred. The build-up could have been for the sake of signaling that it should stay that way. It turned out that this was not the case. It turns out the build-up was clearly for the reason of occupying parts of Ukraine and removing the current government of Ukraine. The issues over NATO were merely the cover for a 1936–40-style exercise in naked, armed aggression.[7]

U.S. Intelligence Estimates

The interesting aspect of this situation is that U.S. intelligence decided to make Russia deployments public knowledge. This was different to how many other potential conflicts have been handled. So very much part of the story from December 2021 through February 2022 was the constant release of material from the U.S. intelligence community about the threat posed by Russia. It is clear that they had concluded that this was a very valid threat, even though some people had a hard time accepting that this was the case. This was a unique effort.[8]

This will be discussed in depth later, but for this war U.S. intelligence played three major roles. First, it notified the world of the impending threat. In this case they did a convincing job and were correct, even though a lot of people, including many people in Ukraine, had a hard time accepting that this was indeed what Russia was going to do.

On the other hand, their estimates of the situation and forecasting how the war was going to develop could not have been further from the mark. This is discussed later. Finally, they provided considerable intelligence support to Ukraine at both the strategic and tactical level. This was extremely helpful for fighting the war and gave Ukraine many advantages during the fighting. This will also be discussed later.

The January Dialogue

As the Russian build-up continued, it was decided that the U.S., NATO and Russia should hold "security talks" on January 10, 12 and 13 starting in Geneva.[9] Russia wanted to discuss security guarantees. Russia was still denying at this stage that it had any plans for an assault. It does appear that the build-up got Russia the attention they wanted. Russia was specifically insisting that it wanted legally binding guarantees that NATO would not expand further eastwards. This would mean a guarantee that Ukraine would not join NATO and probably also excluded NATO membership for the nations of Georgia and Moldova. They also wanted to ensure that certain offensive weapons would not be deployed to Ukraine or other neighboring countries. The U.S. position was that it could not promise that Ukraine would never join NATO. It was also threatening economic sanctions if Russia attacked Ukraine. The U.S. already had existing economic sanctions in place over the Russian annexation of Crimea and Sevastopol. Meanwhile, U.S. President Biden signed into a law a spending bill that would provide $300 million of aid to Ukraine's armed forces.

The talks were unproductive and that was clear in Geneva on Monday, 10 January, the first day of the talks. Neither side modified their positions and there did not seem to be a good middle-ground position. The Russian delegation then met with the NATO Council on 12 January in Brussels and with the OSCE Permanent Council in Vienna on 13 January. These meetings were equally unproductive.

Starting in January, Russia began to slowly and discretely drawn down their large embassy staff in Kyiv. By mid-January Ukrainian intelligence was claiming there were some 127,000 Russian troops in the area, with 106,000 being part of the land forces. There were 35,000 more forces with the two separatists' armies along with 3,000 Russian troops in Ukraine.[10] This gave the Russians a total of 165,000 troops.

So was Russia Actually Going to Attack Ukraine?

Based upon on the buzz in the news and comments by some Western politicians, it appeared at this stage to be only a question of when, not if, that Russia was going to attack Ukraine. Yet, Russia was saying they are not going to attack. I was still hesitant to believe that they were going to do so because it simply did not make military sense to us. The three issues were: 1. Force ratios, 2. Weather and 3. Warning. Our comments on these at the time were:[11]

Force Ratios: First of all, Russia has amassed a 100K+ troops along the border, plus some forces are in a training exercise in Belarus. I gather the actual figure is on the low side of 100,000, vice being near 200,000. On the other hand, the Ukrainian Army, before mobilization is almost 200,000. So, is Russia really massing so it can attack while outnumbered?

Now, there are a few other factors in what is not that simple of a comparison. First of all, Russia can move more troops into the area(s) of interest on short notice. So that buildup of 100K+ could quickly turn into

300K+. If Russia had more than 300K troops in the area, I would become very concerned. But right now, they do not.

Weather: People are making noise like something will happen in February. It is freakin' cold at that time of year. There is snow on the ground. Do they really want to attack then? I would wait until after the spring thaw, like the Germans did in 1941, 1942 and 1943, when you have a nice long summer for your campaign.

Warning: Surprise is a nice force multiplier. I have a chapter on the subject in my book *War by Numbers*. It is now no surprise if an attack comes. Furthermore, they even lack strategic surprise, so Ukraine has been able to lobby for more aid and has received more weapons. Why would Russia help their potential adversary get prepared, which is what has happened over the last couple of months? Ukraine is receiving weaponry and support that it probably would not have otherwise received. So, did Russia really choose to give Ukraine 2–3 months of warning to prepare before they attack them? This seems counter-intuitive.

As I noted at the time:

I may be proven wrong come February and Russia suddenly comes swarming across the border to take the rest of "New Russia," to take Kharkov (the second largest city in Ukraine) and to cross the Pripyat marshes and Chernobyl/Pripyat area to threaten Kyiv, but right now, I am not sure this is the real scenario. I still think the threats are part of a larger negotiation strategy (although I don't rule out that the Russian government has simply made a mistake).[12]

It turns out, in fact, that Russia and Putin made a mistake and attacked.

As I noted in early February:[13]

Apparently, the current U.S. administration is saying that the attack may happen in the second half of this month. To quote from the *New York Times* article by Helen Cooper and David E. Sanger that I found here: U.S. Warns of Grim Toll if Putin Pursues Full Invasion of Ukraine.

"Should Mr. Putin decide to invade, American officials believe he is not likely to move until the second half of February."

So, maybe a five-week campaign season? Two weeks in February and maybe three weeks in March. In 1943, the German offensive past

Belgorod was called off around 24 March 1943 because of mud. Don't know if "mud season" arrives sooner now and have not done any analysis of the currently mobility of the modern Russian army in poor weather conditions, but I am guessing it will still be a problem. The "American officials" quoted in the *NYT* article are apparently aware of this with their next sentence "By that point, more ground will have frozen, making it easier to move heavy vehicles and equipment ..."

So ... five, maybe six, weeks campaign season, then mud.

As they note in the *NYT* article "... the officials warned that if Mr. Putin chose the most aggressive of his options, he could quickly surround or capture Kyiv ..."

Maybe. Back in 1943, the Russians during the Battle of Kursk started their offensive north of Belgorod on 3 August 1943 and took Kiev on 6 November 1943. I am assuming that the 170,000+ Ukrainian Army will have some ability to slow the Russians down (unlike the Afghani army in August of last year).

Force Levels:

I gather Russia currently has around 110,000 troops and according to *NYT* "... the Russian military had assembled 70 percent of the forces it would need to mount a full invasion of Ukraine ... who assessed that Mr. Putin had concluded that he would need some 150,000 troops from 110 battalion tactical groups to conquer Ukraine ..."

So, they will have 150,000 troops "... to conquer Ukraine ...". I gather this includes the "Thirty thousand troops ... now in Belarus."

The Ukrainian Army is 170,000+. Now, I do not know how good the Ukrainian Army is relative to the Russian Army. Suspect the Russian communications, recon, spotting and artillery are pretty good (see: The Russian Artillery Strike That Spooked The U.S. Army | Mystics & Statistics (dupuyinstitute.org)). They will certainly have air superiority (unless NATO decides to directly support Ukraine). So, they will have the advantage. The range of casualty estimates (see below) seem to give credit the Russians with a 1.7-to-1 to 2.5-to-1 advantage in casualty effectiveness.

Still, I do expect the Ukrainian army, on the defensive, in prepared positions, fully warned, recently supplemented, and maybe somewhat motivated to defend their homeland, is something more than just speed bumps. I don't really see how Russia is going to take Kiev in a five-week campaign.

Casualties:
This one gives me real heartburn. My suspicion is that the officials briefed "casualties" and it ended up in the *NYT* as killed. Keep in mind "casualties" include killed, wounded, wounded and later died of wounds, missing and captured (and deserters). The number of wounded usually outnumbers the number killed by 3- or 4-to-1 and sometimes as high as 10-to-1. I do have a full chapter on the subject in my book *War by Numbers*.

The *NYT* says "… potential deaths … of 5,000 to 25,000 members of the Ukrainian military…"

25,000 deaths times three wounded per person killed is 100,000 casualties. 100,000 casualties from a force of 170,000 is almost 60% losses. Are they really talking about an army level force taking 60% losses in a five-week campaign? That has not happened a lot. Do those losses include the various reserves and militias that Ukraine can call up? If so, the numbers mesh together better.

The armed forces of Ukraine are 215,000 active (2022). Their reserves are 250,000 (2022). Available for military service is 11,139,646, ages 16–49 (2015). Fit for military service is 6,979,035 (2015). Reaching military age annually is 470,406 (2021). So, how big of a Ukrainian military are we talking about here? 170K in ground forces, or half-million or more counting reserves, militia and new call-ups? If Ukraine calls up its reserves and draft militia, is Russia really going to take (and hold) a lot of Ukraine with an army of 150,000? Anyhow, a lot of things don't match up here. Perhaps that is because the *NYT* did not properly quote the "officials," perhaps because of the details of some of the scenarios they drafted (which may be improbable), or perhaps because they have garbled their calculations (this has happened before, remember Afghanistan in August 2021).

Anyhow, it is hard for me to evaluate the data in the *NYT* article. In the meantime, I will stick to my opinions given in my first two blog posts on the subject.

My opinion in my first two blog posts on the subject was, "If I was going to invade Ukraine, I would use surprise, overwhelming force and hit them during good weather. This is not what is happening right now. So, I still have a hard time believing we are about to see a major conventional war starting this month."

Ukraine did not Actually Think Russia was Going to Invade

While the U.S. intelligence community had come to the conclusion that Russia was going to invade, or at least that there was a high probability of such, the Ukrainian government held out at least two days before the invasion started that they were not going to invade. The internal workings of the decision-making process is not known to us, but it does appear that the majority of the Ukrainian government did not believe the Russian invasion was going to happen up until almost the last moment. President Zelenskyy also stated this on 22 February, two days before the invasion started.

As significant, the Ukrainian armed forces were not fully mobilized up until this point. While they they were reasonably well prepared just in case, this is somewhat different to being fully mobilized.

In all reality, it was not entirely certain that Russia was going to invade Ukraine until they did.

The History of Mistakes

To put it bluntly, Vladimir Putin made a mistake by invading Ukraine. He still may gain something out of the process, but clearly the decision was made under the assumption that this operation was going to be a lot easier than it was. The fact that the war has now dragged on for over 500 days shows the unintended consequences of such a decision. In the meantime, he: 1. Threw away the advantage of surprise, both tactical and strategic, 2. Chose to attack during a weather shortened campaign season and 3. Attacked with insufficient force. These will all be discussed later, but the point is that this operation was poorly conceived, poorly conducted and a mistake.

Actually, mistakes are quite common among political leadership. Just addressing some of the wars of the last century, one wonders who got the decision-making correct in 1914. Was Austria-Hungary's decision to declare war on Serbia on 31 July 1914 properly thought through? Four years later, the Hapsburg monarchy was removed from power and their country was dissolved. Was the Russian decision to back Serbia made in the middle of 1914 properly thought through? By mid-1918, the Tsarist government had been overthrown, the Tsar and his entire family had been executed, Russia had lost significant territory to nationalistic independence movements and the Russian government was replaced by historically one of the bloodiest and most brutal regimes in world history. On 1 August 1914, when Germany went to war, was this a properly thought-out decision, or was their earlier decision in the summer of 1914 to back Austria-Hungary unconditionally? Before the end of 1918, the kaiser had been overthrown and Germany lost territory in the settlement of the war, and was then thrown into an extended period of economic and political instability. Turkey, then known at the Ottoman Empire, joined the war in October/November 1914. It did not need to. When the war was over, the sultan had been overthrown (which may have happened regardless of the war) and the Ottoman Empire was dissolved, and lost significant amounts of the territory they held. The First World War was the death of four Imperial dynasties in Europe.

But the same holds true for the Second World War. Adolf Hitler's decision to initiate a war on 1 September 1939 led to Germany being divided up into four sections six years later, with Hitler and his wife committing suicide in a bunker in the face of an advancing Soviet Army. Benito Mussolini, who brought Italy into the war later, also ended up with his country conquered, his newly developed New Roman Empire dissolved and him and his mistress dangling from a meat hook in 1945. And then one has to look at Japan, which unilaterally decided to start a war by a surprise attack against the United States on 7 December 1941. The Japanese leader, Prime Minister Hideki Tojo, was executed in 1948 and his country occupied by the United States in 1946. Clearly, this was a series of extremely poor decisions by the leaders of these countries. There seems to be no lack of such examples.

Even in the post-Second World War era, there were many poorly conceived and failed operations. This would include North Korea's decision to invade South Korea in 1950, General Macarthur's advance to the Yalu River in Korea later in 1950, the U.S. intervention in Vietnam from 1965–73, the Soviet invasion of Afghanistan from 1979–89, the Iraqi invasion of Iran in 1979, the U.S. deployment in Lebanon 1982–4, the Iraqi invasion of Kuwait in 1990 and many others that I do not care to exhaustively list right now.

History does not suffer from a lack of examples of important decision-makers reaching very poor and potentially fatal decisions for them and their countries. Whether this is the case with Vladimir Putin has yet to be seen, but clearly the decision on how to initiate the war was a mistake. The decision to go to war at all may also be a mistake. Whether it will be a fatal mistake for Putin and his regime has yet to be seen.

Kyiv will be Conquered in 72 Hours

One of the odd things the U.S. intelligence community did was assume that Kyiv would be conquered in 72 hours. Not sure how they reached such a decision, but in retrospect it clearly was in error. Before the war, the U.S. intelligence community was mostly saying that Kyiv would be taken in

72 hours. Meanwhile, the Ukrainian Defense Minister was saying that Russia "…will not capture either Kyiv, Odesa, Kharkiv, or any other city."[14] There is a big difference between 72 hours and never.

But it was not just the intelligence community, U.S. General Milley, the Chairman of the Joint Chiefs of Staff, also suggested that Kyiv could fall within 72 hours. Now, the U.S. intelligence community is multi-faceted. The CIA (Central Intelligence Agency) is just one central agency in the community. There are also organizations such as the NSA (National Security Agency), the NRO (National Reconnaissance Office) that report to the Department of Defense and the I&A (Office of Intelligence and Analysis) that reports to the Department of Homeland Security, among others. So, it is clear that for whatever reason, they decided that Russia could take Kyiv in 72 hours. This may have been what Russia was planning and also thought. With the massive capabilities of our intelligence community, I have no doubt that we had some awareness of what Russia thought they could accomplish. Did we mistakenly assume that they were correct?

But the Department of Defense has its own intelligence agency, the Defense Intelligence Agency (DIA). Obviously anything of this nature would have been cleared through this organization before General Milley said anything. It light of it being a defense intelligence agency, I do wonder if they did any independent analysis of the potential combat situation, including wargaming out various scenarios. I do not know, but it does appear odd that they independently came to the same conclusion.

On the other hand, one intelligence function in the U.S. government did not agree with the conclusion reached. The small Bureau of Intelligence and Research (INR) at the U.S. Department of State concluded that the Ukrainian Army and people would put up a fight. As the Ukrainian Army numbered at least 170,000 and had some actual combat experience, this is nothing to scoff at. Clearly, they could put up a fight. For some reason, this was being discounted by the Department of Homeland Security, the CIA and the DIA. It was not being discounted by the State Department. The primary analysis that the State Department did was a series of polls taken of the Ukrainian people. This was polling done under contract for the State Department directly for them, so as to get a feel for what the people of Ukraine felt. This told the State Department that they were going to fight.[15] This apparently was not considered in the other analysis conducted by the other U.S. intelligence agencies.

It is possible that the other agencies were gun-shy after having mis-predicted the speed at which the Afghani government fell in 2021. Perhaps the sudden collapse of the entire Afghani Army had conditioned them to think the same would happen with the Ukrainian Army. Regardless, it is clear that most of the

U.S. intelligence community simply got this wrong, and the mistake was in the exact opposite direction of the mistakes they made regarding Afghanistan. It is not very comforting that most of these intelligence agencies made two major mistakes (Afghan and Ukraine) two years in a row, and for different reasons. The U.S. does spend a lot on intelligence.

What also bothers me as an analyst, is that there does not appear to be any solid analytical foundation for their conclusions. I have no idea of what analysis they did, but I would have expected at least the DIA to have wargamed out possible scenarios. I do know for a fact that the CIA used to wargame out possible combat scenarios between countries.[16] But, it does not appear that any such analysis was being done, or if it was, they were dismissing the Ukrainian Army as being as worthless as the Afghani Army was in 2021. As the Ukrainian Army had been actively engaged in combat since 2014, this would be hard to believe.

On the other hand, the State Department's primary analytical tool appears to have been a public opinion survey. It did not include any wargaming and combat analysis. Still, even with this extremely limited piece of analytical material, they were able to reach a conclusion that was a whole lot more correct that what was achieved by the Department of Homeland Security, CIA or DIA, all agencies with considerably more funding. As a tax-payer, I have every right to be concerned about this.

Regardless of the wild inaccuracy of the initial predictions, it appears obvious to everyone that if Russia attacked Ukraine, they would make some progress. They have some highly trained and well-equipped units, they have a more advanced array of equipment and had some recent deployments in both Ukraine in 2014–15 and Syria in around 2012 to the present. It was expected to be a competent Russian Army that had the advantage of air superiority. It was hard to imagine that with air superiority, they would not be able to make some progress somewhere.

Oil Prices and Combat Power

On 5 December, the price of oil was below $70 a barrel (Brent Crude was $69.92). A couple of years ago it was claimed that Russia needed the price of oil to be at $80 or higher to balance their budget. Oil is a significant part of the government revenue, so the incoming revenue varies widely as the oil and gas markets go up and down. Running significant deficits may limit their willingness to explore military options. Perhaps the easiest way to constrain Russian adventurism was to keep the price of oil down.

A month earlier, the price of oil was over $80, but has dropped to a low of $68.87 on 1 December. It then started steadily rising after that to the point where at the end of January it was $91.21. The ratcheting up of tensions was helping the Russian oil market and balancing their budget. By 22 February it was up to $96.84 a barrel. So now, the Russian budget was running in the black.

The Build-up, 21–3 February

On 21 February, the Russian government recognized the Lugansk and Donetsk People's Republics as legitimate countries, a legal status that no other country in the world provided them. That evening Putin ordered Russian troops into the Donbas on a "peacekeeping operation," even though there was nothing more intense than the usual level of sniping and shelling that had been going on for the last six or more years. That night, Putin gave an extended speech on the situation with Ukraine. It went on for less than an hour. To quote from parts of the speech:[17]

> My address concerns the events in Ukraine.... The situation in Donbas has reached a critical, acute stage ... Going back to history, I would like to repeat that the Soviet Union was established in place of the former Russian Empire in 1922 ... The virus of nationalist ambitions is still with us, and the mine laid at the initial stage to destroy state immunity to the disease of nationalism was ticking. As I have already said the mine was the right of secession from the Soviet Union. In the mid-1980s, the increasing socioeconomic problems and the apparent crisis of the planned economy aggravated the ethnic issue, which essentially was not based on any expectations or unfulfilled dreams of the Soviet peoples but primarily the growing appetites of the local elites. However, instead of analyzing the situation, taking appropriate measures, first of all in the economy, and gradually transforming the political system and government in a well-considered and balanced manner, the Communist Party leadership only engaged in open doubletalk about the revival of Leninists principle of national self-determination. Moreover, in the course of power struggle within the Communist Party itself, each of the opposing sides, in a bid to expand its support base, started to thoughtlessly incite and encourage nationalist sentiments, manipulating them and promising their potential supporters whatever they wished. Against the backdrop of the superficial and populist rhetoric about democracy and a bright future based either on a market or a planned economy, but amid a true impoverishment of people and widespread shortages, no one among the powers that be was

thinking about the inevitable tragic consequences for the country. Next, they entirely embarked on the track beaten at the inception of the USSR and pandering to the ambitions of the nationalist elites nurtured within their own party ranks. But in so doing, they forgot that the CPSU no longer had – thank God – the tools for retaining power and the country itself, tools such as state terror and a Stalinist-type dictatorship, and that the notorious guiding role of the party was disappearing without a trace, like a morning mist, right before their eyes. And then, the September 1989 plenary session of the CPSU Central Committee approved a truly fatal document, the so-called ethnic policy of the party in modern conditions, the CPSU platform. It included the following provisions, I quote: "The republics of the USSR shall possess all the rights appropriate to their status as sovereign socialist states."

The next point: "The supreme representative bodies of power of the USSR republics can challenge and suspect the operation of the USSR Government's resolutions and directives in their territory."

And finally: "Each republic of the USSR shall have citizenship of its own, which shall apply to all of its residents."

Wasn't it clear what these formulas and decisions would lead to? Now is not the time or place to go into matters pertaining to state or constitutional law, or define the concept of citizenship. But one may wonder: why was it necessary to rock the country even more in that already complicated situation? The facts remain. Even two years before the collapse of the USSR, its fate was actually predetermined. It is now that radicals and nationalists, including and primarily those in Ukraine, are taking credit for having gained independence. As we can see, this is absolutely wrong. This disintegration of our united country was brought about by the historic, strategic mistakes on the part of the Bolshevik leaders and the CPSU leadership, mistakes committed at different times in state-building and in economic and ethnic policies. The collapse of the historical Russia known as the USSR is on their conscience.

Forgive this long quotation, but it is interesting as Putin clearly lays out the argument for the legal justification for the creation of fifteen independent states out of the former Soviet Union (of which Russia was only one of these fifteen states) and then dismisses this legal justification. He states his disapproval in 1991 of the collapse of the "historical Russia known as the USSR." He is stating that "historical Russia" is the same as the USSR.

More basically, Putin is effectively saying that none of the fifteen sovereign states of the former Soviet Union has any justification to be an independent state. They should clearly be considered to be part of "historical Russia." This would not only include Ukraine, but, of course, Belarus, Georgia, Kazakhstan and ten other countries. It would also include Lithuania, Latvia and Estonia, which joined NATO in 2004. This is a significant statement, as one could them make the interpretation that this argument not only applied to conquering the country of Ukraine, but conquering thirteen other former Soviet countries.

Added to this, Putin claims that the "Soviet Union was established in place of the former Russian Empire." Does this mean that old elements of the Russian Empire, such as Finland and Poland, should also be considered legitimate parts of his Russian state? That could be one interpretation of his presentation.

It is clear from Putin's recounting of history that he had decided none of the former Soviet states had any right to independence and that they were clearly part of "historical Russia" which appeared to include the borders of the former Soviet Union and possibly the borders of the Russian Empire in 1913.

To continue with his speech (after a small gap):

At the same time, the Ukrainian authorities – I would like to emphasize this – began by building their statehood on the negation of everything that united us, trying to distort the mentality and historical memory of millions of people, of entire generations living in Ukraine. It is not surprising that Ukrainian society was faced with the rise of far-right nationalism, which rapidly developed into aggressive Russophobia and neo-Nazism. This resulted in the participations of Ukrainian nationalists and neo-Nazis in the terrorist groups in the North Caucasus and the increasingly loud territorial claims to Russia. ...

A few words about Crimea. The people of the peninsula feely made their choice to be with Russia. The Kiev authorities cannot challenge the clearly stated choice of the people, which is why they have opted for aggressive action, for activating extremists cells, including radical Islamist organizations, for sending subversives to stage terrorist attacks at critical infrastructure facilities, and for kidnapping Russian citizens. We have factual proof that such aggressive actions are being taken with support from Western security services. In March 2021, a new Military Strategy was adopted in Ukraine. This document is almost entirely dedicated to confrontation with Russia and sets the goal of involving foreign states in a conflict with our country. The strategy stipulates the organization of what can be described as a terrorist underground movement in Russia's Crimea and in Donbas. It also sets out the contours of a potential war, which should end, according to the Kiev strategists, I quote further:

"with the assistance of the international community on favorable terms for Ukraine," as well as currently expressed in Kiev, I also quote here – please, listen carefully – "with foreign military support in the geopolitical confrontation with the Russian Federation." In fact, this is nothing other than preparation for hostilities against our country, Russia. As we know, it has already been stated today that Ukraine intends to create its own nuclear weapons, and this is not just bragging. Ukraine has the nuclear technologies created back in the Soviet times and delivery vehicles for such weapons, including aircraft, as well as the Soviet-designed Tochka-U precision tactical missiles with a range of over 100km. But they can do more; it is only a matter of time. They have had the groundwork for this since Soviet era. In other words, acquiring tactical nuclear weapons will be much easier for Ukraine than for some other states. I am not going to mention here, which are conducting such research, especially if Kiev receives foreign technological support. We cannot rule this out either. If Ukraine acquires weapons of mass destruction, the situation in the world and in Europe will drastically change, especially for us, for Russia. We cannot but react to this real danger, all the more so since, let me repeat, Ukraine's Western patrons may help it acquire these weapons to create yet another threat to our country.

No attempt will be made here to analyze, collaborate or dispute the statements made in Putin's speech. That would take a book into itself. Needless to say, lots of the statements made in Putin's speech could not be verified. The statement "we cannot but react to this real danger" clearly lays out the path this presentation is on. It then continues with:

We are seeing how persistently the Kiev regime is being pumped with arms. Since 2014, the United States alone has spent billions of dollars for this purpose, including supplies of arms and equipment and training of specialists. In the last few months, there has been a constant flow of Western weapons to Ukraine, ostentatiously, with the entire world watching. Foreign advisors supervise the activities of Ukraine's armed forces and special services and we are well aware of this. Over the past few years, military contingents of NATO countries have been almost constantly present on Ukrainian territory under the pretext of exercises … Obviously such undertakings are designed to be a cover-up for a rapid buildup of the NATO military group on Ukrainian territory.… Ukraine joining NATO is a direct threat to Russia's security.… We also know the main adversary of the United States and NATO. It is Russia …

Last December, we handed over to our Western partners a draft treaty between the Russian Federation and the United States of America on security guarantees, as well as a draft agreement on measures to ensure the security of the Russian Federation and NATO member states ... that includes Russia's core proposals which contain three key points. First, to prevent further NATO expansion. Second, to have the Alliance refrain from deploying assault weapon systems on Russian borders. And finally, rolling back the bloc's military capability and infrastructure in Europe to where they were in 1997, when the NATO-Russia Founding Acts was signed. These principled proposals of ours have been ignored.

Just to clarify, the Russia proposal for a rolling back NATO's military capability and infrastructure to where they were in 1997 would indicate no NATO presence in Estonia, Latvia, Lithuania, Poland, Hungary, Romania or eight other NATO countries. Obviously, this was a non-starter and not a serious recommendation. This was not a case of trying to prevent NATO overreach, but a case of Russia deciding that that they wanted to turn the clock back twenty-four years.

And then he concludes:

Their one and only goal is to hold back the development of Russia. And they will keep doing so, just as they did before, even without any formal pretext just because we exist and will never compromise our sovereignty, national interests or values. I would like to be clear and straightforward: in the current circumstances, when our proposals for an equal dialogue on fundamental issues have actually remained unanswered by the United States and NATO, when the level of threats to our country has increased significantly, Russia has every right to respond in order to ensure its security. That is exactly what we will do.

With regard to the state of affairs in Donbas, we see that the ruling Kiev elites never stop publicly making clear their unwillingness to comply with the Mink Package of Measures to settle the conflict and are not interested in a peaceful settlement. On the contrary, they are trying to orchestrate a blitzkrieg in Donbas as was the case in 2014 and 2015. We all know how these reckless schemes ended. Now, not a single day goes by without Donbas communities coming under shelling attacks. The recently formed large military force makes use of attack drones, heavy equipment, missiles, artillery and multiple rocket launchers. The killing of civilians, the blockade, the abuse of people, including children, women and the elderly, continues unabated. As we say, there is no end in sight to this. Meanwhile, the so-called civilized world, which our Western colleagues proclaimed themselves the only representatives of, prefers not to see this, as if this horror and genocide, which almost 4 million people are facing, do not exist. But they do exist and only because these people did not agree with the West-supported coup in Ukraine in 2014 and opposed the transition towards the Neanderthal and aggressive nationalism and neo-Nazism which have been elevated in Ukraine to the rank of national policy. They are fighting for their elementary right to live on their own land, to speak their own language, and to preserve their culture and traditions. How long can this tragedy continue? How much longer can one put up with this?

Russia has done everything to preserve Ukraine's territorial integrity. All these years, it has persistently and patiently pushed for the implementation of UN Security Council Resolution 2202 of February 17, 2015, which consolidated the Minsk Package of Measures of February 12, 2015, to settle the situation in Donbas. Everything was in vain! Presidents and Rada deputies come and go, but deep down the aggressive and nationalistic regime that seized power in Kiev remains unchanged. It is entirely a product of the 2014 coup, and those who then embarked on the path of violence, bloodshed and lawlessness did not recognize then and do not recognize now any solution to the Donbas issue other than a military one.

In this regard, I consider it necessary to take a long overdue decision and to immediately recognize the independence and sovereignty of the Donetsk People's Republic and the Lugansk People's Republic. I would like to ask the Federal Assembly of the Russian Federation to support this decision and then ratify the Treaty of Friendship and Mutual Assistance with both republics. These two documents will be prepared and signed shortly.

And from those who seized and continue to hold power in Kiev, we demand an immediate cessation of hostilities. Otherwise, the responsibility for the possible continuation of the bloodshed will lie entirely on the conscience of Ukraine's ruling regime. As I announce the decisions taken today, I remain confident in the support of Russia's citizens and the country's patriotic forces.

Thank you.

At this point, it was clear that something was about to happen in Ukraine. The conflict in Donbas has been effectively in stasis since early 2015. Now war was coming.

Video footage the next morning showed that Russia tanks and other military forces were moving in the areas of the Luhansk and Donetsk People's Republics and the Federal Assembly of Russia authorized the use of military forces outside of Russia. In response, Ukrainian President Zelenskyy called up the Army reservists while Russia abandoned its embassy in Kyiv. Just before 0500 Kyiv time on 24 February, Putin announced a "special military operation" in eastern Ukraine.

It is difficult to consider this as anything other than a blatant declaration of war by Russia on Ukraine. It was not based upon any valid *casus belli*. It would appear from his speech on 21 February that he is arguing that although these nations were established by the organs of the Soviet Union, this was in error and so, therefore, as the Soviet Union is part of the "historical Russia," they should be part of Russia. The UN Charter, of which the Soviet Union was a founding member, as was Ukraine and Belarus, does not define what a proper cause of war is. On the other hand, Article 51 does state, "Nothing in the present Charter shall impair the inherent right of individual or collective self-defence if an armed attack occurs against a Member of the United Nations ...."

The Russian government has put out their arguments out in favor of this war, often relying on belittling or demonizing the Ukrainians, but their arguments have not been taken very seriously by most people outside of Russia. In fact, they really did not do a very clever job of explaining or justifying their arguments, and appeared not to be very concerned with how the rest of the world perceived their actions. It is almost as if they simply did not feel the need to play the international public relations game and could do whatever they wished when they wished to. This, along with their other actions, turned this into a giant public relations mistake that would end up costing them the lives of their soldiers. Their high-handed behavior was inexplicable.

In the end, this whole episode looked more like the actions of Adolph Hitler on 1 September 1939 than anything else that has occurred in Europe in more than eighty years.

Chapter 4

The Ukrainian Army

In 2016, the Ukrainian Army was reported as having a strength of 169,000. In 2021, the armed forces in Ukraine were reported as having a strength of 255,000 active personnel. This figure included Navy and Air Force strengths. In 2016, the Air Force had 36,300 personnel, the Navy had 6,500 personnel and the Special Forces had 4,000. The Ukrainian armed forces also consisted of the separate Ukraine Air Assault Force. This force became an independent branch of the armed forces in 2016 and consisted of 20,000 troops in February 2022 and 7 maneuver brigades. The February 2022 edition of the IISS handbook gave the armed forces a strength of 196,600, which is odd in light of the previous figure of 255,000 for 2021.[1] This included an Army of 125,600, a Navy of 15,000, an Air Force of 35,000, an Air Assault Force of 20,000 and Special Forces of 1,000. They also reported a Gendarmerie and Paramilitary of 102,000. These varying numbers cannot be resolved, but the indications are that even in 2021, just before the start of the war, the Ukrainian Army probably numbered about 200,000 ground troops or higher, including mobilized reserve units.

Ukraine also had 900,000 troops listed in reserve in 2021 according to the IISS estimates.[2] This figure appears to have been a paper strength only, as another 900,000 reserve forces did not suddenly appear in the battlefield shortly after the start of the invasion. They did have a number of active militia units, such as the Azov Regiment. It is not known if these are counted among the 169,000 or the 900,000, but probably the later. These units were part of the National Guard which reported to the Ministry of the Internal Affairs, as do the State Border Guard Service and the National Police. The State Border Guard Service consists of 42,000–60,000 personnel.[3] The National Police has up to 100,000 personnel.[4] There are additional Ministry of Internal Forces that sometimes get added to the figures of people mobilized.[5]

In addition to the National Guard are the Territorial Defense Forces (TDF). In 2014, Ukraine started organizing Territorial Defense battalions from volunteers as the fighting developed at that time. They were reorganized as a stand-alone branch in the armed forces in 2021 and on 1 January 2022 were officially activated. At the start of the current war, they were not actively deployed forces but that changed rapidly as the situation developed, adding tens of thousands of militia to the battlefield, sometimes at critical junctures.

Counting the active militia at the start of the war, the Ukrainian Army probably had more than 200,000 troops, perhaps as many as 210,000–220,000 with mobilization in early 2022.

Still, this was not a level of mobilization expected for a country about ready to go to war. With a population of over 40 million, this was around 0.5% of the population mobilized and the military expenditures in 2020 only made up around 3% of the GDP. In contrast, in 2020 the United States spent 3.74% of its GDP on defense, while the threatening Russia was spending over 4.26% from an economy almost ten times the size.[6] Ukraine clearly could have and should have been better mobilized and better prepared for the war with Russia.

At the start of the war, the Ukrainian Army had around 18 activated maneuver brigades and up to 9 reserve brigades ready to be activated.[7] It appears that 4 or 5 of these brigades had 3 maneuver battalions per brigade, while 13 or 14 of them had 4 or more maneuver battalions.[8] This amounted to at least 74 or so maneuver battalions.[9] Added to that were some 5 regular airborne, air assault and air mobile brigades and 2 Naval Infantry brigades and other such forces which included at least a further 30 maneuver battalions.[10] Therefore, the Ukrainian armed forces could deploy at least 104 maneuver battalions at the start of the war. It was estimated at the time that they were about to be invaded by 150 Russian maneuver battalions or Battalion Tactical Groups (BTGs).[11]

The Ukrainian Army started with war with at least 18 maneuver brigades mobilized which have been identified. It was primarily a mechanized infantry army. According to the list assembled below, Ukraine started with war with 2 regular and 1 active reserve tank brigades and 2 more reserve tank brigades that were not fully deployable in the first 6 weeks of the war. A tank brigade has 4 maneuver battalions, 3 tank and 1 mechanized infantry.[12] It also had an artillery and air defense battalion along with support troops. Ukraine started the war with at least 892 tanks, including 720 T-64s.[13]

The Army had 9 active mechanized brigades. It also had 5 reserve mechanized brigades of which 3 may have been deployed in the first 6 weeks of the war.[14] Each regular mechanized brigade had at least 3 mechanized infantry battalions and probably a tank battalion.[15] A tank battalion usually consisted of 31 T-64s. They also had a collection of infantry fighting vehicles (IFVs) and armored personnel carriers (APCs). The infantry fighting vehicles were usually Soviet-era BMP-2 or BMP-2Ks. The BMP-2 was introduced in the early 1980s, weighs about 16 tons, carries 3 crew and 7 passengers, has

1.3in (33mm) of armor and carries a stabilized 30mm autocannon, a 9P135m ATGM launcher able to fire Konkurs 9M113 (AT-5) or Kornet-M 9M133M (AT-5B) missiles, a 7.62mm coaxial machinegun and an AGS-30 grenade launcher. The BMP-2K is the command version of this vehicle, with 6 crew.

The armored personnel carriers were usually Soviet-era MT-LBs. This is a 1950s Soviet-era design made at the Kharkov Tractor Plant. It weighs about 12 tons, carries 2 crew and 11 passengers, has 14mm of armor and usually carries a 7.62mm machinegun. The Kharkiv Tractor Plant, which is over 90 years old, was still producing MT-LBs in the 2000s. It was a public company that became majority owned by the Russian billionaire Oleg Deripaska in 2007. Control was regained by Ukraine in 2016 when it appeared that parts of the factory were going to be dismantled and transferred. In November 2018, Russia imposed sanctions on the factory and its new owners. The factory was reported destroyed by extensive shelling in late February 2022.

The inventory count of IFVs and APCs, according to open sources was 1,510 IFVs of which 890 are BMP-2s and BMP-2Ks and well over 2,000 APCs, which includes at least 2,090 MT-LBs.[16] They also have artillery, anti-aircraft weapons, anti-tank weapons and the entire range and mix of weapons.

The Ukrainians have 2 mountain assault brigades which had 3 mountain assault battalions and perhaps a tank battalion. This includes 16th Tank Battalion assigned to 128th Mountain Assault Brigade.

Finally, they had 6 motorized and foot infantry brigades, 4 regular and 2 reserve. These had 3 infantry battalions and a tank company.

This is a total of 18 active brigades deploying at least 892 tanks.[17] This is still an armor moderate force with 5.3 tanks per thousand soldiers.[18]

List of Active Ukrainian Ground Forces Brigades[19]

Unit Name	Type
1st Tank Brigade	Regular
4th Tank Brigade	Reserve
17th Tank Brigade	Regular
10th Mountain Assault Brigade	Regular
14th Mechanized Brigade	Regular
24th Mechanized Brigade	Regular
28th Mechanized Brigade	Regular
30th Mechanized Brigade	Regular
53rd Mechanized Brigade	Regular
54th Mechanized Brigade	Regular

56th Motorized Infantry Brigade	Regular
57th Motorized Infantry Brigade	Regular
58th Motorized Infantry Brigade	Regular
59th Motorized Infantry Brigade	Regular
72nd Mechanized Brigade	Regular
92nd Mechanized Brigade	Regular
93rd Mechanized Brigade	Regular
128th Mountain Assault Brigade	Regular

List of Other Ukrainian Ground Forces Brigades[20]

3rd Tank Brigade	Reserve[21]
5th Tank Brigade	Reserve
11th Motorized Infantry Brigade	Reserve
15th Mechanized Brigade	Reserve
33rd Mechanized Brigade	Reserve
60th Mechanized Brigade	Reserve
61st Jager Infantry Brigade	Reserve[22]
62nd Mechanized Brigade	Reserve
63rd Mechanized Brigade	Reserve

It is uncertain if 60th, 61st, 62nd or 63rd brigades were active in the first six weeks of the war. It is fairly certain that 11th, 15th and 33rd were not. The 3rd Tank Brigade did not arrive in the area of Izyum, near Kharkiv, until mid-April. The 5th Tank Brigade was only partly manned and held in the area of Odesa for the first part of the war. The 14th Tank Brigade (reserve) is not listed as it is currently still inactive.

Other separate maneuver battalions include:[23]

12th Tank Battalion
54th Reconnaissance Battalion
74th Reconnaissance Battalion
130th Reconnaissance Battalion
131st Reconnaissance Battalion
143rd Reconnaissance Battalion

The Ukrainian Army consists of eleven artillery brigades, with two of them reserve. Most brigades consist of four artillery battalions and an additional anti-tank battalion with 26th, 40th, 45th and 55th Artillery Brigades. The 44th Artillery Brigade had only three artillery battalions and an anti-tank battalion. They are:

15th Artillery Recon Brigade
19th Missile Brigade
26th Artillery Brigade
27th Rocket Artillery Brigade
40th Artillery Brigade
43rd Artillery Brigade
44th Artillery Brigade
55th Artillery Brigade
107th Rocket Artillery Brigade

Reserve:[24]
38th Artillery Brigade
45th Artillery Brigade

There are three other services that provide ground forces, the Navy, the Air Assault Forces and the Special Forces. The Air Assault Forces consist of five mobilized airborne, air assault and air mobile brigades, two reserve brigades, and their support units. Most brigades consist of three battalions and a tank company. It was reported to have a strength of 20,000 in February 2022. These forces include:

25th Airborne "Sicheshalska" Brigade
79th Air Assault Brigade
80th Air Assault Brigade
81st Air Mobile Brigade
95th Air Assault Brigade

Reserves:[25]
45th Air Assault Brigade[26]
46th Air Mobile Brigade

The Ukrainian Air Assault Forces also include:

132nd Separate Reconnaissance Battalion
148th Howitzer Self-Propelled Battalion

Each brigade is between 1,000 to 2,200 people, ideally including 3 infantry battalions, 3 artillery battalions, a tank company and a reconnaissance company.[27] The Air Assault Forces add up to another 16 maneuver battalions to the Ukrainian Army, if the brigades were fully up the strength (which may not have been the case).

The Special Operation Forces are 4,000 strong and include 2 units that may add 2 or more battalions to the maneuver forces:

3rd Special Purpose Regiment "Prince Sviatoslav the Brave"
8th Special Purpose Regiment "Iziaslav Mstislavich"

The Ukrainian Navy also provided amphibious ground forces, which also had significant combat capabilities:

35th Naval Infantry Brigade (Odesa)
   2nd Tank Battalion with T-80BVs[28]
36th Naval Infantry Brigade (Mykolaiv)
   1st Tank Battalion with T-80BVs[29]

These two Marine or Naval Infantry brigades consist of three infantry battalions, a tank battalion, an artillery brigade with three artillery battalions, an air defense battalion and other supporting units including a reconnaissance company and a sniper rifle company. Other naval ground units of significance include 406th Artillery Brigade (Mykolaiv) of four field artillery battalions, 140th Reconnaissance Battalion and 32nd Rocket Artillery Regiment.

Active militia units that were developed during the first war (2014–15) include:

Donbas Battalion – demobilized September 2016
Dnipro Battalion
Azov Regiment – active in 2022

The Donbas Battalion, or 2nd Battalion of Special Assignment "Donbas," was created in 2014 and is part of the National Guard of Ukraine. It was originally formed by Russian-speaking Ukrainians from Donbas. The battalion was demobilized in September 2016 and the majority of their personnel went into the reserves. They formed a public organization called the Internal Corps of the Donbas Battalion which has operated from October 2016 to the present. They are no longer a combat unit.

The Dnipro Battalion, or the Dnipro-1 Regiment, reports to the Ministry of Internal Affairs of Ukraine as a Special Tasks Patrol Police. It also was created in 2014 and hired Romanians and Georgian military advisors to train their troops. It is still supposedly active, but we have not heard anything from it during the current war.

The Azov Battalion, which then became the Azov Regiment, is still active and was heavily involved in defending Mariupol from February through April of 2022. It provided a large battalion-sized force for Mariupol and has forces deployed elsewhere in Ukraine in 2022 including at Brovary near Kyiv and a new unit raised in Kharkiv. It was formed in May 2014 and was incorporated into the National Guard of Ukraine in November 2014. It has ties to far-right wing groups, connections to neo-fascist ideologies and has made use of symbols borrowed from Nazism. Russia designated it a terrorist organization in August 2022. It was based in Mariupol. Most of members are drawn from Russian speaking regions of Ukraine. It also has a number of foreign fighters.

National Guard of Ukraine

The National Guard of Ukraine is part of the Ministry of Internal Affairs. The National Guard became merged into the Internal Troops of Ukraine in January 2000 as a cost-saving measure, but was reestablished in March 2014. The authorized strength at re-establishment was originally 33,000 troops and the National Guard had considerable policing and security duties. Still, it became the home of the various volunteer battalions that added several capable combat units to the stable, including the Donbas and Azov battalions which had a strength of 900–1,000 troops. According to official figures, by mid-April, the Interior Ministry and the National Guard had lost 308 personnel since war broke out in early 2014. This included 108 from the National Guard's volunteer battalions.

Among the major ground-combat units in the National Guard at the start of the war in 2022 are:[30]

General Directorate of the National Guard of Ukraine – Kyiv
1st Independent Special Purpose Brigade "Ivan Bogun"
4th Rapid Reaction Brigade – Hostomel
- 2 infantry battalions, a tank battalion, an artillery battalion, an AA missile battalion and support units
1st Important State Facilities Protection Regiment – Dnipro
- 3 infantry battalions
2nd Important State Facilities Protection Regiment – Shostka
- 3 infantry battalions

4th Important State Facilities Protection Regiment – Pavlohrad
  • 3 infantry battalions
1st–5th Important State Facilities Protection Battalions – 1 battalion at each nuclear power plant, including Chernobyl, Zaporizhzhia, Khmelnytskyi, South Ukraine and Rivne
Western Operational-Territorial Command – Lviv
  2nd National Guard Brigade "Halychuna" – Lviv
    • 4 infantry battalions
  8th Operational Regiment "Jaguar" – Kalynivka
    • 3 operational battalions
  40th National Guard Regiment – Vinnytsia
    • Assumed to have 3 National Guard battalions
  45th Operational Regiment – Lviv
    • 3 operational battalions
  50th National Guard Regiment – Ivano-Frankivsk
    • 1 operational battalion, 1 infantry company, 2 patrol companies
  13th National Guard Battalion – Khmelnitsky
  32nd National Guard Battalion – Lutsk
Northern Operational-Territorial Command – Kyiv
  1st Operational Brigade – Vyshhorod (Kyiv)
    • Three operational battalions, an artillery battalion, an AA Missile battalion and support units
  25th Public Security Protection Brigade – Kyiv
    • NGU National Honor Guard Battalion
    • 5 patrol battalions
  27th (Transport) Brigade – Kyiv
    • 1st Operational Battalion "Kulchytskiy" – Kyiv
    • 1st–3rd (Transport) Battalions
Central Operational-Territorial Command
  21st Public Order Protection Brigade – Kryvyi Rih
    • 2 patrol battalions
  16th Public Order Protection Regiment – Dnipro
    • 3 patrol battalions
  12th National Guard Battalion – Poltava
  14th (Transport) Battalion – Dnipro
  26th National Guard Battalion – Kremenchug
Eastern Operational-Territorial Command – Kharkiv
  3rd Operational Brigade – Kharkiv
    • 3 operational battalions, tank battalion, artillery battalion, AA missile battalion and support troops

5th Independent National Guard Brigade "Slobzhansky" – Kharkiv
- 4 infantry battalions, support units

15th National Guard Regiment – Sloviansk
- 1st Infantry Battalion

18th Operational Regiment (reinforced) – Mariupol
- 1st Patrol Battalion
- 2nd Special Purpose Battalion "Donbas" – Mariupol
- Special Purpose Reinforced Battalion "Azov" – Mariupol
- Support troops

11th National Guard Battalion – Sumy

Southern Operational-Territorial Command – Odesa

23rd Public Order Protection Brigade – Zaporizhzhia
- 4 patrol battalions

9th Operational Regiment "Gepard" – Zaporizhzhia
- 3 operational battalions

19th Public Order Protection Regiment – Mykolaiv
- 3 patrol battalions

49th Public Order Protection Regiment – Odesa
- 3 patrol battalions, 1 operational battalion

16th National Guard Battalion – Kherson

9th (Transport) Battalion – Zaporizhzhia

34th (Transport) Battalion – Odesa

As can be seen from this listing, there are considerable scattered trained defensive forces throughout Ukraine, including 4th Rapid Reaction Brigade at Hostomel. It does put at least one National Guard battalion in each major city and in some cases three to four battalions, a tank battalion, an artillery battalion and an anti-aircraft missile battalion. This means there is a basic level of resistance in most locales sufficient to challenge a Russian BTG if the Ukrainian National Guard units are fully mobilized. This is before consideration of any available Ukrainian Army forces.

Overall, the National Guard has a total of 20 infantry battalions, 18 operational battalions (probably the same as the infantry battalions), 10 National Guard battalions (probably the same as the infantry battalions), 21 patrol battalions, 2 special purpose battalions, 5 protection battalions, 6 (transport) battalions, 3 tank battalions, 3 artillery battalions, 3 anti-aircraft missile battalions and 3 companies that add up to one more battalion. This is a total of 92 additional battalions or 80 additional maneuver battalions, above and beyond the 100-plus maneuver battalions that make up the Ukrainian armed forces.

Foreign Volunteer Battalions

There have been a number of foreign volunteer battalions, several of which were in place before the start of the war. The latter were:

Georgian Battalion based in Kyiv
1st Chechen Battalion (Dudayev Battalion) of several hundred
2nd Chechen Battalion – newly raised

Since the war started, the independent Belarussian Kastus Kalinouski Battalion, a Foreign Volunteer Battalion and a unit of Russian defectors and dissidents fighting for Ukraine called the Freedom of Russia Legion can be added to this list. This unit was supposedly raised between 27 February and 10 March 2022 from Russian defectors. Many of these units are not under the formal command of the Ukrainian Army.

The Ukrainian Tank Brigades

The exact structure and organization of the Ukrainian Army is not known to us. There are five or six listed tank brigades, although only four of them have regularly been seen in action. It is uncertain if the other two are only partly staffed and primarily maintained on paper.

Nominally, a Ukrainian tank brigade consists of three or four battalions, a hundred or so tanks and several thousand troops.

At the start of the campaign the initial tank brigades were:[31]

1st Tank Brigade: armed with T-64s
    Initially defended Chernihiv
    Reconstituted September 2014[32]

3rd Tank Brigade: a reserve unit with T-72s
    Deployed to Izyum, southeast of Kharkiv, in mid-April 2022

4th Tank Brigade: a reserve unit with T-64s
    Initially defended in Donbas
    Deployed to Kharkiv in the weeks prior to the war

17th Tank Brigade: armed with T-64s
    Deployed to northern Kherson Oblast at the beginning of the war

5th Tank Brigade: A reserve unit with at least 30 T-72s[33]
    Moved to bolster defense at Odesa; unit was not at full strength

14th Mechanized Brigade: Tank company armed with T-64BV type 2017 as of 2017. From around May 2022 the five Ukrainian T-84 Oplot tanks were rumored to be deployed with this unit[34]

Ukraine started the war with at least 892 tanks, including 720 T-64s.[35] This includes 410 T-64BVs, 210 T-64BVs mod. 2017, 100 T-64BM Bulats, about 133 T-72s and between 34 to 134 T-80BVs and 5 T-84Us. With the reserve 3rd Tank Brigade armed with T-72s along with the only partly mobilized reserve 5th Tank Brigade with at least 30 T-72s, all the T-72s are probably accounted for in those 2 units. The remaining Ukrainian Army armor units are almost certainly all armed with T-64s. It appears that the Naval Infantry was equipped with the T-80BVs.

The primary Ukrainian tank is the Soviet-era T-64 tank which was built in the Kharkov Tank Factory. The T-64BV was a mid-1980s Soviet-era version that includes "Kontakt-1" reactive armor and 81mm smoke-grenade launchers on the turret. The T-64BV mod. 2017 is a Ukrainian 2017 modification that included improved reactive armor, updated night sights, satellite navigation system, digital radio and the infrared searchlight removed. The T-64BM Bulat is a Ukrainian 2019 modernization that included improved thermal sights, fire-control systems, radios, a new battlefield information system, a raised turret ring, improved reactive armor, an armor shield above the commander's cupola, 12mm armor for the external fuel tanks, anti-RPG screens, and a new 1000hp engine and transmission.

The T-72s are Soviet-era tanks and not as capable as the Ukrainian T-64s. The T-80BV was a 1985 Soviet-era update that included explosive reactive armor Kontakt-1. The T-80 is based upon the T-64. The T-84 Oplot is a Ukrainian upgrade to the T-80. It includes new armored side skirts, turret-mounted Kontakt-5 reactive armor, auxiliary power unit, thermal-imaging sight, satellite navigation, commander's laser range-finder, muzzle reference system and other improvements. With a high-performance diesel engine, it is fast, capable of doing 40mph on a paved road.

The Kharkov Tank Factory, or the Malyshev Factory, was reestablished in 1945, with the original factory dating back to 1895. At its peak during the Soviet era, it employed 60,000 people. As of 2015, 5,000 people worked at the factory. Tank production declined from 800 tanks in 1991 to only 46 tanks by about 1996, when it began to make hundreds of tanks for export to Pakistan in addition to its work for the Ukrainian Army.

Overall Strength

The Ukrainian Ground Forces started the war with around 74 maneuver battalions. The Ukraine Air Assault Forces added up to 16 maneuver battalions to that total. The Ukrainian Navy has at least 9 maneuver battalions (including the reconnaissance battalion). The Special Forces may have added 2 more. This is around 101 maneuver battalions. The National Guard has about 80 maneuver battalions of various capabilities. At least one of these National Guard battalions is active. There are also at least 2 foreign battalions.

Therefore, 101 maneuver battalions, 1 National Guard battalion and at least 2 foreign battalions adds up to 104 active maneuver battalions. With all the National Guards forces counted, this is a total of around 180 Ukrainian maneuver battalions. This is to face the 150 or so Russian BTGs. This does not count artillery or air defense. It is hard to envision with these forces scattered across Ukraine that one could imagine this war would be over in 72 hours if the Ukrainian armed forces put up any sort of fight.

The Ukrainian war effort was also supplemented by the Territorial Defense Forces (TDF) who seemed to show up at critical junctures. For example, it appears the Russian 2nd Guards Motorized Infantry Division was stopped by primarily TDF forces, with some help from Ukrainian Special Forces, near Pryluki.

Ukrainian Armaments Industry

Ukraine does have its own armament industry. Many of these were former large Soviet-era works such as the Antonov State Enterprise at Hostomel airport, the now destroyed Kharkiv Tractor Plant, the Kharkiv Tank Factory (operational status currently unknown), the Kharkiv Morozov Machine Building Design Bureau, the Luch Design Bureau in Kyiv and the aerospace Yuzhnoye Design Bureau in Dnipro. Some of these companies have been involved in maintaining and developing the existing Soviet-era weapons in the Ukrainian Army. Some have been focused on developing new modern weapon systems, although some of these are still not widely deployed. The end result is that Ukraine already has the ability to make a lot of its own major weapon systems. It also has or had surplus manufacturing capacity in many cases. This includes tanks, IFVs, APCs, artillery, MLRS, ATGMs, shore-to-sea missiles and many other items. Some of these newer systems have been a factor in the current fighting. Among the major new weapon systems being maintain or developed by Ukraine are:[36]

1. Tanks. Upgrades to the T-64, T-80 and T-84 have all been done at the Kharkiv Tank Factory. The most developed tank is the T-84 Oplot of which only ten were built. This is Ukraine's variant of the Soviet-era T-84 main battle tank. This Ukrainian version has been in service since 2000. It is armed with a 125mm main gun, two machineguns, has reactive armor and carries Ukrainian Kombat laser-guided missiles. With a high-performance diesel engine, it is capable of doing 40 mph on a paved road. Each tank costs about $4 million. It was first deployed in combat in May 2022. Only five remain in the Ukrainian inventory.

2. BTR-4 IFV. This Ukrainian 8x8 amphibious wheeled infantry fighting vehicle has been in service since 2011 and first saw action in 2014. It can be armed with a range of weapons from machineguns to 30mm autocannons, ATGMs, grenade launchers and so forth. Each IFV cost up to $1.6 million, depending on armament. As of 2021 only around 67 of these were deployed with the Ukrainian Army and only around 60 of the earlier Ukrainian built BTR-3s. The vast majority of Ukrainian IFVs are Soviet-era BMP-2s. While the BTR-4 appears similar to the Soviet-era BTR-80, this was an all-new production vehicle developed by a consortium that includes the Kharkiv Morozov Machine Building Design Bureau.

3. Kozak-2M1 APC. Built by NPO Practika, this Ukrainian-built 4x4 wheeled APC has been in service since at least 2020. It can carry five crew and eleven personnel in the back. It can be armed with a range of weapons from machineguns to Ukrainian Barrier ATGM 130mm laser-guided missiles. Over 240 are currently with the Ukrainian armed forces, although it is not the most common wheeled APC in the Ukrainian inventory. The Soviet-era eight-wheeled BTR-70s and BTR-80s were more common before the war.

4. Bohdana self-propelled howitzer. This newly developed howitzer was first used in June 2022 at Snake Island. There is only one known prototype. The primary Ukrainian self-propelled artillery pieces are the Soviet-era 122mm 2S1 Gvozdika, the 152mm 2S3 Akatsiya, the 152mm 2S19 Msta and the 203mm 2S7 Pion. The Bohdana is a Ukrainian-designed artillery system that can use the NATO 155mm artillery rounds (vice the Soviet-era 152mm rounds). It is technically still not in service, but has a range of 42 to 50km (the last using rocket-assisted shells). It is at best a weapon for use in 2023 and later. The current shortfalls in Ukrainian artillery are being made up during the war by Western 155mm systems, such as the U.S. M-109, the German PzH 2000 and the Polish-provided AHS Krab.

5. Vilkha tactical multiple-launch rocket system (MLRS). This Ukrainian-made MLRS fires 300mm rockets out to a range of 70 or 130km (the newest M model has a range of 130km). It has a 250kg warhead. It is based on the Soviet-era Smerch MLRS. The Vilkha has been in service since October 2018. Only a small number have been deployed. The primary Ukrainian rocket artillery systems are the Soviet-era BM-21 Grad, although these are now being replaced by far more advanced U.S. systems such as the M270 and the M42 HIMARS.

6. The Skif or Stugna-P Anti-Tank Guided Missile (ATGM). This 130mm guided missile has been in service since 2011 and was used in the fighting in 2014 and 2015. Although designated as an anti-tank missile, it has been used extensively against buildings and even downed a Russian Ka-52 attack helicopter on 5 April 2022. A versatile weapon with multiple warhead options, it has been used extensively in urban warfare. Its effective range is 5.5km in daytime and 3km at night. It is a tripod-mounted launcher that requires a two-, three- or four-man crew and is often vehicle mounted, sometimes improvised. There are also 155mm versions of the system. They are manufactured by the Luch Design Bureau in Kyiv. The guidance system was manufactured in Belarus. It is used alongside many of the NATO systems such as the U.S. FGM-148 Javelin, the UK NLAW and the German Panzerfaust 3.

7. Neptune Anti-Ship Missile System. This recently developed system has only been in service since August 2020. The missile has a range of 280km (174 miles), flies at low altitudes (3–10m) and can execute evasive maneuvers during its approach. It has a 150kg warhead (331lb) that can sink vessels of up to 5,000 tons displacement. This was proved in operations, which alerted the world to the capabilities of this recently developed Ukrainian missile. A battery consists of six launchers. It is also manufactured by the Luch Design Bureau in Kyiv.

History and Cultural Influence

The Ukrainian Army that came into existence in 1991 was simply the old Soviet Army, carved up into pieces. The Soviet Army, in the changing environment of the 1980s, was an army in decline. In 1994, Ukraine joined the Partnership for Peace program. At that point, the Ukrainian Army began to be influenced by American and Western ideas of how an army should be run, including its relationship with civilian authorities. Still, at that point, it was very much a Soviet-style army, officer heavy, no strong Non-Commissioned Officer (NCO) corps and draftee enlisted. Very much involved in the process of advising the development of this army from the early 1990s until 2010 was retired U.S. Army Major General Nicholas Krawciw. Krawciw was born in Lvov in 1935, spent the Second World War in Germany and then migrated to Philadelphia in 1949 and graduated from West Point in 1959. One of my relatives who met Nick Krawciw in Kyiv in about 1999 relayed back to us that "'while he talked like a Ukrainian, he thought like an American." I am not exactly sure what was said that made it appear that General Krawciw "thought like an American" or why that was so obvious to this one Ukrainian, but when the remark was relayed back to Nick Krawciw, he was amused and I think a little bit proud of it. But, this also shows the cultural gap between an American of Ukrainian descent and a Ukrainian.

During some of our joint travels at this time to U.S. Army facilities, General Krawciw did make a few comments on the state of Ukrainian training. During a visit to a 3rd Infantry Division command post exercise in 1999 he gave a brief introductory presentation noting that in the 1980s, we tended to view the Soviet Army as being ten foot tall, but it turns out they were only about four feet tall. I asked him after the presentation about that observation and he went into a detailed discussion of what he had seen from his own observations of Ukrainian Army combat exercises. One observation he made is that Ukrainian visiting commanders (usually senior generals) were always stunned when they were in an American command post and they asked a question. The question would then be answered by whichever American enlisted man happened to be manning the station in question. He pointed out that in the Ukrainian Army (which was still very Soviet-style at that time), an enlisted man would have never directly answered such a question, but an officer would always be there to answer it instead. The officers in the old Soviet system took over a lot of functions of what NCOs do in the American system and there were always extra junior officers available in the Soviet system.

Clearly, the Ukrainian Army was in a state of transition. That older generation of Soviet trained officers was maturing and by 2010 most had retired or otherwise moved out of the Ukrainian Army. But, the Ukrainian Army was then gutted by the Yanukovych regime, dropping to less than 50,000 personnel by 2013. The new Ukrainian Army that has developed from there is hopefully more Western leaning and Western in their style of operating.

The Ukrainian Army already had multiple opportunities to deploy with and work with their Western partners. First, they were part of the KFOR (Kosovo Force). On 1 September 1991 a Ukrainian force of 321 was deployed to Kosovo. This was later merged as part of a Polish-Ukrainian Peace Force Battalion. This force, started in 2000, consisted of 545 Polish and 267 Ukrainian soldiers. In August 2006, the Ukrainian contingent was reduced to 179 soldiers. At the start of the war with Russia there were still forty Ukrainian troops attached to KFOR. They remained there until August 2022. This was a peacekeeping exercise, which does put undue stress on the units. Still, Ukraine has suffered some casualties in these operations.[37]

There were also some Ukrainian citizens in the French Foreign Legion. At the start of the war this number was reported to be about seventy-four. Of those, about twenty had already left their bases without permission, and were suspected of going back to Ukraine for the war.[38]

The Ukrainian Army also deployed to both Iraq and Afghanistan, which were combat zones. Between 2003 to 2011, approximately 5,000 Ukrainian soldiers served in Iraq. Ukraine was the third largest force in Iraq from 2003–5, with over 1,700 soldiers deployed during the early part of the period. For domestic political reasons, this large Ukrainian involvement was quickly reduced. President Yushchenko was actively trying to demonstrate to the Western allies that Ukraine was a worthy ally, but this was not entirely supported by his populace. Eighteen soldiers had died during this deployment and thirty-three had been wounded by the end of 2005.[39] By 2006, this deployment had shifted to a peacekeeping force of around forty soldiers.[40] The deployment to Afghanistan was from 2007–14 and was always a fairly limited support group that only had twenty-six members in 2013. The Ukrainian Army also deployed peacekeeping forces to the Democratic Republic of Congo, Liberia, Sudan, South Sudan, Côte d'Ivoire and the Northern Mali Conflict in 2012.

Of course, this declining level of commitment harkens back to discussions in 2008 when Ukraine was being considered for NATO membership. Clearly, many Ukrainians supported this, and the Ukrainian government was very supportive through 2004. Starting with 2005, the degree of Ukrainian engagement significantly declined, showing an about face. There was obviously still a large minority in the country that was not completely behind integration with NATO. They would take over the government in 2010.

For example, an agreement was signed on 16 November 2009 to create a Lithuania-Polish-Ukrainian Brigade, with the goal of reaching operational status in fall of 2011, but this was delayed due to the election of Yanukovych. The unit was finally formed on 19 September 2014, only after he was gone, becoming operational in early 2016. This Lithuania-Polish-Ukrainian Brigade united Ukrainian units with a brigade consisting of two NATO partners.

Therefore, by 2022, certainly almost all the officer corps and much of the Army had had exposure to NATO standards and had experience working with NATO units. To what extent this Army had developed into a modern well-trained fighting force is more difficult to determine.

Chapter 5

The Russian Army

The Russian Army had a total manpower of 280,000 in 2020. It is one of six parts of the entire Russian Armed Forces which numbered 1,014,000. The Russian Armed Forces are divided into three branches: Ground Forces, Navy and Aerospace. They also have three independent arms of service: the Strategic Rocket Forces, the Airborne Forces and the Special Operations Forces. The existence of a separate Airborne Forces sometimes leads to confusion, as these forces are usually counted in the ground forces of most armed forces, as opposed to being a separate arm. The Ground Forces have 280,000 active-duty personnel as of 2020. It is the largest of the six branches or divisions. Their patron is Saint Alexander Nevsky, who was the Prince of Novgorod three times (1236–40, 1241–56 and 1258–9), the Grand Prince of Vladimir (1252–63) and Grand Prince of Kiev (1246–63).

The Russian Army's training and development has been uneven since the breakup of the Soviet Union in 1991, and during the 1990s it was not the same caliber of army that existed at the height of the Soviet Union. The most recent Minister of Defense, Sergei Shoigu, assumed office on 6 November 2012. He was a civil engineer with extensive experience in disaster response who later became a career politician. Shoigu has limited background in military affairs. Under his leadership the army has continued a series of reforms of the previous Defense Minister, Anatolii Serdyukov (2007–12), to counteract the decline and decay that the Russian Army had undergone since the fall of the Soviet Union. Serdyukov was sacked due to corruption scandals, although he was amnestied in 2014. The reforms they have supported have included conducting more military exercises, increasing spending for rearmament and modernization, with the Russian defense budget now more the 4% of the GDP, and the formation of Battalion Tactical Groups (BTGs). This last change was due to a lack of trained manpower to maintain ready brigades, so these battalions become the ready component of the Russian Army. This may have been less of an improvement and more of an adjustment to minimize a fault. By August 2021, Russia claimed to have around 170 BTGs.

The Airborne Forces had 45,000 troops in 2015. These were organized into four divisions along with four separate combat brigades. The majority of the airborne troops are contracted soldiers vice conscripts. At least one of their divisions was fully manned with contract soldiers as opposed to conscripts. The Special Operations Forces were founded in 2009 and their strength is not reported. It appears to be at least 2,000 people. Between the Ground Forces and the Airborne Forces, the deployable Russian ground army is about 325,000.

Battalion Tactical Groups (BTGs)[1]

One of the major changes in the Russian Army was the focus on keeping BTGs as the primary ready component of the Russian Army as opposed to brigades or divisions. While the regiment and brigade structures of the Russian Army remained in place, the maneuver battalions were the maneuver forces that were maintained at full readiness. As of August 2021, the Defense Minister stated that the Russian Army had around 170 BTGs.

The BTG is not a conceptual development by the Russian Army, but is simply a battalion-sized, task-organized combined arms team. All major armies have utilized this since the Second World War. The Russian Army's current emphasis on BTGs (vice regiments/brigades) is due to a lack of available manpower. They were used an as expedient during the Chechen War and then the Ministry of Defense adopted the idea wholesale in 2013 as a manpower hedge. The Russian Army BTGs and doctrine are built around firepower and mobility, at the expense of manpower.

As a result of the 2014 Zelenopillya artillery strike, many Western analysts believed that Russian BTGs were capable of networking long-range fires in real time (or near real time). It turns out the BTGs can't actually do this. Early in the war it became apparent that many cannot even communicate via secure means, much less target and strike quickly and effectively at long range. This negates much of their supposed combat power advantage. In effect, by stripping the brigade structure down to its component battalions, these smaller units were less robust in capabilities.

As discovered as the war in Ukraine developed, the Russian BTGs appeared unable to execute competent combined arms tactics. This is a fundamental failure as combined arms have been the *sine qua non* of modern fire and movement tactics since the Second World War. This shows up in the lack of effective infantry support. BTG infantry cannot prevent Ukrainian mechanized and light infantry anti-tank hunter/killer teams from attriting their tanks, IFVs, and SP artillery. This is the primary job of infantry in tank units. It is not clear if this is due to ineffective infantry forces or insufficient numbers of them in the BTGs; probably both are true. The net result is that the BTGs lack the mass (i.e. infantry) necessary to take defended urban terrain by assault. At least, not at a reasonable cost in combat losses. The leanness of the

BTG manning (less than 1,000 troops) means that they cannot sustain much attrition without suffering a marked decline in combat power and effectiveness.

It will take a more thorough analysis to determine if the performance of the BTGs is due to inherent flaws in Russian Army personnel and training or flaws in their doctrinal approach. Again, both are probably culpable. In any case, these problems are not likely to be remedied in the short term. Fixing them will take a major reform effort. Regardless, it does not appear that Russia gained any significant advantage from deploying BTGs as opposed to making proper use of their regimental and brigade command structures.

The average BTG is maybe 400 or so personnel, although with attachments from regiment and brigade (which still exist) they may grow to a more Western-sized 800–1,000 people. But, they are mostly supplemented or reinforced battalions of about 400 people, with little in the way of unique capability. They are a little light in firepower, staying power and in support capabilities.

Forces Massed

On 18 February 2022, U.S. ambassador Michael Carpenter reported, "We assess that Russia probably has massed between 169,000–190,000 personnel in and near Ukraine as compared with about 100,000 on January 30. This estimate includes military troops along the border, in Belarus, and in occupied Crimea; Russian National Guard and other internal security units deployed to these areas; and Russian-led forces in eastern Ukraine."[2] This estimate included Russian-backed separatists, which I gather were not part of the previous public estimates of 150,000. It also included "Russian National Guard and other internal security units" which are usually not offensive forces.

The Donetsk People's Republic was estimated to have an armed force of 20,000, while the smaller Lugansk People's Republic was estimated to have an armed force of 14,000. These were almost all ground forces, with them having neither air nor naval forces.

Structure of the Russian Offensive Forces

The Russian Army maintained its structure of armies, divisions, brigades and regiments, even though its ready units were built around the BTGs. The Russian Army consists of ten combined arms armies (5th, 6th, 8th Guards, 20th, 29th, 35th, 36th, 41st, 49th and 58th), nominally two tank armies (1st Guards Tank Army and 2nd Guards Combined Arms Army) and four separate Army Corps (11th, 14th, 22nd and 68th).

The Russian command was organized into four military districts for this operation, referred to as Eastern, Central, Western and Southern. For this operation, elements of the 29th, 35th and 36th Combined Arms Armies were deployed in Belarus under the Eastern Military District.[3] Deployed near the Ukrainian borders were the 41st Combined Arms Army, the 8th Guards and the 22nd Army Corps. The 2nd Guards Combined Arms Army, formerly 2nd Guards Tank Army, was deployed further back, near Kursk. These forces were under command of the Central Military District. Deployed to Voronezh were elements of the 1st Guards Tank Army and Sixth Combined Arms Army. Along the Ukrainian border was the 20th Combined Arms Army. These forces were under command of the Western Military District. Deployed to Crimea were elements of the 49th and 58th Combined Arms Armies. Also in Crimea was the Airborne Forces' 7th Air Assault Division and 11th Guards Air Assault Brigade. These forces were under command of the Southern Military District. The 1st and 2nd Army Corps, representing the DPR and LPR forces respectively, were operating in the Donbas before the start of the war.[4]

The military districts were effectively army-level headquarters. Most of the formations listed as armies were effectively division-level headquarters, with at best a half-dozen brigades reporting to them. Only the 1st Guards Tank Army had multiple divisions reporting to it. Each military district (effectively a small army) commanded from twenty to sixty BTGs. A U.S. Army division usually has nine or ten maneuver battalions.

The 1st Guards Tank Army consisted of three divisions: 2nd Guards Motorized Rifle Division (formed 2013), 4th Guards Tank Division (formed 2013) and 47th Guards Tank Division (formed 2021). It appears that only the 26th Tank Regiment and 7th Reconnaissance Battalion of 47th Guards Tank Division were involved in the initial offensives. The unit was formed from the 6th Tank Brigade as of 1 December 2021, and it appears to have only the tank regiment, the reconnaissance regiment and some other support units. The 1st Guards Tank Army also includes the 27th Guards Motorized Rifle Brigade. As of 15 March its order of battle was:[5]

2nd Guards Motorized Rifle Division
    1st Motorized Rifle Regiment
    15th Motorized Rifle Regiment
    1st Tank Regiment
    147th Self-propelled Artillery Regiment
    1117th Anti-aircraft Rocket Regiment
4th Guards Tank Division
    12th Tank Regiment

13th Tank Regiment
423rd Motorized Rifle Regiment
275th Self-propelled Artillery Regiment
538th Anti-aircraft Rocket Regiment
47th Guards Tank Division
    26th Tank Regiment
       7th Reconnaissance Battalion
27th Guards Motorized Rifle Brigade

The orders of battle for the other Russian armies are a challenge, and some of them appear to have only deployed to Ukraine a single regiment or brigade (i.e. 29th Combined Arms Army and 2nd Guards Combined Arms Army).

The Russian Offensive Plan

On 1 March, six days into the invasion, the Belarussian President Aleksandr Lukashenko in a televised presentation showed a map that detailed the Russian offensive plan. This may be have been deliberate misinformation, but it does appear that the offensive plan was initiated as indicated on this map. Most likely this map was an accurate reflection of the Russian plan. It involved an attack on four axes:

Eastern Military District (drive on Kyiv along the west bank of the Dnieper with 35th and 36th Combined Arms Armies)

Central Military District (drive on Kyiv from the east and from the north along the east bank of the Dnieper with 41st and 2nd Guards Combined Arms Armies)

Western Military District (southwest thrust to the Dnieper to cut the bridges from Kaniv to Dnipro) with 1st Guard Tanks Army, 6th Combined Arms Army (encircle Kharkiv), 20th Combined Arms Army (take northern Luhansk and outflank the Donbas front)

Southern Military District (one grouping composed of an independent Motorized Rifle Division and Russian Airborne (VDV) divisions drives on Odesa, with potential link-up with naval infantry brigade), 58th Combined Arms Army drives on Melitopol from the west and links up with 8th Combined Arms Army with the DPR forces under its command which drives from the East, sealing the land bridge.

It also showed offensive lines moving up to the border of Moldova, causing some to speculate that they were looking to invade that country. Moldova is another former republic of the Soviet Union and the Russian Empire.

Dueling Armies

The deployed strengths of the two sides for this upcoming war can be summarized as follows:

	Russia	Ukraine	Ratio
Total Ground Forces strength:	190,000	210,000–220,000	0.90-to-1
Total maneuver battalions:[6]	150	126 or 205	1.19-to-1 or 0.73-to-1

In effect, it appears that Russia was going to attack while outnumbered. This is never a good idea, although it has worked in a few campaigns (the German attack on France in 1940 and the U.S. invasion of Iraq in 2003).

Dueling Air Forces

The Russian Air Force is a large organization with considerable assets. There is a real mismatch in airpower between Russia and Ukraine. The Ukrainian Air Force can field about 100 modern aircraft, while Russia can field over 1,300. According to some reports before the start of the war, about 500 Russian fighters and fighter-bombers were deployed near Ukraine. Even with this lower number, this is still 500 Russian fighter and fighter-bombers versus Ukraine's 100. Therefore, Russia was clearly going to have air superiority.

A rough count of opposing air forces shows:

Ukraine
MiG-29 – 37 (multirole)
Su-24 – 12 (attack)
Su-25 – 17 (attack/CAS)
Su-27 – 32 (multirole)
Total modern combat airplanes: 98
Total multirole or fighters: 69

Russia (in service)
MiG-35 – 8 (multirole)
MiG-31 – 113 (fighter)
MiG-29 – 259 (fighter)
Su-24 – 274
Su-25 – 193
Su-27 – 172 (fighter)
Su-30 – 119 (multirole)
Su-34 – 131 (multirole)
Su-35 – 103 (multirole)
Su-57 – 5 (multirole)
Total modern combat airplanes: 1,377 (plus 124 modern bombers)
Total multirole or fighters: 910

This does not include Russian naval service aircraft: 22 MiG-29s, 42 MiG-31s, 22 Su-24s, 4 Su-25UTG, 6 Su-27s, 26 Su-30s and 18 Su-33s for a total of 140.

It was clear from the start that Russia would dominate the air. This does not address helicopter and drones.

The big unknown in the calculation of air assets is the considerable air defense assets of both sides. This was a product of the Soviet military system, where there were extensive air defense assets throughout the army. Russia has thirty-five air defense battalions deployed around Ukraine according to some estimates. We have seen these types of significant air defense assets neutralize an enemy air advantage before, as happened between the Egyptians and Israelis in 1973. For several days the Egyptians were able to neutralize the vastly superior Israeli air force. Would this be an option for Ukraine, which has an estimated thirty-nine air defense battalions?[7]

Dueling Navies

Again, this has been an area where Russia has held all the cards. The largest warship in the Black Sea was the rather large Russian cruiser the *Moskva* of 11,490 tons.[8] It was supported by 5 frigates, 1 Corvette, 11 landing ships, gunboats and a collection of other supporting craft.[9] They also had at least 7 submarines, which were mostly based at Sevastopol in Crimea and at Novorossiysk in Russia.[10] This fleet was easily able to get anywhere in the Black Sea along the Ukrainian coastline in a matter of hours. The distance between Snake Island and Sevastopol was only 170 miles (274km).

The largest Ukrainian ship was the frigate *Hetman Sahaydachniy*, which was undergoing refitting in Mykolaiv. It had a displacement of 3,150 tons. This was the only major combat ship or submarine in the Navy. The rest were ASW ships, patrol vessels, gunboats, lesser combat vessels and gunboats, smaller landing ships, or auxiliaries and support ships. It was clear that the Black Sea was going to be dominated by the Russian fleet, and would certainly be assisted by their dominance of the air.

By 3 March 2002, the frigate *Hetman Sahaydachniy* had been scuttled in the port of Mykolaiv to prevent its capture by the Russians. This appears to have taken place on 28 February. On 12 March, a number of Ukrainian ships were captured in the harbor of Berdiansk.[11] A few others were lost elsewhere early in the war.[12] This all effectively removed most of the Ukrainian Navy from the conflict.

Training, Experience, Morale and Motivation of the Two Competing Armed Forces

A unit's combat power is manpower times weapons times human factors. These human factors are significant. Two units of equal strength and similar weapons can have widely varying combat power depending on the other factors. These factors have traditionally included morale, training, experience, leadership (which is different than generalship), motivation, cohesion, intelligence (including interpretation), momentum, initiative, doctrine, surprise, logistics, organizational habits, cultural differences, generalship (vice leadership) and the quality of personnel. All these sixteen elements make up the combat effectiveness of a force.

Let us address each of these elements in turn:[13]

1. Morale: "1) The state of an individual's mental attitude or feeling in respect to what he is, does, or is going to do, as determined by the presence or absence of such psychological factors as confidence in his leaders, recognition of a spirit of sacrifice in others, feeling of comradeship for associates, physical comfort, and hope, 2) a state of mind or feeling attributed to a group of individuals or to an organization."[14]
2. Training: "The process of preparing military individuals and units to perform their assigned functions and missions, particularly to prepare for combat and wartime functions. Covering every aspect of military activity, training is the principal occupation of military forces when not actually engaged in combat."[15]

3. Experience: This is experience in doing one's job, especially experience in a combat environment. Many people consider combat experience of more value than additional training, depending on the particular job. It is obviously different than training. Certainly, gaining combat experience is very different than training and adds to a person or unit's capabilities.

4. Leadership (which is different than generalship): "The art of influencing and directing people to an assigned goal in such a manner as to command their obedience, confidence, respect, and loyalty."[16]

   In this case I have separated leadership into two aspects, one is the training, experience and leadership capabilities of all the non-commissioned officers, the junior officers, and mid-level officers in a combat unit, who make up the leadership of the unit at squad, platoon, company and battalion level. For example, if there is a shortfall in the NCO corps, which is a regular complaint of Soviet-style armies, then it would be apparent in this factor (if it could be measured).

   This factor does not include the man and immediate associates in charge of the unit. This leader is separated to a factor called Generalship (see below).

These four factors, morale, training, experience and leadership are the four factors that explain the majority of differences in combat effectiveness of units, but they do not entirely. There are some other factors that influence combat effectiveness.

5. Motivation:[17] This is related to morale and some people might consider it a subfactor of morale. While morale measures the overall state of a given unit, motivation indicates a possibly temporary condition caused by being inspired by the mission, the commander or the situation. It tends to be a more temporary conditional driven factor than morale.

6. Cohesion:[18] "The quality of characteristic of a unit whereby its members work well together and demonstrate loyalty to each other and to their unit under all circumstances. Cohesion is achieved by training together, living together, and strong leadership. Sometimes called cohesiveness."[19]

   This is related to morale and some people might consider it a subfactor of morale. It tends to represent a capability built up over time within the unit. The German Army in World War I and World

War II was considered by many to be focused on maintaining unit cohesion, as they considered this important. This included raising units by region, keeping unit's regional associations, developing the individual unit heritage, keeping tied to the unit and returning recovered injured soldiers to their original units. The British regimental system also is intended to encourage cohesion. The modern American Army is not considered to be as focused on maintaining unit cohesion.

7. Intelligence (including interpretation): "The product resulting from the collection, evaluation, analysis, integration, and interpretation of all available information that concerns one or more aspects of foreign nations, their areas of operations, and their military establishment, and which is immediately or potentially significant to military and diplomatic planning and operations."[20]

    Note that this definition not only includes gathering of information, which is now often assisted by advanced technical means, but also evaluation, analysis, integration and interpretation. These are clearly influenced by human factors. Certainly, the tendency of Soviet-era armies in the Second World War to grossly exaggerate the damage done to their enemies, including overestimating casualties, is an example of a human failing in the intelligence system. Certainly, the failure of the United States to correctly predict the possible outcome of the first three days of the Russo-Ukrainian War is a similar such error.

    As Dupuy notes: "This is an aspect of leadership, also related to training and experience."[21]

8. Momentum: "The property of continuing forward movement of a military force, as a result of previous success in combat, which is presumed to provide an additive or multiplicative bonus to its combat capability."[22]

    This is usually a temporary condition dependent upon the situation as it develops in combat, but can become significant.

9. Initiative: "The side which possesses the initiative in combat operations has an unquestionable intangible advantage over the opponent. What is not clear at this time, however, is whether this variable can be represented by itself, or whether it can or should be included within leadership, or combined with momentum. It certainly is an element within the larger intangible of general combat effectiveness."[23]

    This is arguably a part of training and leadership, and may be influenced by cultural factors and organizational habits.

10. Doctrine:[24] "Fundamental principles and operational concepts by which the military forces or elements thereof guide their actions in military operations in support of national objectives."[25]

     Doctrinal difference can be significant in the relative performance of military forces. The German doctrinal approaches in the Second World War have since influenced the doctrine of many countries currently in NATO. The Soviet doctrinal approaches in the Second World War are the starting point for the both the Russian and the Ukrainian armies. Many analysts, including this author, consider the German doctrinal approach in the Second World War to be superior than that practiced by the Soviet Union in the Second World War.

11. Surprise:[26] "v. To make an attack at a time or place or in a manner unexpected to the enemy. This is an important principle of war. n. The reaction of a combatant to an unanticipated attack by the enemy."[27]

     Surprise is something that is achieved in combat, often as a result of having an intelligence advantage. It is clearly something related to leadership, generalship and intelligence. It can sometimes be a significant temporary combat multiplier.

12. Logistics: "1) That aspect of military activity providing for the buildup and support of a military forces so that it will be efficient and effective in both combat and noncombat operations. Supplies, equipment, transportation, maintenance, construction, and operation of facilities, provision, movement, and evacuation of personnel, and other like services, are included in logistics. 2) The furnishing of supplies and equipment. See also **administration**."[28]

     As such, logistics is also influenced by training, experience, leadership and doctrine.

13. Organizational habits:[29] This might be partly subsumed by doctrine and leadership, but it is the habits and ways of behavior that an organization exhibits, regardless of the written doctrine. For example, do people report results of combat honestly and openly? Do people argue and debate with commanders over disagreeable orders? This may be related to the factor below, cultural differences.

14. Cultural differences:[30] This is habits or behavior that affect military performance that are displayed by some armies. Such differences may overlap with organizational habits, but are often more deeply ingrained, including respect of authority, willingness to exercise individual initiative, manner of discussing differences, etc. Some of this can be influenced by training and leadership, but no two cultures are exactly the same, the cultural habits of the society they are drawn from is reflected in the army itself.

15. Generalship (vice leadership):[31] This is the capabilities and decision-making of the actual person in charge. In most professional armies, the training and experience of the leader in charge is similar, yet sometimes these leaders make very different decisions in a stressful combat environment. It is hard to quantify or predict this without a deep understanding of the individual leader and how he will react. This is why it is separated from leadership.

16. Quality of personnel:[32] This measures the quality of the personnel that are recruited. The final factor of these sixteen factors is related to recruiting, and perhaps the factor should just be simply called "recruiting." For example, are the line troops educated accomplished individuals, or have they been recruited from prisons? While this is a factor that can clearly be influenced by training and leadership, units recruited from prisons are likely to have a number of problems that other units recruited differently otherwise might not. This will certainly influence the morale and cohesiveness of a unit.

These sixteen factors all play a part in influencing the combat effectiveness of units, which is the major element of the combat power of a unit. There is nothing earthshaking in this construct.

On the other hand, an evaluation of the units of the Russian and Ukrainian sides may reveal some general differences between these two. For example, we suspect that there is a difference in the motivation of the two forces, as Ukrainians are defending their homeland, while the Russians clearly are not. How big of an advantage in combat effectiveness this gives the Ukrainians has never been measured, and may be overshadowed by other factors such as Morale, Training, Experience and Leadership.

Because of the extensive fighting from 2014 and onwards, some of the units on both sides may have considerable combat experience. This probably creates more capable individual combat units among the rank-and-file. Certainly, the experienced Azov Battalion, even though a National Guard unit, fits that description.

Both armies make use of conscripts. The Russian system only has these conscripts for twelve months. This means that these conscripts have less than a year's experience, which clearly works against those units manned primarily by conscripts. After serving a year, personnel may contract to continue service past that year. These are volunteers with at least a year's experience. Russian air assault units are primarily manned by contracted personnel, not conscripts.

Nominally, this would indicate that they are more effective in combat than a unit primarily manned by conscripts.

It is clear that units vary across each army in combat effectiveness and, overall, armies vary between each other in combat effectiveness. It is difficult to tell which force would start this war with superior morale and training. On the other hand, the intelligence analysts who decided that Ukrainian Army would not fight effectively and Russia would win in 72 hours clearly made a very negative judgment as to the combat effectiveness of the Ukrainian Army. This estimate does imply an interpretation of the Ukrainian morale and motivation. They clearly sorely misjudged this and it is questionable what detailed analysis, if any, was used as the basis for this conclusion.

By the same token, it appears that the Russian Army made the same mistake, both under-estimating the Ukrainian Army and over-estimating their own capabilities. This is also difficult to understand as they had experience engaging each other, but this problem of overestimating has often been a common error made by offensive forces.

Chapter 6

The First Day of the War, 24 February 2022

The war started before 5 in the morning, Kyiv time, on 24 February 2022. The first fighting started at 0340 in Luhansk Province on the border with Russia near the village of Milove.[1] At this early stage, it was uncertain whether this was really a full-scale invasion. As Alexey Danilov, the secretary of the Ukrainian National Security and Defense Council, said in an interview in April 2022, "We thought that they were entering the territory of Donetsk and Luhansk regions. We believed that their goal, after the recognition of the "republics", was to take them within the regions. But then, within an hour and twenty [counting from 0340], the offensive began everywhere. I immediately went to the president."[2]

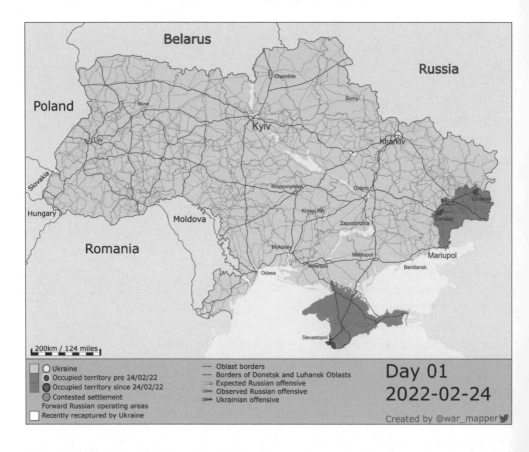

200km / 124 miles

○ Ukraine
● Occupied territory pre 24/02/22
◐ Occupied territory since 24/02/22
◌ Contested settlement
Forward Russian operating areas
☐ Recently recaptured by Ukraine

--- Oblast borders
--- Borders of Donetsk and Luhansk Oblasts
⇢ Expected Russian offensive
➡ Observed Russian offensive
➡ Ukrainian offensive

Day 01
2022-02-24

Created by @war_mapper

Was this a limited and defined operation or was Russia looking for large-scale occupation of Ukrainian territory? Even on the first day, the Ukrainians were not sure until they saw at 0500 that morning that the Russians were attacking "everywhere." The National Security and Defense Council, including President Zelenskyy, convened in Kyiv around 5:30 in the morning. They already had a set of draft solutions prepared, knowing from the start that they were going to fight (a point somehow missed by many of our own intelligence people).

It soon became clear that there were potentially six major areas of operations: 1. Kyiv, 2. Odesa, 3. Kharkiv, 4. The Donetsk and Luhansk provinces, 5. Mariupol and 6. The border area with Crimea.

In the area of Kyiv (population 2,962,180) on the first day there was an armored column driving south down the road from Belarus. It quickly moved the Ukrainian border guards out of the way and continued on down towards Kyiv. At the time it was not known if this was just a Russian column or mixed Russian-Belarussian force. It turns out it was only Russian, for although Belarus was allowing their territory to be moved through to invade Ukraine, they were not actively participating in the offensive.

This column consisted of the 5th Guards Tank Brigade and a considerable element of the 76th Guards Air Assault Division and probably a few other elements, including at least one BTG from Chechens of the 141st Special Motorized Regiment, possibly additional elements from 31st Guards Air Assault Brigade and probably 37th Guards Motorized Rifle Brigade and 64th Motorized Rifle Brigade. The 5th Guards Tank Brigade consisted of 353 vehicles in a 17.6km-long column and the elements of the 76th Guards Air Assault Division consisted of 495 vehicles in a 24.8km-long column.[3] The 5th Guards Tank Brigade was part of the 36th Combined Arms Army, while the 76th Guards Air Assault Division was also assumed to be subordinated to that same army. The 5th Guards Tank Brigade probably consisted of at least four maneuver battalions, while the elements of the 76th Guards Air Assault Division deployed six maneuver battalions.[4]

The march plan had the 5th Guards Tank Brigade arriving at Belaya Soroka on the Belarussian-Ukrainian Border at 0200. The tail of the column would not pass that point until 0400. Meanwhile, the 76th Guards Air Assault Division was starting at Palmira, near Khoyniki, Belarus in the Gomel Oblast. The 76th Guards Air Assault Division was supposed to leave the starting line at 0133 and arrive at Belaya Soroka at 0400, falling in behind the 5th Guards Tank Brigade. They were then to pass down using route P56/T2505. This route crossed the border, cross the Pripyat River, and went past the disabled

Chernobyl Nuclear Power Plant. The column was then to pass through Cherevach, the bridge over the Uzh; then Ivankiv, the bridge over the Terev (Teteriv River); and on to Bayntsi, the bridge over Zdvyzh. It was now on route P02. This is a point still over 14 miles (23km) from Hostomel as the crow flies. The 5th Guards Tank Brigade would have reached that last point at 1100, while the head of the 76th Guards Air Assault Division would reach that point two hours later. The 5th Guards Tank Brigade apparently was to stop there while the 76th Guards Air Assault Division continued on to Stoyanka, the bridge over the Irpin River. This put the head of the column to the west of the outskirts of Kyiv at 1416 on route E40 leading into the city. The whole column was to travel at 23km an hour (14mph) throughout this advance on a rather long and convoluted road.

The march order then has them "concentrating on the blocking line" starting 1455 with the final units in place by 1615. I gather this means they were not expected to enter the suburb of Irpin (population 65,167, 2022 estimate) or the city of Kyiv on the first day. Sunset at Kyiv on 24 February 2022 was at 1730. With sunrise at 0652, attacking in winter meant that Russian Army had a little over ten and half hours of sunlight each day to work with.

Still, it was difficult to consider this single column as a serious threat. It could have been a feint and it probably would have served the Russian Army better if it was. The Russians were reported to only have around 30,000 troops in Belarus. This was probably too small a force to take the large city of Kyiv if there was any form of defense in the area. The 4th Rapid Reaction Brigade was in the Hostomel area. It had two infantry battalions, a tank battalion, an artillery battalion, an AA missile battalion and support units. Also in the area, but not sure when it arrived in the battle area, was the experienced regular army unit 72nd Mechanized Brigade. This brigade had three mechanized battalions, a tank battalion and a full array of supporting units.[5] This force was initially also backed by the 44th Artillery Brigade. It had four artillery battalions, three battalions of 2A36 and 2A65 152mm towed howitzers and one battalion of 2S7 203mm self-propelled howitzers. They were later supported by another artillery brigade.[6] Being the capital city, a significant number of militia could also be raised on short notice. Added to that, the Russian column was supplied down a single two-lane road from Belarus passing through what is often considered marshland. This did not look like a promising direction of attack.

The Ukrainian government was in Kyiv. It was clear from intelligence intercepts before the war that the Russians were looking at the physical destruction of the Ukrainian president and the senior political leadership. At 1910 on the evening of 22 February, a day and half before the war started, the Ukrainian government received the information that an attack on the president would be carried out in the near future.[7]

This set the tone for the first couple of days of operation, with Zelenskyy, who refused to leave Kyiv, operating under the constant threat of being attacked by a Russian special operation targeting him and his government. The United States was also aware of this and was concerned to protect him. As most of U.S. intelligence community was not giving Ukraine much of a chance of withstanding the initial Russian conventional attack, they were clearly looking at withdrawing the Ukrainian government back to Lviv and possibly preparing for a long-term guerilla war, vice an immediate conventional war. Ukraine had other ideas.

The second area of potential operations was Odesa (population 1,015,826). This appeared to be case as on the first day there were reports of an amphibious landing there. There was no indication of the size or location. It turned out that this was a false rumor.

Such a landing so far from the rest of the front looked to be of limited value. It could have also been a distraction or a special operations head-hunting expedition to try to capture/kill some of the people involved in the violence in Odesa in 2013, something that Putin had talked about. But, it turns out no such effort was made, although Odesa was on high alert for the first week of the war and building defenses along its sea front.

On the other hand, on the morning of the first day, the Russian fleet sailed over to Snake Island. This is a small island of 0.08 square miles (0.2 square kilometers) that is only 22 miles (35km) off the coast of the border of Ukraine with Romania and 186 miles (300km) west of Crimea. It is a rock island less than 700m in width, with a single village inhabited by about thirty people. The island was confirmed as part of Romania in 1920 but transferred to the Soviet Union in 1948 by Romania under some rather vague treaty arrangements.

The island has some value for blocking shipments from Odesa down to the Dardanelles. At 1800 the Russian cruiser *Moskva*, the flag ship of the Russia Black Sea Fleet, supported by the patrol ship *Vasily Bykov*, sailed up towards Snake Island and radioed the following message to the garrison holding there: "Snake Island, I am a Russian Warship. I suggest you lay down your arms and surrender. Otherwise, you will be hit. Do you copy?" The garrison commander, Sergeant Roman Hrybov, could be heard discussing the issue with his deputy commander, a female NCO. He said, "Well, this is it. Should I tell him to go fuck himself?" She said, "Just in case." So his immediate response back to the *Moskva* was now the famous phrase, "Russian warship, go fuck yourself."[8]

While this is perhaps not as elegant as the 1775 statement by American Patrick Henry of "Give me liberty or give me death," the attitude of defiance caught the popular imagination and became not only a rallying cry for defiant Ukrainians, but for most of the world, who now saw a smaller country being unfairly attacked by a larger country. It became a repeated slogan and, eventually, Ukraine would issue a stamp in honor of this quote. The audio of the exchange was released by a Ukrainian government official that evening.

The Russian warship did open fire on Snake Island, bombarding it. They then landed forces on that island the same day and captured the island and the garrison of thirteen guardsmen. None had been killed or seriously wounded in the bombardment. Their open defiance in the face of overwhelming odds had earned them respect internationally. On 24 March, all the border guards were returned to Ukraine as part of a prisoner exchange with Ukraine.[9]

Kharkiv (population 1,433,886) is the second largest city in Ukraine and the largest majority Russian-speaking city in Ukraine. It was an objective for the separatists in 2014 but they never really came close to taking it. Even though the city consisted of a majority of Russian speakers, it did not seem to have a desire to be anything but a part of Ukraine. Perhaps, in part, this was because it was doing better economically than its cousins to the south, Luhansk and Donetsk. Back in 2014, the pro-Russian activists tried to assassinate its mayor, who was a member of the Yanukovych-supporting Party of Regions, in an attempt to take it. They failed and the mayor continued in office until his death in December 2020. His death was a result of COVID-19 and the complications from the injuries he received in 2014. Still, Kharkiv was a significant prize, and one that we thought would be a significant Russian target in the first couple of days of battle. It turns out it was not.

Russia had a chance to correct a major failure of their 2014 campaign. While Donetsk and Luhansk were both significant cities, they were cities in decline in the heart of the industrial region of Ukraine. This area was now a struggling rust belt, a sort of "Detroit" of Ukraine. On the other hand, Kharkiv was a vibrate and successful city with an educated class of workers that were leading the country in financial services, manufacturing and high technology. It was part of the former Soviet rust-belt cities (which include Luhansk and Donetsk). It has had a declining population since 1989, although this decline has now mostly stabilized. It had developed a big information technology business, though, and almost all of its business was with overseas customers. A Russian occupation would probably destroy a lot of that business.

This city should have been the prime objective/prize of the early stages of this war. Geographically, it is a city in the middle of a large open plain.

A serious organized Russian advance should have been able to envelop Kharkiv, surround it, isolate it and take it. It does not appear that this was ever attempted or seriously considered. Did the Russian Army consider that it would somehow or the other fall in the process?

In 1943, this city changed hands three times. It was larger (population wise) than Stalingrad was, which is why we examined the operations there for our urban warfare studies. It is just south of Belgorod, which is on the edge of the famous Battle of Kursk battlefields. There were significant Russian forces near Belgorod and at the border between Belgorod and Kharkiv.

From an operational point of view, this probably should have been the primary center of mass for the Russian offensive. It turns out it was not. Instead, Russia had organized a serious effort to threaten Kyiv (which should have been limited to a feint), had advanced forces towards Chernihiv and Sumy, had advanced forces out of Donetsk and Luhansk, had advanced on Mariupol and had advanced forces out of Crimea to take Melitopol and Kherson. While this was all significant, it meant that the advance to take Kharkiv was limited in strength and potency. I think they would have been better served to have concentrated forces in investing and then taking Kharkiv. Instead, what they did was to attempt to take half of Ukraine at once. We shall see shortly how poorly their original plan worked.

The 1st Guards Tank Army was operating to the north of Kharkiv, with the 4th Guards Tank Division in the immediate vicinity of the city. On the first day, Ukraine reported picking up two Russian prisoners from the 4th Guards Tank Division.[10] There were also losses reported near the city that included at least one soldier killed and a tank and a truck destroyed, as shown in videos.[11]

Operations out of the Donetsk and Luhansk provinces were initially fairly limited. Luhansk was reported to have an armed force of 14,000, while the Donetsk People's Republic was reported to have some 20,000 troops. At the start of this war, they each controlled only about half of their respective provinces. The rest of the provinces were under control of Ukraine and well defended by the Ukrainian Army. Their desire was to expand their control and take the rest of both provinces. Of course, Russia recognized these two "people's republics" on the night of 21 February, during Putin's widely broadcast speech.

The forces from Luhansk moved north and westward to start taking back the rest of the province, while the forces from Donetsk advanced on Mariupol, which was Ukrainian held but part of Donetsk Province. These operations initially moved fairly slowly. Not sure Ukraine initially had much facing the areas of the LPR that did not cover the two main cities of Severodonetsk or Lysychansk. On the other hand, the routes to Mariupol, on the Azov coast, were well defended.

Mariupol (population 431,859) would eventually become a story to itself. In the first days of the war, it was just one of many cities in Ukraine and was not under direct threat. This city was part of the Donetsk Oblast and is on the route to Crimea. Effectively, Crimea was completely isolated from the rest of Russia, except for the bridge they had built across the Kerch Peninsula. Was Russia going to try to drive through there to create a land connection to Crimea? Everyone assumed so, but it was well defended. Ukrainian troops had been there since 2014.

So, this attack does not appear to have been a high priority initially. There were other objectives easier to get to as the Russians were attacking across a broad front. In the initial reports of the war, there were lots of shells and missiles exploding around Kyiv and Kharkiv, but there was not much happening around Mariupol.

The sixth area of contention was the lands that bordered Crimea. This was obviously a critical area for Russia as Crimea gets their water from Ukraine. So while Russia had taken Crimea in 2014, Ukraine had the ability to effectively isolate it by cutting off their water. This had already been a source of friction. So, certainly Russia was going to try to expand their control of the area north of Crimea so as to secure water resources. Such an operation would also complicate the defense of Mariupol. On the first day they crossed the borders there.

It was hard to say at this point what Russia's final objectives were. They obviously were going to bomb all major military facilities and airfields. As cities are where many reporters are located, this is what is first reported on. But the question was what did they intend to occupy? This was difficult to tell initially, although the proclamations of their objectives were very expansive, including talking about replacing the Zelenskyy government in Kyiv.

Was the Russian objective to conquer half of Ukraine? This seems very optimistic as it is a very big piece of land to swallow. Were they going to just occupy all of Luhansk and Donetsk oblasts? Maybe, but this is a hard fight over terrain of limited economic value. Were they going to isolate and then try to take Kharkiv? They appeared to make no serious attempt to. Were they really trying to eliminate the Ukrainian government and take Kyiv? Apparently, they thought they could.

While the Ukrainian Army has some defensive capabilities, their biggest problem was that Russia has complete air superiority.

Chapter 7

The Fight over Hostomel Airfield,
24 February–1 March 2022

I t was clear by the end the first day of the war that Russia taking Kyiv was central to their plan. Forces had moved across the border north of Kyiv from Belarus and were marching south towards Kyiv. Before the war, it was claimed that 30,000 troops had moved to Belarus from Russia. This appeared to be the primary assault force for taking Kyiv. It still did not appear to be enough if the Ukrainians were properly positioned and ready to fight.

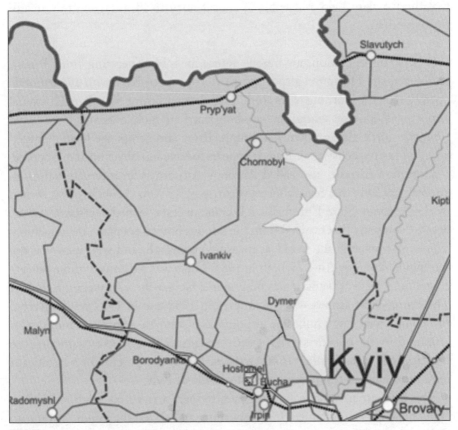

The Kyiv area.

It is claimed that in January 2022, the CIA director William J. Burns travelled to Ukraine and informed the Ukrainian government that Russia intended to capture the airport and that this would allow Russian forces to quickly move into Kyiv and decapitate the government. It is claimed that the American analysts stated that Putin and the Russian government believed that this quick operation would throw Ukraine into disarray, result in the collapse of the Ukrainian military and Russia would be able to install a puppet government. In effect, Russia was relying on a single military move to collapse their opposition. Now, it is hard to know how much of this narrative is correct, as it is based on newspaper reports of classified discussions, but in light of how the rest of the Russian military operations conducted, it does appear that Russia expected a lot from this fairly limited operation.[1]

Still, it does not appear that the Ukrainians were fully convinced that this was the primary threat and initially considered that the Russia's main assault was going to be in the Donbas. They did not announce general mobilization until 25 February, the second day of the invasion.[2] Therefore, it does appear that the Russians held a little bit of a local surprise advantage in this area of the battlefield.

In a separate operation, air mobile forces, possibly operating from Russia, had seized the Hostomel airport north-northwest of Kyiv with an airmobile operation on the morning of the 24th. This clever morning assault on Hostomel airport was done by sending a battalion-sized air mobile assault force down from the north, flying down the Dnipro River and across the large dammed lake that lies to the north of Kyiv. It appears to have initially landed unopposed.

Hostomel Airport, also called Antonov Airport, is an international cargo airport near Kyiv that has a concrete airstrip of 3,500m (11,483ft). It is owned by the Antonov State Enterprise, a Ukrainian state-owned aerospace and air defense company that evolved from the famous Soviet-era plane manufacturer. The largest plane in the world, as measured by weight and wingspan, was the six-engine Antonov An-225, built in 1985. There was only one of these Soviet-era relics in the world and it was housed in a hangar there, at its home airstrip. The Soviet-built airport was constructed in 1959 and in 1989 was converted to a commercial cargo hub. The airport was just north-northwest and 6 miles (10km) from the outskirts of Kyiv, with the large lake formed by damming the Dnipro River just 10 miles (16km) to its east. This was potentially a significant reinforcement and resupply point just outside of Kyiv.

The Russian air mobile force of paratroopers arrived on low-flying Mi-8 "Hip" helicopters and landed in the morning and seized the airport against no real resistance. They were escorted by Ka-52 "Alligator" attack helicopters. This air mobile force flew across the Belarus-Ukrainian border down to Hostomel airport.[3] It was reported to have happened at 0800 with a formation of twenty to thirty-four Russian helicopters.[4] The Mi-8 is a medium-sized twin-turbine transport helicopter that can carry around twenty-four soldiers. They can also be armed. This implies that the initial landing force was only between 480 and 816 troops.[5] Basically, a single reinforced battalion, probably from the 31st Guards Air Assault Brigade.[6]

The landing zone was softened up by Mi-35 and Ka-52 attack helicopters operating out of Belarus. The Mi-35 is an updated version of the Mi-24 Hind close air support helicopter that has been in common usage since the 1970s. It is an impressively armed but large and vulnerable helicopter gunship. It was the Soviet answer to the U.S. Cobra and Apache gunships. The Ka-52 looks a whole lot more like a U.S. gunship and was their 2008 successor to the Mi-24 Hind, smaller with only a two-man crew. One Ka-52 was hit near Vyshgorod, the two crewmen ejecting and the helicopter crashing into the Dnipro River, as did the two paratrooping crew.[7] One Ka-52 was hit by a MANPADS and had to make an emergency landing just outside the airport.[8] It appears that all the Mi-8s made it safely and unloaded their cargo of paratroopers.[9]

By early afternoon it was clear that the airport was in Russian hands and foreign reporters were driving up to their positions and filming them. It appeared to be a well-trained infantry force of at least a battalion in size. The first reporters to arrive at the scene were not aware that the Russians had taken the airport and were quite surprised to discover Russians there. This included Matthew Chance of CNN.[10] The Russian paratroopers, after a moment of consultation with their command, continued allowing the reporters to film them there. They were not hostile or confrontational to the foreign press, and looked competent and professional.

The seizure of this cargo hub was a brilliant initial stroke that set the Russians up just 16 miles (26km) from the Maidan Square in downtown Kyiv. It was clear that this was the first step of the 72-hour plan to remove the Ukrainian government and take Kyiv. This was the only part of the plan that worked.

That afternoon 4th Rapid Reaction Brigade of the Ukrainian National Guard surrounded the airport. This was a NATO standard light infantry brigade that included a battalion of T-64BV tanks, an artillery battery and supporting surveillance drones.[11] It probably outnumbered the Russian defenders at the airport. The T-64 was a Soviet-era tank, first designed in the early 1960s. The upgraded version, the T-64B, first entered service in 1976. The BV version has an armor upgrade package that features enhanced anti-radiation protection and add-on explosive reactive armor. It went into production in 1985. These forces were reported to have also been supported by the volunteer Georgian Battalion, which was based in Kyiv.

Later that afternoon, local Ukrainian forces counterattacked and the fight for the airport went into the night. In Kyiv, on 24 February, the sun rose at 0652 and set at 1730 giving them less than an 11-hour day. That afternoon attack continued into the evening, with the Russians receiving air support from Su-25s. In response, the Ukrainian Air Force also sent in at least two Su-24M bombers and at least one MiG-29.[12]

Between 2000 and 2200 Kyiv time, it was reported that the Ukrainians had retaken the airport, but this may not have been entirely the case. It does appear that they made some progress in closing with the Russian defenders and neutralizing the airstrip. By 1400 the next day, Russia declared that it had control of the airport. The airport and the neighboring town of Hostomel (population 17,534) now appeared to be in Russian hands.

It does seem that the initial force sent by Russia to seize the airfield was not sufficient. It probably should have been a brigade-size force of at least two to three infantry battalions. These forces were probably available if the Russians so choose. It would have required more helicopters in the initial wave, and perhaps subsequent waves of reinforcements. Instead, Russia conducted a single landing in the morning and no air reinforcement during the day. They probably could have used the helicopters in the first wave to transport in a second battalion during the afternoon. This would have helped. It appears that they underestimated the opposition, although it is hard to believe that they were not aware that a Ukrainian National Guard brigade was in the area. Apparently, they simply ignored the fact that they were sending in an unsupported battalion into an area defended by three times their number and equipped with armor. This seemed to be a common mistake made by Russia early in the war.

Meanwhile, it appears that the reinforcing column from Belarus that included the 5th Guards Tank Brigade and most of the 76th Guards Air Assault Division had not yet arrived at Hostomel. They were supposed to be in the area before 1416 according to their march plans. March plans are often optimistic, for in wartime a couple of vehicles stalled out or damaged on the two-line highway they are moving on can slow the units considerably.

It is claimed that the Russians did send a supporting landing force of eighteen Il-76s air transports from Pskov to Hostomel on the first day of the battle.[13] Any reinforcing planes that arrived in the area during the fight were unable to land in the cratered and fought over airfield. According to a newspaper report, U.S.

intelligence provided help that allowed Ukraine to shoot down one Russian transport plane that was carrying hundreds of troops to Hostomel Airport.[14]

An Ilyushin Il-76 can carry as many as a hundred passengers but usually only carries between forty and sixty soldiers on board (as a soldier with his weapons and backpack take up considerable space). Therefore, eighteen Il-76s would indicate a reinforcement of maybe one or two more reinforced battalions. This is still far from an overwhelming force, but would have at least evened the odds. As it was, because the Russians were fighting outnumbered, they were not able to protect the airfield and these troops could not land. The claim that hundreds of passengers were killed when one Il-76 went down is almost certainly an exaggeration.

If fact, the entire story may not be correct, as to date, no wreckage has been found.[15] It is not certain if Russia sent 18 Il-76s to the area to land. Regardless, the cratering of the airfield by the local defenders was probably enough to keep them from landing reinforcements, regardless of what was attempted and the kills later claimed.[16]

The end result is that reinforcements did not arrive, and the Russian airborne battalion ended up rather desperately hanging on at Hostomel until overland reinforcements arrived from Belarus. As this point, the forces employed did not have the strength to make it an effective operation.

The Russians did send a significant reinforcement column to Hostomel down from Belarus. Thanks to U.S. intelligence, the reinforcing column was spotted well ahead of time and location information was passed in a timely manner to the Ukrainian armed forces. The road from Belarus to Kyiv was a single two-lane blacktop. It is hard to move a mechanized column down a single two-lane road. They tend to go down it one vehicle at a time (vice two side-by-side) and each vehicle is spaced out for security and driving purposes. Therefore, suddenly you are looking at a moving military column with at best fifty vehicles a kilometer and if a mechanized battalion is on the move, then it is hundreds of vehicles and a column at least 10km in length.[17] For example, in the initial march plan for the 5th Guards Tank Brigade from 24 February in its march from Palmira Belarus it had 353 vehicles, for a column length of 17.6km and a travel speed of 23km per hour. This averages 50m per vehicle or 20 vehicles per km. The 76th Guards Air Assault Division had 495 vehicles and column that was 24.8km in length using the same density of deployment.[18]

Needless to say, an armored vehicle column stretched out for 40km down a highway was not only visible to U.S. intelligence, but also visible to U.S. commercial satellites. This, of course, was producing scary stories in the media of a Russian 40km column coming down to Kyiv. This basically meant a force of two reinforced brigades, and the Ukrainians appeared to have started with at least a brigade-sized force in the area.[19] Therefore, when the Russian column arrived, and it would take several days to fully deploy, they did not have overwhelming force. At that point they could secure Hostomel and Hostomel Airfield, threaten Irpin and Kyiv, but could not have done a whole lot more than that. The Russians would still have to advance on Kyiv against a considerable defending opposing force that was being supplemented by militia assembling in the city.

The Ukrainian president bravely and correctly stayed in Kyiv and started organizing the defense there. They started raising local militia to defend the city. According to the news reports of the time, some 18,000 rifles were handed out on 25 February.[20] The previous president of Ukraine, Petro Poroshenko, also remained in Kyiv and helped organize resistance, as did the mayor of Kyiv, internationally famous heavyweight boxer and World Champion Vitali Klitschko. There is no question that there was significant militia being assembled in Kyiv, although their strength and capabilities were not known and never tested.

The U.S. in its assumption that this was a 72-hour operation to decapitate the government, did offer to transport the President Zelenskyy to Lviv. He chose to stay, claiming in an unsubstantiated quote on 25 or 26 February, "The fight is here; I need ammunition, not a ride."[21] Whether this is what he actually said, it is hard to deny the "Churchillian" attitude of the resistance that he displayed.

The column from Belarus started arriving in the Hostomel area late on 25 February. This was a day behind the original schedule, taking twice as long as planned to cover the distance. This was effectively a two brigade-sized column that stretched for at least 25 miles (40km). According to one description of the advance, the heavy vehicles tore up the roads as the moved forward and the convoy bogged down immediately. It took more than a day for some units to cross the border into Ukraine. A Russian logbook recorded repeated delays over several days. It also reported Ukrainian attacks with hundreds of injuries and many deaths and destroyed vehicles.[22]

The route from the border of Belarus down to Kyiv ran through an area known as the Pripet Marshes. It is a wet wilderness area that is not well trafficked. Effectively, this single two-lane blacktop road was the only route down. This was hardly enough to move and support a mechanized brigade, or to transport the additional supplies and reinforcements required. They really needed an operational airfield open for re-supply and the Ukrainian air defense was robust enough now that this was not possible. Therefore, by the end of the second day, the Russians had the reinforced tank brigade and the air assault division winding down this road towards Hostomel, the airborne battalion holding Hostomel and not a whole lot else that they could do. This was beginning to look like a dead end from the second day.

The 76th Air Assault Division was supposed to cross at the village of Stoyanka, at the bridge over the Irpin River on highway E40. This was due west of Kyiv. They appeared to have reached there as of the end of the second day, but never attempted a crossing. It was a village to the west of Kyiv and on the west side of the river with a population in 2001 of only 405 inhabitants. Once across the river, following highway E40, there was a wooded area of covering almost 5 miles (4.8 miles or 7.7km) before they would arrive at another water obstacle and the western suburbs of Kyiv. This was not the most promising advance route.

The 5th Guards Tank Brigade crossed the bridge over the Zdvyzh River at Babyntsi and then moved off that march route, probably moving to the south and covering the flank of the 76th Air Assault Division. They appeared to be part of the force covering the west flank of the advance on Kyiv, as opposed to assaulting Kyiv. The 76th Air Assault Division consisted of six maneuver battalions while the tank brigade probably had four.

Meanwhile, for truly mystifying reasons, Russia sent troops from Belarus to seize the area of the Chernobyl nuclear power plant. In 1986, the infamous Chernobyl plant had one reactor explode and then conduct a core melt down. This spread radioactivity elements that seriously contaminated more than 29,000 square miles (100,000 square kilometers) of land. Iodine-131 and caesium-137 were the two primary contaminates. Cesium-137 has a half-life of thirty years, so even some thirty-six years later this is still not an area safe for people. The troops that they sent were not aware of the nature of the area, and were poorly enough informed that they did not immediately recognize the threat they had been placed under. Although the area was nowhere near as radioactive as it was back in 1986, the Chernobyl Exclusion Zone is still not considered habitable again for a further 300 years. There were still some 197 people living in the area, but most of the over 1,000 original residents had left. Most of the area was still abandoned. For some reason, the Russian Army felt that this was an important enough area to occupy, even though it has no clear open routes to any other areas of military importance. It was not an area that was defended or even patrolled by Ukraine.

Among the lead forces in the column advancing from Belarus was the Chechen 141st Special Motorized Regiment, also known as the Kadyrovites. This was a unit originally created from the Kadyrovites, a Chechen paramilitary organization that served to protect the Head of the Chechen Republic, now Colonel General Ramzon Kadyrov, age 46. They were now organized with a combat fighting unit that reported to the National Guard of Russia. On 26 February, Kadyrov confirmed that the regiment has been deployed in Ukraine. According to the secretary of the Ukrainian Defense Council, the Chechens were tasked with capturing and killing the Ukrainian leaders, including President Zelenskyy. They clearly were near the head of this column, with the The Kyiv Independent reporting them being near Hostomel on 27 February.[23] That same day, the Ukrainians also claimed to have ambushed and killed the commander of the regiment, Major General Magomed Tushayev. This claim appears to be optimistic, as it appears that he was still alive on 16 March 2022 according to a video posted in which he states he is still alive. On 1 March, Kadyrov reported that Chechen losses to date had been two killed and six wounded. On 3 March, it was reported that a group of Chechen soldiers had been sent to infiltrate Kyiv and assassinate President Zelenskyy. This effort failed before it ever got near the president, possibly due to intelligence intercepts or intelligence leaks.

The Russian regular forces deployed for this operation included the reinforced paratrooper battalion from the 31st Guards Air Assault Brigade or 104th Guards Air Assault Regiment,[24] the 64th Motorized Rifle Brigade, the 37th Guards Motorized Rifle Brigade and various Special Operations Forces. There are few reports of what fighting the 64th Separate Motorized Rifle Brigade did to the west of Kyiv, but it ended up becoming notorious for its involvement in massacres around Bucha. There are also few reports on what 37th Guards Motorized Rifle Brigade did in February and early March, but it eventually ended up fighting for Makariv to the west of Kyiv. Only elements of the regiment may have been deployed.[25] During the fighting, the Russian Major General Andrei Sukhovetski was killed. He is reported to have died on 28 February at the age of 47. He was the airborne major general (a one-star rank) and was the deputy commander of the 41st Combined Arms Army. According to Ukrainian sources, he was shot by a sniper either at Hostomel or at Hostomel airport. He was the first of several Russian generals to be killed in this war. As he was in Hostomel, this does reinforce the notion that the 41st Combined Arms Army was the operational command in this area at the moment, vice the 29th, 35th or 36th Combined Arms Armies. It is uncertain who had overall command of the area north of Kyiv.

The Russian Special Operations Forces conducted several attempts to penetrate into Kyiv to attack government figures. The earliest effort was on the morning of 25 February, when three Russian saboteurs dressed as Ukrainians soldiers were intercepted and killed in the Obolon District. This was an area of the city 6 miles (12km) north of the center of Kyiv. The last attempt was the effort reported on 3 March conducted by Chechens. Many other attempts were claimed, but the accuracy of this wartime reporting is suspect. Still, the Obolon district was over 8 miles from the front lines on 25 February, making one wonder how the Russian commandos were inserted.

Well outside of Kyiv, the Russians also took the town of Ivankiv (population 9,993 in 2022 estimate) on the morning of 25 February. This town was some 37 miles (59km) to the northwest of Kyiv. The town was on the two-lane road coming down from Belarus and was being defended by Ukrainian air assault forces. This forced the lead elements of the 5th Guards Tank Brigade into the attack.[26] This large column was supposed to be at western edge of Kyiv as of the afternoon on the 24th, and here they were fighting for control of a town 37 miles outside of Kyiv.

The attempt to take this town turned into an extended fight, which continued into the afternoon and evening. The Ukrainian forces were also able to destroy the bridge crossing at the Teteriv River, forcing the Russians to erect a pontoon bridge instead. The fighting at Ivankiv would continue for the following two days, with Russia shelling the town with artillery as their forces bypassed the town and continued on towards Kyiv. This destroyed the Ivankiv Historical and Local History Museum on 27 February with the loss of over twenty works by famous Ukrainian folk art painter Maria Prymachenko (1909–97).

Part of the Russian column had advanced towards the Kyiv suburb of Irpin on the morning of 25 February. A convoy of about eighty Russian special police (OMON and SOBR troops) in six vehicles was ambushed at the E373 bridge over the Irpin River, according to one account. All six vehicles were taken out with heavy casualties, and three Russian special police were captured.[27] There was otherwise no organized attack on Kyiv on the 25th.

During the night of 25 February the Ukrainian civilians blew a 5 foot gap in the dam at Demydiv which separated the mouth of Irpin River from the large Kyiv Reservoir. The water level of the reservoir was several meters higher. This resulted in the Irpin River being flooded during the morning of 26 February in the areas around Demydiv, temporarily removing that village to the north-northwest of Kyiv as a possible advance route. It is not entirely clear what additional problems this expanded water obstacle created downstream for the Russians, but it clearly made it difficult for a while to cross the river near Demydiv. The sluice gates 5 miles upriver at Chervone stopped some the flooding from going further, but this effort did effectively shorten the front by at least 5 miles.[28]

Kyiv itself was first shelled by Russian artillery for 30 minutes on the morning of 26 February. Several attacks were reported to have been repelled on the outskirts of the city. An odd video showing a pointblank engagement between a Ukrainian Stela-10 vehicle (an armored short-range surface-to-air missile transport) and a machinegunned armed Russian MRAP (Mine-Resistant Ambush Protected) armored car clearly showed that elements of the Russian Army were in the Obolon District and clashing with Ukrainian forces.[29] The two vehicles are facing each other and driving down the street, while several civilian cars are driving down the same road, discovering they are in the middle of a battle. Still, it appears that Russia only had a foothold in this urban district and was not advancing further.

Clashes, shelling and skirmishes continue on the 27th, but there was still no clearly organized assault or advance on the city of Kyiv or its suburb of Obolon. The Russian forces advanced into Bucha and engaged in a fight for Irpin, with intense clashes taking place in the open area between Bucha and Irpin.[30] Over the course of the day, Russia IFVs and other vehicle losses mounted, most of them lined up on Vokzalna Street, a block away from the open area. Photographic evidence records thirty-two vehicles destroyed on this street.[31] Some of these were clearly destroyed in a morning actions before 1040. The Ukrainians claimed eleven BMD-2s destroyed by Bayraktars and artillery. The Ukrainian reconnaissance troops and paratroopers then advanced into Bucha and claimed another three or four BTRs.[32] A number of these vehicles destroyed were command vehicles and self-propelled artillery. This indicates that part of this column was spotted parked in the shelter of the town and then later struck with artillery, drones or loitering munitions. Because a collection of BMPs and BDRs are in the rear of the column and many of the command vehicles are in the front, it indicates that this was at least two separate groupings struck on two separate occasions. No other destroyed vehicles are spotted in Irpin or even Bucha on 27 February. The Ukrainians ended up blowing the bridge between Bucha and Irpin.

The Russians also advanced into the small village of Moshchun (population about 794), across the Irpin River just to the east of Hostomel. The area was defended by at least elements of a company of the 72nd Mechanized Brigade, along with a handful of Ukrainian militia men.[33] Moshchun was 8 miles (13km) to the northwest of Kyiv.

Fighting was even lighter on the 28th as the 40km convoy was still winding its way down to Hostomel. The Ukrainians concentrated their fires on Russian forces on highway M06 that morning, causing considerable casualties.[34]

The following day, 1 March, there was more shelling of the city, mostly by missiles, with some of it clearly targeted at critical infrastructure. Five civilians were killed as the Russians had hit the Kyiv TV Tower with a missile

Meanwhile, to the west of Kyiv, an extended fight developed along the line that included the village of Makariv. Moving into the defense of this area was initially the Ukrainian 14th Mechanized Brigade in front of Marakiv and later the 10th Mountain Assault Brigade on its left. Also in the area were elements of the 95th Air Assault Brigade on its right.[35] Facing opposite to them, from right to left (from west to east), was the later infamous 64th Motorized Rifle Brigade, the 37th Guards Motorized Rifle Brigade directly opposite of Makariv and the 5th Guards Tank Brigade to its left.[36] The 64th Motorized Rifle Brigade was reported to have a strength in March of 1,700 men, according to documents captured by Ukraine. The 37th Motorized Rifle Brigade had 659 men deployed in 1 reinforced battalion and it may have been similar in strength to the 64th if the entire brigade was there.[37]

Still, it was clear by 1 March that Kyiv was not going to fall within the first 72 hours. As noted at the time, "this first phase of this campaign is over, and Russia clearly did not win it."[38] At this point, the war was almost a week old and the forces to the north-northwest of Kyiv probably comprised a reinforced airborne battalion and a six-maneuver battalion air mobile division, with other forces arriving that added up to eight or nine more additional maneuver battalions.[39] They were able to advance in the face of the not-as-well trained Ukrainian forces to the outskirts of the Obolon District of Kyiv.[40] They entered that district on 26 February. They only got part way into it, never entirely clearing it.

To the west of Kyiv were three Russian brigades holding the line there. They had been able to expand their control across the countryside, but again taking no significant areas. They would soon be tangled up in a fight for Makariv. Furthermore, the forces outside of Kyiv did not have the strength to continue forward. So ended the initial assault on Kyiv that was supposed to decapitate the government.

Let us look at the reasons this operation failed.

First, the Russian initial plan appears to be optimistic and under-resourced. It does appear that they sent forward primarily brigade-size groups, that otherwise had limited support, to seize major objectives such as Kyiv and Kherson. Supposedly, the Russian Army had deployed about 150,000 troops around Ukraine. According to the reports at time, initially only about 60,000 Russian troops went in. This is rather odd. If you have 150,000 troops, why not use all 150,000 troops? This led to a single-prong assault that came out of Belarus to attack the areas to the north and northwest of Kyiv. This led to a brigade-size group seizing Kherson.... and that was it. They really didn't take too much else, except in the south. Let's discuss the Kyiv operation first.

The attack on Kyiv was poorly conceived. The initial assault consisted of an air mobile assault to take Hostomel/Antonov airport. This was a clever opening maneuver and posed significant Russian forces and a good resupply point just north-northwest of Kyiv. It nicely shows what can be done with air mobile forces (helicopter bound) in an environment when you control the air.

What was missing after that was a massive reinforcement effort. There were several reasons for this:

1. The initial airborne landing was not sufficiently large.
2. The initial airborne landing was not reinforced by a second airborne wave in the afternoon.
3. The Ukrainian counterattack contested the airfield and cratered it.
4. Ukrainian resistance in the area was significant. Before the end of the first day of the attack, they retook parts or all of the airport.
5. The follow-on forces on 25 February were plane bound, vice helicopter bound, and therefore prevented from landing.
6. There was no systematic follow-up or resupply from helicopter borne forces on subsequent days.

This last point is mystifying. If Russia had control of a large airbase, why were significant reinforcements and huge amounts of supplies not shipped in by helicopters, if not airplanes? One could envision a scenario when they take the airbase on day 1, fly in a second wave of troops in the afternoon, fly it at least two waves of reinforcements on day 2 by helicopter, fly in massive reinforcements on subsequent days by plane and helicopter as the airfield was secured and repaired, and then launch a reinforced assault towards Kyiv on day 3 or 4. This is not what happened. Instead, they ended up fighting for control of the airbase on day 2, and then it appeared that they waited for their reinforcements to come down from Belarus. On top of that, it appears they had not real plans to resupply and were struggling with shortages after a few days. By the time they started moving forward again, Ukraine certainly had time to shift forces, reinforce the defense, mobilize the militia and prepare for the assault.

This attack quickly bogged down in the face of determined Ukrainian resistance. While lots of people talk about urban warfare, they never got that far; instead they were occupying airfields, villages and parts of the outskirts of Kyiv. As of 18 March, the Kyiv city administration was reporting their losses as 162 soldiers killed, 648 wounded (a 4-to-1 wounded-to-killed ratio) and

60 civilians killed and 241 wounded (a 4.02-to-1 wounded-to-killed ratio). This is not a lot of casualties for a defending force estimated to be over 18,000 that had started on 24 February.

On the other hand, as it was a helicopter assault on Hostomel, why didn't Ukraine have effective anti-aircraft defense of the area? It was an obvious route, and they knew that Russia had moved 20,000 or more troops into Belarus. They probably had detailed orders of battle, based upon U.S. intelligence. It was pretty obvious which way they were going. Was the Ukrainian air defense degraded and destroyed by the Russians on the first day of the war (I have no reports on this) or was it not properly placed?

The Russians did lose two Ka-52 assault helicopters and one Mi-35 on the first day (24 February), but no Mi-8 transport helicopters. They may have lost an Il-76 on the second day. On 1 March, the Russian lost another Mi-35M helicopter in the Kyiv Reservoir. They did not lose any jet aircraft in and around Kyiv at this time. The Ukrainian lost the An-225 Mriya destroyed on the ground at Hostomel airbase on 24 February, and also eight other commercial or cargo aircraft were also destroyed around Hostomel. On 25 February 2002 a Ukrainian Su-27 was shot down over Kyiv by a Russian S-400 missile, and crashed in a residential complex. The pilot died. On 27 February, an Su-25 was shot down near Kyiv and the following day a Ukrainian Mi-8 was shot down at the cost of three crew. This was all. It was not a heavily contested airspace.

Anyhow, what developed after that became a dreadful unproductive deployment on the part of Russia. They ended up with a force of one or two brigades north-northwest of Kyiv, unable to move forward, facing a determined defense and not properly supported logistically.

It also appears that U.S. or Ukrainian intelligence played a major part in helping to contain and mitigate the Russian attempts to assassinate Ukrainian leaders. It is clear that the United States knew of these plans before the war started, and may have known the details of the Russian plans. That none of these multiple efforts (at least two) were able to penetrate and get near their targets indicates that the Ukrainians probably had some knowledge of the efforts, perhaps complete knowledge.

The failure of the Russians to take Kyiv and decapitate the Ukrainian government in the first days of the war set them up for the extended unproductive fight that they are now in. This was perhaps the single most important Russian operation of the war, and it was poorly conceived and under resourced.

Chapter 8

The Fight over Kherson,
24 February–3 March

The other dramatic and threatening advance early in the war was out of Crimea, into Kherson Province and on to the provincial capital of Kherson. This advance, depending on how it developed could have threatened to cut off the whole of eastern Ukraine from western Ukraine and could have threatened Odesa. It appears to have also been under-resourced.

The Russian forces advanced rapidly out of Crimea and took Kherson by the evening of the first day of the war, 24 February. They secured the Antonovskii bridge in the northeast part of the city and raised their flag in

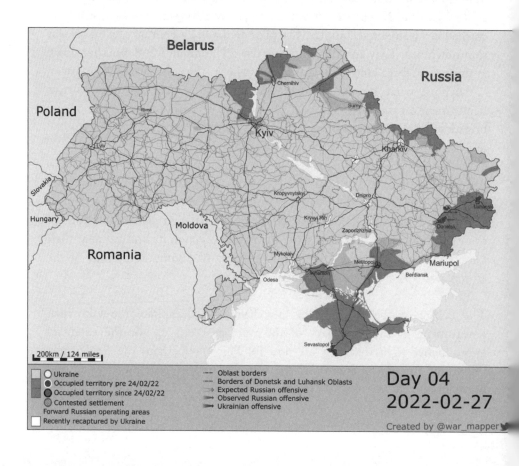

Belarus

Russia

Poland

Kyiv

Kharkiv

Chernihiv

Sumy

Rivne

Lviv

Slovakia

Hungary

Moldova

Kropyvnytskyi

Dnipro

Luhansk

Kryvyi Rih

Zaporizhzhia

Donetsk

Romania

Mykolaiv

Melitopol

Mariupol

Kherson

Berdiansk

Odesa

Sevastopol

200km / 124 miles

○ Ukraine
● Occupied territory pre 24/02/22
● Occupied territory since 24/02/22
◐ Contested settlement
Forward Russian operating areas
Recently recaptured by Ukraine

--- Oblast borders
----- Borders of Donetsk and Luhansk Oblasts
→ Expected Russian offensive
➡ Observed Russian offensive
➡ Ukrainian offensive

Day 04
2022-02-27

Created by @war_mapper

this area of Kherson. The size of this force was probably not much, maybe a single BTG (Battalion Tactical Group) or less and thrown out without much support. Kherson was only about 60 miles (97km) as the crow flies from the Crimean border.

In the early morning of 25 February, the Ukrainian forces recaptured the Antonovskii bridge in a dramatic fight over this rather long bridge (some 4,482ft or 1,366m). This forced the Russians out of Kherson. Later that day, the Russians again seized the Antonovskii bridge. The next day several dead soldiers and destroyed military vehicles could be seen still lying on the bridge. Ukraine still held the city. This bridge was to the northeast of the main area of the city, so seizing the bridge allowed Russian forces to continue north past the city without having to capture the city.

This was an unusually defensible line created by the Dnipro River. The Dnipro River was dammed at Nova Kakhovka to create the Kakhovka Reservoir. No bridges crossed this rather extended body of water, with the reservoir going from just south of Zaporizhzhia (population 710,052 as of 1 January 2022) down southwest to Novo Kakhovka. At Nova Kakhovka (population 45,069 in 2021) there was the Kakhovka Hydroelectric Power Plant and a bridge across that dam. Down river from there were only two other bridges, a railroad bridge at Prydniprovske (the Antonivskyy Zaliznychnyy) and the Antonovoskii bridge. This was an inherently easy area to defend and it appears that it was not really defended. The Russians took the Antonovskii bridge on the 24th and reclaimed it on the 25th. Other Russian forces pushing north captured Nova Kakhovka on the 25th and took the dam and bridge there. By the end of that day, Russian controlled all routes across the Dnipro River.

Operations against Kherson now dragged out, with the Russians claiming to have encircled the city on 27 February. They also occupied parts of the city and took the Kherson International Airport. Early in the morning of 1 March, the Russians renewed their assault on the city but they did not take Kherson until 2 March, some six days after they first crossed the bridge. The Russians had to move up additional forces in the interim to deal with Ukrainian defenders, who may not have been properly reinforced.

According to the mayor of Kherson, the fighting there over the week resulted in the deaths of about 300 Ukrainian soldiers and civilians. Russian tank and vehicle losses in the area show little around Kherson. South of the Dnipro there were only three vehicles reported as destroyed from March.[1] There were no Russian vehicles reported lost on Antonovskii bridge in February or March. There were no destroyed Russian vehicles in Kherson or around the Kherson international Airport in February or March. It does not mean they were not there, it just means they were not recorded, or were pulled out, or reported only in November.

A separate column also had advanced and attacked Melitopol, to the northeast of Crimea, on 25 February taking it by 1 March. This city was the first major city that the Russian Army had captured (they took Kherson the following day). Rushed into the area to defend against the Russian advance out of Melitopol was the 128th Mountain Assault Brigade, which had probably been shifted over from western Ukraine.[2]

These were now the two largest cities taken from Ukraine, and after a week of war, the only two cities seized. Kherson had a pre-war population of 283,649 and Melitopol had 150,768 people (according to the 2021 population estimate). Kherson was the only regional capital captured by Russia in the first eighteen months of this war. The Russians and their allies also held two others, the capitals of the Lugansk People's Republic and the Donetsk People's Republic that were seized back in 2014.

Russia was certainly looking like they were doing what they intended to do in this area. The real danger to Ukraine, though, was what Russia could take after expanding from these areas.

Even before taking Kherson the Russians expanded their operations, advancing northwest beyond to Mykolaiv and starting a battle on the evening of 26 February with a column of reportedly twelve tanks. They entered the outskirts of the city at 1852, according to one account, but were driven back in a battle that lasted around three hours.[3] Russian reinforcements advanced from Kherson on the 28th and launched another attack in the morning before 1100.[4] There were several subsequent attacks over the next few days and fighting on the outskirts of the city, but clearly Russia did not have the forces in place to take Mykolaiv. This was the third sign that the Russian offensives actually did not have a lot of "umpf" (the failure to hold Kherson and the failure to break into Kyiv in the first few days were the earlier signs). Five Russian vehicles were recorded as destroyed around Mykolaiv.[5]

The Russians then continued to advance past Mykolaiv (population 476,101), up the Southern Bug River to Nova Odesa (population 11,690), also not taking that town, and then continued up the Southern Bug to Voznesensk (population 34,050), which they also did not take. There was a Russian armored column that was hit outside the village on 2–3 March, meaning that they were just taking Kherson while the head of the column was 88 miles (142km) further on and was in a serious fight outside of Voznesensk.[6] Lots of blitz here, but one questions if they had enough weight to these forces conduct krieg. The attacking force was reportedly the Russian 126th Coastal

Defense Brigade of 400 men and 43 vehicles. Essentially, a large reinforced company had been flung 90 miles to the northwest of Kherson. It is claimed that most of this BTG was eliminated in a battle over the course of 2 and 3 March.[7] This force retreated from the area.

Not a lot of losses from this advance were reported in photos and videos. No vehicles were recorded outside of Nova Odesa and only one BTR-80 is reported at Voznesensk.[8] There were three other destroyed Russian vehicles at Sashpero Mykolaivka, a village on the edge of the route from Mykolaiv to Voznesensk.[9]

This advance seems like a pointless probe into nowhere, operating under what appears to be the now proven false assumption that somehow or the other the Ukrainians were going to collapse the moment they saw a Russian armor column.

Mykolaiv is a port, even though it is a way up the river. It is the main shipbuilding center on the Black Sea. The largest warship in the Ukrainian Navy and their only frigate, the *Hetman Sahaidachny* (3,150 tons displacement), was undergoing a major refit there. It was scuttled probably on about 28 February 2022. Not sure why they did this, as they ended up maintaining control of Mykolaiv.

At this point Russia was stretched out across about 90 miles from Kherson to Mykolaiv to Nova Odesa to Voznesensk. Needless to say, this was an untenable position that they would soon be pushed back from or withdraw from.

The Ukrainian holding of Mykolaiv was significant. Without control of that, any further operations up the Southern Bug were pointless. Without Mykolaiv, they could not threaten to cut off eastern Ukraine and could not threaten to take Odesa. Mykolaiv is the location of the bridge crossing the Southern Bug on the road to Odesa. It was fairly critical for Ukraine to hold this city of around a half million people, which they apparently did with a mix of forces (elements of the 59th Motorized Brigade, 80th Air Assault Brigade, 36th Naval Infantry Brigade and militia). The Russian forces that advanced appeared to be of limited strength, which was becoming a theme throughout this campaign. It was a force large enough to overcome the hastily organized defenders of Kherson, but not large enough to take any other major population centers. One does wonder if Kherson had been properly defended with two or three battalions to start with, whether the Russian Army would have been able to do anything at all in this area. Was Kherson a city taken on the cheap?

The Russians had enough forces to send a column to Melitopol, to advance after that to Zaporizhzhia Nuclear Power Plant, to push up to Mykolaiv and to push beyond all the way to Voznesensk. By the results, it appears that this was a force that came out of Crimea of maybe three or four BTGs. It may have been more, but it could not have been much more. This really was not a lot for the amount of area they were taking and then had to cover. They then appear to have run out steam, which is not surprising considering.

Russian forces occupied the areas between Melitopol and Kherson, including taking the Zaporizhzhia Nuclear Power plant. They then did not advance further north, probably because of a lack of strength. This left the Ukrainian cities of Mykolaiv (population 476,101 in 2021) and Zaporizhzhiya (population 722,713 in 2021) to their north still securely in Ukrainian hands. The advance did create a large occupied area to the north of Crimea that secured the water supply from Kakhovka Reservoir for the peninsula. To their west, along the Sea of Azov, was the Ukrainian city of Mariupol (population 431,859), which became the next big objective for the forces operating in the south.

There does appear to have been a few things wrong with Russian operations. First, the initial assault on Kherson was conducted with a very limited force. They obviously reinforced that force, correcting the problem and took Kherson six days later. But, overall, it does not look like the forces that came out of Crimea were all that significant size wise. I have seen no estimates of their force strength for this operation, but would not be surprised if it was as low as a half-dozen BTGs. They were basically able to grab one undefended city, and lightly defended nuclear power plant, one lightly defended city, two undefended bridges and a lot of undefended territory in between. They were not able to take anything that was defended in strength.

And then there is the question of where and what the Ukrainian Army was doing. In the process of defending Kyiv, Mariupol, Kharkiv, and the provinces of Donetsk and Luhansk, did they just leave this area under-resourced? Did they even bother to defend the route out of Crimea, where there are only three narrow peninsulas leading to the rest of Ukraine? There were only four roads leading out of Crimea. It does not appear that they defended these at all. That a weak column could run all the way from Crimea to Kherson and take the only road bridge in the area on the first day indicates that there was no opposition in between. This is something of a surprise to me.

It also does not appear that they had a significant force initially defending Kherson. They gathered something together in the area that took the bridge back that same day, but one might guess that the Russian forces hanging on to Kherson initially were a company sized force or less. They fact that the Russians were quickly able to retake it, across a bridge and a large river, indicates that there was not a lot Ukrainians defending there to start with (and apparently even less Russians initially). It just seems like a lot of progress was made in this area with very limited Russian forces against what was even more limited Ukrainian opposition. This is surprising because the Ukrainians probably should have been prepared for an advance out of Crimea.

This odd sideshow of an operation had captured almost the entire Kherson Province from Ukraine in a little over a week. This ended up becoming the most successful Russian operation of the first phase of the war.

Chapter 9

The Attack in Northeast Ukraine and the Advance on Kyiv, 24 February–10 March 2022

Meanwhile in the northeast part of Ukraine, Russian forces were advancing around Chernihiv and Sumy and bypassing Konotop. This was a strange series of operations as it covered lot of ground with very limited forces, some of them not that well trained.

It is the clear that the experienced, trained and more capable Russian forces were committed to advances on Kyiv and out of Crimea. The Russian forces in the area of northeastern Ukraine seemed to consist of a lot of

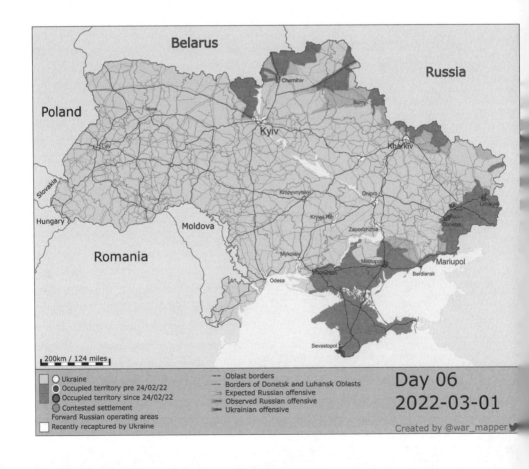

"second-line" forces, many of them using draftees, and often with older, less capable equipment.

Russian tanks had been very similar for over seventy years. The post-war series of tanks started with the T-54 and T-55, which were a series of Soviet main battle tanks that first entered service around 1947. They had evolved from the late war T-44 tank. T-54/55 was the most-produced tank in history with around 100,000 of them made. These main battle tanks were fairly heavy (about 40 tons), well armored (205mm turret front, 100mm hull front at 60 degrees), with a single 100mm rifled gun, a four-man crew and a low profile. That low profile is what made these tanks unique compared to many other tanks in the West. This was partially achieved by limiting the crew height for armor units to 5ft 8in. They were decent tanks in 1955. Some are still in use today.

Their next upgrades were the T-62 and then the T-64. The T-62 was similar to the previous design except it had a 115mm smoothbore gun. The production T-64 had a 125mm smoothbore gun and composite armor. It also reduced the crew to three, making use of an autoloader to replace one of the crew men. The T-64 was at a level of development not previously seen in Russian tanks. With composite armor and an autoloader, it was much more expensive to make then the previous Russian tanks. It continued being updated throughout the Soviet era, with T-64 BM models developed in 1983 and T-64BV models developed in 1985. The T-64BV had reactive armor.

The T-64 was made in Kharkov. As such, when the Soviet Union broke up, the most developed Soviet tank ended up being manufactured in Ukraine. Ukraine further developed the tank with the T-64B M2 models and the T-64BV type 2017. The Ukrainian T-64BM Bulat modernization included additional reactive armor. The tank was further refined in 2019 as the T-64BM2 Bulat with upgraded thermal sights. The Ukrainian development of the T-64BV also included bolt-on reactive armor, and improved thermal imaging, and upgraded night sights.

The next Soviet tank, the T-72, was the mainstay Soviet tank for most of the remaining decades of the Soviet Union. It was also their primary export tank. No T-64s were exported. The T-72 was simpler and easier to build than the T-64. About 25,000 of them were built. It also had a 125mm smoothbore and a three-man crew. At the time of its initial deployment, it was as good as any tank in the world. Over time, it somewhat fell behind in development once the British produced Chobham armor and the United States produced the impressive M-1. At that point, the T-72 was a generation behind.

The upgraded version of the T-72 was the T-80. It also had a 125mm smoothbore and a three-man crew. This was still not a tank that matched a

U.S. M-1. Their next and last Soviet upgrade was the T-90, which also had a 125mm smoothbore gun and a three-man crew. While this was a definite improvement it was also no match for the upgraded M-1A2. In 1991, during the Gulf War, U.S. M-1A2s were matched against Iraqi T-72s. It was a lopsided contest, with the M1-A2 clearly superior in almost all ways.[1]

The T-64s were nominally still in the Russian inventory, although mostly held in reserve as the post-Soviet Russian Army decided to standardize their forces around the T-72 and T-80. The versions they kept were not from 1964, though, but were later revisions. For example, the T-64B was from 1976 and included laser telemeter and a missile guidance system for missiles fired through the gun. While the T-62 was a direct descendent of the T-55, the T-64 was something a little different. It was the expensive Cadillac version of Soviet tanks. The later T-72 was a more affordable main battle tank, although not as capable.

The Russians have since then developed a new advanced fifth-generation tank, the T-14 Amata. While this is an advanced fifth-generation tank, only ten of them have been built to date. As far as we know, none were used in Ukraine. What Russia was primarily using outside of Kyiv and Kherson were the T-80s and T-90s. What they were often using in the operations around Chernihiv, Sumy and Konotop were the older T-72s. As these were older tanks, their reliability and maintenance were not as good.

A tank is notoriously unreliable. In addition to sucking up fuel at a prodigious rate (measured in gallons per mile), they often have a high breakdown rate. It is not unusual to move a column of armor and leave scattered on the side of the road a half-dozen or more broken-down tanks. There are videos of some of these tanks standing on the side of the road.[2] As the Russian Army is primarily a draftee army, then the quality and depth of maintenance and support is often not as good as in a professional army. Added to that, the less reliable older tanks were manned by some of those draftees. Needless to say, this all added up to make for a weaker, less capable force.

The Ukrainian forces they were facing were a mix of experienced regular units, such as the 1st Tank Brigade, and National Guards and reserve units. A lot of the Ukrainian Army was down in the Donbas and at Mariupol, where they had been fighting since 2014. What was holding Chernihiv, Sumy and Konotop was mostly National Guard and reserve units, with the exception of 1st Tank Brigade. As such, these forces tended to hold in and around the cities, and not deploy in a continuous line across a frontier that stretched in excess of 400km.[3]

Therefore, we ended up with a war in the northeast of Ukraine where the Russian forces would advance around the cities, not able to take them, and the Ukrainian forces would huddle inside the cities, holding on.

The Advance in the Northeast

The northeast part of Ukraine includes a number of medium-sized cities that are scattered about. From west to east, they include Chernihiv (population 285,234), Konotop (population 84,787), Sumy (population 259,660) and Okhtyrka (population 47,216). After that we wander into Kharkiv territory. Kharkiv is the second largest city in Ukraine and the largest primarily Russian-speaking city in Ukraine. This will be the subject of a separate chapter.

These urban areas are spread out and limited in number, leaving these cities as "islands" among the farmland and villages of this area. There is not any line of continuous urbanization, meaning each city stands alone. Furthermore, they make up a significant part of populations in these regions. For example, the Chernihiv Province has 1,511 settlements, yet Chernihiv city alone makes up almost a third (29%) of the population of the province. The second largest town is Nizhyn with only 66,983 people, the third largest town is Pryluky with only 52,553 people and no other towns in the province have more than 20,000 people.

Sumy Province is a little more populated and a little more densely populated, containing the cites of Sumy, and the towns of Konotop, Orktyrka, Romny (population 38,305) and Shostka (population 73,197) and a sizeable number of smaller towns and villages. Still, beyond the few larger towns in the direct path of the invasion, it is not very urban.

It appears that the forces used for this advance were not the best prepared Russian front-line forces. These were reserved for Kyiv and other axes. Most of these forces were armed with T-72s (now an over fifty-year-old tank design) and had a large number of conscripts. In some cases, it does not appear that they were told they were going to war. The units appeared to be poorly prepared. The infamous video of a Ukrainian driving by an out-of-fuel tank column and talking to them is from the Sumy area.[4]

The Advance on Chernihiv
Chernihiv came under threat on the first day of the war. It was close to the Russian border and on the route to Kyiv from the northeast. The Russian Army made no serious attempt to take it. Russian forces in the area included elements of the 11th Guards Air Assault Brigade and 74th Motorized Rifle Brigade. Russian soldiers from these units were reported surrendering on the first day of the war, which is surprising. In the case of the 74th Motorized Rifle Brigade, it was an entire reconnaissance platoon along with its commander, Konstantin Buynichev. Ukraine provided photographs of them. Either these units were truly poorly motivated or this was a very clever cover story to conceal the U.S. intelligence the Ukrainians were receiving. The former is more likely.

Also, the Russian 35th Guards Motorized Rifle Brigade was reported operating in the area, and according to one Ukrainian source it took heavy losses in early March. Intercepted communications reported by the Ukrainians indicated that at least 45 soldiers died and it may have been as many as 132. At least one death has been confirmed by name.

The primary regular army brigade in the area was the Ukrainian 1st Tank Brigade. It was supported by an assortment of reserve and territorial units. The 1st Tank Brigade consisted of three tank battalions armed with T-64BMs and a mechanized infantry battalion with BMPs. Each battalion was around 400 troops and 40–50 vehicles.[5] The brigade was supported by three artillery battalions with 2S1 and 2S3 self-propelled howitzers and BM-21 rocket-launchers. Their air defense troops were armed with Stela-10 and Tunguska missile-launchers and guns.[6]

The supporting units included air defense and artillery brigades, giving the Ukrainians considerable defensive firepower with howitzers, heavier rockets and longer-range air-defense systems. This created a tough defense force.

The 1st Tank Brigade was an experienced unit, having been reconstituted in September 2014 and having attacked the separatist forces in January 2015 at Donetsk airport, which cost them of up to two dozen tanks. The brigade remained in the Donbas region, engaged until April 2021. As the Russians did their first massing at the border back in April 2021, the 1st Tank Brigade moved back to its permanent garrison post including the Mizhrichynskyi nature preserve, just outside of Kyiv. Its movement right before and on 24 February 2022 is not known. It was moved from Mizhrichynskyi before the war so as disperse for its own safety in expectation of the opening shots of the Russian offensive.

The Russians did attempt to attack Chernihiv on the first day of the war, but quickly switched to seizing the surrounding territory instead. The details of these operations are not known, but the defense was certainly assisted by the 1st Tank Brigade concentrating its forces near Chernihiv from their dispersed positions.

The failure to take this city was a pattern that would be repeated throughout this offensive. They either assumed it would fall when they showed up or they had intended to bypass it from the start. Chernihiv was bypassed and Russia declared that it was surrounded the following day, except it was not. It was designated by the Ukrainian government a "Hero City" on 6 March. On 10 March, the mayor announced that the city had been completely encircled. This was rather slow progress for an invasion that was already fifteen days old against a city that was less than 50 miles (80km) from the border.

The 1st Tank Brigade was the primary regular army unit defending Chernihiv in its encirclement. Fighting continued around Chernihiv throughout this period, but it was mostly a loose siege operation with occasional artillery shelling. There is no indication that the 1st Tank Brigade took any significant armor losses.[7] During the course of siege, more than half of the city's population fled. Also, on 17 March, the American civilian James Whitney Hill was killed by a Russian artillery strike as he was standing in a food line. He was an American that had moved to Ukraine and was making his life there.

There was some real fighting in and around Chernihiv. According to estimates derived from Ukrainian statements, 300–350 soldiers were killed defending Chernihiv and the surrounding areas. Ukraine claimed on 2 March that 132 Russian soldiers had been killed and 50–100 captured. A Russian Su-34 was shot down over Chernihiv on 4 March 2022, as confirmed by photos. The area was also laced with mines, which the Ukrainians now have to clean up. The mayor of the city estimated that 350–400 civilians had been killed. Russian vehicle losses, as reported by photographic evidence, included fifteen vehicles to the immediate north of the city and three in the city.[8] Further north of the city were another thirty destroyed vehicles that appear to be mostly rear area groupings that were hit by artillery and drones.[9] Among the destroyed targets were five floating pontoon bridges. One wonders if Ukraine, with the help of U.S. intelligence, was deliberately targeting their bridging assets from the beginning of the campaign. There were seventy destroyed vehicles and towed guns just to the south of the city.[10]

The Ukrainian armor column that attacked Brovary on 9 March was from this force that bypassed Chernihiv. It appears to have been a single BTG. Not sure what the overall forces committed to this advance were, but based upon the extremely limited results of this advance, it was probably only three to six BTGs. They did surround Chernihiv, sent a column of 90th Guards Tank Division down to Brovary to get shot up and grabbed a whole lot of area in between, but the fighting was otherwise limited. At least two BTGs were shot up pretty badly.

That the column did not get to Brovary until the evening of 9 March is also an issue. Chernihiv is 46 miles (74km) from the Russian border as the crow flies. The Russians were able to get to the city in less than a day. Chernihiv is 73 miles (117km) from Brovary. Yet, it took another thirteen days for Russian units to get that far. Now, it may not have been the Russian plan to envelop Kyiv from the northeast and east, as they may have considered forces coming down from the north to be sufficient, but it would have been useful if they could have managed to deploy forces to the east of Kyiv before the end of February. There was limited value in sending forces down there on 9 March, as the attack to the north had already stalled out. This meant that Russia was now conducting a piecemeal attack against defenders with interior lines. The outcome is not surprising. It does appear that the Russian decision to move down from Chernihiv to Kyiv was driven by the failure of their previous attacks on Kyiv, and that it was not part of the original plan. If so, this was an improvisation of limited value.

On 31 March, the advancing Ukrainian forces opened the highway connecting Kyiv and Chernihiv and the mayor reported the first quiet night there since the war began. The Russian army withdrew from the area around 4 April, ending the fight.

The Advance on Konotop

Konotop is a weird story, because the Russians advanced on it on 24 February to attack it with a column of up to 300 vehicles (is this one BTG?). Konotop is also less than 50 miles from the Russian border and the Russian forces arrived outside the city on the first day before 1700. The Sumy state administration said that it was surrounded as of 0130 on 25 February. This suggests that there was no real defense along the border, but only at the major cities and towns inside the country.

The mayor of Konotop, a representative of the neo-fascist Svoboda Party, claimed that he was prepared with the militia to fight to the last man for control of the town. He then negotiated with Russians and it was agreed that the Russian forces could pass through (not that any of the accounts actually say this) as long as the residents did not attack them. Russia also agreed not to change the city's government, nor deploy troops in the city, nor obstruct transportation nor remove the Ukrainian flag. Instead, they bypassed it and even moved through it but did not occupy the town. It was reported for Konotop on 26 February that two soldiers and three civilians had been wounded.

The neo-fascist Svoboda Party (Svoboda means freedom) holds only 1 out of 450 seats (0.2%) in the Ukrainian parliament. It held 37 seats in the 2012 election but has been in decline since then. It holds 890 local positions out of 43,122 in regional elections (2.1%), the Mayor of Konotop being one of them.

The advance past Konotop went westward towards Kyiv, although these forces never got as far as the outskirts of Kyiv. In the end, four Russian losses were reported inside of Konotop and there were no losses around the city.[11]

On 3 April, Russian forces had withdrawn from Konotop Raion (county).

The Advance on Sumy

Sumy, the other major city in the northeast, was also not taken. It came close to being one of the early Russian prizes, coming under attack on the first day. The Russian ground forces in the area were commanded by 1st Guards Tank Army, including 2nd Guards Motorized Rifle Division, 4th Guards Tank Division, 26th Tank Regiment of 47th Guards Tank Division, and 27th Guards Motorized Rifle Brigade. A mix of Ukrainian Army forces (including 27th Artillery Brigade) and militia formed the defense. The Russians did enter the city, burning down a church there and getting in a fight near the Sumy State University in the evening (the battle began at 2230). During the night, the Russian forces withdrew from the city (at about 0139).

The Russians pushed into the city two days later, advancing half-way into the city center, according to a twitter post by Zelenskyy. They were then pushed back out by the end of the day, putting the whole city back in Ukrainian hands. It would remain that way. If this account is correct, then it does raise the question as to why a force could manage to penetrate halfway into the city and not manage to deploy troops and supporting forces into the city to hold on to it for a while. It appears that this may have been company size or at best an unsupported battalion-size force thrust into the city that did not have the size or confidence to hold onto their positions. Again, one gets the sense with the back-and-forth in places like Sumy and Kherson that the initial forward Russian forces were simply not that strong.

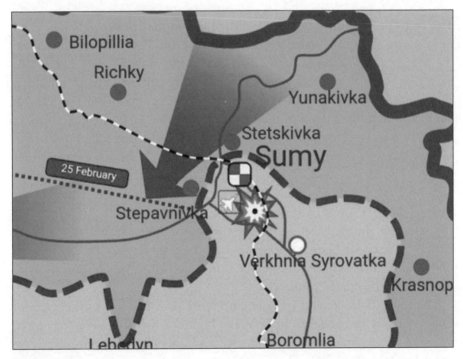

Sumy, *c.* 28 February.

The Russians then partly enveloped the city and held in place around three-fourths of it for the next month, with the city fed by a road from the south. Ukrainian casualties are claimed to be at least 81 soldiers killed, but this source is Wikipedia and does not appear to be properly backed by sources. In an airstrike on 8 March, 4 soldiers were killed along with 22 civilians. At least 25 civilians were killed and maybe over 100 civilians were lost during the month of fighting there. Russian casualties included 104 reported captured as of 11 March. The Ukrainians claimed a hundred Russian tanks destroyed. Most of these claims (96 tanks) come from a strike on Russian armor on 28 February by Bayraktar TB2 drones and GM-31 Grad launchers. As a BTG usually only has around 10 tanks, one wonders what formation or operation was being done that gathered that many tanks together. We doubt these counts of tank losses.

The photographic evidence shows 41 destroyed Russian vehicles in the area around Sumy, including 12 IFVs and 16 tanks.[12] While this is not a complete or entirely reliable count of Russian losses, if a hundred tanks were destroyed there would have been photographic evidence. There is not.

Sumy was relieved/abandoned on 4 April. On this day the governor of Sumy Oblast reported that Russian troops no longer occupied any towns or villages in the province and on 8 April the governor said that the Russians had left Sumy Province.

Two large outlying towns, Okhtyrka just to the south of Sumy and Shostka far to its north, also came under attack on the first day. The Russians threatened the outskirts of Okhtyrka on the first day in the morning and then pulled back that night or the following day. They then did not attempt to take it again but did occasionally shell and direct missiles at the town. Two Danish journalists were fired upon in their car and wounded on 26 February. On 28 February, a military base was hit by an artillery strike that killed more than seventy Ukrainian soldiers. It is this strike that led to claims that a thermobaric (vacuum) bomb was used. This has not been confirmed. The claim that it was a thermobaric bomb was made by the Ukrainian ambassador to the United States. I do not know if there is any other confirming evidence.[13] International law does not prohibit the use of thermobaric munitions, fuel-air explosive devices or vacuum bombs against military targets. During the fighting at Okhtyrka in February, at least ten civilians were killed in addition to more than seventy Ukrainian soldiers.

The town of Trostianets (population 19,797 in 2021), just to the north of Okhtyrka, was also attacked in February. Lightly armed Ukrainian territorial forces of around hundred delayed the Russian forces by felling trees to create obstacles along the roads and then the mayor and some of the men went into

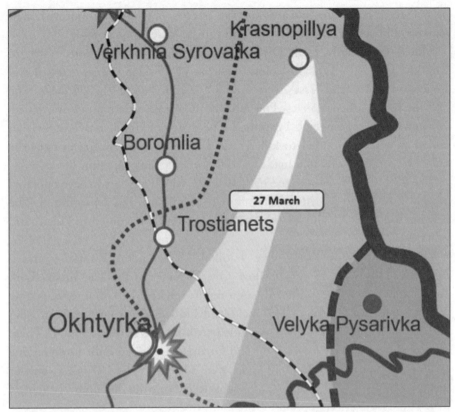

Okhtyrka, after 27 March.

the countryside to maintain a guerilla force. The Russians occupied the town on 1 March.[14]

The Russian 1st Guards Tank Army was deployed across a wide area of the front from around Sumy to north of Kharkiv. They seemed to achieve rather limited results considering this was largest army and the premier army in Russia. The 2nd Guards Motorized Rifle Division was involved in the movements past Sumy and Konotop, before being stopped east of Pryluky, 75 miles (121km) east of Kyiv.[15] Its losses as of 15 March were reported to be 16 killed, 43 wounded, 2 missing and 54 captured for a total of 115 casualties. Its tank losses were considerably higher, with 45 T72B3Ms lost. It lost 85 other vehicles. This division ended up with a wounded-to-killed ratio of 2.69-to-1.

The 4th Guards Tank Division was involved in the attack on Okhtyrka and operations north of Kharkiv. Its losses as of 15 March were reported to be 25 killed, 92 wounded, 18 missing, 21 captured for a total of 156 casualties. The tanks losses between its 2 tank regiments were 62 T-80Us and T-80UEs. It lost 58 other vehicles. This division ended up with a wounded-to-killed ratio of 3.68-to-1. It was stopped at Okhtyrka, but this obviously was not with high personnel losses, although the tank and vehicle losses were notable.

The 47th Guards Tank Division was involved in operations north of Kharkiv. The 26th Tank Regiment losses as of 15 March were 4 killed and 13 wounded. Its tank losses were only 8 T-72B3Ms and T-72 B3M2s. The division lost 9 other vehicles. The 7th Reconnaissance Battalion lost 5 killed, 13 wounded, 2 missing and 1 captured. These are not high losses. The division ended up with a wounded-to-killed ratio of 2.88-to-1. These appear to be the only two combat units that made up 47th Guards Tank Division.

The 27th Guards Motorized Rifle Brigade, which appears to have operated around Sumy, had 7 killed, 28 wounded, 14 missing and 14 captured. The brigade lost 9 T-90s and 21 other vehicles. It had a wounded to killed ratio of 4.00-to-1.

Other army troop losses were 4 killed, 18 wounded, 8 missing and 6 captured along with 15 vehicles lost. Overall losses of the 1st Guards Tank Army, drawn from a captured Russian report released by Ukraine, were only 408 in 3 weeks of fighting.[16] This included 61 killed, 207 wounded, 44 missing and 96 surrendered. This is a wounded-to-killed ratio of 3.39-to-1. There were also two sanitary losses from 2nd Guards Motorized Rifle Division due to illness. Their total equipment losses were 115 tanks and 197 other vehicles lost for a total of 312.[17] This is 0.86 people killed or wounded for every vehicle lost. There is no strong reason to the doubt this report.

One cannot help but make a few observations about this report. First, personnel losses are lower than one would expect, considering their actions, the Ukrainian claims and their heavy armor losses. It would appear that they did not make much active use of their infantry in combat. Second, the armor losses are significant. Of the 115 tanks lost, it is not known how many were broken down, abandoned or captured. In the Oryx count of tanks lost, around one-third were abandoned or captured. Probably some of these were broken down. One does note that there is less than one person killed or wounded per vehicle lost. Third, the number of people missing and captured is high for the overall casualties. They make up 34% of their casualties. These are not the figures that one would expect to see from a force on the offense. At the Battle of Kursk in 1943, units with that high of losses of missing and captured tended to be defenders who were dislodged and partly overrun. These high missing and captured figures from 1st Guards Tank Army indicates poor morale and mishandling of the units. One wonders if the fearsome 1st Guards Tank Army was still somewhat lacking in capability. It was probably made up of a mix of contract soldiers and conscripts, with perhaps the third battalion in each regiment or brigade being conscripts. As such, most of them would not have been sent into Ukraine because of Russian policies. In the end, the 1st Guards Tank Army ended up taking no significant cities, not even Sumy, only 25 miles (40km) from the border, and never got within 100km of Kyiv.

Their opposition appeared to include the Ukrainian 58th Motorized Brigade in addition to National Guard forces and perhaps other Ukrainian regular forces.[18]

On 26 March, Russian forces withdrew from the area. Ukrainian forces in the area of Trostienets had started a counteroffensive on 23 March and led by 93rd Mechanized Brigade reclaimed the town on 26 March. The Russian troops had largely withdrawn the night before the arrival of Ukrainian forces. The advance lead to a reputed fight between 93rd Mechanized Brigade and elements of the 4th Guards Tank Division, where the Ukrainians claimed a major victory.[19] Independent confirmation of this action has not been obtained but it appears to have been grossly overstated.[20]

According to the mayor of the town, who remained in the area during its occupation, over 50 civilians were killed during the occupation of Trostienets.[21] Another seven were killed after the Russians had withdrawn due to mines and other ordnance.[22]

In the case of Shostka, only 30 miles (49km) from Russian border, it was actually besieged for the first couple of days of the war before being occupied by Russian troops. They withdrew in early April. The town of Romny, the home of Ukrainian nationalist poet and writer Taras Shevchenko (1814-1861), was never occupied.

The Value of the Counterattack

What stands out in these accounts is the presence of multiple counterattacks on the part of Ukrainian armed forces. This includes the counterattack at Hostomel on first day of the invasion, the counterattack on the second day of the invasion in Kherson, which briefly reclaimed the city, and the counterattack at Sumy on the third day of the invasion. This points to an army that was confident, competent and willing to fight. While these counterattacks did not save Kherson, they may have saved Sumy and certainly messed up Russian operations north of Kyiv. There is an untold story of how and why these counterattacks were organized and who ordered them.

Losses to Date

On 2 March, the Russian Ministry of Defense stated that 498 troops had been killed and 1,597 sustained wounds since 24 February 2022. They also claimed that 2,870 Ukrainian troops had been killed and 3,700 had been injured. They reported 572 had been captured. The Ukrainian State Emergency Service claimed that more than 2,000 soldiers and civilians had died. The UN human rights office around the same time had recorded the deaths of 136 civilians.[23] Most likely Russian losses were higher than that. The Donetsk People's Republic reported from 19 February–4 March that they had 86 killed and 451 wounded for a wounded-to-killed ratio of 5.24-to-1 (see Appendix I). Ukrainian losses are not known, but there is no reason to doubt the Russian claims of Ukrainians captured.

Chapter 10

The Fight at Brovary, 9–12 March 2022

While Melitopol and Kherson had been taken and Kyiv was being threatened from the northwest, a new threat was emerging from the direction of Chernihiv. Having isolated Chernihiv, the Russians bypassed the Ukrainian defense and moved a column down towards Brovary.

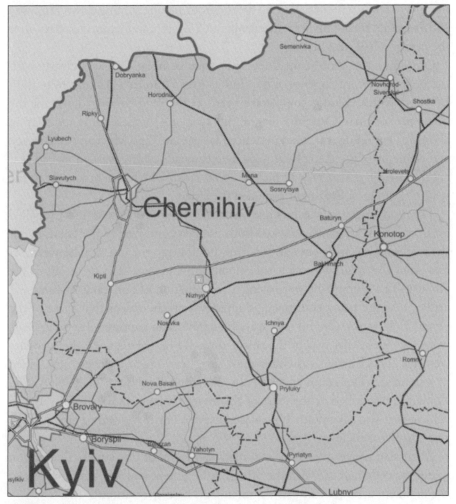

The Kyiv, Chernihiv and Brovary area.

It consisted of at least the 6th Tank Regiment and 239th Tank Regiment of the 90th Guards Tank Division. Nominally, this was at least four BTGs.

But this effort did seem somewhat quixotic. To the west of the Dnipro River were a dozen or more Russian battalions and BTGs, stalled and holding to the northwest of Kyiv. Now coming down on the east were two or maybe four BTGs in a column driving into the suburban village of Brovary. Brovary was a separate village 4 miles (7km) outside of Kyiv on the main highway from Chernihiv to Kyiv. While it was near the eastern outskirts of Kyiv, the Dnipro River was between it and downtown Kyiv. Brovary was a sprawling suburban town with a population of 109,473 (2021 estimate) that stretched for several kilometers.

The ambush site was on the far side of the town around 10 miles (17km) from Kyiv. It was a natural place to defend from anyone coming down Highway M01 towards Kyiv. This was the evening of 9 March, some fourteen days after the invasion had started.

Obviously, the Ukrainians knew they were coming. This was clearly with the help of U.S. intelligence. Chernihiv is over 70 miles (114km) away from Brovary, so this column could have been on the road coming down for the better part of a day. Certainly, lots of time to spot it, prepare for it and a lay an ambush. Defending was the experienced Ukrainian 72nd Mechanized Brigade and elements of the Azov Regiment. The Russian column was ambushed as it entered Brovary. This was all picked up on video which was broadcast to the world.[1] The Azov Regiment provided the video.

The lead tanks in the column were the older T-72s and self-propelled artillery. The Ukrainians attacked both the head and rear of the column, but the road area was wide enough that this did not trap the forces in between. At this point the column knew it was in ambush and started to drive out of the ambush. The Ukrainians were using a combination of anti-tank missiles and artillery. As the firing continued, it appears from the videos that three of the eleven T-72 tanks were hit and at least one was later captured. It also appears from the videos that two of the thirty-three BTRs, APCs and other vehicles were hit. The Russian casualties may have been up to a dozen men killed or wounded.[2] The commander of the 6th Tank Regiment, Colonel Andrei Zakharov, was killed at the start of the attack. It appears he was in the lead vehicle that was taken out. This was a disaster, but it was only a single BTG that lost five vehicles.

A Russian conversation was recorded at the end of this attack. The person under the code name is with the 6th Tank Regiment and was left in charge of the regiment after they lost its commander. The conversation:[3]

Udar: Nitro, I am Udar. I am listening.

Nitro: I am Nitro. I almost lost 6th regiment.

Udar: What?

Nitro: 6th regiment. I can report fully for the moment. I am still gathering [people], lots and lots of losses. They are waiting. The head of the convoy ran into an ambush. The commander of the regiment died. I am trying to get the picture with the regard to the rest.

Udar: Now when you get the picture, when you gather everyone, report to me. Do you read me?

Nitro: They were hitting with artillery, tanks, UAV is flying as I understand Bayraktar. I am trying to clarify the picture with the rest of the losses.

This was a predictable disaster. They kind of had to know, driving down from Chernihiv, they would be spotted and tracked. They kind of knew that any piece of wooded or urban terrain was a potential ambush spot. So the question is, where were their forward recon elements? Why were they not reconnoitering these positions before advancing the entire force in there. This seems negligent, and appears to go back to the idea, that had apparently been drilled in their heads, that the Ukrainians were not going to put up any resistance, even though they already had at Chernihiv, where this unit came from, and of course, had also resisted at Kyiv.

This did not take a lot of resistance. It appears in the company sized engagement that no Ukrainian vehicles or personnel were lost, whereas the Russians lost five vehicles and a dozen people, It was a clear demonstration of the nature of Russian hubris, their failure to operate according to simple military practices, the value of Ukraine's superior intelligence and, of course, the capabilities of the Ukrainian Army.

Also of interest is that the Ukrainians had drones, while the Russians really did not. Furthermore, the Russians clearly were already familiar with the name Bayraktar, a Turkish-built drone that the Ukrainian were now using. At the start of the war, it is estimated that the Ukrainians had a dozen of these new Turkish drones.

As the fighting ended that day, some of the Russian soldiers fled on foot into the nearby woods and village. Furthermore, over the next few days, heavy fighting erupted in the villages east of the ambush site. The fighting there continued for several days, with some civilian casualties. On 12 March, the Russians claimed to have disabled the Ukrainian main radio intelligence center at Brovary with a high-precision strike.[4] This was the last major action we were aware of around Kyiv, although they continued operations in the area for several more weeks. On 29 March the Russians shelled Brovary again.

Subsequent operations were hard to explain. The Russians came down with at least two tank regiments or at least four BTGs. One BTG was clearly shot up on 9 March. But then on subsequent days, their operations to did appear to move any further forward. Brovary was never threatened with seizure and they never got closer to Kyiv. They did take villages to the east of Kyiv and eventually connected back to the columns marching west from Konotop, but the ultimate objective of the campaign, Kyiv, was not really further threatened.

Nominally, the Russians had enveloped Kyiv on three sides. They had expanded enough to the west of the city that the roads going into the city from there were no longer secure. They nominally held outside of Brovary to the east of the city. So theoretically they had encircled three-fourths of it. That said, there were still major political figures regularly going in and out of the city, including the prime ministers of Czech Republic, Poland and Slovenia on 15 March. This made a clear statement that the city was going to be held.

The Russians lacked the force to attack Kyiv and lacked the force to complete the encirclement. As they were certainly still far away from encircling it, it is doubtful they could have held it closed even if they did. According to the Pentagon, Russia committed around one-third of its forces to taking the capital. This consisted of about twenty BTGs to the north and northwest of Kyiv and another twenty BTGs near Chernihiv. It seems that a lot of forces near Chernihiv were still up there, rather than moving down on Kyiv.

Chapter 11

The Air War, 24 February–31 March 2022

The air war opened on 24 February at 0500 with strikes against Kyiv by cruise missiles. The sun would not rise in Kyiv until 0652. This signaled a full-scale invasion of the country, supported by the overwhelming air power from an air force with least 1,400 aircraft, although maybe only 500 were deployed to operate against Ukraine.[1] Ukraine's 69 fighters were overwhelmed in comparison. Russian was expected to have air supremacy to start with and to use the air supremacy to dominate the battlefield.

This is not what really happened, and the failure to do so in light of the extensive resources of the Russian air force is one of more challenging aspects of this war to understand. With 1,400 aircraft, or even 500, one would have expected them to affect a "shock and awe" campaign such as those the United States inflicted on Iraq in 1991, Afghanistan in 2001 and Iraq in 2003. But, it appears that this approach to the dominating use of air power by the Russian Air Force was not part of their doctrine, and therefore not part of their plan.[2] They planned on using air power from the start of the invasion, but it ended up not having the sustained targeted success of an American air campaign. The air campaign was not sufficiently shocking to demoralize the Ukrainians, and their air campaign has therefore not been held in much awe.

On the first day the Russian air force took losses, including helicopters near Kyiv, at least one Su-25 and two Ka-52s and one Mi-8 helicopters. The second day their count of losses may have included an Il-76 transport plane heading to Hostomel airport.[3] These helicopters were taken down by relatively low-tech MANPADSs and anti-tank missiles, and a Soviet-era surface-to-air missile allegedly took out the Il-76. Ukrainian air losses were relatively low in the first two days. The Ukrainian Air Force was scattered before the war began and mostly located in the western half of the country. As such, they were able to maintain their fighter strength, although they made only limited and careful forays with them.

Ukraine lost at least nine aircraft on the first day (24 February). This included four MiG-29s lost in combat, along with an Su-24 and an Su-27 lost on the ground. Nine civilian aircraft were also recorded as heavily damaged or destroyed at Hostomel airfield this first day. The following day only one

Ukrainian aircraft was destroyed, an Su-27 shot down over Kyiv by a Russian S-400 surface-to-air missile. Its pilot died and the plane crashed into a residential complex.

In contrast the Russians lost an Su-25 on the first day, along with three helicopters shot down over the Kyiv reservoir by Ukrainian MANPADSs and anti-tank missiles. They also lost an An-26 on the first or second day of the war (as did the Ukrainians on the first day of the war).[4]

Ukrainian plane losses were still high in the subsequent three days with three Su-25s shot down on the 26th, with two of the pilots being killed near Kherson, ten aircraft lost on 27 February and an Su-27 and Mi-8 helicopter lost on the 28th. Among the ten aircraft lost on the 27th were six MiG-29s caught on the ground as were two Su-24s. Lost in the air was another Su-24 and an Su-25. This is loss of twenty-one modern combat aircraft by Ukraine in the first five days of the war. While this was a favorable exchange by the Russian Air Force, it was not sweeping the Ukrainians from the skies.

As early as 28 February it was becoming obvious that Russia had not swept the skies and established complete air supremacy.[5] They had air superiority, but the Ukraine air force was still active. It appeared from video evidence that several of the Ukrainian MiG-29s survived the first couple of days and were still operating. The Russian's initial strikes did not completely take out the Ukrainian Air Force of ninety-eight modern combat airplanes. It appears to have taken out less than two dozen. The rest appeared to be operational, although careful in presenting themselves.

It is reported that in the final days of February and the first week of March, the Russian Air Force were conducting around 140 low-altitude sorties a day.[6] This figure does not include other sorties. These low-altitude flights did make them vulnerable to MANPADSs, although it protected them from other SAM systems. On 11 March, it was reported by the U.S. Department of Defense that Russia was flying an average of 200 sorties a day compared to 10 by Ukraine.[7] They also reported at this time that Ukraine still had 56 fully operational fighter jets.

This was also when we saw the first use by Ukrainians of the very capable Turkish-manufactured Bayraktar TB-2 Unmanned Air Vehicles (UAV). At the start of war, the Ukrainian Army had six to twelve of them in operation, while the Ukrainian Navy had an additional one to five. There had already been videos of successful strikes by two of them. By 2 March, another six to twelve Bayraktar TB-2 UAVs had shipped to Ukraine from either Turkey or Azerbaijan and Ukraine was setting up a contract to build forty-eight more of these drones in Ukraine. As the war developed, Turkey would continue sending Bayraktar drones to Ukraine, some purchased for them by fundraising efforts conducted by countries that were formerly part of the Soviet Union.

Meanwhile, the Ukrainian Air Force was being replenished. They were getting 29 MiG-29s from Bulgaria, 14 Su-25s from Bulgaria, 28 MiG-29s from Poland and 12 MiG-29s from Slovakia. All these former Warsaw Pact countries were now members of NATO. By 2 March, Ukrainian pilots were in Poland to pick up their MiG-29s, but as of 5 March had still not received any additional aircraft. However, it appears that Ukraine still had most of their original aircraft, though, which is surprising.

Another significant anti-air weapon in Ukrainian hands was their MANPADS, including the Stinger (FIM-92). The U.S.-made Stinger is a great air denial weapon and videos had already shown a couple of Russian planes and helicopters brought down by them. Before the war Ukraine had been supplied with some Stingers by Latvia and Lithuania, two former states of the Soviet Union that were now members of NATO. Poland provided them with the Piorun MANPADS and Ukraine already had hundreds of various Soviet-era Ilga-1, Igla-2, Stela-2 and Strela-3 missiles. Starting in March, an additional 2,700 of former East German Strela-2 (maybe 2,000 operational) were donated to Ukraine by Germany. By 28 February, Germany had announced that it was providing Ukraine with 500 Stingers. The United States was also sending Ukraine more Stingers, with 200 arriving on 1 March. This gave Ukraine an array of thousands of MANPADSs. This quickly provided considerable protection against any low-altitude penetration of Ukrainian air space. Russian attempts to penetrate this airspace at low altitudes ceased by April 2022.[8]

Ukraine also had an entire array of other anti-aircraft systems, including 4 batteries of S-300V1 (SA-12 Gladiator), 6 TOR (SA-15 Guantlet), 72 9K27 BUK (SA-17 Grizzly), 125 9K33 Osa (SA-9 Grecko), more than 150 9K35 Stela 10 (SA-15 Gopher), some 9K41 Stela-01 (SA-9 Gaskin), maybe 10 2K22 Tuguska (SA-190 Grison), up to 300 ZSU-23-4 "Shilka" anti-aircraft guns, and AZP S-60 and ZU-23-2 air-aircraft guns. This totals at least 687 anti-aircraft systems, although at this point, a number of them were already out of action.

Still, these hundreds of anti-aircraft systems and thousands of MANPADSs guaranteed that air space would be contested at least some of the time at some of the locations. Over time, as hundreds more Stingers and other MANPADSs were to arrive, the air space would become contested more frequently.

Five days into the war, it was becoming obvious the Russia would never achieve air supremacy, although it would maintain air superiority.[9] What this meant was that there were limits to when and where Russian airpower could be used. This would greatly complicate operations for the Russian Army.

The subsequent air losses in the month of March can be mostly tracked through reports from photos, videos and so on. As such, most aircraft that were shot down are recorded. These efforts show the following:[10]

	February	March	Total
Ukraine			
Combat Aircraft Lost[11]	21	15	36
Utility Aircraft Lost	2	1	3
Civilian Aircraft Lost	(9)	–	(9)
Unidentified Aircraft Lost	1	1	2
Helicopters Lost	1	12	13
Total	25 (34)	29	54 (63)
Russia			
Combat Aircraft Lost	3	17	20
Utility Aircraft Lost	1	–	1
Unidentified Aircraft Lost	–	1	1
Helicopters Lost	4	12	16
Total	8	30	38

Note that this listing does not include drone losses.

Chapter 12

The Advance on Kharkiv,
24 February–31 March 2022

Kharkiv (population 1,433,886) in my mind is extremely important to this entire war. Not only is it the second largest city in Ukraine, but it is the largest Russian-speaking majority city in Ukraine.

Its unwillingness to join with Luhansk and Donetsk in revolting against the new Ukrainian government in 2014 was significant then. A sniper did try to assassinate the mayor of Kharkiv in April 2014, shooting him in the back and partly crippling him for life. He was a supporter of the Russian-favoring over-thrown Ukrainian President Yanukovych. Yet, he opposed the Russian separatists in Kharkiv. He died of Coronavirus in 2021 while still mayor.

Kharkiv, dated 27 February.

The city's willingness to defend itself now is also significant. It is right next to Russia, just south of Belgorod and the area of the Battle of Kursk. It was fought over four times during the Second World War, once in 1941 and three times in 1943. It was the largest Russian city fought over in the Second World War and the fighting there was used for our urban warfare studies.[1] It is a big sprawling city, 24.3km from north to south and 25.2km from west to east.

The Attack on Kharkiv

Being only 19 miles (31km) south of the border, Kharkiv came under attack early in the campaign from forces advancing from Belgorod. They encountered resistance on the first day, slowing down their advance. They did shell the city the first day, 24 February 2022. It does appear that two columns tried to advance into the city from the north and northwest. The column to the north included two BM-21 rocket launchers and three trucks that were lost near the School of Physics and Technology. The column to the northwest consisted of at least a tank and three MT-LBs IFVs. Both of these were halted with the loss of nine vehicles, including the tank and three IFVs.[2] The 1st Guards Tank Army was operating to the north of Kharkiv, with the 4th Guards Tank Division in the immediate vicinity of the city. On the first day, Ukraine reported picking up two Russian prisoners from the 4th Guards Tank Division.[3] There were also losses reported near the city that included at least one soldier killed, a tank and a truck destroyed, as shown by videos.[4]

On the second day of the war, the Russian advance had reached the northern suburbs of the city, the village of Tsyrkuny. There the Ukrainian Army put up a fight.[5] It was not the best weather for operations.

Heavy fighting continued outside the city the following day with Russian forces entering the city on the morning of the 27th. By the end of the day they were thrown back.[6] Russian recorded armor and vehicle losses were light. In and around the city proper there were only twelve vehicles recorded as destroyed.[7] Clearly two columns of vehicles were shot up on 24 February as they tried to enter the city from the north and the northwest. There were considerable vehicles photographed outside the city, but most of these were posted after April, and as the Russians continued operating in this area, it is more difficult to determine when they were lost.[8] It appears to include at least 25 more vehicles (including 6 tanks and 4 IFVs) lost in the fighting in February and another 11 vehicles (4 tanks, 3 IFVs and 1 helicopter) lost in the fighting in March.

It is not sure what the strength was of the attacking Russian forces, but they did not seem significant. Not sure of the strength of the defenders either. It does seem like, as in the case of number of the other Russian advances, that they led into these suburban and urban areas with mobile forces with limited infantry support. The results were as expected.

On 27 February, the Russian forces were clearly repelled from Kharkiv. The city came under heavy artillery fire on the 28th. It is during these bombardments against the Kharkiv Tractor Plant, Moskovskyi District and Shevchenkivskyi District that cluster munitions were used (no need to use the word "alleged," they clearly leave behind identifiable fragments).

This more or less became the norm for the subsequent month, with Russian forces operating just outside of the city, regularly bringing it under artillery fire. The governor of Kharkiv said that between 24 February and 14 April, at least 503 civilians were killed in the Kharkiv region. Between 24 February to 28 April, 606 civilians were reported killed in the Kharkiv region, according to the National Police. One Algerian student was reported killed by a sniper on 28 February, but I gather most civilians were killed due to artillery, missile and air strikes.

This was a strange operation, so it appears that the Russians never arrived with significant forces to take the city and did not have the forces to surround the city. Part of the reason may have been that Kharkiv was better defended than Chernihiv, Sumy, Kherson, Melitopol, etc. The Russians forces took over three days before they could advance into the city, and they never really seriously attempted to surround it. It is a case where the defenders not only held the city, but they also held the countryside on both sides.

Military casualties are only hinted at with a report on 7 March that 209 people had been killed, including 133 civilians, and 443 people has been wounded, including 319 civilians. This implies Ukrainian military deaths of 76 killed and 124 wounded, a 1.63-to-1 wounded-to-killed ratio. Russian losses are not known, although there is no reason to believe they were higher than Ukrainian losses. Unlike other operations and areas, there are no claims of BTGs getting destroyed, no reports of heavy fighting after 27 February or anything similar. For a city this important, not that much happened.

The 1st Guards Tank Army's Push into Nowhere

The legendary 1st Guards Tank Army was the only tank army involved in the Russian offensive. It had two full divisions, parts of another division and an independent brigade.

The tank army pushed unsuccessfully towards Sumy, not even completely surrounding it, and pushed around the north of Kharkov, also not taking it. Elements then pushed further to the west, in an offensive notable for its insignificance. There were no real political or military objectives here. It was mostly open farmland dotted by villages and towns. The objective of this advance is not known. They did not get as far as Kyiv or any of the other cities on the Dnipro River. What it left was a record of lines of destroyed vehicles scattered across the steppe. The photographs of these destroyed vehicles allow us to observe their routes and "progress."

The 2nd Guards Motorized Rifle Division was involved in some of the fighting around Sumy but its 1st Tank Regiment appeared to have moved on, pushing halfway across the route between Sumy and Kyiv by 27 February. They were stopped east of Pryluky, 75 miles (121km) east of Kyiv.[9] This was with some losses, leaving behind five destroyed tanks on the road towards Pryluky. Pryluky was defended by Territorial Defense Forces only, but they were sufficient in this case.[10] Pryluky (population 52,553 in 2021) has not been taken in the war.

The 4th Guards Tank Division was clearly heavily involved in the fighting around Sumy and Okhtyrka. It did not appear to send any forces further east, putting all of their sixty-two tanks lost by 15 March in the Sumy-Kharkiv area, even though the photographic record does not show this.

Finally, the 26th Tank Regiment of the 47th Guards Tank Division appeared to be involved in the fighting around Kharkiv but nothing further. The independent 27th Guards Motorized Rifle Brigade initially operated around Sumy and ended up losing 63 personnel and 30 vehicles (including 9 T-90s) by 15 March 2022.[11]

Were the Russians Trying to Take Too Much with Too Little?

This does go to the question of the use and disposition of the initial Russian operational forces. They sent significant forces to Kyiv, a force of four to six BTGs to Chernihiv and eventually to Kyiv, forces to surround Sumy and forces to march through Konotop towards Kyiv. This pretty much grabbed most of northeastern Ukraine. Yet, they did not send significant forces to take, threaten or surround Kharkiv. Kharkiv, for all practical purposes, anchored the entire northern flank of the Ukrainian Army holding the areas of Luhansk and Donetsk provinces. A significant Russian armed force driving between Kharkiv and Okyturka, a front over 60 miles wide (100km), could have potentially enveloped the city from the north. Instead, 20,000–30,000 forces were encamped outside of Kyiv and other forces that may have numbered more than 10,000 were taking the rest of northeastern Ukraine. Meanwhile, Kharkiv was holding out, and anchoring the entire line from the north. One can see the Russian line running northwest from Kharkiv to Bohodukhiv (population 14,882), which was never taken, to Okhtyrka. This was mostly open country. A concentrated force of 30,000 pushing in that area would have been hard to stop and probably could have surrounded Kharkiv. That would have started a process that could have put Izyum, then Slovyansk, Kramatorsk, Sievierodonetsk and Lysychansk in danger. Instead, tens of thousands of Russian troops were stalled out in the marsh lands to the north of Kyiv while thousands more were grabbing open ground in the rest of northeastern Ukraine, while Kharkiv held firm.

It does appear that the original Russian plan was to march in columns of troops from everywhere to everywhere, strongly indicating that they really did not expect any real resistance. If that was true, then their planned operations make sense. As that was not the case, then their plan appears to make no sense. A discussion of the Russian thinking behind this is difficult to address without more research, including interviews of the participants and decision-makers. It may be a while before that research can occur.

The 20th Combined Arms Army's Future Operations

The 20th Combined Arms Army, starting around 2 April, appeared to be pushing to the south of Kharkiv towards the southwest. This could have been part of a coordinated plan to continue pushing to the southwest, unhinging the defense of the Ukrainian forces holding in the Donbas. An extended drive to the southwest, through and past Izyum and towards the Dnipro and with the 58th Combined Arms Army down around Zaporizhzhia, could have forced the entire collection of Ukrainian forces holding in the Donbas opposite the LPR and DPR forces to have to withdraw, effectively ceding all of eastern Ukraine to the Russians.

As it was, they refocused on this operation only around Day 38 (2 April).[12] Izyum had only been taken by 1 April (see Chapter 18). This makes this a discussion for a future book, not this one. On the other hand, it would require a significant effort and it does not appear that the 20th Combined Arms Army was currently up to the task, having only two motorized rifle divisions. Furthermore, it is a long drive, potentially over a hundred miles (161km). Drives like that tend to require forces to hold at least one flank while the head of the drive moves forward. It is difficult to believe that the 20th Combined Arms Army had the forces to effectively do this.

If they were serious about this, then perhaps the 1st Guards Tank Army should have also been committed to this area, instead of rather pointlessly pushing to the west from Kharkiv and Sumy. Furthermore, part of the distance could have been covered by 58th Combined Arms Army pushing north and northeast from Melitopol. Yet, it never got as far as Zaporizhzhia.

This is the subject for a future book, but it is clear that the threat was being developed at this time and may have been part of the Russian planning related to withdrawal from other parts of the battlefield.

Chapter 13

The Advance in the Donbas,
24 February–31 March 2022

O f course, this war was supposed to be about the Donbas, but this seemed to be a very secondary area of operation during the early days of the war. Part of the reason for this may have been that this was where experienced, regular Ukrainian Army units were located. Any fighting there was going to hit real resistance, so instead the Russians attacked anywhere but here.

The LPR and DPR both had their own independent stand-alone armies. The LPR had an estimated 14,000 troops and the DPR 20,000 troops.[1]

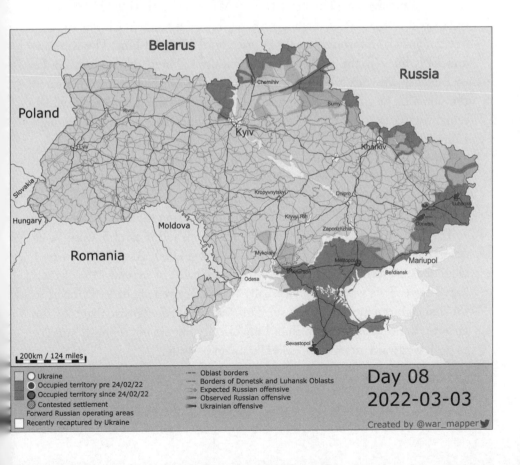

Early in the war the LPR Army was active, advancing to the areas to the north of Luhansk and clearing away the Ukrainians from the Russian border. This allowed them to expand the territory held by the LPR. Clearly, this area was also not very seriously defended by the Ukrainian Army. In the first couple of weeks of the war this allowed the front line to be extended from Luhansk to Novoaidar (taken 27 February), to Starobilsk (assaulted on 24 February, captured on 26 February) and to Svatove (taken 6 March). Meanwhile, Russian forces invaded Luhansk province, taking Baranykivka on 25 February and advanced through Bilovodsk, Vesele, and Starobilsk to Mistky and Svatove. Towns such as Troitske, Bilolusk, Kamianka, Markivka and Novopskov were also taken by the Russians, while the towns of Luhanska, Shchastia (attacked and occupied on 24 February), Petropavlivka and Shyrokyi were taken by LPR forces. The town of Tavilzhanka, in Kharkiv Province on the border with Luhansk and Russia and to the northeast of Ukrainian-held Kupyansk, was taken on 1 March.

This was to north and northwest of Luhansk. The push due west of Luhansk was very limited, taking Pervomalsk on 14 March and little else. The line in the west stood to the east of the line running from Bakhmut to Lysychansk and Severodonetsk and would remain in place until May and June. The Russians and LPR lines by the end of March basically followed the western border of Luhansk Province in the north from the Russian border until it neared the complex of cities of Rubizhne, Severodonetsk and Lysychansk, which remained securely in Ukrainian hands. The line then continued through Luhansk Province past Bakhmut, which was held by Ukraine.

On 6 March, in Starobilsk (population 16,267) there occurred one of the first signs of public protest over Russian occupation. A crowd of inhabitants pulled down the flag of the LPR, burned it and sang the Ukrainian national anthem. The crowd was dispersed by LPR forces firing shots in the air.

The LPR reported some 500–600 of its troops killed as of 5 April in its operations. This is from a force estimated at 14,000. Assuming a 4-to-1 wounded-to-killed ratio, this means that they had lost around 21% of their initial force. This was the only casualty report received about LPR forces in the first eighteen months of the war. This was a limited offensive that took the areas to the north and northwest of Luhansk city, but did not seriously attempt to push westward into solidly held Ukrainian positions.

The DPR's larger army was mostly initially involved in operations against Mariupol. Mariupol was the second largest city in the Donetsk Province and had been under Ukrainian control since the second half of 2014. Furthermore,

T-55A on the streets of Poland during martial law. (*J. Zolnierkiewicz, @ 1981*)

Russian T-62 at the Russian Museum of Military History, Moscow. (*www.kskdivniy.ru/museum/, 20 October 2015*)

Soviet T-64 in Perleberg, East Germany, 1980s. (*Ashot Pgogsyants, ГСВГ, Перлеберг, 1980–1982, 34 ОРБ, 21 МСД*)

Ukrainian T-64BV model 2017, Rehearsal for 2018 Independence Day parade in Kyiv. (*VoildWanderer, 20 August 2018*)

Ukrainian T-64BM2 Bulat, Rehearsal for 2021 Independence Day parade in Kyiv. (*VoidWanderer, 22 August 2021*)

Captured Ukrainian T-64BV used by Lugansk People's Republic, 2022. (*Ministry of Defense of the Russian Federation, Mil.ru, 16 March 2022*)

Ukrainian T-72 during training, 2018. (*Ministry of Defense of Ukraine, 1 February 2018*)

Russian T-72B mod. 1989 on bridge at Kalynivka, Mykolaiv Oblast, Ukraine on 2 March, 2022. (*Ministry of Internal Affairs of Ukraine, 5 March 2022*)

Russian T-80BVM, parade in Murmansk, 2018. (*Ministry of Defense of the Russian Federation, Andrey Luzik, www.mil.ru, 8 May 2018*)

Boris Yeltsin reading a speech on a tank, August 1991. (*Source:* New York Times)

Russian T-80UD tanks firing at Russian Parliament building, October 1993.

Russian T-80BVM during the invasion of Ukraine. (*Ministry of Defense of the Russian Federation Mil.ru, 7 March 2022*)

Captured Russian T-80s used by Ukraine's 93rd Mechanized Brigade, 2022. (*93rd Mechanized Brigade, on or before 9 May 2022*)

Russian T-90A on display in Moscow during 2013 Victory Day Parade. (*Vitaly V. Kuzmin with permission, 7 May 2013*)

Russian T-90A destroyed in Zaporizhzhia Oblast, Ukraine, 2022. (*armyinform.com.ua, 21 March 2022*)

Russian T-14 Amata, Victory Day parade rehearsal, Moscow 2016. It has yet to be deployed in Ukraine. (*Vitaly V. Kuzmin with permission, 11 April 2016*)

East German BMP-1, 1988. (*Bundesasrchiv*)

Russian BMP-2 in South Ossetia during the 2008 South Ossetia War. (*Yana Amelina, August 2008*)

Russian BTR-80 in 2011 Moscow Victory Day Parade. (Vitaly V. Kuzmin with permission, 3 May 2011)

Ukrainian BTR-80, Ukrainian Naval Infantry, 2010. (*Kristopher Regan, U.S. Navy, 17 July 2010*)

Lithuanian U.S.-built M-113A2 with .50 caliber machinegun, 2018. (*Mike Bravo88, 20 December 2018*)

Dutch YPR-765 A1. (*Rasbak*)

Russian 2A36 Giatsint-B towed 152mm howitzer at Saint Petersburg Artillery Museum. (*George Shuklin, on or before 13 October 2007*)

Russian 2A65 Msta-B towed 152mm howitzer with 90th Guards Tank Division, 2017. (*Ministry of Defense of the Russian Federation, Mil.ru, 18 April 2017*)

Ukraine 2S7 Pion self-propelled 203mm howitzer, 43rd Artillery Brigade, 2022. (*43rd Hetman Taras Triasylo Heavy Artillery Brigade, 22 September 2022*)

Russian 2S1 Gvozdika self-propelled 122mm howitzer, Moscow, 2008. (*Andrew Bossi, 3 August 2008*)

Polish 2S1 Gvozdika self-propelled 122mm howitzer, 2008. (*Kapitan Kloss, 2008*)

Ukrainian 2S3 Akatsiya self-propelled 152mm howitzer, 2016. (*www.president.gov.ua, 23 August 2016*)

Russian BM-21-1 Grad 122mm rocket launcher, Saint Petersburg, May 2009. (*Robert Wray, 8 May 2009*)

Ukrainian BM-21 Bastion-1 based on a Ukrainian KrAZ-260 chassis, 2014. (*Nickispeaki, 22 August 2014*)

Ukrainian R-360 Neptune Missile, Kyiv, 2021. (*VoidWanderer, 18 June 2021*)

Ukrainian Launch Vehicle for Neptune Missile, Kyiv, 2021. (*VoidWanderer, 16 October 2021*)

that control stretched all the way to the Russian border, cutting the DPR off from the Sea of Azov.

Needless to say, this area was heavily defended. Fighting before the war from 1–January to 25 February had already cost the DPR Army some 13 killed and 50 wounded (a 3.85-to-1 wounded-to-killed ratio). One of the oddities of this conflict is that of the four major political entities involved in this operation (Russia, Ukraine, LPR and DPR), only the DPR regularly provided updated casualty reports on its website for the first ten or so months of the war. They reported 13 killed and 50 wounded before the war started, and then reported 780 killed and 3,609 wounded (a 4.63-to-1 wounded-to-killed ratio) from 1 January 2022–31 March 2022.[2] They then periodically, once a week, updated these figures. These are the only systematically reported casualties for this war.

Furthermore, the reporting appears reasonable. We have no way of determining if it is accurate, but the wounded-to-killed ratios are in the range of what we would expect. We cannot say this was the case with some of the other reports and estimates we received on other entities operations. For lack of any major argument against, we have assumed that these figures are indeed close to correct. Let us look at their losses over this period:

Date	Killed	Wounded	Wounded-to Killed Ratio	Casualties per day
01.01.22–01.14.22	0	0	0	0
to 01.21.22	0	1	N/A	0.14
01.22.22–01.28.22	1	0	N/A	0.28
01.31.22–02.04.22	2	1	0.5-to-1	0.43
02.05.22–02.11.22	1	3	3-to-1	0.57
02.12.22–02.18.22	0	0	N/A	0
02.19.22–02.25.22	9	45	5-to-1	7.71
02.26.22 – 03.04.22	77	406	5.27-to-1	69.00[3]
03.04.22–03.10.22	122	638	5.23-to-1	108.57
03.11.22–03.17.22	150	885	5.90-to-1	147.86
03.18.22–03.24.22	232	871	3.75-to-1	157.57
03.25.22–03.31.22	186	758	4.08-to-1	134.86
Total	780	3,608[4]	4.63-to-1	

As can be seen, initially the most intense period of operations for the DPR Army was the week of 18–24 March. It also had a lower wounded-to-killed ratio, indicating possibly more losses from direct fire. Not sure what operations were occurring that week that would have caused such losses.

Now, this is nominally from a force estimated to be 20,000 troops. Over the course of the first five weeks of the war this added up to almost 22% of the force being casualties. This is fairly significant and similar to what was being indicated for the LPR forces. We do not know the validity of the initial estimate of the force size, we do not know what reinforcements they received, we do not know of what additional recruits and replacements they received and we do not know of the count of people among the wounded who were returned-to-duty. Still, it does seem that the DPR Army took some of the heaviest losses of all four national armies involved in this conflict.

In any case, initial operations of the DPR Army were focused not on expanding control of the areas about Donetsk (Ukrainian-held Pisky was only 7 miles/11km from downtown Donetsk), nor reclaiming the cities of Slovansk and Kramatorsk which were part of Donetsk Province nor reclaiming the cities of Severodonetsk and Lysychansk which were part of Luhansk Province. Instead, they focused on Mariupol and, as such, their initial operations will be discussed in the next chapter.

Day 12
2022-03-07

Created by @war_mapper

Chapter 14

Melitopol, Berdiansk and Mariupol, 24 February–2 March 2022

Besides their sweeping the area to the north and northwest of Luhansk, the operations in the south were where the Russians achieved their only real successes in the first two months of the war. I am not sure that is what they expected.

Mariupol was a primary objective of the war, everyone knew this was coming. It was well defended and was known to be a tough nut to crack. These lines and units had been in place since 2014. Russia's original operations focused on Kyiv (and Chernihiv and Sumy) and Kharkiv and Kherson (and Melitopol). They also did advance on Mariupol from the east. The advance and operations to the east of Mariupol were probably carried out by a mix of DPR and Russian forces.

Mariupol and the areas around it were defended by at least 3,500 Ukrainian defenders, and suspect it was more than that. The two units in the area were the neo-fascist militia Azov Regiment and the Ukrainian 36th Naval Infantry Brigade. Other units that have been listed inside Mariupol include the 12th Operations Brigade and the State Border Guards Service. The 10th Assault Brigade, 56th Motorized Brigade (whose HQ is in Mariupol) and Territorial Defense Forces were also listed by some as involved, but, those first two units are the ones that were still holding out in Mariupol as of May.

The Azov Regiment, although a volunteer militia that evolved from a football (soccer) club, was also an experienced and highly motivated combat unit that has been involved in fighting since 2014. They are the neo-fascist unit tied to the Ukrainian Army. As far as I know, they are the only proclaimed neo-fascist unit.

Mariupol itself did not come under any form of direct ground attack in the first couple of days of the war. It was, of course, shelled on the first day of the war, being within artillery range of the front lines. On 25 February, forces advancing from DPR territory fought near the village of Pavlopil (population 624 in 2001). The Russian and DPR forces continued advancing forward over the next couple of days, reaching the outskirts of Mariupol on the night of

27 February. The following day the city was surrounded by these forces and electricity, gas and internet connections were cut that evening. It does appear that the local Russian and DPR forces effectively isolated Mariupol, making any amphibious operations near Berdiansk and operations from Melitopol somewhat redundant.

On 1 March, the head of the DPR announced that they had surrounded the nearby town of Volnovakha (population 21,441), 35 miles north of Mariupol. It has a significant Ukrainian Greek population. It had been heavily shelled.

Mariupol was effectively surrounded and isolated on 2 March except for the route out through Volnovakha, which was still holding out. This appears to have been done by the forces that came out of the DPR. They also began shelling Mariupol on 1 and 2 March, with the shelling on 2 March being particularly heavy. The city was without power, gas or water and on 3 March, the vice-mayor of the city stated that they could hold out for five days.

Meanwhile, Russian forces arrived outside Melitopol (population 150,768) on the morning of 25 February and the city's leadership surrendered the city later that day. Then the narrative gets a little confused, with Ukraine claiming to have counterattacked, and the city and surrounding area still being contested over the next couple of days. On the 28th, the Ukrainians actually reclaimed the city hall. Again, it appears that the Russian forces were limited in manpower. On 1 March, after a four-day fight, Russia clearly had control of the city. This fight probably resulted in less than 100 killed on both sides. It is clear this area was not heavily defended and the attacking forces were also somewhat limited. The forces coming out of Crimea had taken Kherson, Melitopol and much of the area between those two cities. The distance between Melitopol and Mariupol was only 107 miles (172km), so Mariupol was being deeply enveloped in addition to the fighting near the city of Mariupol itself.

So, depending on available forces and what Ukrainian resistance there was, it was a distance that could be covered by advancing Russian ground forces in two or more days. But then they conducted an amphibious operation to the west of Berdiansk to further envelop Mariupol on the evening of 25 February.

The amphibious landing at Berdiansk appears to have been rather unnecessary. They were outside Melitopol on 25 February, taking it on 1 March, and they were outside Mariupol on the evening of 27 February. So not sure what the objective of this amphibious operation was unless it was just another way of introducing more forces into the area. Melitopol is only 68 miles (102km) from Berdiansk (population 107,928), and, as far as I know, there were not a lot of Ukrainian forces in between. It would probably have been easier to just advance from Melitopol.

Possibly they just wanted to add some more forces to the operations and the available forces were Naval Infantry. Still, they could have brought them over to Crimea and marched on Berdiansk from the west from there, but that may have taken longer (perhaps). Or, they could have landed them in Crimea before the war started and had them come out of Crimea with the rest of the forces on 24 February.

In any event, they conducted an un-opposed amphibious landing some 70km (43 miles) to the west of Mariupol on the evening of 25 February. This was also to the west of Berdiansk. It was reported by U.S. defense officials to be a force of thousands of Naval Infantry (marines). We never got a good estimate of the size of the operations, but it was reported to have used four landing ships. The Russians had up to 10 LSTs in the Black Sea, which could each can carry 25 APCs or 10 tanks. The sense is that there was more amphibious capability available than what was used here. It is doubtful that the landing was more than brigade-sized. Just as a note, the last **opposed** U.S. amphibious operation conducted by the U.S. Marine Corps was the landing at Tang Island in 1975. There have been no major opposed amphibious operations in the world in the last forty-eight years.

These forces quickly consolidated, advanced and took Berdiansk on 27 February and later connected up with whatever forces were advancing from Melitopol. Berdiansk was not well defended, with local authorities claiming that just one person was killed and another wounded. At least eight Ukrainian small warships and patrol boats were seized.

The real action in Berdiansk did not happen until 24 March, when the Russian landing ship *Saratov* (3,400 tons) was sunk in port and one or two other landing ships were damaged by a Ukrainian missile attack. The commander of the large landing ship *Caesar Kunikov* (2,812 tons) was reported killed on 18 April, but it probably occurred during this attack.

Having control of Berdiansk, which was only 45 miles (72km) away from Mariupol, the Russians now moved to complete the investment of Mariupol (which still may have been open to the west). Mariupol ending up losing power on 1 March and was certainly surrounded and cut off from the rest of Ukraine that same day (we start dating the siege from 2 March). At this point, no outside Ukrainian Army forces were within 60 miles of Mariupol, and it was clearly isolated and was not ever going to be relieved.

Meanwhile, Volnovakha continued to hold out. The DPR claimed to have taken the town on 11 March, although on 12 March the Ukrainian governor of Donetsk Oblast claimed that the town was completely destroyed but they were holding out in the area to prevent a complete encirclement.

Mariupol was now an Alamo-like scenario, an impossible defense while surrounded for the purpose of delaying the enemy. There was no hope for the besieged. I will stop here for now. The extended siege of Mariupol became the stuff of legends and deserves its own account. It turned into the longest continuous battle of the war. It will be a subject of a separate future book.

Chapter 15

The Continued Battle for Kyiv, 10 March–31 March 2022

Meanwhile, the battles to the northwest and west of Kyiv seemed to have lost force and direction after 1 March. A major part of this was the delayed and piecemeal deployment created by the long Russian march of multiple brigades down a two-lane road from Belarus. The lead elements of this column, 5th Guards Tank Brigade and 76th Guards Air Assault Division did not began arriving in the areas around Kyiv until the afternoon of 25 February. Not sure when the entire units were in place. The follow-up battalions in the column, the 64th Motorized Infantry Regiment,

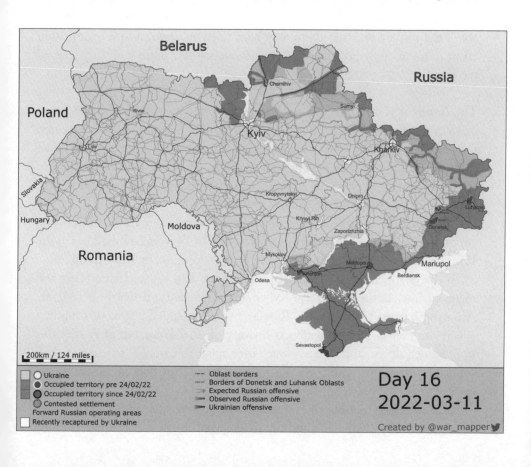

○ Ukraine	--- Oblast borders
● Occupied territory pre 24/02/22	--- Borders of Donetsk and Luhansk Oblasts
◐ Occupied territory since 24/02/22	⇢ Expected Russian offensive
◌ Contested settlement	➡ Observed Russian offensive
Forward Russian operating areas	➡ Ukrainian offensive
Recently recaptured by Ukraine	

200km / 124 miles

Day 16
2022-03-11

Created by @war_mapper

98th Guards Airborne Division, 106th Guards Airborne Division, 155th Naval Infantry Brigade and others, certainly did not arrive and deploy on the battlefield until a day or two or four later. It does not appear that the entire Russian force that came down from Belarus was fully deployed during the first week of the war.

Added to that were the logistics problems. If it was difficult to move the units down this route, then it was also quite a challenge to maintain a steady flow of food, ammunition and fuel to support them. While the units certainly carried three to six days of food and a basic load or two of ammunition with them, the fuel would become an issue shortly, and after a week, so too would the food. There would be plenty of reports of units scrounging around the villages in the area looking for supplies.

Clearly, though, the initial attack on Kyiv had failed. Now there appeared to be a coordinated effort starting around 8 March to attack Kyiv from both the northwest and the east. How coordinated this was is difficult to tell, as there were repeated communication problems and Russian forces on both sides of the Dnipro River were under different commands. Still, it appears with the attack on Brovary on 9 March and the pushes on Makariv and Moshchun at about the same time, that there may have been an attempt at a coordinated effort to try to apply pressure on Kyiv, although at this point it already seemed too late.

The Battle of Kyiv continued until the end of the month. To the northwest of Kyiv, the Russians took Hostomel airport on 24 February and had secured it by 26 February. They then received Russian reinforcements travelling down from Belarus, but they were slow to arrive. The Russians had advanced up to the Kyiv suburbs of Irpin on 25 February, took Bucha and attempted to take Irpin on 27 February, but could not advance further.

The Russians finally managed to advance into Irpin on 6 March and continued contesting for control of the town.[1] On 14 March, a member of the Irpin city council stated that half the town was occupied by Russian forces.

To the northeast of Kyiv, the Russians forces had isolated Chernihiv and marched down to the outskirts of Kyiv, being ambushed at Brovary on 9 March. After the Battle of Brovary, the Russian forces expanded out to surrounding villages and areas. They threatened Brovary on 11 March, but after that this front settled down, and Brovary was never again threatened. Russian control went up to the town and some surrounding areas, but they never got to the eastern or northeastern outskirts of Kyiv.

A considerable number of Ukrainian militia were raised in Kyiv, but they were never really challenged and hardly engaged. Instead, the Russian Army appears to have sat around the areas of Hostomel, Bucha and other towns in the area, and sent reconnaissance forces to the west and south. This included the villages of Makariv and Borodyanka to the west of Kyiv and Ivankiv (taken on 24 February) to the northwest of Kyiv, and then they pushed all the way to the border of Kyiv Province in the northwest.

The Ukrainians did expand their water obstacles in the area to the north-northwest of Kyiv. On the night of 25 February they blew a five foot hole in the dam at Demydiv which flooded five miles of the Irpin River down to a sluice gate at Chervone. Upriver from there was an area that the Russians were using for crossing the river. The Russians had laid pontoon bridges and were advancing. Defending was a battalion of the Ukrainian 72nd Mechanized Brigade. In response, the Ukrainians, this time using sappers, blew the dam wide open and the increased flow of water overwhelming the sluice gate at Chervone, making pontoon bridge crossings difficult to use and stalling out the Russian attack.[2]

The areas behind Demydiv and the Irpin River remained mostly in Ukrainian hands, although they were not particularly secure. The village of Lyutizh (population 2,282 in 2006), some 11 miles (18km) due north of Kyiv, was shelled multiple times throughout March. As the Russian attack had stalled at the suburban town of Irpin, the Russians then attempted to push across the Irpin River to and through the smaller village of Moshchun. This village was around 8 miles (13km) to the northwest of Kyiv and due east of Hostomel. It was attacked by the Russian 98th Guards Airborne Division starting on about 10 March.[3] The 98th Guards Airborne Division may have only had four maneuver battalions.[4] It was opposed by the elements of the 72nd Mechanized Brigade.[5] The Ukrainians choose to blow up additional sluices in the area to increase the water levels in area, flooding out some of the Russian units in the area, including possibly the 155th Naval Infantry Brigade.[6]

The Russian vehicle losses reported around Moshchun were limited, only around ten vehicles, three BTRs and BMDs in the western part of the village and the rest west and northwest of the village, along the Irpin River, along with two pontoon bridges. Some belonged to the 331st Airborne Regiment, 98th Guards Airborne Division.[7] Not sure if any other Russian regiment was involved in offensive operations against Moshchun.

Makariv (population 9,589 in 2021), to the west of Kyiv, was the scene of several fights. The village was taken during the first four days of the war, but clearly there were Ukrainian defenders in the area. On 27 February, it was reported that a Russian column of over fifty vehicles passed through the city.[8] On the morning of 28 February a Russian military convoy in the city was attacked.

On 2 March the Ukrainians claimed to have taken back Makariv completely. This was probably done by the Ukrainian 14th Mechanized Brigade and elements of 95th Air Assault Brigade.[9] Fighting continued over the town on 7–9 March with the Russians having a presence in the town as of 8 March.

The center of the line over the fight for Makariv was the Ukrainian 14th Mechanized Brigade versus the Russian 37th Guards Motorized Rifle Brigade. To the left (west) of the Ukrainian brigade was 10th Mountain Assault Brigade, which arrived in the area sometime between the 7th and 10th.[10] Opposite to it was the Russian 64th Motorized Rifle Brigade. Also in the area, probably to its right, were elements of the 95th Air Assault Brigade. Facing opposite Ukrainians, from right to left (from west to east), was the later infamous 64th Motorized Rifle Brigade (confirmed in the area as of 3 March), the 37th Guards Motorized Rifle Brigade (confirmed in the area as of 1 March) directly opposite of Makariv and the 5th Guards Tank Brigade to its left.[11]

On 8 March, in the tense situation that existed in the town, an elderly couple was killed when their car was machinegunned while driving in the middle of the city by a Russian BMP infantry fighting vehicle. This was caught on video, sending an image to the world of Russian irresponsibility.[12] At least thirteen other civilians had been killed the previous day as a result of the fighting there.[13]

But part of the problem is that with modern technology and cell phones, many civilians were able to report, photograph or make videos of Russian operations and then send them out to other people as they were happening. Ukraine even made a phone app that allowed them to send reports to the Ukrainian Army. So, therefore, any Ukrainian civilian ambling about looked suspicious and in some cases, orders were given to shoot them. This led to an unfortunate increase in brutality, or at least the justification for it. There is no question that some Ukrainian civilians were reporting on Russian positions.

Fighting over the town continued with the Russians in control of parts of the town during this period. On 22 March, the Ukrainian General Staff announced that Makariv had been recaptured, but the mayor of Makariv did not entirely agree.[14] Makariv was still being contested for several days afterwards with some recording that the battle ended on 25 March.

On 23 March, a Ukrainian journalist posted a video showing the brigade commander for the 37th Guards Motorized Rifle Brigade being evacuated. He was reported to have been run over with a tank by his own troops. They were reported to have suffered 50 percent casualties fighting for Makariv.[15] It was reported by Western intelligence as a sign of widespread demoralization in the Russian Army as a result of the war.

Russian vehicle losses in and around Makariv were recorded as twenty-four vehicles based upon photographic evidence, covering the period of fighting from 27 February. They do not include any tanks and only one BMP. There was also one helicopter lost as of 4 March.[16] There were two clusters of Russian vehicles lost on the M06/E40 road to the south of Makariv. First is a group of eleven vehicles all lost around the area labeled Okko to the south-southwest of Makariv.[17] This looks like an attempt to envelop the town from the east. Most of these are posted for 22 March or later, but one vehicle was posted for 1 March. To the southwest of Makariv is another cluster of eight destroyed vehicles, at least five from early March.[18] These two formations point to Makariv being flanked from both the west and the east or being taken and the fighting occurring on a line three to five miles (5–8km) to the south of the town. The 37th Motorized Rifle Brigade was clearly fighting to the south of Makariv on 1 March.

It is unknown whether this brigade was simply a single BTG of 659 men or had a second BTG or even three BTGs.[19] It is possible that it was outmatched and overpowered by the two attacking Ukrainian brigades. Also in the area was the Russian 5th Guards Tank Brigade and the infamous 64th Motorized Rifle Brigade, but it is unknown to what extent they were involved in the Battle of Makariv.[20] But, in general, the Russian regiments and brigades were low on infantry. Their battalions tended to be smaller than Ukrainian battalions. Because they were often organized with the first two battalions made up of contract soldiers and the third battalion being conscripts, the regiments and brigades were often deployed with only two battalions (as was the case with the 76th Guards Air Assault Division). This is because Russian law forbids conscripts from being deployed outside of Russia. Added to that, the majority of losses in warfare are traditionally taken by the infantry. So, the Russian troops at the spearhead of the unit could easily being seeing 50% losses, but the brigade's overall losses could be at a much lower percentage.

This nominally expanded the area under Russian control and cut Kyiv off from the west. Kyiv was never entirely isolated and always accessible from the south. The Russian operations after 11 March were clearly a failure, and mostly left unproductive armed forces sitting around, underutilized and poorly supplied. Still, the areas controlled by Russia had expanded, leaving Kyiv closed from the west, north and east and creating the threat of a surrounded major city coming under siege.

Meanwhile, the city of Kyiv, with a population of around 4.6 million people, was reported by the mayor to have less than a million people. This mass migration, much of it to regions in western Ukraine, temporarily disrupted people's lives and of course, the economy. Still, by the end of the month of March people started returning again to the capital. It was back up to 3.6 million residents by the end of the year.[21]

It was probably the existence of an idle, poorly supply force that resulted in the worst massacre of the war, in and around Bucha. Armed forces, consisting of a collection of young armed men under stress and under pressure, have sometimes been known to conduct depredations on the local civilian populations. This may happen if the force is not forcefully or maturely led. It appears that this force was left to its own means, especially when it came to procuring supplies. It was not led with a firm hand.

The natural outcome was a number of small atrocities that added up over time. In July, after this area had been cleared by Ukraine, the Kyiv police was able to thoroughly examine the area and ended up exhuming 1,346 bodies, almost all of them civilians. There may have also been around 300 people missing. The systematic examination of the bodies revealed that a considerable number of the civilians had been killed by Russian ordnance. The fighting in these areas was really not severe enough to justify all those losses. There were also clearly dozens of civilians who had been executed. Interviews with locals who had remained in the area produced repeated stories of random firing, random shelling, random killing and some civilians deliberately being killed or executed and, of course, a number of sexual crimes. Outside reporters were allowed into the area, where they were able to examine the exhumed bodies and interview the people in the area. It all clearly established that a considerable number of undisciplined and unnecessary abuses were prevalent in this area. The United Nations also independently verified the abuses.

The Makariv area, to the west of Kyiv, was also the scene of over 200 civilian deaths. It was claimed that many were executed or tortured.[22]

It was clear that little discipline was exercised over the Russian troops in this area and the end result was a considerable number of entirely unnecessary and not justifiable civilian deaths. There were multiple war crimes recorded. The units that appeared to be responsible for many of these crimes were two units from Chechnya and the Russian 64th Motorized Rifle Brigade. Personnel in some other Russian units have also been blamed for their actions around Bucha.[23] The two Chechen (Kadyrovite) units were their "spetsnaz" Special Rapid Response Force (SOBR) "Terek" and a police unit called the Special Purpose Mobile Unit (ONOM). These two units were intended for policing operations in Kyiv after it was conquered.

The 64th Motorized Rifle Brigade appeared to have been operating to the northwest of Kyiv at the start of the invasion, under command of the

35th Combined Arms Army. On or before 13 March it was pulled back to the area around Bucha (north of Kyiv).[24] This unit was originally stationed in the Khabarovsk area, in far eastern Siberia. It appears to have not been a very disciplined or controlled unit and was involved in a number of random shootings and other criminal acts.[25] Not sure how much of this was a matter of policy and how much was a matter of negligence by Russian command.[26]

Ukraine has since detailed out each of the crimes and in many cases have charged dozens of Russians in these cases. As of July 2022 they were investigating over 20,000 alleged offenses across Ukraine and had assembled a list of over 600 suspects. Russia, of course, denied responsibility, but the collection of exhumed corpses and large number of detailed stories and witness verifications of such stories made the denials entirely hollow. It is clear considerable mayhem had been conducted by the Russian units. Russia, doubling down on its denial, proceeded on 18 April 2022 to give the 64th Guards Motorized Rifle Brigade honorary guards status by executive order from President Putin. Meanwhile, by 27 May Ukraine had identified eleven suspects from that brigade who they accused of war crimes.[27] In November, it was reported that one member of the unit was interviewed in Russia and confessed to executing a Ukrainian civilian in the Kyiv suburb of Andriivka in March. He stated that he was ordered to shoot civilians by his commanding officer, a lieutenant colonel.[28]

This thoughtless collection of atrocities both here and elsewhere in Ukraine created a new narrative for the world, with the image being that of the brutal, Orc-like Russians abusing the poor brave Ukrainians fighting for their freedom.[29] This became the image established across the world, and the Russian denials were meaningless against the power of the video and television images that the whole world could witness. Russia, at that point, had lost the propaganda war. Of significance, it created a strong negative impression of the Russian military machine and the Russian nation, an image that will take Russia decades to overcome internationally.

Added to that, at this stage, over sixty nations in the world were providing aid to Ukraine. There were also hundreds of foreign national fighters who had joined the war. By Russia's own count, they came from sixty-four different countries, and Russia left out several countries from that count.[30] It is clear that significant portions of the world community sided with Ukraine in this conflict.

The purpose of a military is to serve the interests of the state. In this case, with the extensive brutality and multiple atrocities conducted not only at Bucha but in other places in Ukraine, their failure to establish standards of behavior and to control their soldiers and in some cases entire units proceeded to hand repeated major propaganda victories to Ukraine and created an image of Russia that will endure for decades. It also helped Ukraine garner more aid, more foreign volunteers and more international support. The Russians' military failure to enforce standards of behavior for their troops damaged the nation. The nation's response so far has been to give these men medals.

I am not going to attempt to detail all the crimes and atrocities here. There have been many claims made, and against the backdrop of Bucha, many subsequent claims have been amplified and repeated so as the create an image that this is what is occurring all across Ukraine. While this is partly true to an extent, it does appear that single largest massacre of civilians so far in this war was at Bucha and surrounding areas. Nothing has been uncovered in the eighteen months since then that has been as extensive or serious.[31] It is clear that Russia is not conducting atrocities as a matter of policy, but it also appears that they are not making it a policy to prevent such atrocities. Their continued shelling of urban areas and the large number of civilian losses suffered in this war is a strong indicator of their lack of responsibility. While a war in and around populated areas will never be without civilian casualties, the count of civilian deaths from this war number in the thousands.

The UN Office of the High Commissioner for Human Rights does keep a weekly total of confirmed civilian deaths from the war. Their count as of 31 March was 1,276 civilians killed and 1,981 civilians injured.[32] This was before the areas around Bucha had been liberated. By late April (28th) it was 2,899 civilians killed and 3,235 civilians injured.[33] This was an increase in confirmed deaths of civilians by 1,623 in less than a month. This count is certainly less than the total number of civilians killed. This is only the count that independent UN investigators could confirm. Of those 2,899 deaths, 1,411 of them were in the areas of Luhansk and Donetsk. Of those, 1,317 were in areas held by Ukraine and 94 of them were in the areas held by the forces of the LPR and DPR.

Chapter 16

Odesa, 24 February–31 March 2022

Odesa (population 1,015,826 in 2021) is the third largest city in Ukraine, and is a city where the majority of people speak Russian. When people are talking about the Russian areas of Ukraine such as Crimea, Donbas and Kharkiv, they often add Odesa to this list. Odesa was founded in 1794 by the German-born Russian Empress Catherine the Great as a port for the Russian Empire. As a major port on the Black Sea for the expanding Russian Empire, and later the Soviet Union, it always had a significant Russian population and presence.[1] The second bloodiest fight of the Maidan revolution occurred there on 2 May 2014 when Maidan protestors trapped a group of counter-protesting Russians in the five-story Trade Unions House. Forty-two of them died as a result of fires in the building.[2] A complete list of the dead and their identification has been compiled, and it appears that they were almost all local Russian-speaking Odesans. None were from the Russian micro-state of Transdniestria in the neighboring country of Moldova, as was rumored at the time.[3]

Therefore, it was not surprising that it was expected there would be operations against Odesa from the start of the war and that was the rumor at the time. On 24 February, it was reported that there had been an amphibious landing near Odesa, although the size and location was never given (because it never happened). This was reported for several subsequent days by multiple media sites, even though there was no evidence of this.

It turned out it never occurred. Russian operations against Odesa in the first week of the war consisted of Russian airstrikes on the morning of the 24th targeting the warehouses in the city and military airport in Odesa. Well inland from Odesa, near the border with Transnistria, the radar and air defense systems located in the primarily Moldovan-speaking village of Lipetske (population 3,740 in 2001) were also attacked at a cost of eighteen Ukrainian servicemen killed.[4] There were additional attacks against industrial and military targets in Odesa on 2 and 3 March. On 21 March, Russian warships shelled the port of Odesa, resulting in an exchange with Ukrainian coastal artillery before they withdrew. There were then cruise-missile strikes against Odesa on 25 and 27 March, although the Ukrainian air defense claimed they shot all five of the attacking missiles down.

Russia did take Snake Island on the first day of the war, but that is some 89 miles (143km) to the south-southwest of Odesa. Otherwise, the Russian ground forces were never within 69 miles (111km) of Odesa, as measured by the distance from Mykolaiv.

Odessans did build up sandbag defenses along the coast, along with other efforts, and reporters dutifully noted this volunteerism, but in the end there was no amphibious invasion of Odesa nor any threatened amphibious invasion of Odesa. On the evening of 25 February, the Russians invaded just to the west of Berdiansk, in what was their one major amphibious operation of the war. After that, I think most people understood that Odesa was not in danger from amphibious invasion. It had been prepared and reinforced. The reserve 5th Tank Brigade was near Odesa at the start of the war in addition to the local territorial forces. It was still not fully equipped, having only thirty T-72s, but was structured to have three tank battalions and a mechanized battalion.[5] Its brigade artillery group was armed with Soviet-era 2A36 Gaitsint-towed 152mm howitzers and 2G1 Gvozdika self-propelled 122mm howitzers. In May, it received 100 T-72 M1 tanks from Poland and YPR-765 APCs from Netherlands (Dutch M-113s).[6] This reserve brigade was held around Odesa through May before being placed in the Ukrainian strategic reserve. It appears that Odesa was reasonably well defended against anything that Russia may have landed against them during that time.

Still, the Russian fleet shelled the port on 21 March and the Russian cruiser *Moskva* was still hovering ominously over the horizon in early April. This threat was removed when on 13 April, two Ukrainian-built Neptune anti-ship missiles were fired and at least one hit the *Moskva* while it was around 92 miles (148km) south of Odesa. The ship was hit in the rear at least once, seriously damaged and the next day the Russian fleet attempted to tow it back to Sevastopol. It rolled over while being towed and was left to sink.

According to satellite imagery, the *Moskva* was in port on 7 April. It was reported to have left Sevastopol on Sunday, 10 April. On 12 April, the *Moskva* was located due south of Odesa, having left Sevastopol harbor and sailed to an area due south of Odesa and west of Sevastopol. This movement was almost certainly tracked the entire way by U.S. intelligence. It was recorded by satellite imagery at 18:52 to be located about 92 miles (148km) south of Odesa. It had probably been hit and was on fire at that point.[7] It may have moved some after it have been struck and there were five or six gunboats or other small vessels near it. Before 20:42 the ship was reported by Ukrainian sources to have been hit by at least one of the two Neptune missiles fired at it. It was reported to be on fire. Photos taken during the light of day on 14 April show the *Moskva* listing and smoking.[8] The Russian Navy attempted to tow it back to Sevastopol but it rolled over on the 14th and later that day the ship sank in deep water. Russia claimed that 1 person was killed, 27 were missing and 396 crew members were rescued. Some private estimates put Russian losses from this sinking in the hundreds.[9]

This was a major naval victory as it was the largest warship and only cruiser in the Russian fleet and was the flagship of the Russian Black Sea Fleet. It was the second largest warship sunk in combat since the Second World War and the largest since 1982.[10] It was also the ship that radioed the surrender request to Snake Island on the first day of the war. This completed the propaganda victory of the "Russian warship, go fuck yourself" storyline. Hollywood could not have scripted a better story, as the thirteen brave soldiers on Snake Island survived the bombardment and were returned to Ukraine in prisoner exchanges while the *Moskva* ended up at the bottom of the Black Sea. As the Dardanelles were now closed by Turkey to Russian warships, it cannot be replaced during the war. It was one of three ships of its class.

The Neptune battery was located somewhere near Odesa. The system consists of a mobile launcher with four missiles and is supported by a transport/reload vehicle, a command-and-control vehicle and a special cargo vehicle. These vehicles are modified versions of the Czech Tatra T815-7 eight-wheeled trucks.

The Neptune is an anti-ship cruise missile that was developed by the Luch Design Bureau located in Kyiv. It has a range of 280km. The design bureau was established in 1965 in Kyiv under the Soviet Union. This missile was based upon the Soviet Kh-35 anti-ship missile. This Soviet-era missile was designed in 1983 by Zvezda Design Bureau, first tested in 1985, first displayed in 1992, after the Soviet Union had fallen, and was sold to the Indian Navy in 1996. It only first entered service with the Russian Navy in 2003. None were in service in Ukraine. This missile has an operational range of 81 miles (130km), although in 2015 the upgraded Kh-35U extended this range to 260km or more. Ukraine first revealed its R-360 Neptune missile in 2015, with substantially improved range and electronics over the original Kh-35. First flight tests were conducted in 2016 and Ukraine signed a contract with Indonesia in 2020 to supply them with missiles. It was first deployed with the Ukrainian Army in 2021. At the start of the war, it is not certain how many of these missiles Ukraine had, but it was at least a dozen. On 3 April, it was claimed by Ukraine that the Russian frigate *Admiral Essen* had been hit by a Neptune missile, but the ship was able to continue it missions. The Russian cruiser *Moskva* was then hit on 13 April.

Also of importance was that the *Moskva* was one of the primary anti-aircraft assets of the Russian fleet, and one of only a few air defense batteries available in southern Ukraine. It was armed with eight S-300F SAM launchers and eight full reloads (sixty-four missiles). This loss meant that any attempts to conduct amphibious raids or operations around Odesa or elsewhere in the southwest area of Ukraine were now off the table. Its absence also helped expose Kherson and other parts of the coast to Ukrainian drones and aircraft. With Ukraine having other Neptune batteries, for all practical purposes, Russia had lost control of the western part of the Black Sea. Russia could still conduct operations around Snake Island, but as to be seen, even these became difficult. With this one sinking, Ukraine had clearly secured Odesa, a large segment of the western part of the Black Sea and were now threatening Snake Island. They could also now undermine the Russian defense of Kherson Province. The Neptune missiles, with a range of 280km, could hit Sevastopol from several places in Ukraine. Now it was the Russian fleet that was vulnerable, vice Odesa. It was later reported that the Russian fleet had withdrawn back to Novorossiysk. Although Novorossiysk is actually a large Russian port founded in 1838, it is not a satisfactory anchorage for warships as it lacks a deepwater port. The only Russian deepwater port on the Black Sea is at Sevastopol, where parts of the Russian fleet had to remain.

Odesa was clearly now safe and secure.

Chapter 17

The Advance to Mykolaiv,
25 February–31 March 2022

The other threat to Odesa was overland, from Kherson to Mykolaiv and then across the Southern Bug River, down the M14 road towards Odesa, across the Tylihul estuary and then having to bypass or cross three other water obstacles and then to Odesa. As the crow flies, Mykolaiv is 38 miles (61km) from Kherson and Odesa is 69 miles (111km) from Odesa.

On 25 February, some Russian forces bypassed Kherson and advanced on to Mykolaiv. While this was a far-ranging advance, it does not seem to have been a very large force, at best a BTG or two. If the Russians could barely deploy enough to take Kherson, then one must question the size of the forces that were bypassing Kherson and marching north.

Mykolaiv was a significant city. To start with it had an estimated population of 576,101 in 2021. It was also a major Black Sea port even though it was some 44 miles (71km) up the Southern Bug estuary and the Dniprovska Gulf. At the

The Kherson and Mykolaiv area.

start of the war, the largest ship in the Ukrainian Navy was stationed there, the frigate *Hetman Sahaidachny*; 3,150 tons displacement (3,566 tons fully loaded) with an authorized crew of 193. It was undergoing repair and refitting and was not combat ready. Around 28 February, the Ukrainians decided to scuttle it so it could not be captured by the Russians. While this scuttling strikes me as premature, as the Russians never got near the ship, it probably would not have survived subsequent Russian missile and artillery attacks regardless.

Meanwhile, the Russian forces had advanced to the outskirts of Mykolaiv by 25 February and did nothing further. They never really threatened to go into the city and clearly did not have enough forces to range far and wide outside of the city. The local Ukrainian defenders held the city without much challenge. They also continued to advance further north with a column going to the town of Nova Odesa (population 11,690 in 2021) and then on 3 March to the town of Voznesensk (population 34,050 in 2021).

A serious fight brewed up around Voznesensk on the evening of 2–3 March which resulted in a Russian defeat outside of the town (see Chapter 8). This was probably a company sized force or a single BTG. This was in an engagement with local forces. The Russians organized another attack, possibly using forces brought up from Kherson, and attacked again on 9 March. The second attack took the town and they were able to hold it for three days. We do not know what forces were in Voznesensk that failed to defend it but it is assumed to be some of the same local forces. We do not know what the Russian forces were that took and held it or whether they had been reinforced. We also do not know what Ukrainian forces took it back. It was significant enough of a fight that at least three destroyed Russian tanks and other armored vehicles were left in the town after it was retaken. The local forces then built defenses so that Voznesensk would not be used as a route for advance towards Odesa.[1]

The route from Voznesensk allowed the Russians to advance to the southwest towards Odesa, bypassing the worst of the Southern Bug River and the Tylihul estuary. Odesa was 80 miles (129km) away, as measured in a straight line.

In all three cases (Mykolaiv, Novo Odesa and Voznesensk), it was not able to initially enter the towns, as they were defended. Suspect these advancing elements were less than a battalion in strength. This did produce an advance that thrusted 53 miles (86km) into Ukrainian lines.[2] The later Russian brief three-day seizure of Voznesensk looks like a defensive lapse by the Ukrainian Army that was later corrected. While this advance looks threatening on a map, this isolated push to the north did not seem to otherwise pose much of threat and was not expanded. There the situation remained static until the end of March, although there are claims that the Russians were pushed back from Voznesensk in mid-March.[3]

Chapter 18

The Stalled Advance, 12–31 March 2022

By 12 March, the Russian advance on all fronts had truly and completely stalled. Up at Kyiv, no progress into the city has been recorded since February. No progress outside the city had been recorded since 11 March. The city was nominally surrounded on three sides, but was clearly open from the south, regularly receiving supplies and visitors, and was nowhere near being conquered. The forces holding the city at this point probably outnumbered the forces outside the city, trying to surround it or take it. Pretty hard to besiege a city manned by an army larger than yours.

To the east and northeast of Kyiv were the cities of Chernihiv, Sumy and Konotop. Chernihiv had been isolated since 10 March, but remained well-

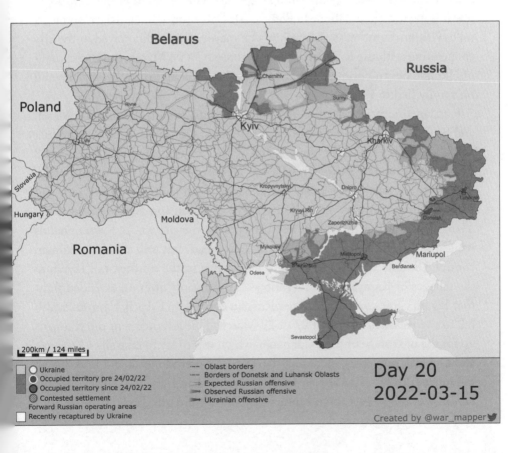

200km / 124 miles

| Ukraine |
| Occupied territory pre 24/02/22 |
| Occupied territory since 24/02/22 |
| Contested settlement |
| Forward Russian operating areas |
| Recently recaptured by Ukraine |

- - Oblast borders
- - Borders of Donetsk and Luhansk Oblasts
⇒ Expected Russian offensive
➡ Observed Russian offensive
➡ Ukrainian offensive

Day 20
2022-03-15

Created by @war_mapper

defended. There had never been a really serious attempt to take it. Sumy, far to the east, was never completely surrounded, although it was fairly isolated. After the first couple of days, it also appears to have been safe and secure, with no real serious attempt to take it. Konotop was still run by the Ukrainian mayor Artem Seminikhin, who remained in control of the city even though Russian forces and supply units were allowed to drive through the city (but not stop).

To the southeast was the second largest city in Ukraine, Kharkiv. It remained solidly in Ukrainian hands with clearly insufficient Russian forces to take it from there. The front line remained contested to the south of Kharkiv. There had been no significant movement along most of the front line since 1 March except for the advances on Brovary and other areas to the east of Kyiv. Even our blog noted on 14 March that there had been no real changes on the ground for the last fourteen days.[1]

Well to the southeast of Kyiv the Russian initiated an offensive in early March. They had taken the town of Balakliia (population 26,921 in 2021) on 3 March and shelled Izyum killing eight civilians. They then pushed down towards Izyum (population 45,884 in 2021) on the Donets River, some 75 miles (120km) southeast of Kharkiv. The mayor of Balakliia stayed in the city cooperating with the Russian occupying forces. On 28 March, the government of Ukraine began criminal proceedings against him and in early April he and his family fled to Russia.

Russian forces advanced to the northern outskirts of Izyum on 4 March and by 6 March were in control of its railway stations and some surrounding neighborhoods. The fight for control of the town started in earnest on 8 March, even though Russian media was claiming it was taken the day before. The northern part of the town was under Russian control by 12 March and Russia claimed to have taken full control of Izyum on the morning of 13 March, but apparently only the northern part of the city was in Russian hands while the southern section was partly enveloped, but still under Ukrainian control. Ukraine was also fighting to hold a line to the southeast of Izyum at the villages of Kamyanka and Tykhotske. It was only after an extended fight that Izyum came completely under Russian control by 1 April. Kamyanka also fell to the Russians on about 27 or 29 March. This advance sent the Russians up for the next stage of their campaign, which was to try to take all of Luhansk and Donetsk provinces, including the cities of Severodonetsk and Lysychansk in Donetsk Oblast, and Slovansk and Kramatorsk in Luhansk Oblast. To date, Izyum was the largest town captured by the 1st Guards Tank Army or 20th Combined Arms Army.

Then the front followed the front line trace past two Ukrainian-controlled major cities in Donestsk Province, Slovyansk and Kramatorsk, and then past two Ukrainian-controlled major cities in Luhansk Province, Severodonetsk and Lysychansk. The front line then ran down towards Mariupol.

Mariupol at this stage was under siege and had been since 2 March. The rest of the cities in the south, such as Berdiansk, Melitopol and Kherson, had all been taken in February or early March and were now part of the rear area of the Russian Army. By 1 March, the Russians had taken only three major cities in Ukraine, Berdiansk, Melitopol and Kherson, and they had not taken anything further by the end of the month.

All indications were that the Russia advance had stalled out. Ukraine had survived the first stage of this war.

Equipment Losses

Thanks to the development of portable phones with cameras and modern media and internet connections, any modern war gets documented by photos and videos as it is occurring. Much like the Vietnam War was the first war shown on TV, these wars are now being shown on the internet through a wide variety of media and sites. During the Nagorno-Karabakh War of 2020, a number of private bloggers assembled lists of tanks and other major weapon systems destroyed or damaged by examining the large number of photos and videos that were coming from the battlefield from the soldiers on both sides, observers in the area and civilians. The end result was that they were able to catalog a detailed listing of tanks and other equipment destroyed by type and sometimes by serial number. This means that people well outside of the war zone can keep track of the losses, system by system, based upon these kind of posts.

The same has been done for the war in Ukraine and some of the same people have been involved in these private accounting efforts. These efforts have the advantage that they are independent of any government control by either side. This is not to say that they are unbiased, but their biases are personal, vice governmental. In its most simple form, this is just a photographic and video documentation of losses, so it is nominally very real and accurate, although not necessarily complete. Within the bigger picture, there are some biases in the data collection. First, it relies upon what pictures were taken, vice those that are not taken. It is certainly possible that a vehicle can get destroyed and not be photographed. These cases are missed in the accounting. Second, it can be biased if one side is doing a better job of documenting the losses. Third, photographs tend to be taken of battlefields that are abandoned or withdrawn from. Therefore, a force that has given up ground is likely to have its losses documented, while a force that holds it ground and maintains operational security is likely to not have its losses fully documented. It is our feeling that some of these efforts are certainly picking up 80 or 90% of actual losses at times. On the other hand, there are clearly times when they are not being picked up and times when one side's losses are being recorded more diligently than the other side. We suspect that is the case for Ukrainian losses vice Russian, but we do not know what percentage of losses are actually being picked up from both sides. We suspect the majority of losses in either case, but it is possible that less of the actual losses of the Ukrainians are being reported.

Regardless of these shortfalls, it is clear that the majority, and in some cases 90% of the losses, are indeed being picked up and posted on Twitter, Telegram and other such accounts. These are then being assembled to provide a narrative for this war. This is provided below.

Equipment losses as documented from photos and videos by Oryxspioenkop (AFVs refers to Armored Fighting Vehicles not identified as Tanks, IFVs or APCs).

Russian Losses (Cumulative)

	2100, 7 March	0800, 11 March	1000, 17 March	0900, 23 March	0900, 30 March	0800, 13 April
Tanks:	141	179	230	267	336	485
AFVs:	89	108	148	179	239	258
IFVs:	131	158	211	259	320	516
APCs:	52	61	69	78	79	95
Jet Aircraft:	10	11	11	12	15	18
Helicopters:	11	11	30	32	32	30

Ukrainian Losses (Cumulative)

	2100, 7 March	0800, 11 March	1000, 17 March	0900, 23 March	0900, 30 March	0800, 13 April
Tanks:	46	49	66	73	79	107
AFVs:	38	42	48	59	62	73
IFVs:	33	36	43	53	60	82
APCs:	28	19	24	27	29	39
Jet Aircraft:	6	7	8	10	10	13
Helicopters:	0	0	1	1	1	3

Note that the time of these losses are as when reported by Oryxspioenkop. It is not the time the losses occurred (which could have been much earlier). It is possible in September to have discovered a tank that was lost in March, but it is difficult to document when it was actually lost. These losses also do not match with Ukrainian government claims or Russian government claims. For example, on 10 March the Ukrainian Ministry of Foreign Affairs was claiming that Ukraine has destroyed 225 tanks, 1,105 armored vehicles, 49 aircraft, 81 helicopters and 12,000 personnel.[2]

Civilian Deaths from the War as Reported by the UN

	Total	Donbas	Other	Notes
31 March:	1,276	425	851	67 in territory controlled by separatists
1 April:	1,325	448	877	
2 April:	1,417	468	949	Bucha casualties have been uncovered
3 April:	1,430	472	948	
4 April:	1,480	474	1,006	
5 April:	1,563	487	1,076	
6 April:	1,611	492	1,119	
7 April:	1,626	499	1,127	
8 April:	1,766	630	1,136	
9 April:	1,793	642	1,151	
10 April:	1,842	656	1,186	
11 April:	1,892	675	1,217	
12 April:	1,932	698	1,234	
13 April:	1,964	703	1,261	
14 April:	1,982	716	1,266	79 in territory controlled by separatists
28 April:	2,899	1,411	1,488	94 in territory controlled by separatists

Again, these are UN figures based upon when they were able to identify and confirm the civilian death, not when it occurred. It clearly does not include all civilian deaths.

Reported Russian Losses

On 2 March: 498 killed and 1,597 wounded (Russian figures)
Around 28 February: Almost 200 Russians captured (Ukrainian figures)
15 March: 1st Guards Tank Army 408 total casualties, including 61 killed, 207 wounded, 44 missing and 96 surrendered[3]
                       Wounded-to-killed ratio of 3.39-to-1
                       Two sanitary losses from due to illness
                       Total equipment losses were 115 tanks and 197 other vehicles lost for a total of 312[4]
21 March: 557 confirmed Russian deaths (BBC)
25 March: 1,351 killed and 3,825 wounded (Russian figures)

Chechen National Guard

As of 1 March: Two killed and six wounded (source Kadyrov)

Reported Losses from Donetsk People's Republic

Date	Killed	Wounded	Wounded-to Killed Ratio	Casualties per Day
02.19.22–02.25.22	9	45	5-to-1	7.71
02.26.22–03.04.22	77	406	5.27-to-1	69.00[5]
03.04.22–03.10.22	122	638	5.23-to-1	108.57
03.11.22–03.17.22	150	885	5.90-to-1	147.86
03.18.22–03.24.22	232	871	3.75-to-1	157.57
03.25.22–03.31.22	186	758	4.08-to-1	134.86
Total	776	3,603	4.64-to-1	

Reported Losses from Lugansk People's Republic

As of 5 April: 500–600 killed

Reported Ukrainian Losses

24 February:	137 killed, including 10 officers (from Zelenskyy, 25 February 2022)
27 February:	Over 470 soldiers captured (Russian claim, 28 February)
Around 3 March:	572 soldiers have been captured (Russian claim)
12 March:	Around 1,300 soldiers have been killed (Zelenskyy, 12 March 2022)

There have been no updates on Ukrainian Army losses since 12 March.

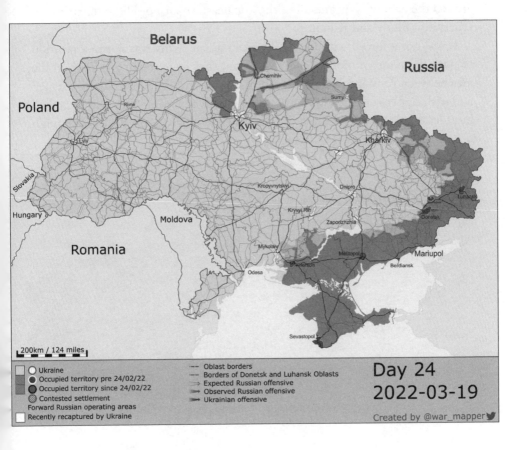

Chapter 19

The Retreat, 30 March–4 April 2022

Faced with multiple failed offensives, an inability to seize any defended town and a seriously overextended army, Russia did something that surprised many people, they withdrew. This withdrawal was conducted around the area of Kyiv and all of the northeastern area of Ukraine, including Chernihiv, Sumy and Konotop.

It was not a forced withdrawal. The Ukrainian Army was not in a position to push them out of most of these areas, but they were starting to push in the area between Kyiv and Konotop. Instead, Russia withdrew, not closely pursued and with few casualties. This reduced the length of the line they had to defend by at least a third. It simplified the war down to a fight from Kharkiv, through

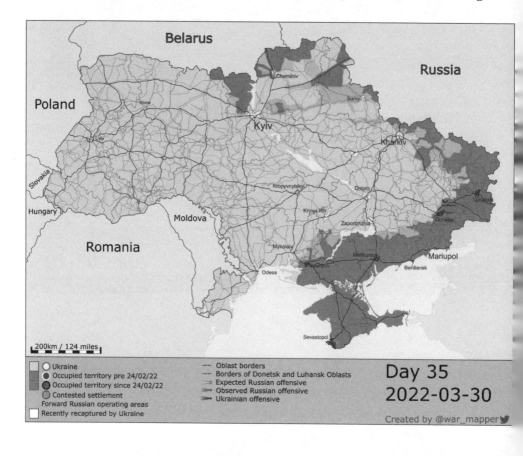

200km / 124 miles

O Ukraine
● Occupied territory pre 24/02/22
◐ Occupied territory since 24/02/22
◉ Contested settlement
Forward Russian operating areas
□ Recently recaptured by Ukraine

--- Oblast borders
--- Borders of Donetsk and Luhansk Oblasts
⇢ Expected Russian offensive
➤ Observed Russian offensive
➤ Ukrainian offensive

Day 35
2022-03-30

Created by @war_mapper

the Donbas, down to Mariupol and over to Kherson. The Russian penetration to Mykolaiv-Novo Odesa-Voznesensk was also abandoned, although these positions were under considerable pressure. It is clear they would have lost that area shortly.[1]

This did simplify the front for Russia and freed up a lot of forces. For obvious reasons, they did not have to defend the Ukrainian-Belarus border which was 690 miles (1,111km) long, although Russian military operations were mostly conducted from the eastern half of this border. On the other hand, Ukraine did have to defend that border, in case Belarus decided to join the war or Russian reinserted troops to attack back through that route. Russia also did not have to defend the area from the Belarussian border to Belgorod Oblast. This was an area some 266 miles (428km) long.[2] Ukraine would obviously still need to defend this area, but Russia did not. A Ukrainian offensive into this area of Russia would be both a military mistake and a political mistake. Russia could hold these areas, the Bryansk and Kursk provinces, with minimal forces. There was not going to be any cross-border fighting here.

This withdrawal clearly freed up a significant number of Russian forces and freed up more Russian forces than it freed up Ukrainian forces. It was to Russia's military advantage, even though it took off the pressure on Kyiv. This left them with a front line of roughly 657 miles (1,057km) running from Kharkiv to Kherson.[3]

Such a sweeping withdrawal could only have been conducted with approval of the top authorities in Russia (including President Putin). When and where this idea was first discussed is not known, nor have we seen the planning or orders for the withdrawal. They telegraphed that withdrawal when on 25 March, the Ministry of Defense held a press conference claiming that the Russian special military operation has mostly met its initial objectives and would move to the second phase of the operation, focused on eastern Ukraine and the Donbas.[4] On 29 March, the Russian Deputy Minister of Defense, while at a meeting in Turkey, declared that its forces would "drastically reduce" operations around Kyiv and Chernihiv.[5]

What we do know is that a limited withdrawal appears to have started to the east of Kyiv as of 30 March and probably earlier to the west and north of Kyiv. There clearly was some preparation for it. Sometime on or several days after 22 March the town of Makariv, to the west of Kyiv, was recaptured by the Ukrainian Army. As of 24 March, it was reported that Irpin was 80% recaptured and on 28 March the mayor announced that the town was fully recovered. The mayor did claim that the Russian military had killed up to 300 civilians and that up to 50 servicemen were killed and about 100 wounded.[6] The low count of serviceman would indicate that there was not a lot of serious back-and-forth fighting over this town, even though the Russians had advanced into it on 6 March and as of 14 March only had control of half of the town.

On 28 March, commercial satellite imagery was showing no Russian forces at Hostomel Airport. Clearly, the Russian forces were withdrawing from these areas. The 29th of March was the last day the Russians shelled Brovary, to the east of Kyiv. They then withdrew. On 31 March, the advancing Ukrainian forces opened the highway connecting Kyiv and Chernihiv and the mayor reported the first quiet night there since the war had begun. On 2 April, Ukraine reclaimed Hostomel Airport along with all the other areas surrounding Kyiv.

Elsewhere in northeastern Ukraine, there were signs of Russian withdrawal. On 26 March, Russian forces withdrew from the area around Okhtyrka in the southern part of Sumy Province. On 29 March, they shelled Brovary one last time and then the Ukrainian Army began to retake villages, starting with villages of Ploske, Svetilny and Hrebelky on 30 March. On 1 April, they reclaimed the villages of Rudnya, Shevchenkove, Bobryk, Stara Basan, Makiyivka, Pohreby, Bazhanivka, Volodymyrivka, Shnyakivka, Salne, Sofiyivka and Havrylivka. The following day the Ukrainian Ministry of Defense reported that the Kyiv Oblast was free of Russian troops. The Ukrainians reported over thirty civilians killed in the fighting to the east of Kyiv. While there are some random unjustified deaths here, this is very different than the scenario they were uncovering at Bucha.

By 1 April, this has turned into a general Russian withdrawal and was conducted simultaneously across the line. By 3 April, most of the Russian forces in these areas had left Ukraine, although Ukraine's follow-up forces were not able to confirm their complete withdrawal until 4 April. But, by the end of the day on 4 April, it was clear that Russians had completely withdrawn from almost all these areas.

The route to Chernihiv was opened as of 31 March. The large town of Konotop was never taken by the Russians, but as of 3 April it was claimed that all Russian forces had left Konotop Raion (county). Sumy, which was never really besieged, was cleared of any threat by 4 April. On 4 April, the governor of Sumy Oblast claimed that Russian troops no longer occupied any towns or villages in the province and had mostly withdrawn. On 4 April, Ukrainian forces has reached villages on the Russian border. They claimed as their peered into Belgorod Oblast that they could not see any Russian troops. It was clear that the Russian had completely withdrawn from Kyiv, Chernihiv, Konotop, Sumy and their respective provinces. Life for the Ukrainian civilians could now return to some degree of normalcy.

It was during the withdrawal that the extent and nature of the civilian killings became apparent in and around Ukraine. The first reports of atrocities at Bucha were reported on 2 April, when 280 bodies were found. This would quickly grow to over a thousand. These atrocities are discussed in some detail in Chapter 15.

The Fight of 90th Guards Tank Division

One division that did leave a lot material behind in the withdrawal was 90th Guards Tank Division. It was originally involved in the fighting around Chernihiv and then pushed down towards Kyiv where one advancing column was shot up at Brovary on 9 March. It continued to expand the area controlled to the east of Kyiv, setting up a west–east line along the villages of Rusaniv, Peremoha, Nova Basan, Novyi Byukiv and Tereshkivka. These areas are all to the west of Pryluky. It was along this line that we see 89 destroyed Russian vehicles (16 tanks and 30 IFVs).[7] Behind this line we see another 73 destroyed vehicles (17 tanks and 14 IFVs).[8] When they were lost is uncertain, as most photographic evidence is dated early April, but clearly there was a push against them by the Ukrainian Army which resulted in considerable casualties. It appears that there was a loss of at least 33 tanks and 44 IFVs from what appears to be mostly 90th Guards Tank Division. Added to that are its losses

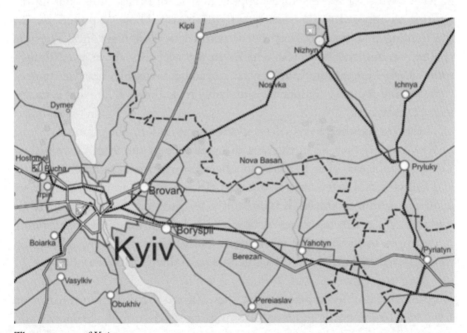

The area west of Kyiv.

from Chernihiv and Brovary, and any losses that were not recorded or vehicles that were recovered and towed back to safety. Clearly, 90th Guards Tank Division was gutted by the beginning of April.

By 2 April, the Ukrainian Army had cleared out of the area east of Kyiv, causing considerable losses to the Russian Army. Meanwhile, the Russian Army could now rebuild and relocate these forces, leading to the next stages of the war, the Battle for Mariupol and the Battle for the Donbas (which will be the subjects of two future books).

Abandoned and Captured Vehicles

There were a number of abandoned and captured vehicles as a result of this withdrawal. These abandoned and captured vehicles were counted as destroyed in the totals given previously, but some of them may have been reusable. Around Kyiv there were at least nine reported captured (one tank and five IFVs), clustered around where the fighting had occurred. It is clear that these were lost or abandoned at the time, not as part of the withdrawal.[9] Not sure how they were otherwise recovered or put to use so they have been counted as losses. There are no other significant collections of abandoned vehicles except for nine north of Kharkiv.[10] There is a surprisingly large number of vehicles reported as captured. This includes eighty-two vehicles to the north and west of Kyiv.[11] Most of these vehicles appear to have been "captured" during the fighting as opposed to the subsequent withdrawal. Those "captured" during the fighting may not have ever been returned to Ukrainian lines. They are counted among the destroyed vehicles in the accounts above, even though some clearly were captured and may have been later reusable. The real count of captured and reusable equipment is probably much lower than what is shown in the tabulations.

There are another 5 vehicles reported captured to the immediate east of Kyiv and another 57 in the area of operations of the 90th Guards Tank Division to the east of Kyiv, 8 around Chernihiv, 10 around Sumy, Trostyanets and Oktyrka and a few around Kharkiv. To the south, around Kherson are another 4 captured vehicles. It is difficult to tell how many of these were really captured. What can been seen is that many of them were in fact "captured" or destroyed in combat, vice taken when the Russians withdrew, although in some cases, their loss was not documented until the Russians withdrew.

It becomes painfully apparent from these figures how costly the drive on Kyiv was. To the north and west of Kyiv, between destroyed, abandoned and captured vehicles, Russia appears to have lost at least 568 vehicles, including

33 tanks and 163 IFVs. To the east of Kyiv, from around Brovary and covering the entire area of the 90th Guard Tank Division's operations to Pryluky, there appears to have been at least 193 vehicles lost, including 45 tanks and 53 IFVs.[12] There are no other collections of losses nearly as significant as these. This all points to the original plan to initially push onto Kyiv as being fundamentally flawed and costly for the Russian Army.

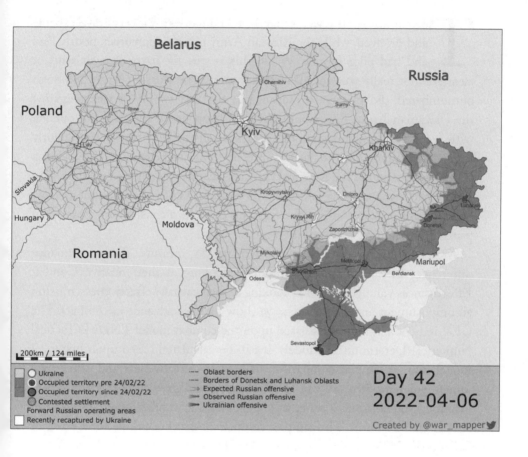

Day 42
2022-04-06

Created by @war_mapper

Chapter 20

An Evaluation of the Two Armies

The narrative of this war is that the Ukrainian Army is very brave, capable and motived, while the Russian Army is very amateurish, poorly lead and had poor morale. While this is true for parts of each army, it clearly is not really true for all of either army. The Russian Army, although outnumbered, did manage to advance in the first couple of weeks against the Ukrainian Army. This would not have happened if they did not operate with a degree of organization and professionalism. They threw some poorly trained conscripts into the battle, especially into northeastern Ukraine, but a significant portion of the Russian Army was made up of contract soldiers, who clearly had some training and some motivation. While the Ukrainian Army had stronger reasons to fight, the Russians did take a considerable number of prisoners in the first weeks of the war.[1]

At The Dupuy Institute we often try to measure the performance differences between opposing armies by looking at their relative Combat Effectiveness Value (CEV) or by looking at their casualty effectiveness, mission accomplishment and spatial effective (how far they advance in combat). The CEV is a combat multiplier based upon the combat model TNDM (Tactical Numerical Deterministic Model). It can be calculated based upon historical model runs. A simpler comparison of casualty effectiveness and other such unmanipulated outcomes can also indicate the degree combat effectiveness assuming you compare a series of engagements at similar force ratios and in similar circumstances. This simpler comparison has been done for a series of Second World War and post-Second World War engagements and is discussed in depth in my book *War by Numbers* (2017). The use of CEVs is discussed in depth in a number of Trevor Dupuy's books, in particular *Understanding War* (1987) and *Numbers, Predictions and War* (1977).[2] The main point is that one can compare the performance of individual armies, and even individual units, relative to each other by looking at their casualty exchange ratios, mission accomplishment and spatial effectiveness over the course of a preferably large number of battalion-, brigade- and division-level actions. To date, this has not been possible to do for this war. Therefore, one is forced to guess a little as to the relative effectiveness of each army.

The first such guess was done by a gentleman named William (Chip) Sayers who was involved with Trevor Dupuy in the early efforts to reprogram the TNDM back in 1992.[3] As such, he had his own personal copy of the TNDM and took the time to set up a hypothetical battle for the first few days of the war and then analyzed it using his "pre-production" version of the TNDM. He notes in his discussion of this effort:[4]

> Having determined that the model is relevant, I could move on to my second objective, which was to determine if the performance of the Ukrainian and Russian Armies was something that should have been foreseeable or was an edge case that couldn't have been predicted. My format was to run a base case with no quality modifier to either side, and then two more where the Ukrainian side was given a Combat Effectiveness Value (CEV) of 1.2 for the second run, and 1.5 for the third. I believe there is every reason to give the Ukrainians a CEV advantage; the only question is to what magnitude.

He then reran the engagements with postulated Ukrainian CEV combat advantage of 1.2 (meaning their forces are 20% more effective than the Russians) and then with a postulated CEV combat advantage of 1.5. The end result was that the engagements run with a Ukrainian CEV of 1.2 more closely fit the actual outcome of the battle. This, of course, is a very fuzzy effort, based upon a combat model run, postulated orders of battles and a comparison to estimated results. Still, it does sort of indicate that Ukrainian combat performance was superior than that of the Russians and that superiority was in the range of a 20% advantage in combat effectiveness. This is not the same as casualty effectiveness, as a 20% advantage in combat effectiveness may indeed result in a casualty exchange rate higher than 20%. Still, it is an interesting indicator.

Theoretically this could be answered by a simple comparison of casualty effectiveness ratio (number of enemy forces killed divided by number of friendly forces killed), except we do not have good data on losses for either side. As of early April 2022, the Ukrainian Army was not reporting their casualties in this war. There were also volunteers fighting for Ukraine, is addition to the Ukrainian Army and National Guard. On 15 April, President Zelenskyy told CNN that the Ukrainian Army has lost between 2,500 and 3,000 troops since the fighting had begun and about 10,000 had been wounded (a wounded-to-kill ratio of 4.00 or 3.33-to-1 depending on the count of killed). Therefore, there is reason to believe that around 3,000 or more Ukrainians had been killed, around 12,000 or more had been wounded and around 4,000

Ukrainians had been captured or were missing.[5] This would be a total of around 19,000 casualties.

The Russian Defense Ministry stated on 25 March that their losses were 1,351 Russians killed and 3,825 wounded (a 2.83-to-1 wounded-to-killed ratio). Very few people accepted this report as complete, valid or even factual. The LPR did report on 5 April that they had lost 500 to 600 killed. The DPR provided weekly reports and by the end of March was reporting 780 killed and 3,609 wounded for a very believable wounded-to-killed ratio of 4.63-to-1. They reported for 1–7 April an additional 212 killed and 706 wounded (a 3.33-to-1 wounded-to-killed ratio) (see Appendix I for a list of the reports from the DPR). This does produce a reported total for the three "Russian" armies of at least 2,943 killed and 8,140 wounded as of 7 April. If you add to that the LPR wounded (estimated at 2,400 or 4 times 600) and the captured and missing (maybe 1,000 total) then you end up with a Russian/LPR/DPR casualty count of 14,483, of which at least 2,943 are killed. Actual losses are probably higher.

So, we do not know what the relative casualty effectiveness was between these two armies. Some people tried to form conclusions based upon the claims made by Ukraine, but these types of claims are traditionally very high. For example, as of 7 June, Ukraine was claiming to have killed 31,250 Russian soldiers. This is probably an overestimate. Meanwhile, as of 5 June, Russia was claiming to have killed 38,257 Ukrainian soldiers.[6] Therefore, was Russia really obtaining a favorable exchange of 1.22-to-1 based upon these casualty estimates? It is doubtful and most analysts assume that both of these estimates are grossly inflated. For example, on 21 August, Ukraine stated that it has lost 9,000 in combat, while Russia claimed that it had lost 5,937 as of 21 September. With LPR having lost at least 600 as of 5 April and DPR reporting 3,151 killed as of 22 September (see Appendix I) then this indicates that Russians killed were at least 9,688. This converts to a 1.08-to-1 ratio in favor of Ukraine based upon the reported losses. The Ukrainian reports are a month earlier than the Russian and DPR reports (and the LPR reports are much earlier) and there are lots of reasons to assume that the Russian reported losses are low. The news service BBC Russia along with the Russian organization Mediazona has assembled its own list of Russian casualties based upon reports and obituaries in local and national Russian papers. This ended up providing a count of 6,476 killed as of 15 September based upon their data-collection efforts, and most likely this is underestimating the number of dead. Not every Russian killed ended up with an obituary or newspaper report about them. So, there is reason to doubt the reported Russian claims of dead. On the other hand, there is also reason to doubt the Ukrainian reports. The report on 21 August of 9,000 killed was preceded by a report on 11 June by the German magazine *Der Spiegel* that an advisor to Zelenskyy had said that about 10,000 Ukrainian soldiers had been killed since the start of the war. These rumors came from in or around the Ukrainian government. So why is the reported number over two months later a thousand less? Did the Ukrainian reported figures on 21 August leave out the National Guard casualties and foreign fighters?

Just to add to the confusion, casualties are those killed, wounded or missing. Those missing clearly make up a considerable number of casualties. The Russian Defense Ministry claimed as of 30 June to be holding 6,000 Ukrainian soldiers in captivity. In early July, the Ukrainian missing person commissioner stated on TV that more than 7,000 people were missing, including soldiers, National Guardsmen, border guards and intelligence officers. Ukrainian President Zelenskyy stated on 18 September that the Russians held more prisoners than Ukraine did. This all indicates that Russia captured a significant number of Ukrainians early in the war. We know from reports at the time that Russian claimed to have captured 2,439 prisoners in the siege at Mariupol, which ended on 20 May. Does this mean that around 3,500 Ukrainians were captured early in the war?

In any case, there are lots of reasons to believe the Ukrainian and Russians casualties during the first month and a half of the war were probably roughly similar in the count of killed and wounded. It is clear that probably thousands of additional Ukrainians were captured during the Russian advance. It is difficult to get an estimate for the total killed by each side, but suspect by the end of March is was probably in the region of 3,000 each, with the total for the Russians, LPR and DPR adding up to a higher figure (see discussion in Chapter 21). Ukrainian General Staff estimates of Russians killed at this time were 17,500 killed as of 31 March.

One could also make an evaluation of their relative combat effectiveness by examining the training and military culture of both armies. They both came from the same core, the Soviet Army, and the officers of the Ukrainian Army were trained in the same schools and according to the same doctrine as the Russian Army. The two countries separated their armies in 1991 and over the next nineteen years the Ukrainian Army was heavily influenced by NATO as part of Partnership for Peace program. The Russian Army was also in that program, but did not train much with the Western allies. It is possible, therefore, that the Ukrainian Army was better trained and certainly more Westernized as of 2010. Then in 2010 Yanukovych was elected to the presidency of Ukraine and over the next couple of years the Ukrainian Army was shrunk to less than 50,000 soldiers.

The Ukrainian Army then had to be rebuilt from 2014 from that reduced core. But even then, they faced problems. In 2014, it was reported that their soldiers were not competitive in pay with the private sector, and the troops were usually on short-term contracts. As a result, they had high turnover of personnel, which probably limited their training and effectiveness, although it did create a pool of civilian personnel with military experience which would be useful later when raising militia.[7] While it is entirely believable that the Ukrainian Army of 2022 is better trained, more Westernized and more competent on the whole than the Russian Army is in 2022, but it more difficult to argue that the differences are particularly large. On the other hand, Ukraine has the advantage of defending their home country, which is certainly a major motivator.

Therefore, considering all the factors discussed above, it is likely that in 2022 the Ukrainian Army is more motivated, has higher morale and maybe better training than the Russian Army. There is not a strong argument, and none based upon any data I have seen, that they are significantly better. There is an argument that they hold 20% or so advantage over the Russians. That may change if the Russians get further demoralized due to their recruiting practices and how the war has been going for them. Still, we have seen lots of evidence that the Russians are more than capable of successfully attacking and defending in the right time and situation.

Now, the equipment losses in the war have been very lopsided. In the first five weeks of the war it appears, based upon photographic evidence, that Russia had lost at least 336 tanks. In contrast, Ukraine had lost only 79 tanks.[8] It is pretty hard to dispute these losses as they are based upon photos and videos of each damaged and destroyed tanks, although this record is not complete or comprehensive. Still, thanks to the overwhelming presence of cell phones and cameras on the battlefield, it is difficult not to believe that a significant number of the lost tanks had indeed been identified and cataloged. This lopsided exchange of tanks of more than 4-to-1 has led some to assume that the casualty exchange ratios are also similar. This is a poor assumption.

The higher Russian tank losses are certainly due in part to there being just so many more tanks in use by the Russian Army. Added to that, Russia was on the offensive. Furthermore, their doctrine tends to emphasize tank-heavy operations. This all adds up. A lost tank does not generate huge casualty losses. In the First World War, Second World War and apparently on the modern battlefield, the majority of losses are among infantry who are hit by high-explosive rounds. Tanks usually suffer around one casualty per tank lost, with over half of those wounded.[9] Still, it is possible that the high Russian tank and other armored fighting vehicle (AFV) losses do indicate several hundred more Russian dead than the Ukrainians have suffered. One could end up seeing a something like a 5-to-4 exchange ratio as a result.

But, unless something unusual happens, such as the Russian Army becomes completely demoralized in 2023, as happened to the Russian Army in 1917, then the two adversaries are probably roughly equal in capability, with Ukraine holding the edge. In the end, what will matter is the amount and quality of the equipment they receive (which does favor the Ukrainians) and the numbers of troops deployed.

Chapter 21

An Evaluation of the War

This being the first major modern conventional war of the twenty-first century, it will probably be mined for lessons learned for decades to come. Here are a few preliminary observations, based on what we have seen and culled from open-data sources. These points should be viewed with caution, as more refined analysis is certainly to come.

U.S. Intelligence

First, is the role that U.S. intelligence assets played on the battlefield. The Battle of Brovary drove home the point that Ukraine was the army that has the intelligence advantage. As I noted on 2 April:[1]

> The Ukrainians have conducted a helicopter strike using missiles at a fuel depot near Belgorod, inside of Russia. This is a town I have been to a couple of times researching the Battle of Kursk. I don't recognize the area (1:25): https://www.youtube.com/watch?v=66XrGQcKnJc. They had previously hit an ammo dump near Krasny Oktyabr around 30 March. See (1:15): https://www.youtube.com/watch?v=cKqhr_pWYbA
>
> The strike at Belgorod brings out a point that I have not discussed yet in this blog. **It does appear that Ukraine is getting significant help from the U.S. intelligence assets.** I have no evidence of this and am not aware of any other reporting on this. Still, I find it hard to believe that Ukraine flew two or more helicopters dozens of miles across enemy territory, dodging radar, dodging their air force, and dodging their extensive SAM capability, to strike at a depot in Russia, **if they did not know the path was clear.** It is possible that a couple of guys took a high risk operation figuring they could get in and out of there by flying low, but most likely, the Ukrainians knew exactly what the radar coverage and SAM coverage was and flew between or around it. Ukraine probably does not have that intel capability. The U.S. does.
>
> There have been several other incidents in the war that point to Ukraine having good intelligence. This includes 1) the picking off of six Russian generals, 2) the preplanned ambush that halted the Russian armored

column at Brovary, and 3) the attack on the airbase near Kherson that took out at least ten Russian helicopters. Each of these may have been caused by Ukrainian planning and acumen, but they are easier to explain if Ukraine has considerable help from U.S. intelligence assets. It is pretty hard to conceive that Ukraine flew two+ helicopter into Russia to strike near Belgorod without knowing what was in the area.

So, I hate to be conspiratorial, but it does appear that U.S. intelligence is providing considerable help and assistance to the Ukrainian Army. It does appear that Ukraine holds an intelligence advantage in this war.

I did provide an update to this posting before the end of April,[2] some of the points of which were reinforced by reporting from other sources. These include:

1. The United States gave Ukraine exactly when and where Russian missiles and bombs were intended to strike, allowing Ukraine to move air defenses and aircraft out of harm's way. See article "U.S. intel helped Ukraine protect air defenses." Also see "Mystery of early Russian failures in Ukraine explained with new revelations of US intelligence help."

2. It does appear that U.S. intelligence notified the Ukrainians on 24 February (the first day of the invasion) about Russian attempts to reinforce the recently seized Hostomel airport and this resulted in the Ukrainians shooting down a reinforcing transport plane with hundreds of troops on board. We have no independent confirmation that this occurred but are guessing this is the case. We have also updated our account "The Assault on Kiev: The Assault on Kiev – part 1 of the discussion on the First Phase of the War | Mystics & Statistics" (dupuyinstitute.org).

3. Of course, my original blog post was based upon a number of other events I had seen, in particular the helicopter strike on the Russian depot near Belgorod.

4. I also noted in that blog post that this might include: "1) the picking off of six Russian generals, 2) the preplanned ambush that halted the Russian armored column at Brovary, and 3) the attack on the airbase near Kherson that took out at least ten Russian helicopters."

5. I also flagged in my daily war posts that Ukrainian ability to resupply Mariupol with helicopters may have also been possible due to U.S. intelligence.

6. I also flagged in my daily war posts that the tracking and targeting of the sunken Russian cruiser *Moskva* may have also been done using U.S. intelligence.

In any case, I suspect there is more to come on this story.

It does appear that Russia is fighting at a disadvantage because of U.S. intelligence. The Dupuy Institute conducted the only study on the subject I am aware of using real-world data. It was based upon 295 cases of divisional-level combat. This was 149 division-level engagements from the Western Front in 1943–45 and 146 division-level engagements from the Eastern Front in 1943. The Eastern Front consisted of 91 engagements from the Battle of Kursk and 55 cases from the battles in and around Kharkov in 1943.

This is discussed in depth in Chapters 10 and 11 of my book *War by Numbers* ("The Combat Value of Superior Situational Awareness" and "The Combat Value of Surprise"). The entire report is available at TDI – The Dupuy Institute Publications. It is SA-1. Measuring the Value of Situational Awareness (May 2004) (Office of the Secretary of Defense Net Assessment) (2 Vols). The report includes the data used for the analysis.[3]

The findings in our situational awareness report are a little complex, but as it is based upon real-world combat data, division-on-division combat, it is therefore worth considering. It was not widely accepted at the time as it was producing a much lower advantage for superior situational awareness than a lot of people thought should be the case, especially those advocating a Revolution in Military Affairs (RMA).[4] Still, as our work was based upon 295 real-world cases, it is difficult to argue that there is not validity in the results This was based upon a comparison of little knowledge as opposed to some knowledge as opposed to considerable knowledge of the enemy. We had few historical cases of no knowledge and complete knowledge. It does appear that the overall advantage of superior situational awareness in division-level combat is around 25% at best (often it is considerably less), plus there is an increased chance of obtaining surprise (which adds to the combat advantage). If the entire Ukrainian Army had that superior situational awareness (which is probably not the case), then this would completely explain the combat effectiveness advantage of the Ukrainian Army over the Russian Army. But, it is clearly a part of the combat advantage that the Ukrainian Army holds over the Russian Army.

Generals Lost

The following Russian generals were reported to have been killed as of 7 April 2022:

1. Major General Andrei Sukhovetsky, aged 47, Deputy Commander, 41st Combined Arms Army, 28 February 2022, near Hostomel.

2. Major General Andrei Kolesnikov, Commander, 29th Combined Arms Army, reported 11 March 2022, near Mariupol. Unconfirmed.
3. Major General Oleg Mityaev, Commander, 150th Motorized Rifle Division, reported 15 March 2022, near Mariupol. Unconfirmed.
4. Lieutenant General Yakov Rezantsev, Commander, 49th Combined Arms Army, reported 25 March 2022, at Chornobaivka airfield in Kherson Raion. Unconfirmed.

These Russian generals were claimed to be killed but the claims have been refuted:

1. Major General Magomed Tushayev, Commander, Chechen National Guard units, reported 26 February 2022.
2. Major General Vitaly Gerasimov, Chief of Staff, 41st Combined Arms Army, reported 8 March, near Kharkiv.
3. Lieutenant General Andrey Mordvichev, Commander, 8th Guards Combined Arms Army, reported 18 March 2022, at Chornobaivka airfield in Kherson Raion.

No Ukrainian generals have been reported killed, which is unusual.

An Evaluation of the Original Russian Deployments

During the discussion of the operations in this book, I did comment on Russian deployments and strategy, but wanted to summarize them here for the sake of developing the narrative.

First, Russian invaded with too few forces. Their initial forces were between 150,000 and 190,000. It is not clear if those intelligence estimates included the estimated 14,000 LPR or the 20,000 DPR forces. But regardless, as the Ukrainian Army was at least 169,000 in strength, this was not enough to produce favorable combat ratios, especially as Ukraine had the advantage of defense and terrain.[5]

Second, the initial partial utilization of the forces resulted in a piecemeal offensive. They did not initially move in with all of their forces, holding back some for several days before committing them. Early U.S. intelligence reports were that only 60,000–90,000 Russian troops had initially invaded Ukraine.[6]

Third, the range and selections of objectives were overly ambitious and scattered. So instead of concentrating their forces to ensure they could surround and take some valuable locales such as Kharkiv, they instead went after Kyiv,

Chernihiv, Sumy, Konotop, Kharkiv, etc. all at the same time. The end result is that they actually took none of their objectives in this area.

Fourth, the Russian Air Force did not "shock and awe" the Ukrainian Armed Forces. In part, because they did not deploy their entire air force in the operation, in part because U.S. intelligence helped Ukrainian assets to disperse or move assets to enable them to survive such strikes, in part because they did not obtain high sortie rates per day in the first couple of days and in part because this was really not part of Russian doctrine. As such, the heavy bombing Ukraine suffered in the first few days of the war was not sufficient to seriously degrade their defensive capabilities. It was very different to what the United States did against Iraq in 1991.

It is clear that the Russian Army needed to be focused primarily on surrounding and taking a high-value target (such as Kharkiv) instead of trying to do everything. By trying to do too much with too little, they ended up effectively accomplishing almost nothing. This was a major strategic and planning failure.

Urban Warfare

The Dupuy Institute did three urban warfare studies back in 2002 to 2004. These did not seem to receive a lot of attention, although our immediate customer seemed to value them. These three reports did not cast urban warfare as the next greatest problem in warfare, as some urban warfare analysts seemed to be postulating, In fact, their publication forced the RAND Corporation to reverse their opinion and publish a follow-up report that confirmed our findings that urban warfare decreased levels of fatigue and DNBI as compared to non-urban warfare.[7] But, in general the findings from our urban warfare reports have held up over the last twenty years. They demonstrated, by doing comparative analysis of division-level urban engagements with division-level non-urban engagements, that: 1. Urban warfare slows down casualty rates, 2. Urban warfare slows down advance rates and 3. Fatigue and DNBI declines in an urban environment.

We also noted in our original study back in 2002, and later summarized in the book War by Numbers, that:[8]

The vast majority of urban terrain encountered will be flanked by nonurban terrain. Operations in the nonurban flanks will potentially advance at a pace two to four times that of the urban operations. Under normal circumstances the urban areas will be bypassed on one or both flanks and will be threatened with envelopment within a few days of an operation beginning. Furthermore, as the attacker is usually aware that faster progress can be made outside the urban terrain, the tendency is to weigh one or both flanks and not bother to attack the city until it is enveloped. This will, of course, result in either the defender withdrawing from the urban terrain, which is what traditionally has occurred, or an assault and eventual mop-up operation by the attacker of the enveloped defenders. This has been the consistent pattern in the past and will likely continue to be so in the future for those cases where urban terrain, regardless of its increased size or density, has nonurban flanks.

In the current war in Ukraine, this appears to still be the case. Cities such as Chernihiv, Konotop and Sumy were bypassed, but never taken. Mariupol was also bypassed, and had to be taken in a multi-month "mop-up" operation. Because the surrounding terrain for most of these cities was relatively open, the cities more or less served as "defensive islands" on the battlefield, especially in February and March 2022. This was not because they were uniquely defensible, although they were more defensible than much of the surrounding terrain. Probably the primary reason they became defensive islands was that this is where the people were, and, therefore, where the Ukrainian National Guard units and Territorial Defense Forces were located.

Infantry Shortage

One of the problems of a modern mechanized army is that they tend to have a shortage of infantry. While combat simulations tend to give a lot more combat value to mobile fighting machines such as tanks and infantry fighting vehicles, infantry are needed to help take and hold ground, especially in difficult terrain. This became apparent in and around some of the fights in urban areas.

The Russian organization amplified this tendency, for every regiment or brigade tended to only have two maneuver battalions because the third one was conscripted and remained in Russia. Furthermore, their battalions, companies, platoons and squads are small. For example, the 37th Guards Motorized Rifle Brigade deployed a reinforced battalion with an assigned strength of 708 but an effective strength of 659. It consisted of 3 companies with the following strengths: 7th Company – 65 men, 8th Company – 64, 9th Company – 51; and two recon platoons of 24 and 15, a sniper platoon of 16, an anti-tank platoon of 22, an engineer company of 24 and a flamethrower platoon of 7. This gives them at best an infantry strength of 288. This was fairly typical of Russian organizations and most of the maneuver battalions and BTGs deployed less than 300 infantry. If these units took casualties, they were quickly depleted.

Russian divisions such as 76th Air Assault Division only deployed 6 infantry battalions for a total infantry strength of less than 1,800.

Ukrainian battalions tended to be a little bigger. They were organized using seven-man squads vice the Russian six-man squad. Added to that, when units dismount they tend to leave men behind to man the BMPs. Therefore, a Russian infantry battalion may have only something like 137 dismounts, while a Ukrainian battalion could have around 223.

A Ukrainian mechanized brigade could have around 900 infantry.[9] For example, the defenders at Sumy were only National Guard forces and Territorial Defense Forces. But, they were only facing a single Russian motorized rifle brigade which probably had around 900 to 1,200 infantry.[10] This limited Russian force was supposed to take and occupy a city of over a quarter million people. This seems ambitious.

Of course, if there is an infantry shortage, the obvious response is to make up the shortfall through using heavy weapons, in particular using artillery to shell enemy villages, towns and cities. This is what seems to have been done. Many Russian operations appeared to have consisted of heavy shelling of urban areas before sending in the infantry. This was, of course, to be expected given their infantry shortages and the danger of depletion of these infantry units. It also meant that taking of urban areas was slower and more destructive. We would see this scenario play out in Mariupol in spades.

Lessons Learned

There will probably be dozens of lessons learned reports prepared by various armies and independent contractors across the world, some going into considerable depth. Without much discussion, let us highlight a few major points here:

1. The return of artillery – because of the majority of fighting the United States has been involved in consists of Vietnam (1965–73), the Gulf War (1991), Afghanistan (2001–21) and Iraq (2003–present), the primacy of artillery as one of the three combat arms of the army has declined. It is clear that in the Russo-Ukrainian War that artillery is still important. It was in the defense of Kyiv, but will become even more important in the fighting after March. It is clear that artillery is now going to be used extensively in a major conventional war, will consume considerable ammunition and force countries to further develop their production. While this is primarily a discussion for later books, the trends showing that artillery has returned to its traditional

pre-dominate position on the battlefield first started to appear in the first six weeks of this war.

2. The development of drones – the extensive use of drones by Ukraine and the subsequent high Russian armor losses is a major change from past wars. This was heralded by the war over Nagorno-Karabakh in 2020 when Azerbaijan was able to effectively establish air superiority using drones and was able to eliminate over a hundred Armenian tanks.[11] This clearly heralded the age of drone warfare, although they had been used in earlier conflicts (such as by Russia in Georgia in 2008). Ukraine clearly held the advantage over Russia from the start of this war. Drones are the poor man's air force, so the Russian Air Force has relied on its air force, while Ukraine has relied on its drones. As such, Russia still has air superiority, but Ukraine gets considerable play because of its drones.

3. Shoot and scoot – with improved intelligence through satellites, drones and other means, coupled with highly accurate one-shot one-kill munitions, the emphasis in operations is now to "shoot and scoot" or for firing units to change positions shortly after firing. This has always been an element in modern combat, but as shown in Ukraine, it is clearly something that has become standard.

4. Inability to concentrate – because of the development of highly accurate munitions and improved ability to spot concentrations (especially with drones), the concentration of forces on the battlefield has become more dangerous and tends sometimes to result in high casualties. Mass is one of the nine principles of war.[12] Clearly if it becomes difficult to mass forces because of firepower, then they will first have to mass their firepower.

5. Dispersion – units are much further dispersed across the battlefield. This is definitely in part because of increased lethality of the weapons. It is also because of the vast expanse of terrain being fought over and the low numbers of forces initially committed to the battlefield. Density of deployment is a fraction of what it was in the theater in 1943. For example, at the Battle of Kursk in July 1943, the density of deployment for the attacker averaged 1,914 men per km. During the mobile operations around Kharkiv in February, March and August 1943 the densities for the attacker averaged 1,504.[13] Deployment densities in Ukraine are now considerably less, in the last quarter of 2022 this was around 387 soldiers per km.[14]

6. Old lessons need to be relearned – the real lesson of this war was that as much as things have changed in the over seventy-five years

since the Second World War, many, many things have not changed. Therefore, amid modern tanks, modern aircraft, modern one-shot fire and forget munitions, helicopters, rockets, drones, satellites, etc., there were also a lot of elements that looked like the Second World War and among the trench lines in the Donbas, elements that looked like the First World War. Not so much a Revolution in Military Affairs (RMA) but an evolution in military affairs. As such, there were basic lessons of conventional warfare that needed to be relearned by both the participating armies and the observing armies (including the U.S. Army). We are now seeing a large conventional war between two modern and similarly capable armies.[15] A lot of it looks like what we have seen before.[16] We have found that over the last twenty years that the U.S. Army has been focused on other missions, counter-insurgency, counter-terrorism, military assistance and training. They are now having to re-examine how they should be fighting conventional warfare.

Drone Warfare

This war is not the first to use drones. Work on drones for the U.S. military started in earnest in the 1980s. Some drones were used by Russia in their brief 2008 war in Georgia. The first extensive use of drones though occurred in the Nagorno-Karabakh War of 2020, when the Azerbaijani armed forces employed drones as a sort of a poor man's air force, destroying many of the 170 tanks that Armenia lost. These losses were confirmed through video and photographic evidence.[17] While it was not the first use in war of the highly capable Turkish-built Bayraktar TB-2 drone, their use early in this war brought them widespread attention.

At the start of this war, Ukraine was better equipped with drones. They had: 1. The small spindly multi-rotor Ukrainian-built R18, introduced into service in 2019 and capable of dropping up to three hand or anti-tank grenades, 2. Two Special Forces drones, the small fixed-wing Punisher drone with a 3kg (6.6lb) bomb and the smaller Spectre drone with a payload of 4lb and 3. Around a dozen or more Bayraktar TB-2s. They had just started deploying the Bayraktar TB-2, a Turkish-made drone of significant capability. Not only was it able to track and spot enemy AFVs, it was able to launch MAM-C glide bombs and MAM-L at them. These Bayraktar drones accounted for considerable Russian tank losses early in this war, as had been the case in the Nagorno-Karabakh War. Ukraine purchased twelve of these drones in 2019, and started receiving them in the same year. The Ukrainian Navy purchased six TB-2s in 2021. They became operational in 2021. That same year a joint venture was established to produce forty-eight more drones in Ukraine. In January 2022 Ukraine had at least a dozen Bayraktars operational. Each drone is reusable and has a payload of 150kg (330lb). They have been effective since the start of the war, although there predominance in news reports have declined since the first weeks of the war. As the war developed, Ukraine received more drones from other nations to supplement this capability.[18]

In contrast, the Russian drone fleet was not well developed, consisting mostly of light observation drones. They had an air force that allowed them to have air superiority, so had not invested in the drones that could be used to strike at Ukrainian armor. That would change as the war continued.

In many respects, the development of drones was not something that changed the nature of warfare. It was more that it allowed poorer countries to develop an air power capability with firepower that it otherwise would not have. This is significant, as it means countries such as the United States will possibly always encounter drones in future operations and cannot be assured of air supremacy, as has been the case for most of their operations since 1941.

Also, "loitering munitions" such as the RAM II, ST-35 Silent Thunder, Switchblade, Phoenix Ghost and Warmate must be considered. The RAM II is a Ukrainian-built UAV-type loitering munition with a 3kg warhead. The ST-35 Silent Thunder is a new Ukrainian-built loitering munition first demonstrated in 2019. It has a 3.5kg warhead. The Switchblade 300 and larger Switchblade 600 are American-built UAV-type loitering munitions that have been provided in large numbers since the start of the invasion. More than 700 were sent to Ukraine early in the war.[19] The Phoenix Ghost is another UVA-type loitering munition similar to the Switchblade, but with a warhead bigger than the Switchblade 300. With a loiter time of up to 6 hours, it can also conduct surveillance. It appears that 121 of them were provided to Ukraine in May 2022.[20] The Warmate is a Polish-built small loitering munition with a 1.4kg (3.1lb) warhead. These are nominally similar to drones in that they can circle over an area looking to acquire a target, and then dive in for the one-shot kill. Some of these systems were in the hands of the Ukrainians at the start of the war. The Russian Army did not use any loitering munitions during this first stage of the war. The only one they had available was the Kalashnikov KUB-BLA. It only cleared state tests in November 2021 and was only first used in Ukraine in March 2022.[21] It has a payload of 3kg.

The War in Georgia in 2008

The Russo-Georgian War of 2008 is an interesting operation. Shooting started in Ossetia on 1 August, but the Russian Army did not enter the fray until 8 August. On 13 August, Russia had taken the city of Gori, effectively dividing Georgia in two, and then advanced towards the Georgian capital, Tbilisi. On 15 August, they were 25 miles (40km) from the capital. They then halted. Some eight days after the Russian intervention had started, Russia had defeated the two Georgian brigades that were defending in front of the capital. The other three Georgian maneuver brigades were not in position to hinder the Russian advance. Certainly, Russia was in position to take the capital city of Tbilisi, which it did not do. Instead, they signed a ceasefire with Georgia on 16 August and began withdrawing from Georgia on 22 August.

This was a case where Russia had overpowered its neighbor in a little more than a week. It was done at a low cost. Only four tanks were reported as destroyed along with eight aircraft. Georgia losses were a lot heavier, with 44 tanks destroyed along with a whole lot of other equipment. It clearly showed Russia's superiority over its neighbor. A pattern had been established, reinforced by the seizure of Crimea in 2014 with no casualties. It appears the ease of these operations distorted their decision-making in 2022.

This case still showed a constrained and controlled Russian intervention that did not permanently add any more territory to their control. They appeared to still be concerned about international public opinion and responsive to it. Up until March of 2014, Russian has played at the border with many countries, with Transnistria being set up as an independent country in 1992, as was Abkhazia also in 1992 and South Ossetia in 1990. Russia had never taken such a brazen step as to actually annex a territory. That they first did with Crimea in March 2014. This was the point that the Russian approach to these issues changed. Still, it was a big step to go from its bloodless seizure of Crimea in 2014 to the decision to launch a full-scale invasion of Ukraine in 2022. Russia behavior in 2008, under President Medvedev and Prime Minister Putin, was different to that of Russia in 2022.

Would Russia Have Stopped at Ukraine?

This is a bigger geopolitical issue but if Russia has achieved much of its initial objectives in Ukraine, and settled on a ceasefire or peace with the seriously reduced Ukraine under new leadership, would this have been their last step?

Russia does have the option of applying pressure to many of its neighbors. This includes Belarus, where the current president and dictator, Aleksander

Lukashenko, appears to have moved closer to the Kremlin in an attempt to shore up his control of the country. The country was seriously shaken with extensive protests after the presidential election in August 2020 and now has an active opposition movement outside its borders than includes a Belarussian battalion fighting for Ukraine. Belarus shares a border with three NATO countries (Poland, Lithuania and Latvia) in addition to Ukraine and Russia. There is also the democratic Armenia, which is tangled up in a conflict with Azerbaijan over Nagorno-Karabakh. It is now relying on Russian peace keepers to control the conflict there. It might include Moldova, a small democratic country of less than 3 million people, of which a half-million live in the Russian-speaking breakaway Pridnestrovian Moldavian Republic (Transnistria), an independent and mostly unrecognized country on the border with Ukraine. Then there is Khazakhstan and the other smaller "stans" (Turkmenistan, Kyrgyzstan, Uzbekistan and Tajikistan). Finally, there is Georgia, which already fought a brief war with Russian in 2008. Its current leadership is now much more Russian-leaning than its leadership was at that time. Each of these countries are in a potentially difficult position if Russia applies pressure to them or threatens to occupy them. They are somewhat geographically isolated. All nine of these countries were formerly part of the Soviet Union, as was Ukraine, Azerbaijan and the three NATO Baltic states. Belarus, Kazakhstan, Kyrgyzstan and Tajikistan are all in the Russian-led Eurasian Union, which is the organization that was at the center of the political violence in Ukraine in 2013. Armenia, Belarus, Kazakhstan, Kyrgyzstan and Tajikistan are all part of the Russian-lead Collective Security Treaty Organization (CSTO). That Russia can pressure these countries does not mean that they would or will, but so far, the track record has strongly indicated otherwise.

And then there are the four former members of the Soviet Union that are not threatened by external pressure. This would include the three Baltic states of Lithuania, Latvia and Estonia. It also includes Azerbaijan, which is sandwiched between Russian and Iran. The three Baltic states are protected by being in the NATO alliance since 2004, but they are concerned enough about the situation that they are now significant contributors to Ukraine's defense. Azerbaijan, thanks to its oil wealth, has been able to run an independent foreign policy, some of this in opposition to Russia interests. Still, it is a nation of 10 million people located next to Russia (145 million people excluding Crimea), Iran (87 million people), Armenia (3 million people) and Georgia (4 million people). This whole region is near the NATO country of Turkey (85 million people).

Other countries that share a common border with Russia include Finland which has just joined NATO. NATO member Poland shares a border with the

Russian enclave at Kaliningrad and, of course, with Belarus and Ukraine. In the far east Mongolia, China and North Korea also share a border with Russia.

Nearby Sweden does not share a border with Russia, but has had to repeatedly deal with violations of its sea space by suspected Russian submarines. It is still not a member of NATO, although that expected to change soon.

One can only hazard to guess what Russia might do if they had succeeded in Ukraine. The map that Lukashenko was briefing on 1 March did show operations continuing up to the Moldavan border. Perhaps Russia would have done nothing further and return to being a responsible member of the world community. Not sure many people would consider this the most likely scenario.

The Development of the Russian Army over Time

The development over time of the armies and military doctrine of the Russian Empire (1721–1917), the Soviet Union (1922–91) and now the Russian Federation could be the subject of an entire book, and several have been written about this.[22] I will only attempt to briefly address this in the broadest of terms here.

The two major combat events that helped defined Soviet Army doctrine for the future was the Brusilov Offensive carried out by the Russian Empire in 1916 and the German spring offensive on the Western Front in 1918. The Brusilov Offensive consisted of a broad attack across an extensive front, while the German spring offensive comprised attacks in multiple echelons in an attempt to punch through British positions. If we look forward to the Battle of Kursk in 1943, we see the Russian Army defending in a layered multiple-echelon defense and also attacking with two or more echelons. Moreover, on 12 July, we see the Russian Army launch a broad front offensive that stretched from the Seventh Guards Army to the Fifth Guards Tank Army to Fifth Guards Army to the Sixth Guards Army to the First Guards Tank Army. The infamous Battle of Prokhorovka, if narrowly defined as fight on the tank fields of Prokhorovka, was just one German division-level engagement that day on the southern side of the Kursk bulge in a day that included fifteen German division-level engagements on that side. Here we see a doctrinal approach to war influenced by the First World War, almost twenty-five years after the war was over.

There were also other operational tendencies that showed up during the Battle of Kursk. One of the most striking of these was the tendency for Soviet Armor brigades to periodically launch unsupported armor counterattacks, often without artillery support, air support and sometimes a shortage of infantry. There was also a lack of well-developed infantry, often hastily recruited at the last moment and thrown into battle. Along with that was a lack of a well-developed trained Non-Commissioned Officer (NCO) corps. Command was driven from the top down, resulting in a lack of independent command and consequently a lack of initiative. In their air force, there was a lack of direct close air support. Overall, even though the Soviet Army during the opening phase of the Battle of Kursk was on the defensive, had prepared works, outnumbered their German opponents, had as much equipment and most of their equipment was as good as their opponents, they still lost over three times the troops as the attacking Germans.[23]

Now, of all the factors listed above, about the only one we did not see in this current war is fighting in echelon. What we did see was a broad front attack conducted starting on 24 February. There are lots of reasons to consider this approach to be flawed. We also see Russian armor conducting unsupported attacks. This tendency was also noted in the First Chechen War (1994–6). Their infantry still remains poorly developed, often using one-year conscripts, and there is still no real NCO corps. It still appears to be a command-driven army that shows a lack of initiative. Their air force, while carrying out considerable bombing, is not doing much direct close air support.

This is an army that learned some of the wrong lessons from the First World War, successfully fought the Second World War with this flawed doctrinal and training approach and then did not significantly improve in the interim. Perhaps reinforced by their success in the Great Patriotic War, they did not feel the need and the urge to re-examine and reform the army. It did not help that they were restricted from accessing and studying German archival records, as they rather consistently overestimated German casualties and the effectiveness of their operations. Since the fall of the Soviet Union the Russian Army has been underfunded and under-resourced. The weaknesses of this army was demonstrated in the First Chechen War and it does not appear in subsequent operations that they have improved it. In fact, they have accepted the weaknesses by keeping the BTGs combat capable at the expense of maintaining fully operational regiments and brigades. It was an army that was in serious need of reform in 1943 and still needs to today.[24]

Casualties

The number of soldiers lost in this war may have been roughly equal in the first six weeks of combat and there were at least 3,000 killed on each side. This is discussed in some depth in the previous chapter.

For the Russians their casualties include 500–600 lost by the LPR by 5 April and 988 for the DPR through 7 April.[25] The Russian Defense Ministry did report on 25 March that their total losses were 1,351 dead and 3,825 wounded, for a wounded-to-killed ratio of 2.83-to-1. Most people consider this report to be incomplete or low. This is a total of at least 2,839.

The one independent source for Russian casualties are the reports from BBC Russia and Mediazona, an independent Russian group. They have assembled listings of Russians who died from newspapers reports, obituaries, other media reports, personal reports and so on. It is a list of people lost by name and in many cases by date, unit and location. It is certainly reasonably accurate as to who they report as killed, but clearly they have not gotten the names of every person who was killed. So it is naturally an undercount. Whether it is an undercount by 50% or a factor of ten is more difficult to determine, but suspect the undercount is in the lower end of the range.

About 72% of the people they are counting as killed have a clear date as to when they were killed.[26] Their listings of these people show:

Week of	Number Reported Killed by Name
24 February–2 March 2022	520
3–9 March	582
10–16 March	440
17–23 March	250
24–30 March	332
31 March–6 April	189
7–13 April 2022	144

This is 2,313 killed from 24 February through 6 April. This is clearly an undercount of Russian losses in the war. Assuming they only represent 72% of the counted losses (actually I suspect the reporting was more complete early in the war), then this would imply that actual counted losses for this period were 3,202. Then there are the LPR and DPR losses. It is not known if these losses overlap or not. Are Russians serving with the LPR and DPR and if they are lost, are they counted in the BBC Russia and Mediazona losses (most likely), are they counted in the LPR and DPR losses (not sure), or both. Finally, there are those that are not counted by BBC Russia and Mediazona. We suspect this number was lower earlier in the war than it was later.

The BBC Russia and Mediazona reports all point to Russian, LPR and DPR losses for the first six weeks of the war being at least 4,790 (3,202 + 600 + 988). The total Russian killed may be higher and could easily be another 1,600 or more higher, but it is certainly not as high as the Ukrainians claims of 17,500 killed by 31 March 2022.

Wounded may be around four times the number killed for both sides. The only systematic and regularly reported wounded-to-killed figures come from the DPR, which reports 3.95-to-1 for the period covering 1 January–4 July 2022. It is unknown how these figures account for died-of-wounds, which are those wounded who made it to a treatment center but later died while under medical care. In the modern battlefield, they make up 2–5% of the wounded. It is assumed in the DPR figures that they are counted as wounded.[27] The UK-based RUSI did note in its report in November 2022 that wounded represented about 80% of the casualties for the Ukrainian side. This meshes with a wounded-to-killed ratio of 4-to-1. It also noted that 40% of the wounded personnel sustained permanent injuries.[28]

It appears that Ukraine also had around 3,500 troops captured. Russia also had some troops captured but this was probably only a couple of hundred. Therefore, total losses could be as of the end 7 April 2022:

Ukrainian: 3,000 killed (as reported) + 12,000 wounded (estimated) + 3,500 captured (estimated) + 500 missing in action (estimated) = 19,000.
Russian: 600 LPR killed (as reported) + 988 DPR killed (as reported) + 3,202 Russians killed (based upon estimate derived from Mediazona) + 2,400 LPR wounded (estimated) + 12,808 Russian wounded (estimated) + 4,310 DPR wounded (as reported) + 200 surrendered (guesstimated) + 500 missing in action (guesstimated) = 25,008.[29]

This implies that Russian losses were slightly higher than Ukrainian losses. Ukrainian figures for killed are based upon two reports, both directly from Zelenskyy. He stated on 12 March that their losses had been 1,300 killed. On 15 April, he stated that their losses had been from 2,500–3,000 killed and 10,000 wounded. This figure of 10,000 wounded would be a 4-to-1 wounded to killed ratio if the killed figure of 2,500 was used. There is reason to suspect that Zelenskyy would tend to downplay their losses or that Ukrainian reporting was not complete. One could just as easily assume that the Ukrainian killed were 4,500 or 5,000 based upon parity with the Russian losses.

The next reports we have for Ukraine casualties was on 21 August when Ukraine stated that they had lost nearly 9,000 killed. Ukrainian figures may be understated and may not include National Guard (which would include the Azov Regiment) or foreign fighters. On 11 June, Der Spiegel claimed that an advisor to Zelenskyy said that about 10,000 Ukrainian soldiers had been killed since the start of the war. If we do a straight-line estimate back covering the first six weeks of the war, then the 11 August statement (24 weeks into the war) implies that losses through 7 April were 2,250 killed. If we do a straight-line estimate from the 11 June claim (around 15 weeks in), then this implies that losses through 7 April were 4,000 killed. There is not better data on Ukrainian losses in this period.

This is all very fuzzy and imprecise, but would rather have a developed estimate than nothing at all. The only confirmed unit-loss report we have is from the Russian 1st Guards Tank Army, which had some of its records captured by the Ukrainian Army.[30] These records reported that the 1st Guards Tank Army lost through 1900 on 15 March: 61 killed-in-action, 207 wounded-in-action, 44 missing-in-action, 2 ill and 96 taken prisoner of war. This is arguably a 3.39-to-1 wounded to killed ratio, although certainly a number of the prisoners of war were wounded, and certainly a number of the missing-in-action were either killed or wounded. Note that with total casualties of 410 over the course of 20 days, this comes out to 20.5 a day. The 1st Guards Tank Army was one of effectively six to seven Russian army-level organizations invading Ukraine, nominally making the argument that Russian casualties through the middle of March were less than 3,000 and less than 500 killed. This does not agree with Ukrainian claims, which put Russian dead as of 15 March at more than 13,500.

The records do report heavy tanks losses, including the 1st Tank Regiment of the 2nd Guards Motorized Rifle Division losing 45 T-72 B3M tanks, the 13th Tank Regiment of the 4th Guards Tank Division losing 44 T-80s UE tanks and the 12th Tank Regiment of the 4th Guards Tank Division losing 18 T-80 U tanks. It is unclear if these were damaged, destroyed or damaged and destroyed tanks. The 1st Tank Regiment/2nd Guards Motorized Rifle Division reports 6 killed and 9 wounded, 13th Tank Regiment/4th Guards Tank Division reports 2 killed and 13 wounded, while the 12th Tank Regiment/4th Guards Tank Division reports 5 killed and 27 wounded. This makes the argument that losses were less than 1 man per tank killed, with a total of 62 casualties in these 3 regiments among 107 tanks damaged or destroyed.

Civilian casualties reported by the UN are 2,899 killed and 3,235 injured as of 28 April 2022. This is clearly an underestimate. The total losses through the end of March for this war could be over 9,000 killed, including civilians.

War of Movement vice a War of Attrition

Any war that lasts longer than six weeks become a war of attrition. This was a statement that we included in a book called 'Understanding World War II', which we have still not completed. It was based in part on the German campaigns in France in 1940 and on the German campaign in Russia in 1941.

After the first six weeks or so of "maneuver warfare" the war really turned into one where the winner was going to be side with the larger available resources. This appears to be the case here, where the war of maneuver lasted for about six weeks, from 24 February–7 April. This was the period in which superior mobility, momentum, air power and large quantities of armor should have given Russia an edge. Their failure to properly develop that resulted in a campaign that cannot be considered to be anything less than a significant failure for Russia.

The war since then has really been a war of attrition, although there are still some moments of considerable movement. Much like conventional wars in the past, this war will end up being decided by who has the equipment, manpower, motivation and popular support to continue the fight. It has been over seventy-five years since the last major conventional war in Europe, and this modern war looks more like one of those older wars, and parts of it even look like the First World War.

Chapter 22

The Salvation and Creation of the Nation of Ukraine

Vladimir Putin created the modern state of Ukraine. This is a state that clearly is now going to be around for decades, if not centuries. The year 2022 is their 1776. It is the year they unified their country and finally and firmly broke with their past as a member of the Russian Empire and the Soviet Union. It is the year it clearly asserted itself as Ukraine.

As I noted on my blog on 13 April:[1]

> At this point in time, more than six weeks after the war has begun, it looks like the nation of Ukraine has been saved. More important, it looks like Ukraine, as a single defined nation, has developed into a unified whole. The Russian speaking Kharkov, the second largest city in Ukraine, is united with Kiev and with Lvov against Russian aggression. In many respects, this has created the modern nation of Ukraine, just like the American Revolutionary War was the defining event that created the United States of America.
>
> This has not always been the case with Ukraine, with part of the country identifying closely with Russia, with large parts of the country being primary Russian speakers, including Kharkov and Odessa, in addition to the Donbass. This drove Ukrainian politics, from the 2004 presidential campaign of Russian-leaning Victor Yanukovych, the subsequent Orange Revolution, the 2010 election of Russian-leaning Victor Yanukovych, his subsequent attempt to join Putin's Eurasian Union instead of the European Union, and of course his overthrow with the Maiden Revolution in 2013–2014 that led to the extended conflict with Russia; the establishment of the Lugansk and Donetsk Republic and the Russian seizure of Crimea in 2014. This set the stage for the current war. What the current war has done is create a unified Ukraine that is independent and clearly willing to fight for that independence. There is now no doubt that Ukraine will remain an independent state for decades, if not centuries to come. It will become part of the European

Union, it will not become part of the Eurasian Union, nor a vassal of Russia or a Russian Empire. We shall see if it becomes part of NATO.

That said, it still has a long, extended fight on its hands, where a country over three times its population and almost ten times its economy has seized and looks like it intends to hold on to major parts of its eastern regions. Not sure for how long that will play out, and whether this is a war that reaches a negotiated settlement in six months, or a war that continues on for years, or achieves an armistice for now only to return back to war later. But what is clear, is that Ukraine as a nation is going to continue to stand, and the primary reason for that is they were willing to fight for their independence multiple times, in the protests of 2004, in the protests of 2013–2014, in the fighting of 2014–2015 and in the war of 2022.[2] Sadly, sometimes freedom and self-determination have to be earned by blood.

Enough said. The state of Ukraine clearly exists, having fought multiple times to establish itself. Regardless of the outcome of this war, the state of Ukraine is not going away. Where lies its eastern boundaries, and whether the Donbas or Crimea will be part of this state of Ukraine, has not yet been established. But, the state of Ukraine has clearly been established. Vladimir Putin's policies have achieved the exact opposite of what he was trying to achieve. He has only himself to blame.

Appendix I

Donetsk People's Republic Losses

The reported losses of the Donetsk People's Republic:

Date	Killed	Wounded	Wounded-to-Killed Ratio	Casualties per Day
01.01.22–01.14.22	0	0	0	0
to 01.21.22	0	1	N/A	0.14
01.22.22–01.28.22	1	0	N/A	0.28
01.31.22–02.04.22	2	1	0.5-to-1	0.43
02.05.22–02.11.22	1	3	3-to-1	0.57
02.12.22–02.18.22	0	0	N/A	0
02.19.22–02.25.22	9	45	5-to-1	7.71
02.26.22–03.04.22	77	406	5.27-to-1	69.00[1]
03.04.22–03.10.22	122	638	5.23-to-1	108.57
03.11.22–03.17.22	150	885	5.90-to-1	147.86
03.18.22–03.24.22	232	871	3.75-to-1	157.57
03.25.22–03.31.22	186	758	4.08-to-1	134.86
Total	780	3,608[2]		4.55-to-1
04.01.22–04.07.22	212	706	3.33-to-1	131.14
04.08.22–04.14.22	209	691	3.31-to-1	128.57
04.15.22–04.21.22	225	760	3.38-to-1	140.71
04.22.22–04.28.22	110	451	4.10-to-1	80.14
04.29.22–05.05.22	99	358	3.62-to-1	62.29
05.06.22–05.12.22	78	495	6.35-to-1	81.86
05.13.22–05.19.22	108	516	4.78-to-1	89.14
05.20.22–05.26.22	104	383	3.68-to-1	69.57
05.27.22–06.02.22	74	280	3.78-to-1	50.57
06.03.22–06.09.22	62	260	4.19-to-1	46.00
06.10.22–06.16.22	67	388	5.79-to-1	65.00
06.17.22–06.23.22	68	349	5.13-to-1	59.57
06.24.22–06.30.22	51	207	4.06-to-1	36.86
07.01.22–07.07.22	109	260	2.39-to-1	52.71
07.08.22–07.14.22	54	238	4.41-to-1	41.71

Date	Killed	Wounded	Wounded-to-Killed Ratio	Casualties per Day
07.15.22–07.21.22	31	193	6.23-to-1	32.00
07.22.22–07.28.22	19	195	10.26-to-1	30.57[3]
07.29.22–08.03.22	87	472	5.43-to-1	79.86
08.04.22–08.11.22	106	466	4.40-to-1	81.71
08.12.22–08.18.22	127	368	2.90-to-1	70.71
08.19.22–08.25.22	64	331	5.17-to-1	56.43
08.26.22–09.01.22	79	297	3.76-to-1	53.71
09.02.22–09.08.22	64	357	5.58-to-1	60.14
09.09.22–09.15.22	95	438	4.61-to-1	76.14
09.16.22–09.22.22	69	252	3.65-to-1	45.86
09.23.22–09.29.22	67	357	5.33-to-1	60.57
09.30.22–10.06.22	67	297	4.43-to-1	52.00
10.07.22–10.14.22	79	166	2.10-to-1	35.00
10.15.22–10.20.22	71	495	6.97-to-1	94.33[4]
11.21.22–10.27.22	104	354	3.40-to-1	65.43[5]
10.28.22–11.02.22	102	364	3.57-to-1	77.67[6]
11.03.22–11.10.22	105	441	4.20-to-1	68.25[7]
11.11.22–11.17.22	100	412	4.12-to-1	73.14
11.18.22–11.24.22	84	271	3.23-to-1	50.71
11.25.22–12.01.22	71	428	6.03-to-1	71.29
12.02.22–12.08.22	58	248	4.28-to-1	43.71
12.10.22–12.16.22	74	226	3.05-to-1	42.86
12.16.22–12.22.22	43	not reported	—	—
Reported Total (12.22.22)	4,176	17,379		4.16-to-1

Appendix II

The Russian Force Structure and Operational Plan

By Sasho Todorov, esquire[1]

Sourcing

It is important to stress that there is still a great deal that we do not know about the opening month of the war. With the conflict still raging, we are a long way away from having the detailed official histories of the war which will help confirm or deny longstanding rumors or suspected information. Any reconstruction of the chaotic opening month of the war is thus a first draft of history, based on eyewitness reports, identified wreckage, rumors and intuition. This does not mean that there is no value in attempting to piece together such a draft. In fact, if Russia's objectives and initial thinking are to be ascertained, it is critical. Yet, humility must be retained, and a first draft is just that, a work to be improved upon as more information is released over time.

The following was assembled via the collation of multiple sources of open-source intelligence. For vehicles and incidents, this included Russo-Ukrainian War Spotting,[2] a database of confirmed vehicle wreckage which includes location and unit, if confirmable and Geoconfirmed, a volunteer team which identifies the locations of images and videos.[3] Twitter was also scoured for any reports and to help add context to incidents. The unfortunately named website Russian Torturers, a searchable database of the doxed personal information of Russian soldiers published by the Ukrainian prosecutor's office, was also of assistance in locating Russian units.[4] Between these sources, and others, a decent idea of the location of almost every maneuver formation in the Russian ground forces could be identified.

In addition, when going over the formations it is important to stress that Russian formations and ranks do not align with Western ones. Russian major generals are one-stars and command brigades and divisions. Russian lieutenant generals are two-stars and command armies. Russian colonel generals are three-stars and army generals four-stars, and they command military districts. In addition, a Russian army is a substantially smaller force than a NATO army, far more akin to a division- or corps-sized formation. Many Russian armies only command two organic maneuver brigades (29th only commands one). Given that most maneuver brigades only deployed two maneuver battalions (due to the third being manned by conscripts), this means that several of the Russian armies only comprised four to six maneuver battalions. In short, when reading the terms involved, the reader should shift their expectations of the size of the force substantially downward.

The question of the actual size of the formations discussed also covers how many maneuver units a Russian brigade or division actually deployed. The general rule of thumb from before the war that Russian units would deploy two of the three maneuver battalions in a regiment appears to have held up. Russian maneuver brigades are built around a maneuver regiment, while Russian divisions are built around three, though occasionally four. A good estimation is thus two maneuver battalions per brigade, and six or eight per division.

This becomes more complicated with the Russian Airborne Forces (the VDV). Two of the four airborne divisions (98th and 106th) only contained two regiments, not three. While the Russian Airborne Forces had a higher proportion of contract soldiers than other units, the airborne regiments still seem to have been limited to deploying only two of their three maneuver battalions.

Finally, this discussion will center on the maneuver units of the Russian regular ground and air assault forces and the separatist militaries. While these composed the bulk of Russian forces, they were supplemented by units from the Russian National Guard, including SOBR (equivalent to mechanized SWAT teams), OMON (militarized riot police) and Kadryov's personal army from Chechnya.

The Overall Operational Plan

From tracking the disposition of Russian forces at the start of the war, and their initial movements, the Russian invasion in February of 2022 appears to have had three key objectives.

First, the encirclement of Kyiv from both sides of the Dnieper and its seizure, with the goal of decapitating the Ukrainian government.

Second, the encirclement of the eleven Ukrainian regular brigades in the Donbas front along the Barvinkove-Velika Novosilka/Lozova-Huilyapole line.[5]

Third, and finally, the taking of Odesa and the cutting off of Ukraine from the Black Sea.

The end results of such an operation are clear. Even if the Ukrainian government were to be able to somewhat recover and reestablish itself in western Ukraine, it would be left economically isolated and with a skeleton regular military. At that point Russia would be free to impose harsh terms, likely with substantial annexations of territory. Most importantly, there'd be no need to engage in a costly replay of the previous Ukrainian insurgent effort in western Ukraine. Instead, Russia could satisfy itself with the public trial and execution of every post-2014 Ukrainian leader it got its hands on and the integration of what were supposed to be friendly, or at least apathetic, territories.

As discussed in Chapter 5, Russia assembled either three or four primary groupings to accomplish these three objectives, each organized around a military district.

The Eastern Military District: Western Kyiv and the Ukrainian Government

Moving from north to south, the first grouping was centered around the Eastern Military District (EMD). This consisted of 35th and 36th Combined Arms Armies (CAA), as well as a corps-sized airborne grouping under the head of the Russian Airborne Forces (VDV), Colonel General Serdyukov. There is a question of whether or not the Central Military District (CMD) was a distinct grouping during the initial invasion. If it was not, then 41st CAA, which will be discussed later, was also under the EMD.[6]

This grouping was aimed both at Kyiv and screening the offensive on Kyiv from the west. If the CMD was involved at the start, then the EMD's operations would be limited to the west bank of the Dnieper. If not, then the EMD handled the north–south offensive on Kyiv from both banks of the river. From west–east, the forces were: 35th CAA, 36th CAA, the airborne grouping and potentially 41st CAA (CMD) on the east bank of the Dnieper. These forces totaled between 6 and 9 brigades (if 41st CAA is counted), a tank division (41st CAA), 3 airborne divisions and 1 airborne brigades comprising 8 airborne regiments, and a potential Spetznaz brigade.

The 35th CAA, with three brigades (38th and 64th Motorized Rifle and 69th Covering Brigades), screened the offensive on Kyiv from the far west along the line of Radcha (on the Belarussian border), Kukhari and Makariv. It arrayed primarily southwestward at the region in between the Kyiv exurbs and Malyn and protected the Russian ground lines of communication for the assault on Kyiv. Given 64th Motorized Rifle Brigade's infamous involvement in war crimes in Bucha, it may be the case that 35th CAA's unit boundary extended into the Kyiv suburbs. However, this appears to be unlikely, as most of 64th's identified vehicle losses place it on the Borodyanka-Makariv axis.

Rather, Bucha appears to have been a convenient "hunting ground" in the rear areas of the EMD's operations.

To the east of 35th CAA, 36th CAA, with two brigades, 37th Motorized Rifle and 5th Tank were tasked with encircling Kyiv along its western suburbs, from Makraiv to Stoyanka. The 35th CAA does not appear to have been tasked with the assault on Kyiv proper, with that mission instead going to the corps-sized airborne grouping.

The Question of the Airborne

To 35th CAA's east was a powerful grouping of airborne units. This included at least three confirmed divisions, 76th Air Assault, 98th Airborne and 106th Airborne, as well as 31st Guards Air Assault Brigade, which made the famous assault on Hostomel. In addition, 155th Naval Infantry Brigade also fell under command of this group when it arrived at the front. In total this amounted to 8 airborne regiments, or 16 deployed airborne battalions and 1 tank battalion, and 1 Naval Infantry brigade. In addition, men of 45th Airborne Spetznaz Brigade are also confirmed to have been in the area, though it is unclear if the entire formation was there. Its mission is easily apparent when confirmed vehicle losses are mapped. Southeast of Irpin there is a distinct line where infantry fighting vehicles rapidly shift from being nearly entirely BMD/BTR-D, the unique vehicles of the Airborne Forces, to BMPs, the chariot of the motorized rifle and tank brigades. Kyiv, and the glory of taking it, appears to have belonged to the Airborne Forces.

This grouping of airborne units was commanded by Colonel General (three-star) Serdyukov, the head of the Russian air assault forces, who would later be replaced in this position following the airborne's failure to take the city. The grouping raises several questions as to how it was organized and how it fell within the Russian command structure. Colonel General Serdyukov was of the same rank as Colonel General Chaiko, the head of the EMD, the only such case of a primus inter pares situation in the EMD grouping. In addition, Russian air assault troops form a theoretically independent chain of command within the Russian ground forces and retain a politically distinct mission. Finally, the pre-war organization of the airborne troops was not designed for such a concentrated application. Unlike the CAAs, the airborne force structure lacks organic separate artillery, long-range missile and anti-air brigades, key capabilities for a larger formation. In short, the airborne forces grouping appears to have been ad hoc and was likely dependent on the resources of the EMD. This helps to explain why such a large concentration of Russia's ostensibly best infantry could not seize, let alone push past, Irpin.

The assignment of Kyiv to the Airborne Forces aligns with a similar allocation of airborne units for the taking of the other centerpiece city, Odesa. In addition, the use of the airborne as a decapitation force had a long history within Russian and Soviet military practice. The 1979 invasion of Afghanistan similarly began with an air landing on Kabul and the decapitation of the old government. The Airborne Forces, as Russia's premier expeditionary force within the Russian-dominated Collective Security Treaty Organization (CSTO), were likely to partner with the Spetznaz and Federal Security Bureau (FSB) forces infiltrated into Kyiv to seize the city and hunt for the pre-war Ukrainian government.

The Forces Left Behind

The EMD is the district with the most units which cannot be identified in the opening weeks of the fighting. First, 18th Static Division on the disputed Sakhalin Island (near Japan) was retained in place. Second, no unit from 5th or 29th Combined Arms Army, nor 68th Army Corps or 40th Naval Infantry Brigade, appears in Ukraine proper (going by reports, confirmed losses or even just rumors) until well past the initial weeks of the war. A single tank rumored to be from 29th CAA's only maneuver unit, 36th Motorized Rifle Brigade, appears around Malyn, northwest of Kyiv, in late March. Meanwhile, 68th Army Corps' 39th Motorized Rifle Brigade and the Pacific Fleet's 40th Naval Infantry Brigade first appear in both reports and confirmed losses at the end of March, while covering the retreat of the Russian Army from Kyiv.

This leaves the question: where was 5th CAA? The 5th CAA was a powerful force, composed of two motorized rifle brigades (57th and 70th) and a motorized rifle division (127th). The 127th, in particular, is the only fully formed Russian division which cannot be placed in the initial fighting. It is confirmed that these units were transferred to Belarus. In addition, the units were in theater, as 5th CAA appears to be the primary formation committed to the Donbas when the emphasis of the war shifted there in April. The likeliest possibility is that 5th CAA was maintained as a grouping in Belarus and pointed towards NATO, to deter potential intervention across the Belarussian border. This is reinforced by the fact that Russia also retained in place the motorized rifle brigade and division stationed in Kaliningrad, and the motorized rifle brigade along the Norwegian border.

As for the Russian Airborne Forces, only one brigade was not deployed during the initial fighting, 83rd Air Assault Brigade. This unit would first see combat around Mariupol in late March.

The Central Military District: Northeastern Kyiv

More than a year on, there is an open question as to whether the CMD formed its own grouping, or whether it was part of a "Central Grouping" alongside the Western Military District (WMD). What does not help is the inconsistent language regarding the topic in the report published by RUSI which had been produced with the help of several top Ukrainian military officials.

In truth, whether it was or was not an independent grouping makes little difference for the Russian operational plan. The CMD was by far the smallest of the four groupings, and its axes of advance were mostly there to support the efforts of the EMD to its west and the WMD to its south. The CMD was composed of five to six brigades and a large tank division.

Continuing the west–east discussion of forces, the bulk of the Central Military District's forces were concentrated in 41st CAA. Composed of 35th, 55th and 74th Motorized Rifle Brigades, and 90th Guards Tank Division (a particularly large division with four regiments), 41st CAA's mission was to punch through the Ukrainian 1st Tank Brigade around Chernihiv, move down the eastern bank of the Dnieper, seize the E95 highway corridor and take northeastern Kyiv. Given that western, not eastern, Kyiv, is the center of the Ukrainian government, this mission was a supporting offensive for the primary effort of the Eastern Military District. This helps explain why 41st CAA's deputy commander was killed early in the war while in Hostomel. If the CMD grouping did not exist, then 41st CAA would have fallen under the EMD's grouping, as previously mentioned.

It was to be met in eastern Kyiv by 2nd Gds CAA, which had a 300km drive to make from the northeastern border near Kursk. It traveled down the E101 highway to near Nizhyn, but hooked south and then west to avoid the city, which remained in Ukrainian hands throughout the fighting. It instead finished by taking the H07 highway and reaching Brovary from the east. It did so with only one brigade which can be placed during the opening of the war, 21st Motorized Rifle Brigade. However, its second brigade, 15th Motorized Rifle Brigade, can be placed in the sector by mid-March and 30th Motorized Rifle Brigade also joined the force at an unspecified later date. If the CMD grouping did not initially exist, then 2nd Gds CAA likely fell within the WMD led "Central Grouping" of forces.

The Russian Forces in Tajikistan

The only units of the CMD not deployed in theater were the three motorized rifle regiments of 201st Military Base in Tajikistan. This Russian presence was particularly important given the return of the Taliban to power in Afghanistan in August 2021.

The Western Military District: the Dnieper from Kyiv to Kremenchuk and the Northern Pincer of the Donbas Front

In prewar commentary, the WMD was often presented as the premier grouping of the Russian army, as it was the one which bordered NATO. It contained the forces that would fight for the infamous "Suwalki gap" between Kaliningrad and Russia, a region that many a NATO officer is glad to never hear of again when they retire. These included 11th Army Corps centered in Kaliningrad, 6th CAA around St. Petersburg, 1st Guards Tank Army ("GTA"), the crown jewel of the Russian military, around Moscow and 20th CAA along the Ukrainian frontier. The WMD deployed 5 brigades, 1 tank regiment and 4 divisions (3 motorized rifle and 1 tank).

The 1st GTA was arrayed south of 2nd Gds CAA, along a 120km front spanning the border north and south of Sumy from Bilopillya to Velyka Pysarivka. Alleged copies of the orders for its 96th Separate Reconnaissance Brigade were captured and published by the Ukrainian Security Service (SBU). The regions specified for intensive recon within the orders align with the initial movements of 1st GTA. They indicate that 1st GTA was responsible for the southeastern quarter of Kyiv, south of Brovary, as well as the bridges across the Dnieper from Kaniv to Cherkasy. While the front would reach close to Kremenchuk, that city appears to have been the responsibility of 6th CAA.

The 1st GTA contained some of the most prestigious units of the Russian ground forces, 2nd Guards Motorized Rifle Division, 4th Guards Tank Division and Moscow's own 27th Guards Motorized Rifle Brigade, the Kremlin's traditional coup-proofing force. These units were first in line to receive the newest equipment, with 2nd Guards Motorized Rifle Division's 1st Tank Regiment being supposedly the intended first recipient of T-14 Armatas. It also had 47th Tank Division, then still being formed, meaning that only 26th Tank Regiment was deployed. This powerful concentration was aligned against what was supposed to be the weakest portion of the Ukrainian line, with only Territorial Defense Forces (TDF) units in its way.

To the south of 1st GTA was 6th CAA, which was aligned against Kharkiv. It consisted of its organic two maneuver brigades, 25th and 138th Motorized Rifle brigades, and two of the three brigades of the Northern Fleet and Arctic Command around Murmansk, 200th Arctic Motorized Rifle and 61st Naval Infantry brigades. These four brigades were to encircle and take Kharkiv and then push south down the M03 towards Kremenchuk.

The most concentrated force in the WMD belonged to 20th CAA. The 20th CAA was the formation directly responsible for the Ukrainian frontier during peacetime. While in early reporting the CAA was claimed to be responsible for Northern Luhansk and Kharkiv Oblast southeast of Kharkiv, these reports appear to be faulty. Rather, the two motorized rifle divisions of 20th CAA, 3rd and 144th, were instead packed into a corridor east of Kharkiv and were aimed at breaching the Siversky Donetsk River at Izyum and Balakliia. This was to form the northern pincer for the encirclement of the eleven Ukrainian regular brigades aligned along the Donbas front. Ukrainian command believes, based on its intelligence, that the northern prong was to ideally pass through Barvinkove, closer to the Donbas front, or Lozova, to the east. It would meet 58th CAA coming up from the north along the Dnieper and complete the destruction of most of Ukraine's standing army.

The 11th Army Corps in Kaliningrad

Russia did not leave its frontier with NATO in the north defenseless. The WMD left behind the forces of 11th Army Corps (the Baltic Fleet) centered in Kaliningrad, 79th Motorized Rifle Brigade and the still forming 7th Motorized Rifle Division. However, 336th Naval Infantry Brigade, and its landing ships, were transferred to the Black Sea. In addition, 80th Arctic Motorized Rifle Brigade of the Arctic command remained in place along the border with Norway.

The Southern Military District: The Southern Pincer of the Donbas Front and Odesa

While prewar coverage of the Russian Army centered on the WMD, due to it facing NATO, the SMD was the more experienced command and was given the most resources. It was the only formation to approximate a NATO army, or even army group in size. In total the SMD had five maneuver brigades, three motorized rifle divisions, an airborne brigade and a division, and the combined forces of the separatist militaries, the Donetsk People's Republic's 1st Army Corps and the Lugansk People's Republic's 2nd Army Corps. This concentration was necessary due to it being the only military district with two axes of advance, both in opposite directions.

East of the Dnieper: the Fixing and Destruction of the Ukrainian Forces in the Donbas Front

The SMD's objectives are cleanly divided in two by the Dnieper River. To the east, 8th and 58th CAA's sought to fix the eleven regular Ukrainian brigades deployed to the Donbas front with the separatist corps, while encircling them with 58th CAA.[7]

The 8th CAA was seemingly paradoxically both one of the largest and smallest Russian forces deployed during the invasion. It was only composed of one motorized rifle division, 150th. However, it also exercised operational control of the nearly 40,000 men of the DPR and LPR militaries. The DPR's forces have been estimated by the Rondeli Foundation at 4 mechanized brigades, 2 mechanized regiments and an additional brigade's worth of independent maneuver units. The LPR's forces have been estimated by the Foundation at 3 mechanized brigades and 1 brigade's worth of independent units, representing 19 maneuver battalions. The prewar total of 1st and 2nd Army Corps is thus in the region of 9 brigades and 2 separate regiments, encompassing up to 40 maneuver battalions. The mission of 8th CAA was simple. It fixed the 11 Ukrainian brigades in the Donbas front while moving against Volnovakha and Mariupol from the east with 150th Motorized Rifle Division and DPR units.

There it would be met by 58th CAA. The 58th was one of the larger Russian formations, being composed of 2 motorized rifle divisions, 19th and 42nd, as well as 2 mechanized brigades, 136th Motorized Rifle and 810th Naval Infantry. It encircled Mariupol from the west, while sending 19th Motorized Rifle Division and 136th Motorized Rifle Brigade northwards in an axis from the Dnieper to near Volnovakha. These forces were to cut the highways from the Dnieper bridges at Zaporizhzhia and Dnipro to the Donbas front and would meet 20th CAA as it came southward, completing the encirclement of the Donbas front.

This eastern SMD grouping also appears to have contained the Caspian Sea Flotilla's 177th Naval Infantry Regiment, though it is unclear if the unit was deployed from the start or sent to Mariupol out of the SMD's reserve.

West of the Dnieper: Odesa and the Economic Blockade of Ukraine

While SMD's 8th and 58th CAAs sought the destruction of the Ukrainian regular army in combination with the WMD's 20th CAA, the SMD's 49th CAA sought the destruction of Ukraine's economy. This is because 70% of Ukraine's exports and imports go by the Black Sea, especially its critical grain exports, and 75% of this flow (i.e., more than 50% of the total) is routed through the ports around Odesa. The mission of 49th CAA was to seize Odesa and the entirety of the Ukrainian Black Sea coast west of the Dnieper River delta.

To do so it was allocated three mechanized brigades, its organic 34th and 205th Motorized Rifle Brigades and 126th Coastal Defense Brigade, as well as the understrength 20th Motorized Rifle Division (two regiments and a tank battalion, formerly of 8th CAA). It was further reinforced by 7th Mountain Air Assault Division and 11th Guards Air Assault Brigade, a five-regiment (ten battalion) airborne grouping. The importance of Odesa can be gleaned from the fact that the Russian Airborne Forces was only launched at two objectives, both of them cities: Odesa and Kyiv. As was discussed in Chapter 5, the selection of those two critical cities for airborne commitment may also have been an internal acceptance of the low quantity of leg infantry dismounts in the standard Russian motorized rifle units.

The 49th CAA was also reinforced by the Baltic Fleet's 336th Naval Infantry Brigade, which had been brought down with its landing ships from Kaliningrad. This force initially remained at sea, with the goal of landing west of Mykolaiv to help maintain the operational tempo by seizing junctions along the coastal highway and unhinging the Ukrainian defensive line. However, after some tentative landings failed, it was never committed from sea and instead was deployed as a regular mechanized unit later on.

Armenia and Georgia

Russia's formerly hegemonic position in the Caucasus was based on two pillars: its occupation of Abkhazia and South Ossetia post-2008, and the two brigades of 102nd Military Base stationed in Armenia to deter Azerbaijan. In total these forces comprised roughly four brigade equivalents (two in Georgia and two regular motorized rifle brigades in Armenia).

Overall Assessment of Russian Force Distribution

On the night of 23 February, Russia had committed the entirety of its regular ground forces to one of seven general tasks:

1. The offensive on Kyiv. This covers the EMD and CMD, as well as 1st GTA of the WMD and the airborne grouping under Serdyukov. A total of 5 armies, containing 12–13 maneuver brigades, 3 divisions (2 reinforced) and the Airborne Forces grouping of 3 airborne divisions and 1 airborne brigade. This totaled 30–32 BTGs, 16 airborne battalions and 1 tank battalion.

2. The destruction of the Ukrainian regular army in the Donbas front. This comprised 6th and 20th CAAs of the WMD, 8th and 58th CAAs of the SMD and the 2 corps of the separatist militaries. A total of 17 brigades or brigade equivalents (11 separatist) and 5 divisions. Unlike the Russian military, the separatist forces were completely mobilized, and conscripts were liable for service at the front. They likely thus had their full complement of 4 maneuver battalions each. The force

dedicated to the destruction of the Ukrainian regular army thus likely totaled 42 BTGs and up to 40 separatist maneuver battalions.

3. The conquest of Ukraine's Black Sea coastline west of the Dnieper River. Only a single CAA (49th) was dedicated to this task, though it was composed of 4 brigades, 1 understrength division and a Russian Airborne Forces grouping of 1 division and 1 brigade. This totaled 12 BTGs, 1 tank battalion and 10 airborne battalions.

4. A general operational reserve deployed either in Belarus or near the Russian border with Ukraine. This consisted of 5th and 29th CAAs, 68th Army Corps, 40th Naval Infantry Brigade and 83rd Air Assault Brigade. This reserve totaled 5 brigades, 1 division and an airborne brigade, or 16 BTGs and 2 airborne battalions.

5. Maintaining a minimal posture to deter NATO and Japan. This includes 80th Arctic Mechanized Rifle Brigade on the border with Norway, 11th Army Corps in Kaliningrad and 18th Static Division on Sakhalin. A total of 1 brigade and 2 divisions, containing 28 maneuver battalions due to conscripts remaining on station in these units. In addition, it is likely that a significant portion of the deployed operational reserve, especially 5th CAA, served the same purpose by being stationed in Belarus near the frontier with Poland.

6. Maintaining the Russian sphere of influence in the CSTO. Between 4th Military Base in Abkhazia, 7th in Ossetia, 102nd in Armenia and 201st in Tajikistan, the force, which included conscripts, comprised 7 independent maneuver battalions, 3 regiments and 2 motorized rifle brigades, or 27 maneuver battalions.

7. The conscript-manned maneuver battalions left behind in garrison, likely totaling approximately 80 battalions. However, this force was more illusory than real, as it could only be activated should Russia declare war, and the bulk of their supporting resources had been stripped and sent to supplement the units deployed to Ukraine.

To summarize, on the night of 23 February, 102 BTGs, 26 airborne battalions and up to 40 separatist battalions were poised to invade Ukrainian territory. In immediate reserve sat another 16 BTGs and 2 airborne battalions. Already deployed into Ukraine were substantial infiltration teams of the Spetznaz, tasked with assassinating members of the Ukrainian government. Behind them were more Spetznaz teams, tasked with grabbing Ukrainian officials for public trial and execution, and the riot police and swat teams of the Rosgvardia for the suppression of local resistance. The question was whether the prewar assumption of both of Russia and the West, that the Ukrainian populace wouldn't fight, would be proven correct.

Appendix III

Mapping the War in Ukraine from February to Mid-March

By Sasho Todorov, esquire

Sourcing and Methodology

These maps were assembled using the same sources and methodology as Appendix II, which discussed the Russian organizational chart and operational plan. The underlying software used was the U.S. Army's released web client for military mapping, map.army.

Much as with Appendix II, the astute reader will notice at times fairly significant differences from this section and the mainline text of the book. Compared with the mainline text, these maps, much like Appendix II, have significantly greater elements of supposition and intuition, as well as a looser bounds regarding what information is considered confirmed or debunked. If the mainline text is an analysis of the information that we solidly know, the reader is advised to treat Appendices II and III as the best attempt to illustrate information that is more likely than not. Even as we were preparing this (January 2023), significant amounts of previously unknown information have been released. Hopefully, over time, even more information comes. In short, do not treat these appendices as gospel, merely a best effort at writing a first draft of history.

Map 1: The Russian Operational Plan (Chapter 5 and Appendix II)

This map is fairly self-explanatory, with an individual arrow having been given to each of the primary axes of advance. It does bring into stark relief the heavy Russian investment in the destruction of the Ukrainian brigades along the Donbas front.

It also reveals why the question of whether the Central Military District was an independent grouping is a bit irrelevant (though still interesting). Both of the CMD's thrusts could just as easily have belonged to another military district.

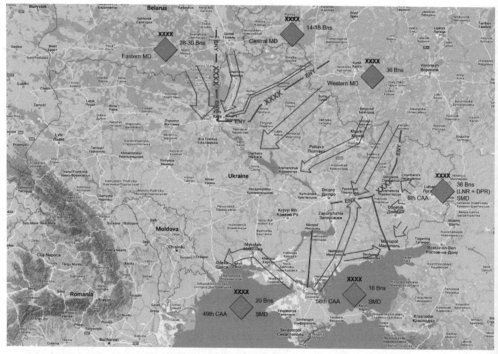

Map 1. The Russian operational plan (Chapter 5 and Appendix II).

Of note for subsequent maps is that the formation level for Russian armies will differ due to their wide variation in size (from 2 to 36 maneuver battalions). Some are labeled as Division equivalents (XX), most as Corps equivalents (XXX), and those of the SMD are labeled as full armies (XXXX) due to their size and independent axes of advance.

Map 2: The Movements of the Uncommitted Ukrainian Brigades (Chapter 4)

This map charts the movement of the uncommitted Ukrainian brigades at the start of the fighting. Of note, as will be discussed later, Ukraine did not pull any of the brigades already along the Donbas front for other uses. Instead, it relied on uncommitted units still in their cantonments. Keep in particular mind the odyssey of 128th Mountain Brigade from its garrison near the Hungarian border to south of the Dnieper bend.

An astute reader will notice in subsequent maps that Ukrainian light infantry units have no size signifier. Those symbols represent the local Territorial Defense Forces (TDF). As there is no conclusive information as to the size of particular TDF groupings, the reader is advised to instead treat them as particularly noteworthy hubs of Ukrainian TDF mobilization.

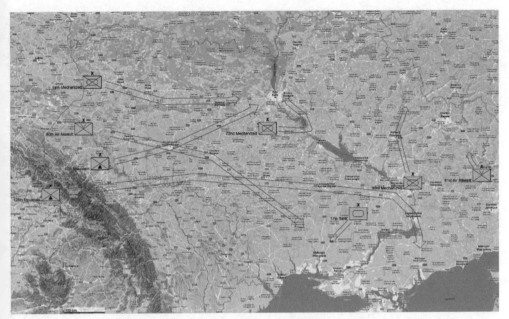

Map 2. The movements of the uncommitted Ukrainian brigades (Chapter 4).

Map 3: The General Operations Around Kyiv (Chapters 6, 7, 10, 18, 19)

This map highlights the general operations with the Eastern Military Districts sector, with the Battle for Kyiv receiving special attention in the next map. What is immediately apparent is the constrained nature of Russian movement. The EMD was forced to move both its units and logistics along only two north–south highways from the Belarussian border, both of which cross the Teteriv River at Ivankiv. This constrained road space is what produced the infamous traffic jam towards Kyiv, which limited the ability of the Russians to move up units and supplies in early March.

Due to this, 35th Combined Arms Army would attempt to seize another bridge over the river (and push Ukrainian artillery out of range) by sending 69th Covering Brigade, a mechanized infantry unit, southwest towards Malyn. This effort was stopped by local Territorial Defense Forces (TDF) supplemented by units from 10th Mountain Assault Brigade.

The forests along the northwestern flank of the EMD's drive would see lively artillery action by both sides, with the Ukrainians bringing up longer ranged assets by mid-March to begin hitting Russian logistical hubs along the highway. In addition, Ukrainian Special Forces used the forests and the dispersed nature of the Russian defensive lines to engage in hit and run attacks on Russian convoys.

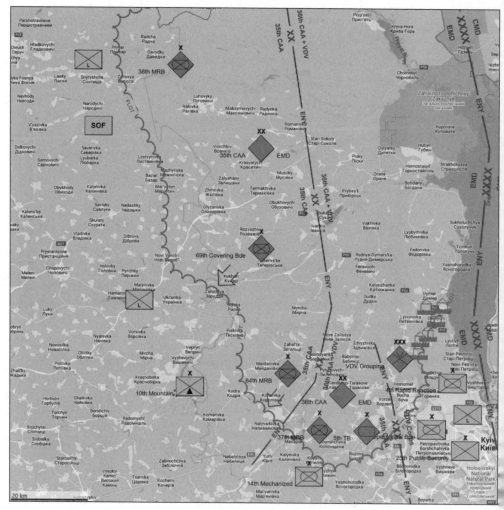

Map 3. The general operations around Kyiv (Chapters 6, 7, 10, 18, 19).

Map 4: The Battle for Kyiv (Chapters 6, 7, 10, 18, 19)

Kyiv was a constantly evolving battle over the first two weeks of the fighting, as both sides brought in additional forces as quickly as they could. The 31st Air Assault Brigade arrived via helicopter at Hostomel on the first day of the fighting, while 76th Air Assault Division and 5th Guards Tank Brigade would link up with it soon after. It was a regiment from 76th which performed the disastrous attempted assault into Irpin on 27 February. The small 98th Airborne Division would be the primary Russian formation fighting for Moshchun (to the northeast of Irpin), with 155th Naval Infantry Brigade being deployed to reinforce that effort once it arrived in the region. Meanwhile, 106th Airborne

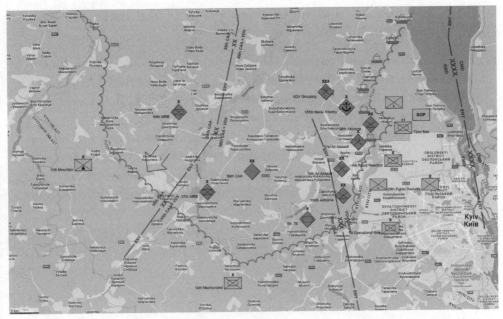

Map 4. The battle for Kyiv (Chapters 6, 7, 10, 18, 19).

Division filled the gap forming between 5th Guards Tank Brigade and 76th Air Assault Division.

On the Ukrainian side, 14th Mechanized Brigade was under substantial pressure as it tried to prevent Kyiv from being cut off from the west. Makariv in particular formed a hotspot in the fighting for the entirety of the battle. By early March, this burden was substantially lightened thanks to the arrival of 10th Mountain Assault Brigade, who also had elements around Malyn.

Yet, it was the Kyiv Territorial Defense and the Irpin sluice gates which may have been the two greatest Ukrainian assets. When the fighting began Ukraine only had two mechanized brigades around Kyiv: 1st Operational Brigade and 4th Rapid Reaction Brigade. The TDF greatly helped compensate for the superiority in Russian regular forces. Moshchun was a particularly shining example of the combined Ukrainian effort. It was held by the TDF, including members of the International Legion, a battalion from 72nd Mechanized Brigade (the rest of the brigade was on the eastern side of the city) and Ukrainian Special Forces.

Map 5: Chernihiv and the Eastern Flank of the Battle for Kyiv (Chapters 9, 10, 15, 19)

It is difficult to conclusively map a battle as fluid as Chernihiv. The Ukrainian 58th Motorized and 1st Tank Brigades fought hard to keep the Chernihiv and Nizhyn pockets linked, with substantial help from the TDF. To the south, the TDF also defended the key road hub of Priluky.

Russian efforts to push on east of Kyiv were greatly constrained by having to squeeze their logistics through the two small roads in between Nizhyn and Priluky. This forced them to divert half of 90th Tank Division to try and help support the closing of the Chernihiv-Nizhyn pocket, to no avail. This reduction

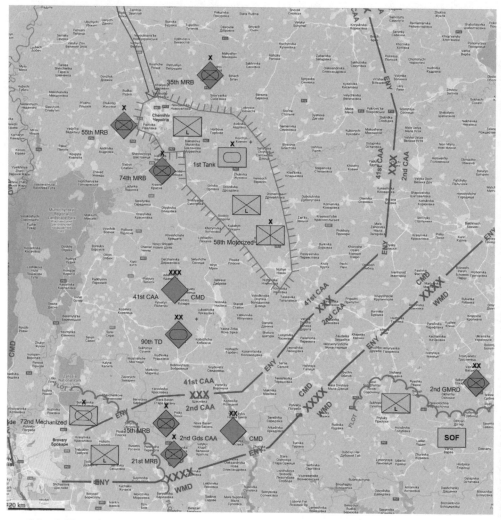

Map 5. Chernihiv and the Eastern flank of the battle for Kyiv (Chapters 9, 10, 15, 19).

in pressure for the push on eastern Kyiv, including Brovary, permitted the Ukrainians to shift one of 72nd Mechanized Brigade's battalions to the fight for Moshchun.

One puzzling element of the battle is the lack of support given by 2nd CAA to assisting 2nd Guards Motor Rifle Division after it was halted east of Priluky.

Map 6: The Operations around Sumy (Chapters 6, 9, 18, 19)

While the TDF may have played a critical role in supplementing Ukrainian forces around Kyiv and Chernihiv, the Priluky-Sumy-Okhtyrka arc was the site of by far its most impressive work. The 1st Guards Tank Army, the pride of the Russian ground forces, found itself halted and badly attritted almost solely by Territorial Defense units, with assistance from Ukrainian Special Forces. The only Ukrainian regular troops in the sector for most of the initial weeks of the war were elements from 93rd Mechanized Brigade near Okhtyrka, though that brigade fully concentrated in the region once Kharkiv had been stabilized.

The reasons for this defeat are apparent from the way 1st Guards Tank Army, especially 2nd Guards Motorized Rifle Division, plunged into Ukraine without consolidating its lines of communication. What did not help in this regard was the overly tank-heavy nature of the force. The 2nd Guards Motorized Rifle Division would find itself halted on 27 February at

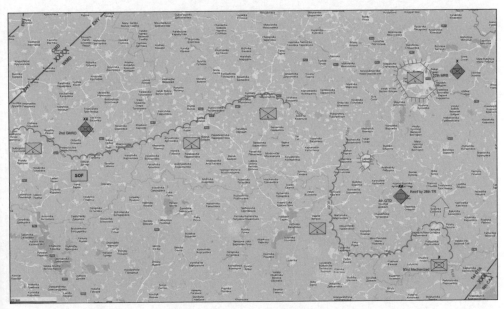

Map 6. The operations around Sumy (Chapters 6, 9, 18, 19).

Perevolochna, east of Priluky, with significant vehicle losses. It would go no further for the rest of the battle, and, puzzlingly, 2nd Guards Combined Arms Army did little to assist it from the north. A potential note of the difficulties in coordination between different military districts.

By 15 March, 1st Guards Tank Army had lost 318 vehicles, including 132 tanks and 67 IFVs. Within a week, well before the general planned Russian withdrawal, the badly attritted 4th Guards Tank Division would be being steadily rolled back by the now concentrated 93rd Mechanized Brigade, including a costly defeat at Trostianets. Meanwhile, 27th Guards Motorized Rifle Brigade, the traditional bodyguard unit of the Kremlin, would find itself fruitlessly besieging Sumy until the April retreat. The siege lines were apparently not too tight as the Sumy TDF frequently sallied out to hit Russian logistical convoys as they skirted around the city.

Map 7: Kharkiv and the Siversky Donetsk River (Chapters 6, 12)

The sector around Kharkiv proper was the only location where the Ukrainians created an overmatch in regular mechanized units. While elements of 93rd

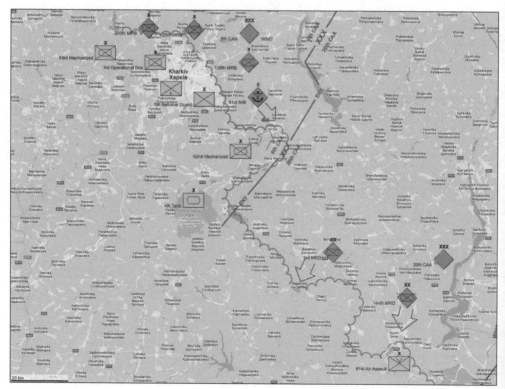

Map 7. Kharkiv and the Siversky Donetsk River (Chapters 6, 12).

Mechanized Brigade (the most northwestern Ukrainian brigade) may have been around Oktyrkha, the bulk of the brigade began the war by being deployed to Kharkiv. There it inflicted a sharp blow on the Russian 200th Motor Rifle Brigade around Derhaci, which opened the door for 93rd to be shifted fully to Okhtyrka in early to mid-March.

Chuhuiv would be the site of particularly fierce fighting, with the Russian 61st Naval Infantry Brigade losing a battalion commander in one of 92nd Mechanized Brigade's counterattacks. The Kharkiv TDF would make a strong showing as well, with it being among the first of the TDF units to coalesce into proper units, as opposed to self-mobilized light infantry groupings.

However, the fight around Kharkiv was primarily a fight for the Siversky Donetsk River. To the southeast of the city was the breakthrough corridor for the northern pincer of the Russian attempted envelopment of the Donbas. The two motor rifle divisions of 20th Combined Arms Army were a powerful concentrated force. Despite obtaining bridgeheads at Husarivka and Izyum, their advance would be contained by 4th Tank and 81st Air Assault brigades. Only once it stalled out did 20th CAA begin to assist 6th CAA, mostly around Chuhuiv.

Map 8: The Donbas and Zaporizhzhia Front (Chapters 6, 13, 14)

For the purposes of decluttering, the units defending Mariupol are depicted as a division-sized formation. These included the Azov Regiment, 36th Marine Brigade and the Mariupol TDF.

As noted in Map 2, the Ukrainians did not pull any of the brigades committed to the Donbas front for service elsewhere. The sheer scale of the commitment is easily apparent. Eleven regular brigades, three of them air assault brigades, and the Azov Regiment in Mariupol. To destroy this force, the Russians aimed to fix it with 8th CAA, while enveloping it from the north with 20th CAA and from the south with 58th CAA coming up from Crimea.

While 20th CAA's offensive may have been contained at the Siversky Donetsk River, 58th CAA had open space to operate between the Dnieper and Volnovkha (held by 56th Motorized Brigade). It was only the arrival of 128th Mountain Assault Brigade, rushed from the Hungarian border to Melitopol, which prevented 19th Motor Rifle Division from cutting the supply lines of the Donbas forces where they crossed the Dnieper River. By doing so, 128th Brigade may well have been the single most impactful Ukrainian unit of the early war.

Yet, this wasn't enough to prevent 58th CAA from linking up with 8th CAA around Mariupol. In addition, the road hub of Volnovakha would be

Map 8. The Donbas and Zaporizhzhia front (Chapters 6, 13, 14).

lost, with the southeastern apex of the Ukrainian Donbas front being under extremely heavy pressure.

Map 9: The Battle for Mykolaiv (Chapters 6, 8, 14, 16, 17)

Mykolaiv may be the most dynamic of the battles that occurred in February and March. Remarkably, the Ukrainian 59th Motorized Brigade was able to remain intact as a force, despite having been overrun at the exit from the Crimean isthmus by 49th and 58th CAAs (see the blue line for its retreat path).

The 59th Brigade would first seek to establish a position at Kherson but was outflanked by the Russians via the bridge over the Dnieper at Nova Khakova. The seizure of the bridge was accomplished by the Russian 11th Air Assault Brigade, in one of the more impressive Russian actions of the war. The 11th Brigade's commander, Colonel Denis Shishov, would be wounded while personally leading the operation. He would later be promoted to command of 76th Air Assault Division. Meanwhile, 59th Motorized Brigade managed to join 35th Marine Brigade and TDF forces in Mykolaiv, where they successfully defended the city.

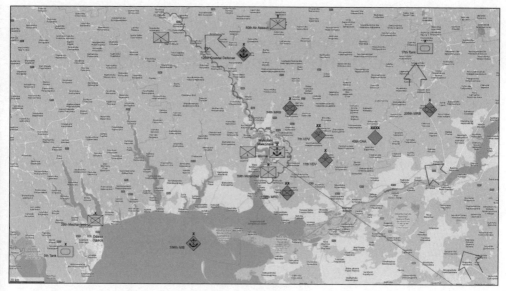

Map 9. The battle for Mykolaiv (Chapters 6, 8, 14, 16, 17).

While too late to prevent the seizure of the Nova Khakova bridge, elements from both the Ukrainian 17th Tank and 80th Air Assault brigades had already arrived to help stabilize the situation by 25 February. They would form the Ukrainian southern flank and would contain Russian attempts to push northwards. Elements of 80th Brigade would help the Voznesensk TDF stop 126th Coastal Infantry Brigade's attempt to outflank Mykolaiv by seizing the bridge over the Bug River there. The 205th Motor Rifle Brigade's push along the Dnieper occurred later in March but is included to help the reader fully visualize the fighting.

The 336th Naval Infantry Brigade remained at sea for much of the fighting, which forced the Ukrainians to keep 28th Mechanized Brigade in Odesa to face the threat. The Ukrainian 5th Tank Brigade was also near Odesa but was at only a fraction of its paper strength during this time period.

Appendix IV

Definitions and Conventions

Russian place names are used for all areas of the Russian Empire and the Soviet Union up through 1991. From 1992 and on, Ukrainian place names are used for Ukrainian cities. Starting in 2014, Russian place names are used for the areas controlled by the Lugansk and Donetsk People's Republics and for all the areas of Crimea and Sevastopol. Below is a list of the cities and areas using both their Russian and Ukrainian place names.

Russian	Ukrainian
Kiev	Kyiv
Kharkov	Kharkiv
Lvov	Lviv
Odessa	Odesa
Chernigov	Chernihiv
Sumy	Sumy
Konotop	Konotop
Lugansk	Luhansk
Donetsk	Donetsk
Mariupol	Mariupol
Berdyansk	Berdiansk
Melitopol	Melitopol
Kherson	Kherson
Mykolaiv	Mykolaiv
Sevastopol	Sevastopol
Crimea	Crimea

Definitions

AFV – Armored Fighting Vehicle (including tanks, IFVs and APCs)
APC – Armored Personnel Carrier
CAA – Combined Arms Army
CMD – Central Military District
EMD – Eastern Military District
GTA – Guards Tank Army

IFV – Infantry Fighting Vehicle
Oblast – a province
OMON – Special Purpose Mobile Unit, a Russian special police unit
Raion – a county, a subdivision of a province
SMD – Southern Military District
SORB – Special Rapid Response Unit, a Russian special police unit
TDF – Territorial Defense Force
VDV – Vozdushnodesantnye voyska Rossii or the Russian Airborne
WMD – Western Military District

Conventions

Villages – settled areas with a population of less than 10,000. Usually, their population is 3,000 or less.

Towns – settled areas with a population of greater than 10,000 or was greater than 10,000 in the last two decades. Usually, their population is in the 10,000–40,000 range.

Cities – any urban area with a population of greater than 100,000.

Notes

Dedication

1. Conversations with Nicholas Krawciw, around 2005–10.
2. A picture of the aftermath of the explosion can be seen in my in my book, Christopher A. Lawrence, *America's Modern Wars: Understanding Iraq, Afghanistan and Vietnam* (Casemate Publishers, Philadelphia & Oxford, 2015), after p. 192.
3. Also see 1. "TDI Profile: Nicholas Krawciw" by Susan Rich, *International TNDM Newsletter*, Volume 2, Number 4, December 1998, p. 28, 2. "Interview: Col. Nicholas Krawciw, newly nominated brigadier general" by Ika Koznarska Casnova, *Ukrainian Weekly*, Sunday, 18 December 1983, p. 10, 3. Wikipedia, "Nicholas Krawciw," 4. Tom Carhart, *West Point Warriors: Profiles of Duty, Honor, and Country in Battle* (Warner Books, New York, 2002), pp. 157–88. Some of this account was directly relayed to the author during the twenty years he worked for him.

Chapter 1

1. The term "New Russia" encompasses the areas of the Donbas (Lugansk and Donetsk, the areas of Kharkov, Crimea, the areas north of Crimea (Kherson and Zaporizhzhia) and Odessa and even more territory. It was actually the name of a governorate (province) from 1764–83 and from 1796–1802 that encompassed these areas and more.
2. See the 2018 survey by the Razumkov Centre.
3. Five marshals were created on 20 November 1935, but three were purged and executed in 1937–9.
4. The others being the Second World War aces Ivan Kozhedub and Alexander Pokryshkin. legendary Soviet Marshal Georgy Zhukov (four times) and the Soviet Union leader Leonid Brezhnev (four times), who probably did not deserve a single one of those awards.
5. In 2009 Putin is quoted as saying, "'You certainly should read' Anton Denikin's diary, specifically the part about 'Great and little Russia, Ukraine. He says nobody should be allowed to interfere between us. This is only Russia's right.'" See *Kyiv Post*, 24 May 2009 at Putin: 'You certainly should read' Anton Denikin's diary; specifically the part about 'Great and little Russia, Ukraine. He says nobody should be allowed to interfere between us. This is only Russia's – May. 24, 2009 | KyivPost.
6. According to Richard Pipes, a total of 1,236 violent attacks on Jews had been recorded between 1918 and 1921 in Ukraine. Of those, 493 were carried out by the soldiers of the Ukrainian People's Republic, which was led by Symon Peluyura; 307 of the attacks were conducted by independent Ukrainian warlords, which would include Nester Makhno; 213 were conducted by General Anton Denikin's White Army; 106 were conducted by the Red Army; and 32 by the Polish Army. See Richard Pipes, *A Concise History of the Russian Revolution* (Vintage Books, New York, 1996), p. 262.

   These claims of Petlyura's responsibility were also a major part of the trail of Sholom Schwartzbard, who assassinated Symon Pelyrya in France on 25 May 1926. In the 1919–20 pogroms in Ukraine, he lost all fifteen members of his family. Even though he confessed to the murder, he was acquitted by the French jury after 35 minutes of deliberation because of the pogroms.

My great-aunt by marriage, Polyana, was a girl of around 9 in Radomyshl, Ukraine during this time. We visited the town in summer of 1996. It had significant Jewish settlement at the turn of the last century with a population of 7,503 Jews in 1897, who made up two-thirds of the town (see History of Radomyshl (archive.org) on the Radomyshl Ukraine website maintained by Eli Kislyuk). We then discussed this with her and her older brother in Moscow. According to her, Nestor Makhno's troops were collecting food and goods from them and other houses in the neighborhood. Some neighbors across the street were killed because they argued with them. They then moved during the Civil War to Kiev, which are the time was under control of Denikin. She was stopped in the street by some of his soldiers and asked to pronounce some Ukrainian words that Ukrainian Jews often pronounced with a Yiddish accent. She was able to pronounce them in perfect Ukrainian, even though Jewish, and was allowed to continue on her way. Aunt Polya later moved to Moscow, became an engineer and served with the Soviet Army in the Battle of Stalingrad.

7. There was a force of up to 3,000 gathered in the summer of 1941 by Ukrainian nationalist partisan leader Taras Bulba-Borovets to assist the German Army, which eventually became the Ukrainian National Revolutionary Army. During the war 250,000 Ukrainians joined the Nationalist Military Detachments (VVN), the Brotherhoods of Ukrainian Nationalists (DUN), the SS Division Galicia, the Ukrainian Liberation Army (UVV) and the Ukrainian National Army (UNA). There were many Ukrainians who served as volunteers in the German Army, including as Hilfswilliger (Hiwis), effectively auxiliary volunteers. It is claimed that either 53,000 or 80,000 Ukrainians served the SS Division Galicia, specifically organized to be manned by Ukrainian volunteers. In the initial call-up in the summer of 1943, 42,000 men were called up, only 27,000 were fit for military service and only 13,000 were enlisted.

Hundreds of thousands of Ukrainians and Russians were serving at Hiwis by mid-1943. There were also tens of thousands of Russians who fought for the German Army during the Second World War, many with the German Army as Hiwis, also in the Kaminsky Brigade, and 40,000 or more with the Russian Liberation Army, also called the Vlasov Army. One division was fully raised and two more partly raised. It is claimed that 113 "Eastern" battalions were raised. Other formations raised, primarily from Russian "White" emigres, include the Russian Corps of over 10,000 and the XV SS Cossack Cavalry Corps of over 20,000.

8. This loss estimate is from a range of sources that added up to over 30,000 killed. Source: Dupuy Insurgency Spread Sheet (DISS), "2. Ukrainian Independence Movement (1944–1954)," unpublished. The majority of casualties are recorded from 1944–8, although fighting continued through 1953. Wikipedia, "Ukrainian Insurgent Army" gives two sets of figures for Soviet losses: 8,788 dead (which is clearly low) and 14,600 dead and missing for period covering only late 1944–early 1945.

9. Dmitri Volkogonov, *Stalin: Triumph and Tragedy* (Prima Publishing, Rocklin, CA, 1992), page 531. The full quote is, "On 12 April 1946, Interior Minister Kruglov sent a long account of events during March. It mentioned that in the western regions of the Ukraine 8,360 partisans had been either killed or captured, along with eight mortars, twenty machine-guns, 712 sub-machine-guns, 2,002 rifles, 600 pistols, 1,766 grenades, four printing presses and thirty-three typewriters. Also captured were a number of local leaders of the Ukrainian Nationalist Formation, while some 200 troops of the Interior and Security Ministries, as well as of the Red Army, had been killed."

10. The DISS records 95,552 insurgents killed (versus 32,451 Soviet losses and 1,597 Polish losses). Wikipedia reports 153,000 killed.

11. It has been translated into English by *RT* (the former Russia Today TV network) at https://www.youtube.com/watch?v=GjMnTo85S4A.

Chapter 2

1. The Act of Declaration of Independence of Ukraine was adopted by the Supreme Soviet of the Ukrainian SSR on 24 August 1991, the Independence referendum was approved by the voters on 1 December 1991, the meeting of Yeltsin, Kravchuk and Shushkevich that declared the Soviet Union dissolved was held on 8 December, the head of the Soviet Union, Mikhail Gorbachev, resigned on 25 December and the Supreme Soviet of the Soviet Union voted to dissolve the Soviet Union the following day.

2. A copy of the memorandum can be found here, Budapest Memorandums on Security Assurances, 1994 – Council on Foreign Relations (archive.org).

3. In the case of Albania and Croatia, they were invited to join NATO in April 2008, their accession protocols were signed in July 2008 and their accession into NATO was on 1 April 2009, which was particularly quick in that it only took a little less than twelve months. It is possible in 2008 that Ukraine's accession could have occurred on the same schedule, but this is doubtful considering the other political issues and challenges in both Ukraine and in some of the twenty-six NATO member nations.

   In recent time we have seen Czechia, Hungary and Poland invited to begin accession talks in July 1997 and on 12 March 1999 (about twenty months later) these former Warsaw Pact nations became members of NATO. Bulgaria, Estonia, Latvia, Lithuania, Romania, Slovakia and Slovenia were invited to begin accession talks in November 2002. On 29 March 2004 (about sixteen months later) they became members of NATO. Montenegro was invited to join NATO on 2 December 2015, they signed their accession protocol in May 2016 and became a member of the alliance on 5 June 2017 (about eighteen months later). North Macedonia was invited to join NATO in July 2018, the accession protocol was signed in February 2019 and they became a member of the alliance on 27 March 2020 (about twenty months later). In July 2022 NATO invited Finland and Sweden to join the alliance. The ratification process for these two countries is still in progress at the time of writing (December 2022), with Hungary and Turkey still not having approved.

4. The exchange rates at the time were 5-to-1 to a UAH, giving the Ukrainians a defense budget of 2.12 billion in US dollars. In 2012 the exchange rate was 8-to-1 giving the Ukrainians a defense budget of 2.05 billion in US dollars. The exchange rates dropped in 2013 and 2014 to 8.1 and 11.0 respectively, further reducing the buying power of the Ukrainian defense budget.

5. See Reuters, "Ukraine Leaders seeks cash at Kremlin to fed off crisis," dated 17 December 2013 at Ukraine leader seeks cash at Kremlin to fend off crisis (cnbc.com).

6. See *The Guardian*, "Ukraine's bloody crackdown leads to call for sanctions," dated 1 December 2013 at Ukraine's bloody crackdown leads to call for sanctions | Ukraine | The Guardian.

7. This narrative is from an interview that Putin gave in 2015. See "Putin describes secret operations to seize Crimea," 8 March 2015 at AFP, Putin describes secret operation to seize Crimea (yahoo.com).

8. *TCH Ukraine*, 13.12.16, "Poltorak put ground troops as an example of reforms in Ukraine" at Poltorak put ground troops as an example of reforms in Ukraine - Ukraine - tsn.ua.

9. For example, the poisoning in 2020 of Alexi Navalny using the nerve agent Novichok and then his arrest in 2021, the use of Novichok nerve agent in 2018 to attack two Russian citizens in London and kill one UK citizen, the assassination of former Deputy Prime Minister Boris Nemtsov in 2015 near the Kremlin, the use of radioactive Polonium-210 to kill a Russian dissident in the UK in 2006, and gunning down of investigative reporter Anna Politkovskaya in 2006, and many others.

10. See BBC News, "Ukraine soldiers killed in renewed Sloviansk fighting," 5 May 2014 at Ukraine soldiers killed in renewed Sloviansk fighting - BBC News.

11. BBC News, Ukraine, "Near Volnovakha killed 16 soldiers – MOH," 22 May 2014 at 16 soldiers killed near Volnovakha - MoH - BBC News Ukraine and *Kyiv Post*, "Ukrainian army death toll in Volnovakha soars to 18," 23 May 2014 at Ukrainian army death toll in Volnovakha soars to 18 - May. 23, 2014 | KyivPost.

12. The clash in Odesa on 2 May 2014 resulted in a higher death count of forty-eight killed, of which forty-two lost their lives in the burning of the Trade Union House.

13. *The Guardian*, Shaun Walker, "Ukraine says it controls Donetsk airport after fighting leaves dozens dead," dated 27 May 20124 at Ukraine says it controls Donetsk airport after fighting leaves dozens dead | Ukraine | The Guardian.

14. Reuters, "Battle at Donetsk Airport," 26 May 2014 at Battle at Donetsk Airport (newsweek.com).

15. The city morgue reported 33 insurgents and 2 civilians killed. The mayor of Donetsk said the casualties stood at 40, as well as 2 civilians. There were 43 insurgents reported wounded. See Jim Roberts, "Ukraine Government Claims Control of Airport; Up to 50 Separatists are Killed," dated 27 May 2014 at Ukraine Government Claims Control of Airport; Up to 50 Separatists Are Killed | Mashable; see *The Guardian*, Shaun Walker, "Ukraine says it controls Donetsk airport after fighting leaves dozens dead," dated 27 May 20124 at Ukraine says it controls Donetsk airport after fighting leaves dozens dead | Ukraine | The Guardian.

16. This clearly included Chechens, as observed by reporters. According to the *Kyiv Post*, the prime minister of the DPR stated that thirty-four of the dead were sent back to Russia. See *Kyiv Post*, "Donetsk militants send 34 pro-Russian separatists bodies to Russia," dated 30 May 2014 at Donetsk militants send 34 pro-Russian separatists bodies to Russia – leader - May. 30, 2014 | KyivPost. Also see *The Guardian*, Elena Kostyuchenko, "Battle of Donetsk airport: the story of one Russian fighter, dated 27 June 2014 at Battle for Donetsk airport: the story of one Russian fighter | Ukraine | The Guardian. Among the dead was world kick-boxing champion Nikolai Leonov, a native of Dnipropetrovsk, Ukraine.

17. See BBC News, "Ukraine crisis: Kiev forces win back Mariupol," 13 June 2014 at Ukraine crisis: Kiev forces win back Mariupol - BBC News.

18. Actual losses were certainly higher, but both sides appear to have understated their losses and grossly overstated the opposing side's losses. A partial listing of Ukrainian losses by name is provided in Wikipedia, "Battle of Krasnyi Lyman."

19. The political provisions of the association agreement, the Preamble, Article 1, Titles I, II and VII, were signed on 21 March 2014 by Ukrainian Prime Minister Yatseniuk. What was signed on 27 June 2014 was the economic part of the association agreement, including Titles III, IV, V and VI, related Annexes and Protocols. This completed the association agreement with the EU.

20. This section is drawn from a blog post made by Dr Shawn Woodford, "The Artillery Strike That Spooked the U.S. Army," posted on 29 March 2017 to The Dupuy Institute run *Mystics & Statistics* blog. See The Russian Artillery Strike That Spooked The U.S. Army | Mystics & Statistics (dupuyinstitute.org).

21. See Dr Phillip A. Karber, "'Lessons Learned' from the Russo-Ukrainian War: Personal Observations, The Potomac Foundation, 8 July 2015" at RUS-UKR LESSONS for edit (wordpress.com).

22. See Wikipedia, "Zelenopillia rocket attack."

23. Tom Parfitt, *The Telegraph*, 11 July 2014, "Ukraine promises 'retribution' as at least 19 soldiers killed in rebel rocket attack" at Ukraine promises 'retribution' as at least 19 soldiers killed in rebel rocket attack (telegraph.co.uk). Also see FAS Military Analysis Network, "9K51 BM-21 *Grad* (Hail)" at BM-21 122-mm Multiple Rocket Launcher (fas.org).

24. See Bellingcat Report, "Origin of Artillery Attacks on Ukrainian Military Positions in Eastern Ukraine Between 14 July 2014 and 8 August 2014," dated 17 February 2015 at

Bellingcat Report – Origin of Artillery Attacks on Ukrainian Military Positions in Eastern Ukraine Between 14 July 2014 and 8 August 2014 – bellingcat.

25. Michael Weiss and James Miller, "Russia is Firing Missiles at Ukraine", 17 July 2014 at Russia Is Firing Missiles at Ukraine – Foreign Policy.

26. Major General (Ret.) Bob Scales, "Russia's superior new weapons," *Washington Post*, 7 August 2016 at Russia's superior new weapons - The Washington Post.

27. Phillip Karber and Joshua Thibeault, "Russians New-Generation Warfare," *Association of the United States Army*, 20 May 2016 at Russia's New-Generation Warfare | AUSA.

28. See Wikipedia, "Dual-Purpose Improved Conventional Munition" at Dual-Purpose Improved Conventional Munition – Wikipedia; Wikipedia, "List of land mines" at List of land mines – Wikipedia; Wikipedia, "Plunging Fire" at Plunging fire – Wikipedia; Human Rights Watch, 1 February 2000, "Chechnya Conflict: Use of Vacuum Bombs by Russian Forces" at Chechnya Conflict: Use of Vacuum Bombs by Russian Forces | Human Rights Watch (hrw.org); and "Tornado-G 122mm MLRS" at Tornado-G 122mm MLRS Multiple Launch Rocket System data fact sheet | Russia Russian army vehicles system artillery UK | Russia Russian army military equipment vehicles UK (armyrecognition.com).

29. See Shawn Woodford, "Mass Fires vs. Precision Fires on the Battlefield of Tomorrow," *Mystics & Statistics* blog, 20 July 2016 at Mass Fires vs. Precision Fires on the Battlefield of Tomorrow | Mystics & Statistics (dupuyinstitute.org).

30. See Shawn Woodford, "What does A2/AD look like?," 24 September 2016; "Betting on the Future: The Third Offset Strategy," 23 September 2016; and "Army and Marine Corps Join Force to Define Multi-Domain Battle Concept," 3 February 2017, *Mystics & Statistics* blog at What does A2/AD look like? | Mystics & Statistics (dupuyinstitute.org) and Betting On The Future: The Third Offset Strategy | Mystics & Statistics (dupuyinstitute.org) and Army And Marine Corps Join Forces To Define Multi-Domain Battle Concept | Mystics & Statistics (dupuyinstitute.org).

31. Of the over 2,500 blog posts made on our blog site *Mystics & Statistics*, the most widely read post is "The Russian Artillery Strike That Spooked the U.S. Army."

32. Strelkov is a *nom de guerre* based upon the word for rifleman, shooter or rifle, similar to the character Stelnikov in the film *Doctor Zhivago* (1965) directed by David Lean. The movie and character was drawn for Boris Pasternak's 1957 Nobel Prize-winning novel *Doctor Zhivago*. Pasternak was forced to reject the Nobel Prize by the Soviet government.

33. Shaun Walker, Oksana Grytsenko and Leonid Ragozin, *The Guardian*, 3 September 2014, "Russian soldier: 'you're better clueless because the truth is horrible,'" at Russian soldier: 'You're better clueless because the truth is horrible' | Ukraine | The Guardian.

34. These included 10 soldiers from 331st Guards Airborne Regiment, 1 soldier (a driver) from 8th Guards Mountain Motorized Rifle Brigade, 4 soldiers from 31st Guards Air Assault Brigade and 2 soldiers from 6th Tank Brigade. See Ksenia Baranova, *Gazeta.ru*, 17 September 2014, "We came to our senses – we ended up in Ukraine: Nine Kostoma paratroops who returned from Ukraine are going to serve again," at Nine Kostroma paratroopers who returned from Ukraine are again going to serve Gazeta. Ru (archive.org); YouTube video, *Life News*, dated 9 January 2015, "Desantniki RF Akhmetov i Ilmitov" at Десантники РФ Ахметов и Ильмитов | LifeNews – YouTube; and YouTube video dated 18 March 2015, "Viiskovoslizhbovtsi RF, Yaki brali uyact v boiovikh diyakh na skhodi Ukraini" at Військовослужбовці РФ, які брали участь в бойових діях на сході України – YouTube. Also see Wikipedia, "Battle of Ilovaisk."

35. Viacheslav Shramovych, BBC, 29 August 2019, "Ukraine's deadliest day: The Battle of Ilovaisk, August 2014," at Ukraine's deadliest day: The battle of Ilovaisk, August 2014 – BBC News.

36. Amos C. Fox, "The Donbas in Flames: An Operational Level Analysis of Russia's 2014–2015 Donbas Campaign," *Small War & Insurgencies*, 2022, p. 10.

37. Other sources say they came within 5km (3 miles) of Mariupol on 4 September, before being pushed back to 20km (12.5 miles) east of the city. See Ewen MacAskill and Shaun Walker, *The Guardian*, 5 September, 2014, "Heavy shelling in Ukrainian port of Mariupol hours before agreed ceasefire" at Heavy shelling in Ukrainian port of Mariupol hours before agreed ceasefire | Russia | The Guardian.

38. Oleksandr Sivachuk, *Ukrainian National News*, 21 September 2014, "60–65" of military equipment in units destroyed on the front line – P. Poroshenko.

39. Oksana Grytsenko, *Kyiv Post*, 10 October 2104, "'Cyborgs' pledge to defend ruined Donetsk airport," at 'Cyborgs' pledge to defend ruined Donetsk airport – Oct. 10, 2014 | KyivPost. They state, "In one night along on Sept. 28, nine soldiers were killed there, according to official data. On Oct. 3, four more people died, including two from the Right Sector. At least two soldiers were also killed on Oct. 6, Chorny said." and "On Oct. 8 alone five people [civilians] were killed and 24 wounded, Donetsk city authorities reported." The BBC reported on 29 September 2014 that seven Ukrainian soldiers died and three civilians were killed in other incidents. See 'Seven Ukraine troops die' in deadliest post-truce attack – BBC News. A later quoted interview with Ukrainian military spokesman Colonel Andriy Lyssenko stated that a total of 9 soldiers had been killed and 27 wounded in the past 24 hours. The article also stated that 3,200 people have died in fighting since April.

40. See Shaun Walker, "Ukrainian forces and pro-Russia rebels clash over Donetsk airport," *The Guardian*, 1 October 2014 at Ukrainian forces and pro-Russia rebels clash over Donetsk airport | Ukraine | The Guardian. Joanne Mariner of Amnesty International stated, "It is impossible to tell who is responsible for any particular attack, but it does seem that residential areas have been hit by Ukrainian forces firing from the airport. However, the rebels also bear responsibility as they have been stationing artillery in residential area and firing from there, in clear contradiction of the laws of war."

41. There is no good reliable accounting of losses for this operation, just the scattered one-side claims. On 28 September, Ukraine admitted to 9 killed and 27 wounded. Wikipedia in their article "Second Battle of Donetsk Airport" records for Ukraine that they suffered 23 killed between 28 September and 14 October, 12 killed between 15 and 28 October and 125 killed between 29 October and 21 January for a total of 160. The DPR says that is lost 43 killed in the fighting (which continued until 21 January). This figure seems low.

42. Press Release, Office of the High Commissioner for Human Rights, dated 8 October 2014, "Protracted conflict in eastern Ukraine continues to take heavy toll on civilians" at Protracted conflict in eastern Ukraine continues to take heavy toll on civilians | OHCHR.

43. Amos C. Fox, "The Donbas in Flames: An Operational Level Analysis of Russia's 2014–2015 Donbas Campaign," *Small War & Insurgencies*, 2022, p. 13.

44. Fergal Keane, BBC News, 2 December 2014, "Ukraine, Russia and the ceasefire that never was" at Ukraine, Russia and the ceasefire that never was – BBC News. They put the total killed in eastern Ukraine since April at more than 4,300 people.

45. This is according to Wikipedia, "List of aircraft losses during the Russo-Ukrainian War." They consisted of a Mi-8 MT shot by small arms at Kramatorsk airport while on the ground; two Mi-24s shot down on 2 May near Slovyansk by small arms or RPGs. An Mi-8 was damaged. Two men were killed and one was captured, the disposition of the rest of the crew Is not known; and a Mi-24 shot down a machinegun near Slovvansk. All crew survived.

46. It appears at least one claim was correct, as there is a picture provided of the downed Mi-24. See Vesti, "DPR authorities report two helicopters show down in Donetsk," 26 May 2014 at DPR authorities report two helicopters shot down in Donetsk (vesti.ru). The Wikipedia article "List of aircraft losses during the Russo-Ukrainian War" does not list these aircraft.

47. This, of course, was denied by the Ukrainian government, who claimed it was an errant Russian missile; but the evidence is overwhelming that it was done by Ukrainian aircraft. No Russian aircraft were yet operating in the area.

48. Other losses listed included two Mi-24s forced to land on 4 June 2014 due to separatist fire. One of the helicopters burned on the ground due to the damage; an Mi-8 crashed near Zmeivsky on 21 June; and on 2 July an Su-25 crashed due to a technical problem while landing at Dnipropetrovsk.

49. There has been an extensive investigation of this incident by the Dutch Safety Board. The EU Joint Investigation Team determined in 2018 that the Buk used originated from 53rd Anti-Aircraft Missile Brigade of the Russian Federation. Furthermore, the conversations of the Russian officers involved have been recorded and released in 2014 and the Buk was observed in that area at that time. Russian counterclaims that it was shot down by a Ukrainian fighter have also been widely reported, but there does not appear to be any factual basis for accepting these claims.

50. Sophie Tanno, "Dutch Court finds two Russians, one Ukrainian separatist guilty over downing of flight MH17," 17 November 2022 at Dutch Court finds two Russians, one Ukrainian separatist guilty over downing of flight MH17|Cable News Network (cnn.com).

51. Other losses in August include a Mi-8 MT that crash-landed after being hit by gunfire in Donetsk province on 7 August; a MiG-29 shot down in the Luhansk region on 17 August, the pilot ejected and was rescued; a Mi-8 shot down in Luhansk region on 17 August; a Su-24M shot down in Luhansk region on 20 August; an Mi-24 shot down in Donetsk province on 20 August with both pilots killed; a Mi-8 crashed on landing in Donets on 27 August; and a Su-25 shot down near Starobeshevo by a surface-to-air missile on 29 August, pilot ejected and was able to reach Ukrainian-controlled territory four days later. No other Ukrainian losses were reported for 2014. It appears from the above narrative that total Ukraine losses were 1 Su-24, 4 (vice 6) Su-25s, 2 MiG-29s, 1 An-26, 1 An-30, 1 Il-76, 5 (vice 7) Mi-8s and 5 Mi-24s. This matches closely with the reporting in November 2014 (see below).

    The Wikipedia article "List of aircraft losses during the Russo-Ukrainian War" has six Su-25s and seven Mi-8s in their totals. The other two are probably the Su-25 that is a DPR claim on 19 June and the Su-25 that crashed on 2 July. The other two Mi-8 were probably the Mi-8 that crashed on 21 June and the Mi-8 that crashed on 27 August. I have discounted the DPR claim and consider the other three to be operational accidents not directly related to combat.

52. Chris Pocock, "Ukraine has Lost 22 Aircraft to Rebel Forces," 26 November 2014 at Ukraine Has Lost 22 Aircraft to Rebel Forces | Defense News: Aviation International News (ainonline.com). Also see: "20.11.14 A representative of the Ukrainian Air Force spoke in London about the losses and prospects of the country's military aviation" at militaryparitet.com.

53. This is 108 killed among the protestors and other individuals and 13 killed among law-enforcement and government forces. See Office of the United Nations High Commissioner for Human Rights, "Accountability for killing in Ukraine for January 2014 to May 2016," p. 3.

54. On 26 February there were two people killed as result of clashes in Simferopol, Crimea. On 14 March 2014 there were two people killed in clashes in Kharkiv. On 2 May 2014, 48 people were killed in Odesa. Office of the United Nations High Commissioner for Human Rights, "Accountability for killing in Ukraine for January 2014 to May 2016," p. 3.

55. Office of the United Nations High Commissioner for Human Rights, "Accountability for killing in Ukraine for January 2014 to May 2016," p. 11. The wounded were given as 21,671 injured, which seems low compared with the number killed.

56. It also included 43 Malaysians, 27 Australians, 12 Indonesians and 10 from the UK. No Americans were on the flight, which is somewhat unusual, as Americans tend to be everywhere.

57. Amos C. Fox, "The Donbas in Flames: An Operational Level Analysis of Russia's 2014–2015 Donbas Campaign," *Small War & Insurgencies*, 2022, p. 13.
58. This is official data from the Ukrainian German Staff covering the period from 15 January–18 February 2015. See Hromadske International, "the Best of the Worst: What 2016 was like for Donbas," 9 January 2017 at The Best of the Worst: What 2016 Was Like for Donbas (hromadske.ua).
59. Hromadske International, "The Best of the Worst: What 2016 was like for Donbas," 9 January 2017 at The Best of the Worst: What 2016 Was Like for Donbas (hromadske.ua).
60. This idea is drawn from the paper by Amos Fox, although he broke it into only four phases. See Amos C. Fox, "The Donbas in Flames: An Operational Level Analysis of Russia's 2014–2015 Donbas Campaign," *Small War & Insurgencies*, 2022.
61. The phrase "manufactured insurgency" is somewhat pejorative and borrowed from the writing of Amos C. Fox (see "The Donbas in Flames: An Operational Level Analysis of Russia's 2014–2015 Donbas Campaign," *Small War & Insurgencies*, 2022). There clearly was a significant number of locals who were disgruntled with the overthrow of Yanukovych and the new government in Kyiv, but there does not appear to have been enough discontent on its own to have generated an effective insurgency that would actually take ground from Ukraine. The virulence of the insurgency was certainly magnified by the presence of Russian actors and forces in the Donbas region. In fact, it is doubtful the cities of Luhansk or Donetsk would have been occupied by the separatists without the outside actors. Therefore, one is left to call it a "manufactured insurgency," as without such help, there was not enough intensity to have created the conditions for a LPR and DPR to be declared. One only has to look at the events in Kharkiv in contrast to see that.
62. See Hromadske International, "the Best of the Worst: What 2016 was like for Donbas," 9 January 2017 at The Best of the Worst: What 2016 Was Like for Donbas (hromadske.ua). The figure of 211 Ukrainian soldiers killed in 2016 was from the General Staff of the Armed Force of Ukraine as of December 2016. The number of non-combat losses was 256 for 2016.
63. BBC News, "Ukraine conflict: Moscow could 'defend' Russia-backed rebels," 9 April 2021 at Ukraine conflict: Moscow could 'defend' Russia-backed rebels – BBC News.
64. BBC News, "Ukraine conflict: Moscow could 'defend' Russia-backed rebels," 9 April 2021 at Ukraine conflict: Moscow could 'defend' Russia-backed rebels – BBC News.
65. TASS, "Over 50 battalion tactical groups to fight enemy drones in southern Russia drills, dated 2 April 2021 at Over 50 battalion tactical groups to fight enemy drones in southern Russia drills – Military & Defense – TASS.
66. A battalion tactical group tends to consist of 400–600 people, and sometimes can be as large as 1,000, depending on attachments. Over 50 BTGs would indicate that there were far more than 15,000 troops.
67. Clement Charpentreau, *Aerotime Hub*, 14 April 2021, "Ukraine flies its first Turkish-made armed drone over Donbas" at Ukraine flies its first Turkish-made armed drone over Donbas (aerotime.aero).
68. These claims were estimated from Zelenskyy's spokeswoman. See Christopher A. Lawrence, "83,000 Russian Troops?," *Mystics & Statistics*, 13 April 2021 at 83,000 Russian Troops? | Mystics & Statistics (dupuyinstitute.org).
69. It also reports 115 injured: 85 servicemen and 30 civilians. See "Review of the social and humanitarian situation in the territory of the Donetsk People's Republic as a result of hostilities in the period from October 30 to November 5, 2021." Dated 5 November 2021 at Review of the social and humanitarian situation in the territory of the Donetsk People's Republic as a result of hostilities in the period from October 30 to November 5, 2021 – Commissioner for Human Rights in the DPR (ombudsman-dnr.ru).

70. TASS, 27 October 2021, "Ukrainian forces seize village of Staromaryevka – Donetsk Republic" at Ukrainian forces seize village of Staromaryevka – Donetsk Republic – World – TASS. This could very well be a claim made for propaganda purposes, and the village was in Ukrainian hands for years. For example, see "Staromaryevka – Ukrainian village that almost started a war," JAMnews, 4 December 2021 at War in Ukraine and life in a frontline village of Staromaryevka (jam-news.net).

71. For example, see Wikipedia, "Russo-Ukrainian War." This is based upon a date established by the Ukrainian government for the "the beginning of the temporary occupation of Crimea and Sevastopol by Russia" based upon a date inscribed on the Russian medal "For the Return of Crimea." The Ukrainian parliament officially designed this date as the start of the war. On the other hand, the President of Russia in 2015 stated that he did not order the operation against Crimea until the night of 22–23 February and in 2018 the Foreign Minister stated that the start date on the medal was a mistake made due to a "technical misunderstanding." The date of 20 February 2014 for the start of the first war in Ukraine is clearly questionable.

72. This does provide for a population for Donetsk of 4,056,405 and for Luhansk of 2,101,653. See Population by Region as of February 2022 at Population of Ukraine (ukrcensus.gov.ua).

73. This is 1,903,707 for the "Respublicka Kryim and 513,149 for "g. Sevastopol." Drawn from Russian Federal State Statistics Service dated 1 January 2021.

Chapter 3

1. This is according to an interview with Alexy Danilov, the secretary of the National Security and Defense Council. See Sevgil Musayeva, Ukrainska Pravda, 22 April 2022, "Alexey Danilov: Russia will disintegrate during our lifetime," at Oleksiy Danilov: There must be a completely new state – sincere, frank, such as our president is now | Ukrayinska Pravda. Also see Ukrainska Pravda, 31 October 2021, "Russia is pulling troops to the border with Ukraine and this is not an exercise – The Washington Post," at Russia is pulling troops to the border with Ukraine and this is not an exercise – The Washington Post | Ukrayinska Pravda.

2. See Wikipedia. The 2016 figures were the most recent figures for ground forces in early 2022 while the total active personnel figure was from 2021.

3. Christopher A. Lawrence, "Russian Invasions," *Mystics & Statistics*, 5 December 2021 at Russian Invasions | Mystics & Statistics (dupuyinstitute.org).

4. These were the figures given by Ukraine. No reliable figures had been provided since then. See Poltorak put ground troops as an example of reforms in Ukraine – Ukraine – tsn.ua.

5. See Transparency International website at Home – Transparency.org . While this index is far from perfect and very fuzzy, primarily being based upon "perceptions," it does have the advantage of being independent and nominally neutral.

6. Three other countries in NATO were rated worse: Turkey, which joined NATO in 1952, North Macedonia, which joined NATO in 2020, and Albania, which joined NATO in 2009. They were ranked and scored 96/38/8%, 87/39/? and 110/35/25% respectively.

7. While some may choose to debate this conclusion, I am not interested in discussing it further. I think events here have clearly established what were the primary goals of Russia. The reference to 1936–40 is specifically a reference to the bloodless *Anschluss* in 1936 when Hitler unified Austria with Germany, the Italian annexation of Ethiopia in 1936, the German support of political turmoil in Czechoslovakia (hybrid warfare?) and then the annexation of the Sudetenland in 1938, the seizure of all of Czechoslovakia later in 1939, the Italian invasion of Albania in 1939, the German and Soviet Union invasion of Poland in 1939, the Soviet Union occupation and annexation of Bessarabia (now most Moldovia), Lithuania, Latvia and Estonia in 1940, and the Soviet seizure of land from Finland by war in 1940.

8. One could argue that it was similar to the case made against Iraq about developing weapons of mass destruction that was presented leading up to the invasion of Iraq in 2003. I do have a hard time comparing these two efforts, as it is clear that the case against Iraq was very much heavily pushed by senior political leaders at that time and, of course, the case turned out to be entirely false. The United States did invade Iraq in 2003 based upon a false *casus belli* that was certified by the majority of the US intelligence community.

9. Trevor Hunnicutt and Andrew Osborn, Reuters, 27 December 2021 at https://news.yahoo.com/1-u-russian-officials-set-035411514.html.

10. Matthew Chance, Kylie Attwood, Emmet Lyons and Ami Kaufman, CNN, 19 January 2022, "Ukraine wars Russia has 'almost completed' build-up of forces near border," at Ukraine warns Russia has 'almost completed' build-up of forces near border | CNN.

11. Christopher A. Lawrence, "So Is Russia going to actually attack Ukraine?," *Mystics & Statistics,* dated 22 January at So Is Russia going to actually attack Ukraine? | Mystics & Statistics (dupuyinstitute.org). The reference to *War by Numbers* is to Christopher A. Lawrence, *War by Numbers: Understanding Conventional Combat* (Potomac Books, Lincoln, NE, 2017).

12. This is quoted from our post of 22 January. As of 7 February, we still did not think this was going to occur. See *Mystics & Statistics* post of 7 February 2022, "The Russo-Ukrainian War of 2022 – part 1." As I note in that post, "If I was going to invade Ukraine, I would use surprise, overwhelming force and hit them during good weather. This is not what is happening right now. So, I still have a hard time believing we are about to see a major conventional war starting this month."

13. Christopher A. Lawrence, "The Russo-Ukrainian War of 2022 – part 1," *Mystics & Statistics,* 7 February 2022 at The Russo-Ukrainian War of 2022 – part 1 | Mystics & Statistics (dupuyinstitute.org).

14. See: Grayson Quay, "Russia 'will not capture' any of Ukraine's cities, Ukrainian defense minister says," *The Week,* 13 February 2022 at Russia 'will not capture' any of Ukraine's cities, Ukrainian defense minister says.

15. Nothing has been publicly published on this, although it is not classified. I was made aware of it through conversations with people in the State Department.

16. Specially, Trevor Dupuy's old company, DMSI, held a contract for multiple years for this purpose. I was working there at that time.

17. It has been translated into English by RT at https://www.youtube.com/watch?v=GjMnTo85S4A. The statement "The virus of nationalist ambitions is still with us" starts at 1102 into the video.

Chapter 4

1. IISS, or International Institute of Strategic Studies, is the commonly used open-source estimate of countries strengths. That said, the strength of the Ukrainian Army is confusing, being 169,000 in 2016 and 125,600 in 2022. The size of their armed forces is 255,000 in 2021 and 196,600 in February 2022. See The Military Balance: The Annual Assessment of Global Military Capabilities and Defence Economics, 2022 (London, UK, published February 2022).

2. IISS report the same figures for 2021 and 2022.

3. 42,000 in 2016 according to Unian, "Avakov announces large-scale 'cleansing' among generals," dated 17 August 2016 at Avakov announces large-scale "cleansing" among generals | UNIAN and up to 60,000 in 2022 according to Ukrainian Military Pages, "One million Ukrainians in uniform protests Ukraine from Russians," dated 9 July 2022 at One million Ukrainians in uniform protects Ukraine from Russians (ukrmilitary.com).

4. Up to 100,000 National Police in 2022, according to Ukrainian Military Pages, "One million Ukrainians in uniform protests Ukraine from Russians," dated 9 July 2022 at One million Ukrainians in uniform protects Ukraine from Russians (ukrmilitary.com).

5. For example, there is the up to 11,000 civilian personnel that are in the National Police, about 60,000 in the State Emergency Service of Ukraine, there are employees of the State Migration Service of Ukraine (their customs service) and there were about 30,000 people in the Security Service of Ukraine (SBU) before the war began. This last service is the successor service since 1991 to the former Soviet Committee for State Security (KGB). None of these are combat troops, per se, but they sometimes get added into quoted totals.

6. US and Russian figures are from SIPRI, the Stockholm International Peace Research Institute.

7. The 2022 IISS listing had 4 tank brigades, 9 mechanized brigades, 2 mountain brigades, 4 motorized infantry brigades and 1 light infantry brigade. This is a total of 20 maneuver brigades, which does not match the listing below.

8. As of 2017, 10th Mountain Assault Brigade, 24th, 28th, 30th and 72nd Mechanized Brigades were reported with 3 mechanized battalions and an unnamed tank battalion. As of 2017, 17th Tank Brigade is reported with 3 tank battalions and an unnamed mechanized battalion. As of 2017, 53rd Mechanized Brigade is reported with 3 mechanized battalions, an unnamed tank battalion and 24th Motorized Infantry Battalion "Aidar." As of 2017, 54th Mechanized Brigade is reported with 3 mechanized battalions, an unnamed tank battalion and 25th Motorized Infantry Battalion "Kyivan Rus" and 46th Motorized Infantry Battalion "Donbas-Ukraine." As of 2017, 92nd Mechanized Brigade is reported with 3 mechanized battalions, an unnamed tank battalion and 22nd Motorized Infantry Battalion "Kharkiv." As of 2017, the 93rd Mechanized Brigade is reported with 3 mechanized battalions, an unnamed tank battalion and the 20th Motorized Infantry Battalion "Dnipro." As of 2018, 128th Mountain Assault Brigade was reported with 16th Tank Battalion. As of 2019, 61st Jaeger Infantry Brigade was reported with an unnamed tank battalion. We suspect some of these are "on-paper" organizations or errors in the sources.

9. A maneuver brigade or battalion is an infantry, mechanized infantry, armor or cavalry unit. It is not an artillery unit, helicopter unit or air defense unit. These are the units that make up the front-line combat units of an army. The count of total maneuver battalions is 67 battalions, plus 12th and 16th Tank Battalions and the 5 separate reconnaissance battalions for a total of 74 plus any fifth or sixth battalion under these brigades. It is uncertain if the 10th Mountain Assault Brigade had a fourth battalion (a tank battalion), and is not counted as such.

Some brigades may have more than 4 battalions, 14th (1st Motorized Battalion), 28th (5th Reserve Battalion, formed February 2022), 30th (2nd Motorized Battalion), 53rd (24th Mechanized Battalion "Aidar", 43rd Mechanized Battalion), 54th (25th Separate Motorized Battalion, 45th Separate Assault Battalion), 72nd (12th Motorized Battalion), 92nd (22nd Separate Mechanized Battalion), 93rd (20th Separate Motorized Battalion, 49th Motorized Battalion 'Carpathian Sich') and 128th (15th Separate Mountain Assault Battalion) brigades. For 128th Brigade, this is in addition to 16th Tank Battalion that we do count part of 128th. In some cases, these were battalions added in 2014–15 and were possibly later disbanded. In some cases, they are battalions that have been added since the current war has started. The Ukrainian brigades have grown in size as the war has continued. This would potentially add up to another 12 battalions to the count of Ukrainian battalions.

The 24th Separate Assault Battalion "Aidar" with 53rd Mechanized Brigade is referenced in a video posted on twitter on 18 January 2023, see Dan on Twitter: "80. Moving quickly south of Optyne. Earlier in January, released (likely earlier filmed) of 24th Separate Assault Battalion 'Aidar', 53rd Mechanised Bde taking out a Russian at the former fruit processing plant at 48.547679, 38.017045 h/t @azyakancokkacan https://t.co/VMIeTHoFhS" / Twitter.

10. Each of the five regular airborne brigades have 3 maneuver battalions, plus there is 1 independent maneuver battalion (132nd Recon), the 2 Naval Infantry brigades have 4 maneuver battalions plus there was an independent recon battalion (140th Recon), the Special Forces can be counted as 2 more battalions, plus there is the Georgian battalion, the Chechen battalion, the Azov Battalion and perhaps others.

11. The Russian battalion tactical group, or BTG, is a reinforced maneuver battalion. They are described in more depth in the next chapter. Because a BTG often includes a tank company, then they are not always the equivalent of a Ukrainian maneuver battalion as the tank battalions with the mechanized brigades are counted separately, when they are often divided out with one tank company with a maneuver mechanized battalion. A later count in January 2023 by Sasho Todorov of battalions from his reconstructed order of battle gave the Russians up to 130 BTGs and maneuver battalions and the LPR and DPR a total of 37 maneuver battalions.

12. In 2017, 1st Tank Brigade is reported with three tank battalions with 56 T-64BM Bulats.

13. 410 T-64BVs, 210 T-64BVs mod 2017, 100 T-64BM Bulats, about 133 T-72s and between 34 and 134 T-80BVs and 5 T-84Us. See Wikipedia, "List of Equipment of the Armed Forces of Ukraine" and David Axe, Forbes, 15 December 2021, "Ukraine's Tanks Could be Better Than Russia's. It Might Not Matter" at Ukraine's Tanks Could Be Better Than Russia's. It Might Not Matter. (forbes.com). Global Security, "Ukraine – Ground Forces Equipment" at Ground Forces Equipment – Ukraine (globalsecurity.org) is showing 620 T-64s, 100 T-64 BM Bulats, 133 T-72s, no T-80s and 5 T-84 Oplats.

The T-64 was built at the Kharkiv tank factory. In the 2021 IISS listing for Ukraine it was reported to have only 34 T-80s. Other sources report about 100 T-80BVs were restored to service in 2015. We do have a report from personal conversations that 1st Tank Battalion of the Naval Infantry was armed with only 22 T-80s, because of a shortage of the tank.

14. The 60th, 62nd and 63rd Brigades.

15. This exact organization of the army in February 2022 has yet to be revealed. This is our best guess based upon multiple sources.

16. Counts are from Wikipedia, "List of Equipment of the Armed Forces of Ukraine," which is primarily based upon the 2021 IISS listing. The Wikipedia listing is being updated to include equipment received since the war started.

17. The actual count of deployed tanks works out to be: 9 tank battalions with tank brigades (9 x 31 = 279), 9 tank battalions with mechanized brigades (9 x 31 = 279), 12th and 16th tank battalions (2 x 31 = 62), 4 tank companies with the motorized infantry brigades (4 x 10 = 40), 5 tank companies with air assault divisions (5 x 10 = 50), 1st Tank Battalion with the Naval Infantry (22 tanks) and 2nd Tank Battalion with the Naval Infantry (31). This is a total of 763 tanks out of an estimated 892 tanks available.

It is possible that 5th Tank Brigade had about 30 T-72s and 3rd Tank Brigade had about 100 T-72s. It is uncertain if 10th Mountain Assault Brigade had a tank battalion and is not counted as such. Some of the other reserve units may have also had tanks assigned to them at the start of the war. The same with some National Guard units such as 4th Rapid Reaction Brigade.

18. 892 tanks versus 169,000 people. According to definitions created by Trevor Dupuy, force can be considered armor heavy in the proportion of tanks exceeds 6 per 1,000 troops. See, Colonel T.N. Dupuy, *Attrition: Forecasting Battle Casualties and Equipment Losses in Modern War* (NOVA Publications, Falls Church, VA, 1995), p. 89.

19. This listing is assembled from various secondary sources, so is far from definitive. It is drawn from a tweet by Paris Paroinen @Inkvisiit, dated 22 June. The Ukrainian Military

Pages at Ground Forces (ukrmilitary.com) provides a listing for 31 December 2021 that matches the listing of these twenty-seven brigades. That listing also includes in the Reserve Corps a 66rd Mechanized Brigade, a 68th Jaeger Brigade, 71st Jaeger Brigade, 110th Mechanized Brigade and 115th Mechanized Brigade that are not listed elsewhere. It does not list 11th Motorized Infantry Brigade, 15th Mechanized Brigade, 33rd Mechanized Brigade and 62nd Mechanized Brigade. All four of these brigades are listed in Wikipedia, "Mechanized Infantry (Ukraine)." The Wikipedia article "Ukrainian Ground Forces" does list twenty-five of the twenty-seven brigades listed here, omitting listings for 4th Tank Brigade and 11th Motorized Infantry Brigade. The MilitaryLand website provides a listing of all Ukrainians brigades and many smaller units at Armed Forces | MilitaryLand.net.

20. The 3rd Tank Brigade was first mentioned in action on 11 April 2022 near Izyum (https://twitter.com/Militarylandnet/status/1513609624410284042).

   The 5th Tank Brigade was first mentioned in combat at the end of August 2022 near Kherson (https://twitter.com/UAWeapons/status/1564713937073049602), but we do believe it was deployed near Odesa and partly activated before then.

   The 60th Mechanized Brigade was first referenced with a missing serviceman on 4 April 2022 near Kherson (https://www.facebook.com/photo/?fbid=1003960436914465&set=g.679413519875806). This does not mean the brigade was deployed there as the serviceman could have been with another unit, including a TDF unit.

   The 61st Jager Infantry Brigade was first mentioned in action on 24 June 2022 near Kherson (https://www.facebook.com/61opbr/videos/815760919408467). At this point, it has been reorganized as a mechanized brigade.

   The 62nd Mechanized Brigade was first mentioned in action on 14 October 2022 near Donets (https://www.victims.memorial/people/serhii-byba).

   The 63rd Mechanized Brigade was first mentioned in action on 30 April 2022 near Kherson(https://www.facebook.com/photo/?fbid=120597320604131&set=pb.1000795084 85716.-2207520000).

   We have found no references in 2022 to 11th, 15th or 33rd Mechanized Brigades being in action.

   On the other hand, the Ukrainians stood up 110th and 115th Mechanized Brigades by April, which were new combat formations created after the war started. According to MilitaryLand.net, 110th has been active since 10 April 2022, while 115th has been active since 1 March 2022. The 115th Mechanized Brigade's Facebook page was created on 31 July 2020, although the name was not changed to the brigade's name until 4 August 2022. The first posting to that page was from well before the war started, although these appear to be mostly political.

   This is all preliminary work, and we are sure more specific data will be available over time.

21. This brigade may not have been active in the first six weeks of the war. See David Axe, "Ukraine had Mobilized its Tank Reserves. They're Already on the Attack," Forbes, 18 April 2022 at Ukraine Has Mobilized Its Tank Reserves. They're Already On The Attack. (forbes.com).

22. This brigade was converted to a mechanized brigade in 2022.

23. Other units that may now be active include: Separate Presidential Brigade (with five battalions), 1st Special Purpose Brigade active as of 4 March, 2022, 65th Mechanized Brigade active as of 1 April 2022, 66th Mechanized Brigade active as of 18 April 2022, 68th Jager Infantry Brigade active as of 8 April 2022, 110th Mechanized Brigade active as of 10 April 2022, 115th Mechanized Brigade active as of 1 March 2022, 129th Reconnaissance Battalion, 71st Jager Infantry Brigade active as of 24 February 2022 and 77th Airmobile Brigade.

   Also listed on the MilitaryLand website are ten separate rifle battalions (4th, 6th, 12th, 14th, 19th, 23rd, 41st, 42nd, 45th and 214th). The status of them is not known.

Also six battalions were formed as part of 7th Center of Volunteer Corps activated as of 27 March 2022.

24. The 45th Artillery Brigade appears to have been activated in late February and initially was deployed near Kyiv starting 4 March 2022. See In Ukraine time to kill, not die, – interview with the commander of the 45th brigade Oleg Faidyuk – News Agency Aloud/Vgolos.

The prisoner of war from 38th Artillery Brigade was interviewed in the Russian video released on 30 May 2022.

25. The 45th Air Assault Brigade was first mentioned in action on 17 May 2022 near Zaporizhzhia (https://twitter.com/Newsweek/status/1526653455103930369).

The 46th Air Mobile Brigade was first mentioned in action in mid-July at Kherson based upon an email with a Ukrainian service member.

26. According to MilitaryLand.net, this unit was demobilized on 31 December 2020.

27. See the 2017 organization chart for the Ukrainian Airborne Force at Wikipedia "Ukrainian Air Assault Forces" as posted in 2023.

28. See MilitaryLand.net at https://twitter.com/militarylandnet/status/1579919692525080577.

29. The Naval Infantry tank battalions had 31 tanks. Before the start of the war, 36th Naval Infantry Brigade only had 22 tanks because it had T-80s and Ukraine was struggling to get enough serviceable. The source is a Ukrainian Naval Infantry officer contacted in January 2023.

30. This order of battle is almost drawn entirely from the Wikipedia article "National Guards of Ukraine." It has been trimmed back to focus on the combat and maneuver battalions.

31. David Axe, Forbes, August 5, 2022 "It Seems Ukraine is Struggling to Form Tank Brigades," at It Seems Ukraine Is Struggling To Form Tank Brigades (msn.com).

32. David Axe, Forbes, 31 March 2022, "Ukraine's Best Tank Brigade has Won the Battle of Chernihiv" at Ukraine's Best Tank Brigade Has Won The Battle For Chernihiv (forbes.com).

33. David Axe, Forbes, 20 April 2022, "T-72s to the Rescue? Ukraine's 5th Tank Brigade Could Roll Into Battle Any Day Now." at T-72s To The Rescue? Ukraine's 5th Tank Brigade Could Roll Into Battle Any Day Now. (forbes.com).

34. David Axe, Forbes, 29 May, 2022, "Ukraine Made Just A Handful of Speedy T-84 Tanks. Now They're on the Front Line," at Ukraine Made Just A Handful Of Speedy T-84 Tanks. Now They're On The Front Line. (forbes.com).

35. 410 T-64BVs, 210 T-64BVs mod 2017, 100 T-64BM Bulats, about 130 T-72s and between 34 and 130 T-80BVs and 5 T-84Us. See Wikipedia, "List of Equipment of the Armed Forces of Ukraine" and David Axe, Forbes, 15 December 2021, "Ukraine's Tanks Could be Better Than Russia's. It Might Not Matter" at Ukraine's Tanks Could Be Better Than Russia's. It Might Not Matter. (forbes.com). In the 2021 IISS listing for Ukraine it was reported to have only 34 T-80s. Other sources report about 100 T-80BVs were restored to service in 2015. Global Security, "Ukraine – Ground Forces Equipment" at Ground Forces Equipment - Ukraine (globalsecurity.org) is showing 620 T-64s, 100 T-64 BM Bulats, 133 T-72s, no T-80s and 5 T-84 Oplats.

36. Inspiration and one of the sources for this section is the New Voice of Ukraine article dated 27 August 2022 called "Top Ten Most Effective Ukraine-made weapons." Their lists of weapons also included 1. A1-CM Furia UAV. The reconnaissance and fire control drone has been in service since 2020. 2. Zoopark-2 artillery locating radar. It has been in service since 2003. 3. Bukovel UAV countermeasure system. It has been in service since 2016.

37. This includes three Ukrainian soldiers reported to have died during their deployment.

38. See the Telegraf, 8 March 2022, "KFOR: Ukrainian soldiers to remain in Kosovo" at KFOR: Ukrainian soldiers to remain in Kosovo – Telegraf.rs.

39. OCHA Services, December 2005, "Ukraine withdraws last troops in Iraq" at Ukraine withdraws last troops in Iraq – Iraq | ReliefWeb.

40. Sergeant Rodney Foliente, 11 December 2008, "Ukrainians complete mission in Iraq" at Ukrainians complete mission in Iraq | Article | The United States Army.

Chapter 5

1. This write-up is based upon the work of Dr Shawn Woodford as discussed in the Mystics & Statistics blog post of 11 April 2022 called "Some initial observations on the Russian Army Battalion Tactical Group (BTG) concept" at Some initial observations on the Russian Army Battalion Tactical Group (BTG) concept | Mystics & Statistics (dupuyinstitute.org).

2. Source was the twitter feed that day of Kaitlin Collins, CNN.

3. Elements of 5th Combined Arms Army may have also been deployed to Belarus but does not appear to have been deployed to Ukraine in February or March.

4. The initial deployed order of battle for the Russian Army has been repeated across multiple sources. Its accuracy cannot be confirmed. See CSIS Briefs, 1 June 2022, "Russia's Ill-Fated Invasion of Ukraine: Lessons in Modern Warfare at Russia's Ill-Fated Invasion of Ukraine: Lessons in Modern Warfare | Center for Strategic and International Studies (csis.org) and https://www.politico.com/f/?id=0000017d-a0bd-dca7-a1fd-b1bd6cb10000.

5. Partly derived from the lost listing from 15 March. Units below regiment are not listed with the exception of 7th Reconnaissance Battalion.

6. For the Ukrainian minimal figure this represents about 88 maneuver battalions from the Ukrainian Ground Forces, up to 22 maneuver battalions for the Air Assault Force, the 9 maneuver battalions from the Ukrainian Navy, 2 from the Special Operations Forces, 1 battalion from the Azov Regiment and 2 foreign battalions for a total of 124. The figure of 203 represents the inclusion of all National Guard battalions.

7. The count includes 38th Air Defense Missile Regiment, 39th Air Defense Missile Regiment, 1039th Air Defense Missile Regiment and 1129th Bila Tserkva Air Defense Missile Regiment, which probably consist of three air defense battalions each; plus the air defense battalion with each of the twenty-seven active maneuver brigades.

8. The *Moskva* was part of the Slava class of 11,490 tons full load and a crew of 418 enlisted men and 66 officers.

9. The five frigates were the *Ladnyy, Pytivyy, Admiral Grigorovich, Admiral Essen* and *Admiral Makarov*. The multi-role Corvette was the *Mercury*. The first 2 frigates were built in 1980–1 as part of the Krivak class of 3,575 tons full load and 200 crew. The other 3 frigates were built in 2016 and later as part of the Admiral Grigorovich class of 4,000 tons full load and 200 crew. The Corvette was completed in 2022 with sea trials underway in May 2022. It was part of the Stergushchiy class of 2,200 tons full load and 90 crew.

   The eleven landing ships were *Nikolay Filchenkov, Orsk, Azov, Novocherkassk, Caesar Kunikov* and *Vamai, Minsk, Korolev, Kaliningrad, Georgy Pobedonosets* and *Olenegorksy Gornyak*. The first 2 ships were built in 1975 and 1968 and were part of the Alligator class of 4,700 tons full load and 55 crew. They could carry 300–425 troops and 20 tanks. The next 9 were built from 1986–90 and were part of the Ropucha class of 4,080 tons full load and 87–98 crew. They could carry 340 troops and 10 main battle tanks.

   Other Black Sea naval forces included 2 high-speed landing craft, 6 ASW Corvettes, 9 seagoing minesweepers, 14 anti-saboteur boats, 6 guided missile Corvettes, 1 missile Corvette, 4 missile boats, 4 patrol ships, 2 base minesweepers, 3 landing craft, 4 intelligence vessels and a range of auxiliaries, oilers, oceanographic and other support ships. None of the combat ships were larger than 1,100 tons full load. The intelligence vessels and support ships were often much larger.

10. The submarines were *Alrosa (*B-871), *Rostov no Danu* (B-237), *Novorossiysk* (B-261), *Staryy Oskol* (B-262), *Krasnodar* (B-265), *Velikiy Novgorod* (B-268) and *Kolpino* (B-271). They were all diesel attack submarines, 1 Kilo class and 6 improved Kilo class submarines of 3,075 to 3,100 tons and a crew of 52.

11. Specifically, the anti-submarine Corvette *Vinnytsia* of 990 tons, damaged on 24 February and later sunk, the patrol vessel *Korets* of 1,620 tons, patrol boat *Akkerman* of 54 tons and the patrol boat Vyshhorod of 54 tons.

12. Specially, the patrol boat Slovyansk of 168 tons as sunk by an air-launched anti-ship missile, the patrol boats *Kremenchuk* and *Lubny* of 54 tons were lost during the Siege of Mariupol, the minesweeper *Henichesk* of 96.5 tons, the command ship *Donbas* of 5,520 tons was lost during the Siege of Mariupol and the hydrographic boat *Dmitry Chubai* of 148 tons.

13. This listing was assembled in Christopher A. Lawrence, "What Makes up Combat Power?," dated 8 December 2017 in the blog *Mystics & Statistics* and in Lawrence, *War by Numbers*, p. 17. It is based upon Dupuy, *Numbers, Predictions and War*, p. 33, but his listing was under a subject heading of "Intangible Factors" and included 1. Combat effectiveness, 2. Leadership, 3. Training/experience, 4. Morale, 5. Logistics, 6. Time, 7. Space, 8. Momentum, 9. Intelligence, 10. Technology and 11. Initiative. These were intended to address the intangible or not easily measurable factors that influence combat, and therefore combat modeling. Obviously, factors such as time, space and technology are intangibles that do not measure human factors. Logistics and intelligence I have kept in this list, even though their relationship to human factors is tangential.

14. This quote is from Trevor N. Dupuy, Curt Johnson, Grace P. Hayes, *Dictionary of Military Terms: A Guide to the Language of Warfare and Military Institutions* (The H.W. Wilson Company, New York, 1986), pp. 152–3. Over the decades, I have come to appreciate that this is the best single dictionary of military terms. Sadly, it is out of print and is not likely to go back in print.

15. Ibid., pp. 219–21.

16. Ibid., p. 135.

17. This factor has been added by Christopher A. Lawrence and was not part of Trevor Dupuy's original listing. This is not discussed in Dupuy, *Numbers, Prediction and War*.

18. This factor has been added by Christopher A. Lawrence and was not part of Trevor Dupuy's original listing. This is not discussed in Dupuy, *Numbers, Prediction and War*.

19. Dupuy, Johnson and Hayes, *Dictionary of Military Terms*, pp. 50–1.

20. Ibid., p. 121.

21. Dupuy, *Numbers, Predictions and War*, p. 38.

22. Dupuy, Johnson and Hayes, *Dictionary of Military Terms*, p. 152.

23. Dupuy, *Numbers, Predictions and War*, p. 39.

24. This factor has been added by Christopher A. Lawrence and was not part of Trevor Dupuy's original listing.

25. Dupuy, Johnson and Hayes, *Dictionary of Military Terms*, p. 75.

26. This factor has been added by Christopher A. Lawrence and was not part of Trevor Dupuy's original listing.

27. Dupuy, Johnson, Hayes, *Dictionary of Military Terms*, pp. 210–11.

28. Ibid., p. 139.

29. This factor has been added by Christopher A. Lawrence and was not part of Trevor Dupuy's original listing.

30. This factor has been added by Christopher A. Lawrence and was not part of Trevor Dupuy's original listing.

31. This factor has been added by Christopher A. Lawrence and was not part of Trevor Dupuy's original listing.

32. This factor has been added by Christopher A. Lawrence and was not part of Trevor Dupuy's original listing.

Chapter 6

1. This is based upon an interview with Alexy Danilov, the secretary of the National Security and Defense Council. See Sevgil Musayeva, Ukrainska Pravda, 22 April 2022, "Alexey Danilov: Russia will disintegrate during our lifetime," at Oleksiy Danilov: There must be a completely new state – sincere, frank, such as our president is now | Ukrayinska Pravda.

2. Sevgil Musayeva, *Ukrainska Pravda*, 22 April 2022, "Alexey Danilov: Russia will disintegrate during our lifetime," at Oleksiy Danilov: There must be a completely new state – sincere, frank, such as our president is now | Ukrayinska Pravda.

3. This is from the march plan taken from Michael Schwirtz, Anton Troianovski, Yousir Al-Hlou, Masha Froliak, Adam Entous and Thomas Gibbons-Neff, "How Putin's War in Ukraine Became a Catastrophe for Russia," *New York Times*, 16 December 2022 at How Putin's War in Ukraine Became a Catastrophe for Russia – The New York Times (nytimes.com). It was provided to the *New York Times* by the GUR, Ukraine's military intelligence service.

4. They were 2/104th, 1/104th, 2/234th, 1/234th, 1/237th and 2/247th. Their march column also included the OMON, SOBR "Belgorod," 1140th Artillery Regiment, and a tank company from 124th Tank Battalion armed with T-72 B3s. It did not include the third battalion of each regiment, possibly because the first two battalions of each regiment were contract soldiers while the third battalion was conscripts. According to Russian law, conscripts are not allowed to serve outside of Russia.

5. This includes an artillery regiment, an anti-aircraft missile artillery battalion, engineer battalion, maintenance battalion, logistics battalions, reconnaissance company, sniper company, electronic warfare company, signal company, radar company, CBRN-defense company and a medical company. It was reported in 2017 to have had a motorized infantry battalion, but possibly that had been transferred.

6. See David Axe, "Ukraine's Artillery Did The Most Killing Around Kyiv, Ultimately Saving the City from Russian Occupation," Forbes, 25 December 2022 at Ukraine's Artillery Did The Most Killing Around Kyiv, Ultimately Saving The City From Russian Occupation (msn.com).

7. Sevgil Musayeva, *Ukrainska Pravda*, 22 April 2022, "Alexey Danilov: Russia will disintegrate during our lifetime," at Oleksiy Danilov: There must be a completely new state – sincere, frank, such as our president is now | Ukrayinska Pravda.

8. This translation is from the YouTube video by *The Guardian*, dated 25 February 2022 at 'Go fuck yourself', Ukrainian soldiers on Snake Island tell Russian ship – audio – YouTube. An alternate translation is given by Alex Abramovich in the *London Review of Books* on 28 February 2022 as:
   Russian warship: "Snake Island, I, Russian warship, repeat the offer: put down your arms and surrender, or you will be bombed. Have you understood me? Do you copy?"
   Ukrainian 1 to Ukrainian 2: "That's it, then. Or, do we need to fuck them back off?"
   Ukrainian 2 to Ukrainian 1: "Might as well."
   Ukrainian 1: "Russian warship, go fuck yourself."
   The actual Ukrainian phrase used was "иди на хуй" which translate as "go to a dick" or more like "go sit on a dick."

9. A nice description of the action and its aftermath is provided by Luke Harding, "'Russian warship, go fuck yourself': what happened next to the Ukrainians defending Snake Island?," *The Guardian*, 19 November 2022 at 'Russian warship, go fuck yourself': what happened next to the Ukrainians defending Snake Island? | Ukraine | The Guardian.

10. Gerrard Kaonga, "First Prisoners of War as Ukraine Captures Russian Soldiers, *Newsweek*, 24 February 2022 at First Prisoners of War as Ukraine Captures Russian Soldiers (newsweek.com).

11. Brendan Cole, "Russian Tank Convoy Blown Up in Videos as Ukraine Fights Back Invasion," *Newsweek*, 24 February 2022 at Russian Tank Convoy Blown Up in Videos As Ukraine Fights Back Invasion (msn.com).

Chapter 7

1. See Michael R. Gordon, Bojan Pancevski, Noemie Bisserbe and Marcus Walker, Wall Street Journal, 1 April 2022, "Vladimir Putin's 20-Year March to War in Ukraine – and How the West Mishandled It" at Vladimir Putin's 20-Year March to War in Ukraine – and How the West Mishandled It – WSJ; Patrick J. McDonnell, Los Angeles Times, 10 April 2022, "Russia lost the battle for Kyiv with its hasty assault on a Ukrainian airport" at Russia lost the battle for Kyiv with its hasty assault on a Ukrainian airport – Los Angeles Times (latimes.com); Stijn Mizer and Joost Oliemans, Oryx, 13 April 2022, "Destination Disaster: Russia's Failure at Hostomel Airport" at Destination Disaster: Russia's Failure At Hostomel Airport – Oryx (oryxspioenkop.com); and Andreas Rüesch, Neue Zürcher Zeitung, 8 April 2022, "Der Mythos von Russlands Elitetruppen wird in der Ukraine entzauber" ("The myth of Russia's elite troops is being disenchanted in Ukraine") at Ukraine: The myth of Russia's elite troops is being disenchanted (nzz.ch).

2. *Russia's War in Ukraine: Military and Intelligence Aspects* (Congressional Research Service, Washington DC, 14 September 2022), p. 5.

3. Andrew McGregor says there were 30 Ka-52s, which seems high. See Andrew McGregor, 8 March 2022, "Russian Airborne Disaster at Hostomel Airport" at Russian Airborne Disaster at Hostomel Airport | Aberfoyle International Security (aberfoylesecurity.com).

4. This detail is from Wikipedia, "Battle of Antonov Airport"; Sebastien Roblin, 19Fortyfive website, "Pictures: In Battle for Hostomel, Ukraine Drove Back Russia's Attack Helicopter and Elite Paratroops" at Pictures: In Battle for Hostomel, Ukraine Drove Back Russia's Attack Helicopters and Elite Paratroopers – 19FortyFive. The Wikipedia page says 20–34 helicopter, while Roblin specifically states 34. There is no way of verifying the accuracy of this, but it is difficult to believe that such detail was simply invented.

5. Note that Sebastien Roblin claims only "up to 300 elite Russian airborne soldiers."

6. Sebastien Roblin claims the unit was 11th Guards Air Assault Brigade, while Andrew McGregor, 8 March 2022, "Russian Airborne Disaster at Hostomel Airport", states it was 31st Guards Air Assault Brigade. See Russian Airborne Disaster at Hostomel Airport | Aberfoyle International Security (aberfoylesecurity.com). The Twitter account @ GirkinGirkin maintained by Igor Girkin on 25 February 2022 shows two captured soldiers from 11th Guards Air Assault Brigade. It is not clear where this video was taken. On 7 March, the deputy commander of the brigade was killed in action near Kharkiv. Other sources strongly indicate that it was 31st Guards Air Assault Brigade at Hostomel. See На кладбище Ульяновска с начала войны появились 42 могилы десантников, о смерти 21 из них не сообщалось публично (zona.media) and 'Are There Even Any Left?' 100 Days of War in Ukraine For an Elite Russian Unit – The Moscow Times.

7. Videos of the event are at Pictures: In Battle for Hostomel, Ukraine Drove Back Russia's Attack Helicopters and Elite Paratroopers – 19FortyFive.

8. Stijn Mizer and Joost Oliemans, *Oryx*, 13 April 2022, "Destination Disaster: Russia's Failure at Hostomel Airport" at Destination Disaster: Russia's Failure At Hostomel Airport – Oryx (oryxspioenkop.com). This is based upon a video on twitter on 18 March 2022 by @RALee85.

9. The interview titled "The only easy day was yesterday. Hostomel. Special Unit 'Omega'," dated 10 November 2022, on the National Information Portal claims that two helicopters were destroyed on the runway that morning. This claim is not repeated in other sources. It is at The Only Easy Day Was Yesterday. Hostomel. Special Unit "Omega" – Teletype. The Wikipedia page "List of aircraft losses during the Russo-Ukrainian" provides a slightly different account, with one Mi-35 lost over the reservoir and two Ka-52s damaged near the airport, one that was later destroyed. The listing "Russo-Ukrainian War Spotting" records two Ka-52s lost and one Mi-8 lost at Hostomel Airport, although the Mi-8 helicopter may

have been lost later. See Search · Russia · WarSpotting – documenting material losses in Russo-Ukrainian war.

10. See CNN report of 24 February, "CNN reporter: This shows just how close Russian forces are to the Ukraine capital" at CNN reporter: This shows just how close Russian forces are to Ukraine capital | Watch (msn.com).

To quote the report: "Matthew, tell us what you're witnessing there. Stop, stop. We may get ...

Jim, we've come out of the center of the Ukrainian capital Kiev and we are here at Antonov airport which is about 25 kilometers, 15 miles, or so out of the center. These troops you can see over here, stand up Lewis, these troops you can see over here, they are Russian airborne forces. They have taken this airport. They've allowed us to come in and be with them as they defend the perimeter of this air base here, where helicopter borne troops, these troops, were landed in the early hours of this morning to take and to form an air bridge to allow for more troops to come, and as you can see, these are Russians forces. You tell they are Russian, I have spoken to them already. You can tell they're Russian. They've got that orange and black band to identify them as Russian forces. I've spoken to the commander on the ground there within the past few minutes and he said they are now in control of this airport and within the past few seconds just before you came to us, they were engaged in a firefight, presumably with the Ukrainian military, which says it is staging a counteroffensive to try and take back this this this airport.

We can tell you now, I'm standing outside the perimeter of this Antonov air base and it has not been taken back by the Ukrainian military. It is the Russian military. You can see them now moving back to a different position. Who's the Ukrainian military who say they are now in control? This is about I would say about 20 miles from the center of the Ukrainian capital and so it just shows us now for the first just how close Russian forces have got towards the center of the Ukrainian capital. It's not just ... I've been to officials earlier, Ukrainian officers, and they're saying that the plan isn't just to surround the Ukrainian capital. They fear now that the plan is to take the capital to decapitate the leadership of Ukraine and to replace that leadership with a pro-Russian government. That's what Ukrainian officials are telling us now, they think is the Russian plan, and I can tell you, it is a very tense situation.

We've been expecting to see Ukrainian military forces, well, we didn't even know, frankly, we didn't even know that, you know, the Russian forces are going to be here. We assumed this was the Ukrainian forces, so went up to them and saying, hey, we've come from Kiev, you know, but it only emerged during the conversation that they're all Russians and there are no Ukrainian military forces in sight, although I can hear them because they've been shooting ferociously in the post in the past few minutes or so we're sort of in the defensive position behind this wall here, and we've got our car here with the crew here as well. And, you know, as the Russian airborne troops defend this position that they've taken on the outskirts of Kiev, Jim."

11. Unit identification from Sebastien Roblin.

12. Videos of two Su-24Ms provided in article by Sebastien Roblin.

13. This was probably only based only upon a single Ukrainian intelligence report. See Anthony Blair and Felix Allen, *U.S. Sun*, 24 February 2022, "Russia on Run: Ukrainian troops recapture Kyiv Airport in major blow to Vladmir Putin after day of fierce fighting" and Aditya Tarar, *Hindustan News Hub*, 24 February 2022, "In the direction of Kiev, 19 Russian Il-76s are flying to land, – Bellingcat."

14. See NBC News, 26 April 2022, Ken Dilanian, Courtney Kube, Carol E. Lee and Dan De Luce, "U.S. intel helped Ukraine protect air defenses, shoot down Russian plane carrying hundreds of troops." The statement in this report is not specific: "That near real-time intelligence-sharing also paved the way for Ukraine to shoot down a Russian transport

plane carrying hundreds of troops in the early days of the war, the officials say, helping repel a Russian assault on a key airport near Kyiv." Also see Mike Brest, *Washington Examiner*, 26 April 2022, "Ukraine shot down Russian plane with help from US intel: Report" at Ukraine shot down Russian plane with help from US intel: Report (msn.com), and *Daily Sun*, 26 April 2022, "US provided Ukrainian military with real-time info that allowed it to shoot down Russian troop transport carrying hundreds of soldiers in early days of war."

15. On the other hand, as of September 2022 no wreckage of the transport plane has been found, adding some doubt to this story. The interview titled "The only easy day was yesterday. Hostomel. Special Unit 'Omega'," dated 10 November 2022, on the National Information Portal describes the action there. It is at The Only Easy Day Was Yesterday. Hostomel. Special Unit "Omega" – Teletype.

16. Although we still do not have confirmation that Russia attempted to land significant reinforcements at this field in the first two days of fighting.

17. According to US Army doctrine with a close march column, the distance between vehicles varies from 20–25m and at a density of 40 to 50 vehicles per km along the route. See ATP 3-21.8, *Infantry Platoon and Squad*, paragraphs 5–19. Soviet doctrine, *c*. 1986, also looked at similar densities of 40 vehicles per km and 25m between vehicles. See *The Sustainability of the Soviet Army in Battle* (Royal Military Academy, Sandhurst, September 1986), pp. 528, 530.

18. This is from the march table provided in Michael Schwirtz, Anton Troianovski, Yousir Al-Hlou, Masha Froliak, Adam Entous and Thomas Gibbons-Neff, "How Putin's War in Ukraine Became a Catastrophe for Russia," *New York Times*, 16 December 2022 at How Putin's War in Ukraine Became a Catastrophe for Russia – The New York Times (nytimes. com). It is presented in the plate section.

19. The 76th Guards Air Assault Division has six airborne battalions, an artillery regiment and tank company. It was certainly a reduced division, or effectively a brigade-sized organization. Not listed in its order of march were its maintenance battalion, engineering battalion, communications battalion, material support battalion, military hospital, postal station, airborne support company, MBC defense company and anti-aircraft missile regiment.

20. See Adam Taylor, "As Russians advance on Kyiv, ordinary civilians heed calls to fight for Ukraine however they can," *Washington Post*, 25 February 2022 at https://www.washingtonpost.com/world/2022/02/25/ukraine-civilians-weapons-molotov/.

21. Glenn Kessler, *Washington Post*, 6 March 2022, "Zelensky's famous quote of 'need ammo, not a ride' not easily confirmed" at Zelensky's famous quote of "need ammo, not a ride" not easily confirmed (msn.com).

22. From Michael Schwirtz, Anton Troianovski, Yousir Al-Hlou, Masha Froliak, Adam Entous and Thomas Gibbons-Neff, "How Putin's War in Ukraine Became a Catastrophe for Russia," *New York Times*, 16 December 2022 at How Putin's War in Ukraine Became a Catastrophe for Russia – The New York Times (nytimes.com). This account appears to be primarily based upon a single interview of a Russian soldier and one Russian unit logbook they obtained. The Russian unit the logbook belonged to is not identified. It is not known if this was the situation throughout the convoy, but the convoy did take twice as long for the head of the column to arrive at its objective as originally planned. It also appears that column was stretched out for days, with the tail being much more than 2 hours behind the head, as originally planned.

23. Specifically, the *Kyiv Independent* reported the destruction of fifty-six of the Chechen tanks by Ukrainian missiles. I am hesitant to include in this account these types of unconfirmed one-sided casualty reports. To start with, I do not know if the regiment had fifty-six tanks.

24. The 104th Guards Air Assault Regiment is part of 76th Guards Air Assault Division, of which the I and II battalions were in the column driving down from Belarus.

25. A personnel roster was obtained listing the soldiers by name. It provided a total for soldiers assigned and soldiers present by name. This included the Bn HQ (3 soldiers including the commander Lt C. Dmitrii Shabayev), Bn staff (3 soldiers), 7th, 8th, and 9th companies (10 vehicles and 67 soldiers assigned and 65 present, 10 vehicles and 67 soldiers assigned and 65 present, and 10 vehicles and 66 soldiers assigned and 61 present respectively), a mortar battery (11 vehicles and 57 soldiers assigned and 49 soldiers present), an anti-tank platoon (3 vehicles and 22 soldiers), 1st reconnaissance platoon (3 vehicles and 26 soldiers assigned and 24 present), a signal platoon (2 vehicles and 12 soldiers), a support platoon (14 vehicles and 21 soldiers assigned and 19 present), a medical platoon (4 vehicles and 14 soldiers assigned and 9 present), a sniper platoon (1 vehicles and 17 soldiers assigned and 16 present), the 2nd Tank Company (13 vehicles and 42 soldiers), 4th Howitzer Battery (12 vehicles and 44 soldiers assigned and 42 present), 2nd Rocket Battery (20 vehicles and 57 soldiers assigned and 55 present), a water section (5 vehicles and 9 soldiers assigned and 7 present), an anti-aircraft gun battery (8 vehicles and 35 soldiers assigned and 34 present), the 2nd reconnaissance platoon (3 vehicles and 23 soldiers assigned and 15 present), an electronic reconnaissance platoon (1 vehicles and 6 soldiers assigned and 2 present), an engineering company (12 vehicles and 25 soldiers assigned and 24 present), a NBC platoon (1 vehicle and 3 soldiers), a flamethrower platoon (1 vehicle and 7 soldiers), a signals platoon (3 vehicles and 12 soldiers), an electronic warfare platoon (3 vehicles and 12 soldiers), a radar reconnaissance section (1 vehicle and 3 soldiers assigned and 2 present), an evacuation and workshop company (5 vehicles and 20 soldiers assigned and 19 present) and elements of the Bde sustainment battalion (26 vehicles and 35 soldiers). This appears to be a fully fleshed out large BTG with a total of 708 officers and men assigned and 659 present and a total of 182 vehicles, including 10 or 13 tanks.

26. Photographic evidence records two T-72Bs and a BTR-80 destroyed near Ivankiv. See Dan on Twitter: "7. On 25/02/22, UAF destroyed a key bridge in Ivankiv on the Teteriv River. RuAF forces nevertheless bypassed Ivankiv continuing to Kyiv. RuAF entered Ivankiv on 26th but fighting continued in or around for a week. Here some 5th Guards Tank Brigade losses. https://t.co/T7rSlBebdG" / Twitter.

27. The vehicles were three KamAZ 6x6 armored trucks, a GAZ-66 4x4 truck, A Tiger all-terrain armored truck and a BTR armored personal carrier. See Tim McMillan, "Know no mercy: The Russian Cops Who Tried to Strom Kyiv by Themselves," *The Debrief*, 20 May 2022, at Know No Mercy: The Russian Cops Who Tried To Storm Kyiv By Themselves – The Debrief. A review of ukr.warspotting.net showed the following vehicles destroyed in the area on 25 February: 1 R-142NSA command and signals vehicle, 1 KamZA Avtozaks from Rosgvardiya and on 26 February: 1 KamAZ Avtozaks from Rosgvardiya. These are both before the brigade. Beyond the bridge posted for 28 February (even though they were probably destroyed on 25 February) are 3 KamAZ Avtozaks from Rosgvardiya, 1 Ural Federal from Rosgvardiya and 1 BTR-80. Posted for 29 March near these other five vehicles is 1 UAZ-394511 "Esaul" from Rosgvardiya.

28. See James Marson, "The Ragtag Army Than Won the Battle of Kyiv and Saved Ukraine, *Wall Street Journal*, 20 September 2022 at https://archive.ph/cBRhl.

29. See "Russian War Ukraine – Ukrainian Armored Vehicle Totally Ignores Direct Machine Gun Fire – YouTube," on YouTube at – Russian War Ukraine – Ukrainian Armored Vehicle Totally Ignores Direct Machine Gun Fire – YouTube.

30. At least one Russian APC and six soldiers were killed according to reports and photos.

31. According to a count of destroyed and captured vehicles taken from ukr.warspotting.net and dated 27 February, this included 12 BMD-2s, 8 BTR-Ds, 2 BTR-82A(M)s, 2 BMD-1KSh-A command and staff vehicles, 1 V119 Artillery Direction Fire vehicle from 104th Air Assault Regiment, 1 R-149MA1 command and staff vehicle, 2 120mm2S9 Nonas, 1

KamZA 6x6 Tanker, 1 BREM-D armored recovery vehicle, 1 9A35 Stela-10 and 1 9S932-1 "Barnaul-T" automated system for air defense units. One vehicle posted 3 March was also spotted in this area.

32. Interview with one Ukrainian participant is provided on YouTube from Ukrainian Military TV, "Intelligence Officer about Fight for Bucha and Irpin – Volodymyr Korotia: I am a Warrior," https://youtu.be/YeclqoQbjJc?t=340. This video appears to be from official sources.

33. Paul Sonne, Isabelle Khurshudyan, Serhiy Morgunov and Kostiantyn Khudov, "Battle for Kyiv: Ukrainian valor, Russian blunders combined to save the capital," *Washington Post*, 24 August 2022 at Battle for Kyiv: How Ukrainian forces defended and saved their capital - Washington Post (archive.org).

34. According to ukr.warspotting.net the easternmost cluster of losses on the highway is in the eastern part of Berezivka and up to the river. This first cluster consists of 25 vehicles, including 17 trucks and 6 tanks. They are posted between 6 March and 3 April 2022. It includes one T-72B in the lead and 5 more tanks further back. There are 16 items of equipment, including most tanks, identified as belonging to 5th Guards Tank Brigade and two trucks are assigned to 37th Motorized Rifle Brigade. The two trucks reported for 37th Motorized Rifle Brigade and 6 nearby trucks were all posted for 6 March. The other 8 kills on the road were posted for 19 March, including 2 tanks. To the south of the road are 9 more kills posted between 21 March and 3 April, including 4 tanks. One wonders if this was 3 or more separate groups of vehicles hit on different days.

A little further south is a cluster of 16 vehicles. They are all posted between 19 March and 20 April, with 12 of them posted for 19 and 20 March and 14 of them are identified as with 5th Guards Tank Brigade.

In western Berezivka is 1 152mm 2S3(M) "Akatsiya" posted 2 April and further west are 11 more vehicles, somewhat scattered, with one posted for 26 February (a T-72B) and 10 posted between 30 March and 5 April 2022. Around the area labeled Okko are 11 more vehicles, mostly dated from 22 March–5 April, including 2 tanks (T-72B3s). These last groupings may have been involved in operations against Makariv than against Kyiv.

This is a total of 73 vehicles in at least 6 separate clusters and possibly killed on different days. The reports for this action from the Office of the President of Ukraine claimed that, "According to confirmed estimates, by 14.00 more than 200 units of various equipment in the directions of Irpin-Zhytomyr highway were destroyed and damaged." See *TSN Ukraine*, 28 February 2022, "'If you knew …': Arestovich on the destruction of military equipment of the invaders" at War Ukraine: Arestovych told about the destruction of military equipment of the occupiers in the directions of Irpin – Zhytomyr – Ukraine – tsn.ua. It appears that these reported kill claims are overstated.

35. The 10th Mountain Assault Brigade and 14th Mechanized Brigade's positions are confirmed by media reports from Ukrainian journalists as well as footage posted by the units themselves. The 10th Mountain Assault Brigade's location on the western flank of Makariv in particular can be confirmed due to footage released by the unit showing captured T-80 BVMs. The 64th Motorized Rifle Brigade was the only Russian unit equipped with that model in the sector around Kyiv. The first time the 10th is confirmed to be in the region was on 10 March when it released a report that it had shot down an SU-25 from one of the Eastern Military District's Assault Aviation Regiments. Until 6 March it had apparently been covering the border with Belarus around Volyn.

The 14th Mechanized is first confirmed to have been involved in the battle for Makariv on 2 March, in a post by the Ukrainian General Staff. This was followed up by obituaries for three of its members after a battle on 8 March 2022.

Media reports and the Ukrainian General Staff post claim that 95th Air Assault Brigade participated in the fighting around Makariv on 2 March. However, the brigade was confirmed to have been around Horlivka in the Donbas, with it breaking into the city in a local attack on 1 March, just a day before it was reported to be near Makariv, nearly 400 miles away. The likeliest answer is that a formation was raised from volunteers and other manpower at the 95th's garrison in Zhytomyr (only 50 miles to the west of Makariv) and was then deployed as an independent battalion to reinforce the operations west of Kyiv.

36. Russian unit deployments were confirmed from photographs of losses on the ground, including unit signs on the wreck and the model of the lost vehicle. The site used to review these losses was ukr.warspotting.net. The 64th Motorized Rifle Brigade, 37th Guards Motorized Rifle Brigade and 5th Guards Tank Brigade each operated a different tank model (T-90BVM, T-72B3, T-72B, respectively), which greatly assists in locating the units. We suspect the 76th Air Assault Division's tank company has T-72B3s, and their IFVs were BMDs vice BMPs. They left very little equipment on the battlefield, making it harder to place them. One T-72B3 was left in Dmytrivka alongside a BMD-2 and a small grouping of losses from the 5th Tank Brigade. The date on the photos is 31 March, but they are all rusted out, so it looks like that they were pretty old wrecks. It does indicate that elements of the 76th Air Assault Division did indeed go down that road through Dmytrivka and then hooked to the left (eastward) to enter Kyiv from the E-40.

From right to left, 64th Motorized Rifle Brigade can be identified northwest of Makariv as early as 3 March, thanks to a video posted by a group from the Ukrainian Territorial Defense Forces showing a captured T-80BVM on a road 8.5 miles to the north of Marariv. Images of a destroyed T-8-BVM 9.5 miles to the north-northwest of Makariv were posted for 10 March. Two more destroyed T-80BVMs were posted for 13 March, both by 10th Mountain Brigade, one of them being geolocated to Nalyvaikivka, 4.5 miles to the northwest of Makariv.

The first photos of confirmed vehicle losses from 37th Guards Motorized Rifle Brigade were uploaded on 1 March, though the vehicle itself may have been destroyed beforehand. This wreck was located in Sytnyaki, 6 miles to the southwest of Makariv. A photo dated 4 March shows a destroyed T-72B3 on the E40 highway just north of Kopyliv, 4.5 miles to the southeast of Makariv. This allows the placing of 37th Brigade in the middle of the Makariv battlezone, with 64th brigade to its west and 5th Guards Tank Brigade to its east.

The 5th Guards Tank Brigade was one of the spearhead units of the push on Kyiv, with a captured Russian timetable published by the *New York Times* showing that it was the lead element of the column which came down along the western bank of the Dnieper. This column also contained 76th Air Assault Division, which was supposed to assist in taking Kyiv on the first day of the war by attacking from the west along the E40 highway. The first photo of a destroyed T-72B in the sector was posted for 26 February, with the wreck being located on the E40 near Severynivka (12 miles west of Kyiv and 7.5 miles southeast of Makariv). The furthest west that a T-72B wreck can be identified is Kalynivka, just south of Makariv but the bulk are east of Kopyliv and west of Stoyanka, where the E40 crosses the Irpin River and enters Kyiv. In short, the brigade was in the sector by the third day of the war.

37. These figures are based upon Russian military personnel records released by the Ukrainian Military Intelligence Directorate on 4 April 2022 and 26 March 2022 respectively. See https://gur.gov.ua/content/voennye-prestupnyky-neposredstvenno-uchastvuiushchye-v-sovershenyy-voennykh-prestuplenyi-protyv-naroda-ukrayny-v-h-bucha-voennosluzhashchye-64-otdelnoi-motostrelkovoi-bryhady-35-oa-vvo.html and https://gur.gov.ua/content/voennosluzhashchye-batalonnoi-taktycheskoi-hruppy-37-otdelnoi-motostrelkovoi-bryhady.html.

38. Christopher A. Lawrence, "The Russo-Ukrainian War of 2022 – Day 6 (ground actions)," *Mystics & Statistics* blog, dated 1 March 2002 at The Russo-Ukrainian War of 2022 – Day 6 (ground actions) | Mystics & Statistics (dupuyinstitute.org).

39. This includes 76th Air Assault Division with six maneuver battalions, at least one battalion of 31st Guards Air Assault Brigade and elements from 141st Special Motorized Regiment. Other units that may have been added to the area were a second battalion of 31st Air Assault Brigade, 98th Guards Airborne Division, probably with only four maneuver battalions, and 106th Guards Airborne Division, probably with only four maneuver battalions. Also, 155th Naval Infantry Brigade moved into the area by 7 March, according to the Ukrainian General Staff.

It appears that 31st Air Assault Brigade had their BMD IFVs brought up by 26 February. This could have been done by a second battalion. The 106th Guards Airborne Division had two confirmed s lost around Irpin, establishing its presence in the area. A member of 137th Regiment (106th Guards Airborne Division) was killed in action on 6 March 2022 in Ukraine and a member of 51st Regiment (106th Guards Airborne Division) died on 5 March . A member of the division's artillery regiment died on 10 March. It would appear that the division was, at the latest, around Kyiv by 5 or 6 March.

Other Russian forces in the area may have included elements of 45th Spetznaz Brigade in Hostomel airport in February based upon photographic evidence.

The defending Ukrainian forces were 4th Rapid Reaction Brigade (three maneuver battalions), the volunteer Georgian battalion and elements from 72nd Mechanized Brigade. Covering the west of Kyiv were various reserve and militia units, possibly including 112th Brigade of the Territorial Defense Forces (five battalions?). Other units that may have been in the area were 1st Operational Brigade (four maneuver battalions) and 25th Public Security Protection Brigade (six battalions).

40. Certainly, the initial Russian airborne battalion that deployed there was well trained and I assume that most of the column that came down had at least professional soldiers in it, although a professional soldier in the Russian Army may not have more than a year of experience. In contrast, the Ukraine National Guard Brigade was almost certainly made up of part-time soldiers and probably not at the level of training and experience as the Russians. So, in actual combat operations, it is assumed that the Russians had the advantages in training and experience.

Chapter 8

1. This includes two BMD-2s on highway T2206 posted for 8 and 11 March, and GAZ Tigr-M on highway P57 posted 5 March. These are well outside the Kherson battle area

2. See Michael Schwirtz, "Dug in on the front lines, Ukrainian soldiers fight to repel t' Russian onslaught," *New York Times*, 22 April 2022 at Ukraine's Forces, Dug In on Fr Line, Fight to Repel Russia – The New York Times (nytimes.com). The brigade's h base is in Mukachevo in far western Ukraine.

3. The time and duration of the battle is as given by Wikipedia, "The Battle of Myk These times are not supported by their reference footnotes, so the source Is not clear

4. The time is drawn from General Staff of the Armed Forces of Ukraine: Oper Information on 11.00, 28.02.2002 regarding the #russian invasion at (20+) Faceboc

5. This includes three to the southwest of the city consisting of two BMP-2s po 6 March 2022 and a BDR-D also posted 6 March. There was a MT-LBVM/' 3 March to west northwest of the city and a BMD-2 posted for 30 April to t' northwest of the city. None of these were near the city. Considering the nat operations and the fact that this ground was retaken reasonably soon by the Ukr do not suspect that a lot of destroyed vehicles were towed out of the area.

6. See Yaroslav Trofimov, "A Ukrainian Town Deals Russia One of the War's M Routs," *Wall Street Journal*, 16 March 2022 at A Ukrainian Town Deals Russ' War's Most Decisive Routs – WSJ.

7. According to Yaroslav Trofimov's article in the *Wall Street Journal*, the Russians left behind almost 30 of their 43 vehicles and 10 Russian soldiers were captured. The Ukrainians estimated 100 Russian troops died and at least 11 dead Russian bodies were recovered. In Voznesensk 10 civilians were killed and 2 more died after the battle after hitting a land mine.

8. This was a BTR-80 posted for 4 March 2022. It was located right at the southern entrance of the town.

9. A KamAZ 6x6 tanker posted for 17 March, a Ural-375D posted for 19 March, and a 122mm 2S1 "Gvozdika" posted for 10 March 2022. These were clearly deployed to support operations.

Chapter 9

1. Some of the details of this are still classified.

2. See YouTube video posted by *The Guardian*, "Ukrainian citizen confronts Russian soldiers after tank runs out of fuel," https://www.youtube.com/watch?v=14gVDF2b1vA, although in this case they say they are out of fuel.

3. The distance in a straight line from Chernihiv to Sumy is about 250km. The distance from Sumy to Kharkiv is more than another 140km.

4. See this video posted by *The Guardian*, "Ukrainian citizen confronts Russian soldiers after tank runs out of fuel," https://www.youtube.com/watch?v=14gVDF2b1vA. The dialogue, which is friendly, between the Ukrainian driver and the crew of an APC (armored personnel carrier) is worth repeating. It goes:
Ukrainian Driver: "Are you guys, broken, broken down?"
Russian crewman: "Out of fuel."
Driver: "Can I tow you back … to Russia?"
Crewmen: [laughter]
Driver: "Do you know where you are going?"
Crewmen: "No, no … To Kyiv, fuck off! What do they say on the news?"
Driver: "Well, while everyone is on our sides, yours and prisoners surrender well, because the boys also do not know where they are going. And I asked the whole column of people like you: no one knows where they are and where they are going."

5. Some reports give the entire brigade at about 100 T-64s, or about 30 a battalion.

6. David Axe, Forbes, 31 March 2022, "Ukraine's Best Tank Brigade has Won the Battle of Chernihiv" at Ukraine's Best Tank Brigade Has Won The Battle For Chernihiv (forbes.com).

7. The T-64 BM is something of a unique weapon, and few of them have shown up in the various photos of destroyed equipment that have circulated during this war.

8. There was a cluster of eight vehicles on route M01 that were all recorded on 24 February 2022. These were clearly the forces approaching Chernihiv on the first day and their losses included 4 MBP-2(K)s, of which 3 were credited to 74th Motorized Brigade. Another 7 vehicles were closer to the city, including a T-72B3 and a T-72B Obr. 1989 (74th Motorized Brigade) on route M01, both posted for 25 February. The other 5 vehicles are off the main road and include a T72B3 Obr. 2016 posted for 2 April and 4 trucks posted for 27 April (but probably destroyed weeks earlier). In the northeastern part of the city were 2 T-72B Obr. 1989s and a R-166-0.5 signals vehicle. All 3 vehicles were from 35th Motorized Rifle Brigade and posted for 26 February.

9. There was a cluster of eight of them near the village of Ukrposhta, near highway T2512, posted from 30 March–12 April. This appears to be a cluster of vehicles that was shot up by either artillery or drones. It included two PP-2005 floating bridges. Further down T2512 towards the village of Burivka are two T-72Bs posted for 5 and 8 April from 80th Tank Regiment and a 152mm 2S3(M) "Akatsiya" SP artillery posted for 9 April. To the

northwest near the town of Horodnya are another 19 vehicles, with 17 of them clustered like they were a rear area grouping targeted by artillery or drones. Posted as destroyed on 25 February are 3 PP-2005 floating bridges, 3 KamAZ 6x6s, 3 TMM-3 bridge layers, a MTP-A@ recovery vehicle, 2 PTS-2 tracked amphibious transports, a BAT-2 heavy engineering vehicle, a KamAZ-5350 with KS-45719-7M crane, a KamAZ-5350 with OEV-3523 excavator, a BMP-2(K) and a R-419L1 communications station. This clearly was another rear area grouping targeted by artillery or drones. Other losses were a T-72A from 80th Tank Regiment posted for 16 April and a T-72B posted for 5 April.

10. In the town of Sehstovytsya were 2 clusters of 8 and 15 destroyed vehicles. The western group was dated from 4–20 April and included 5 KamAZ 6x6s trucks. The eastern group was dated from 8 April–6 May 2022. The only combat vehicle was a MT-LB IFV, dated 5 April. The rest were trucks, 14 KamAZ 6x6s.

In the village of Kolychivka, just outside of Chernihiv, were 4 AFVs, a T-72B OBr. 1989 posted on 18 March, a BMP-2(K) posted on 7 March, a T-72B Obr. 1989 from 228th Motorized Regiment posted on 10 March and a BTR-82A(M) from 228th Motorized Rifle Regiment posted on 7 March.

Further down the M01 road were 19 more vehicles, with only 4 of them AFVs, all posted between 22 March and 14 June 2022, with some from 228th Motorized Rifle Regiment and 55th Mountain Motorized Rifle Brigade. They included 3 AFVs all in the village of Ivanivka: a BTR-82A(M) from 228th Motorized Rifle Regiment posted on 3 April, a BTR-80 posted on 31 March and a T-72B3 posted on 29 March. To the south of Ivanivka and the road intersection of M01 and E95 were 4 152mm @A65 "Msta-B" towed howitzers, dated 22 March. It looks like an entire battery was eliminated here.

To the east of there were another 24 destroyed vehicles, including 10 AFVs (3 tanks). One BMP-2(K) was identified with 74th motorized Rifle Brigade. They were posted from 11 March–24 May 2022.

There was only one vehicle to the west of Chernihiv, a Ural-4320 tanker from 80th Tank Regiment posted on 8 April 2022.

11. They are one 1 MT-LUB M1980 "Blade" IFV posted on 10 March, one BRM-1K reconnaissance vehicle posted on 25 February, and in downtown Konotop a R-1479MGg command and staff vehicle posted on 25 February and a 9P149 Shturm-S antitank system posted on 24 February 2022. Some of these downtown vehicles may have broken down first.

12. Eight tanks lost around Sumy include a T-72B on 4 March at the village of Hutnystske, a T-72B3 Obr. 2016 posted on 3 March at the village of Brovkove just southwest of Sumy, a T-90 (!) from 27th (Guards) Motorized Rifle Brigade just to the southeast of Sumy posted on 27 February, a T-72B3 posted on 25 March and a T-72B3 Obr. 2016 posted on 27 March at the village of Vorozhba further southwest of Sumy, a T-72B3 Obr. 2016 posted on 2 April further southeast of Sumy, and two T-72B3 Obr. 2016 from 1st Tank Regiment posted on 28 February near Krasnopillia (perhaps the evidence of the strike that claimed to kill 96 tanks).

One BMP-2(K) dated 27 February was lost at the village of Hutnysktsku. Other losses near Sumy include two 152mm 2S19 "Msta-S" from 2nd (Guards) Motorized Rifle Division posted on 1 March and another 152mm 2S19 "Msta-S" posted on 26 March southeast of Sumy.

There are considerable losses around and in Trostyanets. To the west tanks include T-80U from 4th (Guards) Tank Division posted at Bilka on 4 April and a T-80U from 4th (Guards) Tank Division posted at Stanova on 28 February.

Other AFVs include BMP-2(K) posted at Boromlia on 29 March and 1 BMP-2(K) from 15th Motorized Rifle Regiment posted on 31 March.

Other vehicles and weapons lost include 152mm 2S19 "Msta-S" from 275th Self-propelled Artillery Regiment (4th Guards Tank Division) posted at Bilka on 17 March, an

R-149MA3 command and staff vehicle from 1st Motorized Rifle Regiment posted on 26 March and a 152mm 2S19 "Msta-S" posted 31 March.

In and on the outskirts of Trosyanets are 4 tanks, 7 other AFVs and 3 other vehicles. They include 2 BMP-2(K)s posted on 26 March, a BMP-2(K) from 4th (Guards) Tank Division posted on 24 March, a T-80BV from 423rd Motorized Rifle Regiment (4th Guards Tank Division) posted on 26 March, 2 152mm 2S19s "Msta-S" from 275th Self-Propelled Artillery Regiment (4th Guards Tank Division) posted on 26 March, a KamAZ 6x5 posted on 27 March, a T-80UK and a T-80U both from 4th (Guards) Tank Division posted on 27 February, a T-80UE-1 from 4th (Guards) Tank Division posted on 26 February, 2 BMP-2(K)s posted on 24 March and 2 BMP-2(K)s from 4th (Guards) Tank Division posted on 24 March and 1 April 2022.

To the west, southwest and south of Trostyanets 1V13(M) battery fire control center from 4th (Guards) Tank Division posted on 28 February, at the village of Chupakhivka are two T-80Us from 4th (Guards) Tank Division posted on 27 and 28 February and two T-80BVs from 423rd Motorized Rifle Regiment (4th Guards Tank Division) posted on 27 February and at the western edge of Okhtyka are a KamAZ-63968 "Typhoon" a KamAZ 6x6 and an Msh-5350.1 command vehicle all from 96th Reconnaissance Brigade and posted on 24 February.

The 4th Guards Tank Division was reported, based upon their own unit records, as of 15 March to have lost 62 T-80Us and T-80UEs.

13. For example see Is Russia Using Thermobaric Weapons in Ukraine?

14. It appears the town was attacked the first day. Other sources claim that the town was taken on 1 March after a week-long fight. See Shaun Walker, "'Barbarians': Russian troops leave grisly mark on town of Trostianets," *The Guardian*, 5 April 2022 at 'Barbarians': Russian troops leave grisly mark on town of Trostianets | Ukraine | The Guardian and Robert Menkick, "Legendary Stalingrad tank division destroyed as Ukraine reclaims key town", *The Telegraph*, 27 March 2022, 1849, at Legendary Stalingrad tank division destroyed as Ukraine reclaims key town (telegraph.co.uk). These two reports do contradict each other. Also see HB Ukraine, 2 March 2022, 0350, "Russian troops completely occupied Trostyanets: they created a 'headquarters' and broke all roads – the head of the Sumy Regional State Administration," at Trostyanets – the occupiers completely occupied the city in the Sumy region – news of Ukraine / NV. The later date of occupation of the town on 1 March does not mesh with the account of their resistance by a hundred lightly armed men on the first day of the invasion.

15. This is an assumption based upon the maps of confirmed lost Russian vehicles. The 2nd Guards Motorized Rifle Division had vehicles strung out along the Sumy–Nedryhailiv–Romny road and the surrounding region, coming to a halt just east of Pryluky. Their opposition may have been the Ukrainian 58th Motorized Brigade and local National Guard forces.

16. See Ukraine General Staff Facebook post of 16 May 2022 at (20+) Facebook.

17. The total number of vehicles lost is 312 by count, which differs slightly from the totals given in the report.

18. A captured Russian 1st Guards Tank Army intelligence report records 58th Motorized Brigade as their opposition. The brigade had one member, Inna Derusova, killed in action in Okhtyrka on 24 February. The unit's cantonment was at Konotop.

19. See Robert Menkick, "Legendary Stalingrad tank division destroyed as Ukraine reclaims key town", *The Telegraph*, 27 March 2022, 1849, at Legendary Stalingrad tank division destroyed as Ukraine reclaims key town (telegraph.co.uk) and SOFREP website, "Ukrainians Obliterate the Elite Russian 4th Guards Tank Division 15 Miles from Russian Border," dated 28 March 2022 at Ukrainians Obliterate the Elite Russian 4th Guards Tank Division 15 Miles From Russian Border | SOFREP.

20. It is reported that Russians occupied the town with about 800 troops. See Thomas Gibbons-Neff, Natalia Yermak and Tyler Hicks, "'This is True Barbarity': Life and Death Under Russian Occupation," *New York Times*, 3 April 2022 at 'This Is True Barbarity': Life Under Russian Occupation - The New York Times (nytimes.com). Some of the other headlines are claiming that 4th Guards Tank Division was destroyed. These claims do not mesh well with an occupying force of only 800 troops. It is also worth noting that 4th Guards Tank Division was already down sixty-two tanks as of 15 March.

21. Shaun Walker, "'Barbarians': Russian troops leave grisly mark on town of Trostianent," *The Guardian*, 5 April 2022 at 'Barbarians': Russian troops leave grisly mark on town of Trostianets | Ukraine | The Guardian. As they note, "On a two-day visit to the town, the Guardian found evidence of summary executions, torture and systematic looting during the month of occupation …".

22. See Ukrinform, 17 April 2022, 1645, "Five children killed by Russian mines and tripwires in Trostianets at Five children killed by Russian mines and tripwires in Trostianets (ukrinform.net).

23. "Moscow says 498 Russians killed in Ukraine since invasion started," Aljazeera, 2 March 2022 at Moscow says 498 Russians killed in Ukraine since invasion started | Russia-Ukraine war News | Al Jazeera.

Chapter 10

1. Video is here, only 1 minute 18 seconds long, https://www.youtube.com/watch?v=4g68MmLrGvM.

2. Videos referenced from YouTube include: *Guardian News*, "Russian tanks seen being ambushed on outskirts of Kyiv, Ukraine," *The Telegraph*, "Ukraine destroy Russian tank column in Brovary near Kyiv," *The Sun*, "Ukrainian town of Brovary near Kyiv littered with destroyed Russian tanks," ABC News, "Russian tanks, armored vehicles ambushed outside Kyiv," CNN, "'Structured ambush': Video appears to show strike on Russian tanks," and ITV News, "'Russian commander killed' as military vehicles destroyed near Kyiv's outskirts." The main video of the column being attacked originally came from the Azov Regiment.

   An examination of the maps at ukr.warspotting.net provided the following count of vehicles destroyed at Skybyn, a suburb just to the northeast of Brovary on the road from southwest to northeast: a T-72AV from 6th Tank Regiment, a T-72A from 6th Tank Regiment, a BTR-82A(M), a T-72A from 6th Tank Regiment and a BMP-2(K). All these vehicles were posted on 10 March 2022. An additional eight vehicles are further back, including an MT-LB posted on 1 April, an R-149MA1 command and staff vehicle also posted on 1 April, a T-72B Obr. 1989 posted on 30 March, an MT-LB IFV posted on 9 March, a T-72B posted on 30 March, a T-72A posted on 27 March, a T-72B Obr. 1989 from 6th Tank Regiment posted on 4 April, a T-72A from 6th Tank Regiment posted on 11 March. Even further back were an additional nine vehicles: T-72B from 90th (Guards) Tank Division posted on 4 April, BMP-2K from 6th Tank Regiment posted on 1 April, T-72B posted on 5 April, T-72B posted on 3 April, T-72A posted on 5 April, MT-LB IFV posted on 5 April, a REM-KL recovery vehicle posted on 27 March, a Ural-4320 tanker from 6th Tank Regiment posted on 4 April and a T-72B posted on 30 March. Most of these last two groups were probably not part of the initial fight.

3. Drawn from Sky News video: Ukraine war: 'Lots and lots of losses': Military vehicles destroyed in Brovary, north-east of Kyiv | World News | Sky News.

4. *Business Standard*, New Delhi, 12 March 2022, "Russia disables Ukraine military's main radio intelligence facility" at Russia disables Ukraine military's main radio intelligence facility | Business Standard News (business-standard.com).

Chapter 11

1. According to RUSI, "The VKS had deployed a fast-jet force of around 350 modern combat aircraft for operations in Ukraine." See Justin Bronk with Nick Reynolds and Jack Watling, *The Russian Air War and Ukrainian Requirements for Air Defence* (Royal United Service Institute for Defence and Security Studies (RUSI), London, 7 November 2022), p. 6.

2. This argument is presented by William (Chip) Sayers in his *Mystics & Statistics*, 16 June 2022 blog post "VVS View of Air Superiority," at VVS View of Air Superiority | Mystics & Statistics (dupuyinstitute.org).

3. Both the Ukrainian Special Communications Agency and the US officials claimed that one or two Russian Il-76s was shot down over Vasylkiv (25 miles south of Kyiv) and Bila Tservkva (85 miles south of Kyiv). To date, no wreckage has been located.

4. It is reported that two An-26s were lost on 24 February. They are identified as Ukrainian Air Force *59 blue* near Zhukivtsi and Russian Air Force *RF-36074* crashed near Voronezh. On 27 February a Ukrainian Antonov Airlines An-26-100 (identified as *UR-13395*) was confirmed to be destroyed in Hostomel.

5. This was noted on our blog on 28 February. See Christopher A. Lawrence, *Mystics & Statistics*, 28 February 2022, "Contested Air Space over Ukraine?" at February | 2022 | Mystics & Statistics (dupuyinstitute.org).

6. This is in accordance with Bronk with Reynolds and Watling, *Russian Air War*, p. 14. I am not sure of these sources for this figure, they appear to be Ukrainian. This count does not include all Russian aircraft and helicopter sorties.

7. Matt Seyler, ABC News, 11 March 2022, "Ukraine using drones to 'great effect' on Russian forces: Pentagon Updates" at Ukraine using drones to 'great effect' on Russian forces: Pentagon updates – ABC News.

8. This is according to Bronk with Reynolds and Watling, *Russian Air War*, p. 1.

9. In addition to my *Mystics & Statistics* blog post on 28 February, this was also noted by the US Department of Defense. See Julie Coleman, Yahoo News, 28 February 2022 "Ukraine and Russia are still fighting for control of the skies 5 days into the way, US defense official says" at Ukraine and Russia are still fighting for control of the skies 5 days into the war, US defense official says (yahoo.com).

10. This list is primarily developed from the Wikipedia article "List of aircraft losses during the Russo-Ukrainian War" which relies on multiple sources. We have reason to believe this is a fairly complete listing.

11. Combat aircraft include such planes as MiG-29s, Su-24s, Su-25s and Su-27s.

Chapter 12

1. See: U-1, U-2 and U-3, Measuring the Effects of Combat in Cities, Phases I, II and III at TDI – The Dupuy Institute Publications. Also see Chapter 16, Urban Legends and Chapter 17, The Use of Case Studies in Lawrence, War by Numbers.

2. On Kharkivski Hwy near the School of Physics and Technology were five vehicles: two 122mm BM-21s "Grad" and three KamAZ 6x6s, all from 200th Motorized Rifle Brigade and posted on 24 February. At the northwest entrance to the city at Lesia Serdiuka St and Hwy E40 were four IFVs all posted on 24 February: three MT-LBVM/K from 25th Motorized Rifle Brigade and a T-80BVM from 200th Motorized Rifle Brigade.

3. Gerrard Kaonga, "First Prisoners of War as Ukraine Captures Russian Soldiers," Newsweek, 24 February 2022 at First Prisoners of War as Ukraine Captures Russian Soldiers (newsweek.com).

4. Brendan Cole, "Russian Tank Convoy Blown Up in Videos as Ukraine Fights Back Invasion," Newsweek, 24 February 2022 at Russian Tank Convoy Blown Up in Videos As Ukraine Fights Back Invasion (msn.com).

5. See YouTube video (2.07), https://www.youtube.com/watch?v=qDIQf10kHzY.
6. A YouTube video of some of the fighting is at (1.59): https://www.youtube.com/watch?v=UreR-qYgZwU and (2.46): https://www.youtube.com/watch?v=ndTla7HQiFw.
7. On Kharkivski Hwy near the School of Physics and Technology were five vehicles: two 122mm BM-21s "Grad" and three KamAZ 6x6s, all from 200th Motorized Rifle Brigade as posted for 24 February. Scattered about the city were three GAZ Tigr-Ms posted for 27 February. At the northwest entrance to the city at Lesia Serdiuka St and Hwy E40 were four IFVs all posted for 24 February: three MT-LBVM/K from 25th Motorized Rifle Brigade and a T-80BVM from 200th Motorized Rifle Brigade.
8. Of significance to the east-southeast of Kharkiv is a MT-LB near Mala Rohan posted on 30 March, a T-72B from 59th Tank Regiment near Mala Rohan also posted on 30 March, an MI-8 transport helicopter near Biskvitne posted 25 March, an BTR-82A(M) from 59th Tank Regiment near Biskvitne posted 29 March and a T-72B Obr. 1989 near Biskvitne posted on 30 March. To the east of Kharkiv lies a Vityaz DT-10PM articulated tracked carrier from 138th Motorized Rifle Brigade at Vilkivka posted on 30 March, an unknown tank at Verkhnya Rohanka posted on 28 April and a P-230T command vehicle at Oleksandrivka posted on 9 March. To the northeast of Kharkiv is a MT-LBVM/K from 25th Motorized Rifle Brigade at Bobrivka posted on 16 April, but may have been lost on 24 February. There are some other vehicles from 25th Motorized Rifle Brigade that were posted later. To the north of Kharkiv on highway E105 is an MT-LBVM/K from 200th Motorized Rifle Brigade at Ruska Lozova posted on 27 February, a 122mm BM-21 "Grad" from 200th Motorized Rifle Brigade at Ruska Lozova posted on 26 February and further north up the road is a GAZ Tigr-M at Alisivka posted on 24 February. To the north-northwest of the city are several significant clusters of vehicles, including one of seven vehicles consisting of two T-72s from 237th Tank Regiment posted on 19 March and three 152mm 2S3(M)s "Akatsiya" from 200th Motorized Rifle Brigade also posted on 19 March. Another five vehicles in the area posted later may also be part of this grouping, including two T-80BVMs from 200th Motorized Rifle Brigade posted on 1 and 8 May, a nearby T-72B and T-80BVM from 200th Motorized Rifle Brigade posted on 8 May and 20 April, and a MT-LB from 200th Motorized Rifle Brigade posted on 15 May. To the northwest of there, near Slatyne and Prudyanka, is a cluster of seven vehicles on highway T2117, all from 200th Motorized Rifle Brigade. They include a KamAZ 6x6 posted on 5 March, a Ural-4320 posted on 28 February, three 122mm BM-21s "Grad" posted on 26 February, a KamAZ 6x6 posted on 26 February and a 1V110 BM-21 "Grad" battery command vehicle posted on 25 February. It is clear that a BM-21 battery was destroyed in this area on about 25 February, probably by artillery or drones. Also scattered about was a MT-LBVM/K from 200th Motorized Rifle Brigade posted on 28 February and a 2S5M (for 2K22M Tunguska AA system) from 200th Motorized Rifle Brigade posted on 27 February and a cluster of three vehicles near Chornohlazivka all from 138th Motorized Rifle Brigade including a T-72B3 posted on 14 March and two MT-LBs posted on 7 March.
9. For example, just beyond Perevelochna and before Pryluky on highway H07 there are four destroyed T-72B3s Obr. 2016 from 1st Tank Regiment (2nd Guards Motorized Rifle Division) posted on 27 February. This is a village more than halfway between Sumy and Kyiv. There is also a BRM-1K reconnaissance vehicle and a Ural-4320 from 2nd (Guards) Motorized Rifle Division posted on 3 March.

Further back (further east) are another eight vehicles on the same road but near Sribne. This included another T-72B3 Obr. 2016 from 1st Tank Regiment, two KamAZ 6x6 trucks, two KamAZ 6x6 truck and a 9A33BM OSA-AKM TELAR from 117th Anti-aircraft Missile Regiment, a Ural-4320 tanker and KamAZ 6x6 truck from 2nd (Guards) Motorized Rifle Division. They are all posted as of 27 February.

10. Source: conversation with a regional Ukrainian newspaper in January 2023.
11. Note that only one of these vehicles, a T-90A, lost on 27 February and destroyed in the southeast section of Sumy, is reported as belonging to this brigade.
12. In particular see Mykhaylo Zebrodskyi, Jack Watling, Oleksandr V. Danylyuk and Nick Reynolds, *Preliminary Lessons in Conventional Warfighting from Russia's Invasion of Ukraine: February – July 2022* (Royal United Services Institute for Defence and Security Studies (RUSI), London, 2022), pp. 34–43.

Chapter 13

1. These were IISS estimates and we have no idea of their accuracy. Considering the heavy losses reported by the Donetsk Peoples Republic, the total may have been higher, or they were counting Russian troops among their losses. On the other hand, the Lugansk Peoples Republic forces did not seem to have anywhere near the presence on the battlefield as the DPR forces.
2. See the webpage of the Human Rights Ombudsman in the Donetsk People's Republic by Daria Morozova at The overview of the current social and humanitarian situation in the territory of the Donetsk People`s Republic as a result of hostilities in the period from 26 March to 01 April 2022 – Human rights Ombudsman in the Donetsk People's Republic (ombudsman-dnr.ru). They provide a casualty report from 1 January–17 March 2022 and then another one covering 25–31 March 2022. This leaves out seven days in March. This is probably a missing weekly report.
3. There was no report for this week, but the cumulative figures in the subsequent weeks provide the figures for this week.
4. The total given in their cumulative report is 3,609. It is not clear when the one extra wounded person occurred.

Chapter 15

1. An examination of destroyed and captured vehicles by ukr.warspotting.net shows four areas of activity in Irpin. There are Russian losses in the northeast corner of Irpin near the Irpin military hospital showing five destroyed vehicles posted between 28 March and 1 April, and there are two vehicles around the Giraffe Mall on Soborna Street. The lead vehicle is dated 4 March and the trailing vehicle is dated 30 March. These may have been part of the attack on 27 February that came down this same street and was destroyed one block further back. There are twelve vehicles destroyed in the western part of Irpin dated between 8 March and 6 April. One 120mm 2S9 "Nona" is dated 8 March and one BMD-2 is dated 10 March. The rest are dated 25 March or later. Finally, there are five destroyed vehicles to the south of Irpin between the town and the river dated between 12 March and 19 April. One BMD-4M is posted on 12 March, while the rest of the vehicles are posted on 29 March or later.
2. See James Marson, "The Ragtag Army That Won the Battle of Kyiv and Saved Ukraine," *Wall Street Journal*, September 20, 2022 at https://archive.ph/cBRhl.
3. An examination of Warspotting (ukr.warspotting.net) shows a large cluster of destroyed and captured vehicles from 441st Air Assault Regiment, 98th Guards Airborne Division, just to the west of Moshchun. The first destroyed BMD from 98th Guards Airborne Division was uploaded on 8 March. A captured command and control vehicle is posted at Moshchun on 1 March.
4. The 98th and 106th Guards Airborne Divisions only had two regiments. If they deployed their two battalions manned by contract soldiers to Ukraine and not their assumed third conscript battalion, then probably both divisions only had four maneuver battalions. There are no reports at this time of either of them having deployed a tank company in Ukraine.
5. See the video "Battle Facts. Battle for Moshchun," 11 April 2022 at BATTLE FACTS. BATTLE FOR MOSHCHUN. – EVIDENCE OF RUSSIAN AGGRESSION AND

WAR CRIMES (mkip.gov.ua). This is a source from the Ukrainian government. Also see YouTube, "Brutality of war on Ukraine's front lines," *Washington Post*, April 2022 at The brutality of war on Ukraine's front lines – YouTube and "Aerial shots show extent of destruction in Moshchun, near Kyiv," AFP News Agency, April 2022 at Aerial shots show extent of destruction in Moshchun, near Kyiv | AFP – YouTube and "Video shows how Ukraine defeated Russians in key battle," CNN, May 2022.

6. Sudarsan Raghavan, Jon Gerberg and Heidi Levine, "In bloodied frontline town, Ukrainian forces push Russians backs," *Washington Post*, 30 March 2022 at In bloodied frontline town, Ukrainian forces push Russian – The Washington Post.

7. Losses include in the western part of the village a BTR-D from 331st Airborne Regiment posted on 30 March, a BMD-2 from 331st Airborne Regiment posted on 24 March and a BMD-2 dated 5 April. Along the Irpin River area are three BMD-2s from 331st Airborne Regiment posted on 18 March, two BTR-Ds from 331st Airborne Regiment posted on 6 April and a PP-22005 floating bridge posted on 7 April. On the road well behind them to the west is a T-80Bv posted on 19 April and up the Irpin River to the north is another PP-22005 floating brigade posted on 8 April and a BREM-1 armored recovery vehicle posted on 30 March.

8. Violetta Orlova, "A huge column of Russian equipment passed Makariv, headed to Kyiv – eyewitnesses," Unian, 27 February 2002, 1337 at A huge column of Russian equipment passed Makariv, sunk to Kiev – eyewitnesses – UNIAN. The report specifically states it was 15 tanks, 25 armored personnel carriers and 15 Urals-4320 off-road 6x6 trucks.

9. Elizaveta Kalitventseva, "Ukrainian military liberated the village of Markariv in the Kyiv region from the Russian occupiers," Ukrainian National News, 2 March 2022, 1830 at Ukrainian military liberated the village of Makariv in the Kyiv region from the Russian occupiers – news on UNN | 2 March 2022, 18:30.

10. The first time 10th Mountain Assault Brigade is confirmed to be in the region was on 10 March when it released a report that it had shot down an SU-25 from one of the Eastern Military District's Assault Aviation Regiments. Until 6 March it had apparently been covering the border with Belarus around Volyn.

Inside of Belarus there was a Russian movement of units by rail towards Brest in the first week of the war. That was probably 5th Combined Arms Army. The 10th Mountain Assault Brigade may have been held around Volyn until the Russian intent was read. As soon as it was safe they shifted 10th over to Kyiv.

11. The 64th Motorized Rifle Brigade can be identified northwest of Makariv as early as 3 March, thanks to a video posted by a group from the Ukrainian Territorial Defense Forces showing a captured T-80BVM on a road 8.5 miles to the north of Marariv. Images of a destroyed T-8-BVM 9.5 miles to the north-northwest of Makariv were posted on 10 March. Two more destroyed T-80BVMs were posted on 13 March, both by 10th Mountain Brigade, one of them being geolocated to Nalyvaikivka, 4.5 miles to the northwest of Makariv.

The first photos of confirmed vehicle losses from 37th Guards Motorized Rifle Brigade were uploaded on 1 March, though the vehicle itself may have been destroyed beforehand. This wreck was located in Sytnyaki, 6 miles to the southwest of Makariv. A photo dated 4 March shows a destroyed T-72B3 on the E40 highway just north of Kopyliv, 4.5 miles southeast of Makariv.

The 5th Guards Tank Brigade was one of the spearhead units of the push on Kyiv. The first photo of a destroyed T-72B in the sector was posted on 26 February, with the wreck being located on the E40 near Severynivka (12 miles west of Kyiv and 7.5 miles southeast of Makariv). The furthest west that a T-72B wreck can be identified is Kalynivka, just south of Makariv but the bulk are east of Kopyliv and west of Stoyanka, where the E40 crosses the Irpin River and enters Kyiv. In short, the brigade was in the sector by the third day of the war.

12. Peter Beaumont, "Russian soldiers accused of firing on civilian vehicles in Ukraine," *The Guardian*, 9 March 2022 at Russian soldiers accused of firing on civilian vehicles in Ukraine | Ukraine | The Guardian.

13. Specially, thirteen civilians were killed on 7 March 2022 as a result of an air strike on a bakery and bread factory in the town.

14. He announced this on 23 March, say that Russians still controlled 15% of Makariv.

15. The journalist was Roman Tsimbalyuk and the brigade commander was Colonel Yuri Medvedev, who was later reported to have died. See Western official: Russian tank commander run over and killed by his own angry troops | The Times of Israel and Mutinous Russian troops ran over their own commander, say western officials | Ukraine | The Guardian.

16. At the north entrance to Makariv were six trucks: 4 KamAZ 6x6s posted on 1, 8, 12 and 22 April and 2 Ural-4320 posted on 14 April. These were probably all lost in March. At the northwest entrance to the town are another eight vehicles, including: 9A317 TELAR (for Buk-M2) posted on 16 March, 9A317 TELAR (for Buk-M2) posted on 27 February, 9A317 TELAR (for Buk-M2) posted on 7 March, MT-LB IFV posted on 18 March, a KamAZ 6x6 posted on 27 February, 152mm 2S3(M) posted on 22 March, a 122mm BM-21 "Grad" posted on 22 March and an MT-LB Ambulance from 64th Motorized Rifle Brigade posted on 22 March. Another ten vehicles in and around the town (mostly downtown) include: a Ural-43206 from 37th Motorized Rifle Brigade, a Ural-4320 tanker from 37th Motorized Rifle Brigade, 1 BMP-2(K), a KamAZ 6x6 tanker, a KamAZ 6x6 from 37th Motorized Rifle Brigade, 2 KamAZ 6x6s, 2 Ural 4320s and a KamAZ KMV-20V boom crane truck. These were all posted between 30 March and 13 April 2022. They are were probably all lost in March. Finally in the eastern part of the town was a MI-8 transport helicopter posted on 4 March.

17. These are described in a previous footnote on the area labeled Okko, but most interesting is that the westernmost collection of these vehicles include two tanks and four IFVs. One BRM-1K reconnaissance vehicle is posted on 1 March. The other five vehicles are posted from 22 March–2 April.

18. There are eight vehicles in and around the town of Sytnyuaky: A T-72B posted on 1 March, a 122mm BM-21 "Grad" posted on 15 March, two Ural-4320s posted on 3 and 28 March, a MT-LB IFV posted on 1 March, 2 BMP=2(K)s assigned to 37th Motorized Rifle Brigade and posted on 1 and 4 March, and a MT-LB M1980 "Blade" ambulance assigned to 37th Motorized Rifle Brigade and posted on 11 March.

19. In 2017 the brigade consisted of three motorized rifle battalions and a tank battalion. See Eastern Military District | VBO (archive.org).

20. For example, the Wikipedia article for the Battle of Makariv only lists 37th Guards Motor Rifle Brigade as involved.

21. All these figures are drawn from Kyiv Mayor Vitali Klitschko in an interview with *Der Spiegel* magazine on 30 December. See "Klitschko: Kyiv's population returns to pre-war level" by *Kyiv Independent*, 30 December 2022. Wikipedia gives the population of Kyiv as of 1 January 2021 at 2,962,180 and for the metro region at 3,475,000. We are aware of relatives who moved from Kyiv to Lviv in March and returned to the city in April.

22. For example, see Makarov head: "We found more than 200 people killed by Russians" - MIPL.

23. In particular 234th Airborne Regiment of 76th Airborne Division. An article in the *New York Times*, 22 December 2022, "Caught on Camera, Traced by Phone: The Russian Military Unit that Killed Dozens in Bucha" has placed the blame for thirty-six murders on

them. See Caught on Camera, Traced by Phone: The Russian Military Unit That Killed Dozens in Bucha – The New York Times (nytimes.com). Also see Erika Kinetz, Oleksandr Stashevskyi and Vasilisa Stepanenko, "How Russian soldiers ran a 'cleansing' operation in Bucha," AP News, 3 November 2022 at How Russian soldiers ran a 'cleansing' operation in Bucha | AP News. Also, members of 155th Naval Infantry Brigade have been accused, but no members of either unit have been indicted by the Ukrainian prosecutors, who do seem to be systematically collecting evidence and processing the charges.

24. It is reported to have taken losses on 1 March in the Borodyanka region of Bucha Raion according to Russo-Ukrainian WarSpotting.

25. For an unverified description see Polish News, 24 May 2022, "Ukraine. Bucha. Who are the soldiers of the 64th Independent Motorized Rifle Brigade, the unit responsible for war crimes against the Ukrainian?" at Ukraine. Bucha. Who are the soldiers of the 64th Independent Motorized Rifle Brigade, the unit responsible for war crimes against the Ukrainians? – Polish News.

26. The brigade commander was Lieutenant Colonel or Colonel Azatbek Omurbekov, age 39. See Azatbek Omurbekov – Wikipedia.

27. As reported by Melissa Bell, CNN, on video at Watch: CNN tracks alleged war crimes committed by Russia's 64th brigade – CNN Video. Also see Carlotta Gill, "'Such Bad Guys Will Come': How One Russian Brigade Terrorized Bucha," *New York Times*, 22 May 2022 at 'Such Bad Guys Will Come': How One Russian Brigade Terrorized Bucha – The New York Times (nytimes.com). They report eighteen people killed by the brigade in the second half of March and ten Russian suspects identified. See Jeffrey Gettleman, "Ukraine singles out Russian soldiers for atrocities in Bucha." *New York Times*, 29 April 2022 at Ukraine Identifies Russian Soldiers in Bucha Atrocities – The New York Times (nytimes.com).

28. See Alex Shprintsen, Terence McKenna and Anastasiya Ivanova, CBC News, 3 November 2022, "While Putin denies war crimes in Ukraine, a Russian soldier confesses to executing a civilian," at While Putin denies war crimes in Ukraine, a Russian soldier confesses to executing a civilian | CBC News.

29. The Ukrainians themselves began calling the Russian's Orcs, as a part of the wartime slang. The Orcs are creatures from the fantasy novels of J.R.R. Tolkien.

30. See Christopher A. Lawrence, "The Russo-Ukrainian War – Day 324," *Mystics & Statistics* blog, 13 January 2023 at The Russo-Ukrainian War – Day 324 | Mystics & Statistics (dupuyinstitute.org). The countries that we know have volunteers fighting for Ukraine that were not on that list included Georgia (a battalion), Belarus (a battalion), Chechnya (two battalions) and even Russia (a battalion).

31. This is stated nine months into the war. The DPR and Russia still control and hold Mariupol, where there have been multiple unconfirmed reports of many civilian deaths. These have not been fully investigated. In one of the more famous incidents in Mariupol, a theater full of civilians was hit and it was claimed 600 civilians were killed. A later UN investigation clearly established that this was the case, but they estimated that about a dozen civilians were killed.

32. See UN Human Rights Office of the High Commissioner, *Ukraine: Civilian Casualty Update 1 April 2022.*

33. Ibid. Update 29 April 2022. As the areas around Bucha were not liberated until early April, we feel that this later report better reflects the situation.

Chapter 16

1. One does note that in the 1991 Ukrainian independence referendum that 85.38% of the Odesa Oblast voted for independence.

2. Six protesters were killed in the fighting earlier that day, four anti-Maidan protesters and two Euromaidan supporters.

3. A list of the protesters who died are at Odessa tragedy: the names of 47 of the 48 who died during the riots on May 2 became known | News of Odessa (dumskaya.net). Of the forty-eight people killed, forty-six were from Odesa or the Odesa region, one from Mykolaiv Oblast and one from Vinnytsia. None were Russian citizens or from neighboring Transnistria.

4. A total of twenty-two servicemen were reported killed in the Odesa Oblast this day.

5. See SOFREP, 23 April 2022, "Slovenia Sending Tanks to Ukraine, Ukrainian Tank Brigades on the Roll."

6. See David Axe, Forbes, 18 April 2022, "Ukraine Has Mobilized Its Tank Reserves. They're Already on the Attack." David Axe, Forbes, 17 May 2022, "Watch the Ukrainian Army Form a New Brigade with Donated Tanks."

7. See www.navalnews.com, H.I. Sutton, 15 April 2022, "Satellite Image Pinpoints Russian Cruiser Moskva as She Burned," at Satellite Image Pinpoints Russian Cruiser Moskva As She Burned – Naval News.

8. Pictures are in this article: "Sunken Russian warship Moskva: What do we know?," BBC, 18 April 2022 at Sunken Russian warship Moskva: What do we know? – BBC News.

9. There are claims that the ship had 510 on board and it is reported that its complement is 485 (419 enlisted and 66 officer). The Russian claims of losses and rescued crew only reported adds up to 424 crew members. Turkey did report rescuing 54 personnel from the ship according to the Lithuanian Minister of National Defense. See "Turkish ship rescues over 50 Russian sailors from naval cruiser Moskva" at Turkish ship rescues over 50 Russian sailors from naval cruiser Moskva (trtworld.com). The videos shown by Russia of the surviving crew show 100 to 240 sailors in it, along with the captain. There is a strong suspicion that at least 61 other crewmembers died or are missing.

10. The Argentina Cruiser *General Belgrano* was torpedoed and sunk on 2 May 1982 with a loss of 323 lives. It displaced 9,575 tons when empty and 12,242 tons fully loaded. The *Moskva* is reported to displace 9,380 tons standard and 11,490 tons full load.

Chapter 17

1. The references to this fighting are limited. See France 24 news report dated 14 March 2022, "Voznesensk resists Russian takeover: City occupied 3 days, now freed & preparing to defend" at Voznesensk resists Russian takeover: City occupied 3 days, now freed & preparing to defend - France 24; CNN, March 9, 2022, "Video shows firefights between Ukrainian and Russian troops in streets of Ukrainian city of Voznesensk" at (33) Video shows firefights between Ukrainian and Russian troops in streets of Ukrainian city of Voznesensk (cnn.com); and Andrew Harding, "Ukraine: The small town which managed to block Russia's big plans," BBC News, 22 March 2022 at Ukraine: The small town which managed to block Russia's big plans – BBC News. This last article may be discussing the fight on 2–3 March, and gives the impression that only one attack was made on Voznesensk.

2. This is 26 miles (42km) up route P06 to Nova Odesa and another 27 miles (44km) up route P06 to Voznesensk.

3. See *Daily Kos*, 17 March 2022, "Ukraine update: Ukraine retakes 75 miles of Russian-held territory, pushes toward Kherson." These claimed appeared to be based upon the taking of the village of Posad-Pokrovskote (population 2,349 in 2001), in between Mykolaiv and Kherson. There is no clear indication that the alleged occupation of this village forced the Russians to retreat from around Voznesensk.

Chapter 18

1. See Christopher A. Lawrence, "The Russo-Ukrainian War of 2022 – Day 19 (ground actions)," Mystics & Statistics, 14 March 2022 at The Russo-Ukrainian War of 2022 – Day 19 (ground actions) | Mystics & Statistics (dupuyinstitute.org).

2. As reported on the twitter site @MFA_Ukraine for 10 March 2022.
3. See Ukraine General Staff Facebook post of 16 May 2022 at (20+) Facebook.
4. The total number of vehicles lost is 312 by count, which differs slightly from the totals given in the report.
5. There was no report for this week, but the cumulative figures in the subsequent weeks provide the figures for this week.

Chapter 19
1. There are claims that they started losing control of this area in mid-March.
2. This is measured as the border between Ukraine and Bryansk Oblast (114 miles/183km) and Kursk Oblast (152 miles/245km). This is effectively the area from Gomel and Chernihiv to Sumy. The total Ukrainian/Russian border is 1,426 miles (2,295km) of which 1,227 miles (1,974km) is a land border and 199 miles (321km) is a sea border.
3. This is calculated by the line from Troitske to Kherson, which is at least 441 miles (710km). Of that, 120 miles is the Kakhovka Reservoir, which probably does not need to be seriously defended, maybe just a few AA batteries and some mobile forces. This leaves a front line of 321 miles (517km) that needs to be seriously defended. See Christopher A. Lawrence, "Length of Front Line Trace in Ukraine," *Mystics & Statistics*, 15 November 2022 at Length of Front Line Trace in Ukraine | Mystics & Statistics (dupuyinstitute.org) Added to that is the length of the border between Belgorod Oblast and Ukraine, which is 336 miles (540km). These are rough estimates and the real front line could be up to 26% longer counting every twist and turn.
4. *Russia's War in Ukraine*, p. 11.
5. *The Economist*, 28 March 2022, "Russia say it is changing its war aims in Ukraine," article updated on 29 March. See Russia says it is changing its war aims in Ukraine | The Economist.
6. Violetta Orlova, "'Killed crushed by tanks': up to 300 civilians were killed in Irpin – mayor," Unian, 30 March 2022 at Irpin News – Up to 300 civilians killed in Irpen – UNIAN.
7. Going from west to east this includes three vehicles lost around Ploske and Svetylnya: a BTR-82AT from 15th Motorized Rifle Brigade posted on 31 March, a T-72B Obr. 1989 posted 28 March and a BTR-82A(M) posted on 30 March.

   Continuing along what appears to be the final stopping line are nine vehicles just east of Rusaniv and four vehicles in Peremora. They include: four BMP-2(K) with three from 21st Motorized Rifle Brigade posted on 12, 18 and 28 March, and a T-72B3 and T-72B3 Obr. 2016 with one from 21st Motorized Rifle Brigade and posted on 3 March, a BMP-2(K) from 21st Motorized Rifle Brigade posted on 3 March, a BMP-2(K) from 21st Motorized Rifle Brigade posted on 30 March and a T-72B3 from the 21st Motorized Rifle Brigade posted on 7 April. At Peremora were a BMP-2(K) from 21st Motorized Rifle Brigade posted on 3 April, a BTR-82AT from 15th Motorized Rifle Brigade posted on 30 March and two BMP-1KSh command and staff vehicles posted on 30 March and 8 April. This all looks to be a line held for part of the month by the 21st and 15th Motorized Rifle Brigades.

   Along the line between Peremora and Nova Basan were two T-72B3s from 21st Motorized Rifle Brigade at Lukyanivka posted on 24 and 25 March, three BMP-2(K) from 6th Tank Regiment at Lukyanivka posted on 24 March, an MT-LB from 21st Motorized Rifle Brigade at Lukyanivka posted on 25 March, a BTR-82A(M) from 15th Motorized Rifle Brigade on route H07 posted on 7 April, two T-72B3s from 21st Motorized Rifle Brigade on route H07 posted on 31 March and 1 April, a MTO-UB1 maintenance vehicle on route H-7 posted on 1 April and a 9A317 TELAR (for Buk-M2) near route H07 posted on 10 March.

   In Nova Basan were two T-72Bs posted on 31 March and 1 April, a T-72AV posted on 11 April, two BTR-82AT from 15th Motorized Rifle Brigade posted on 1 and 2 April, six BTR-82A(M) from 15th Motorized Rifle Brigade posted on 31 March and 1, 2 and 3 April, two GAZ Tigr-Ms posted on 2 and 3 April, a T-72AV from 239th Tank Regiment posted on 2 April, a Ural-420 posted on 5 April, an R-166-0.5 signals vehicle posted on 1 April, an R-149MA1 command and staff vehicle posted on 1 April and a MT-LB M1980 "Blade" posted 1 April. On the route to Novyi Bykiv were 1 AV14(M) battler command and forward observer vehicle posted on 1 April and a 220mm TOS-1A posted on 1 April.

In Novyi Bykiv were two 9T452 transloaders for BM-27 "Uragan" MRL posted on 1 and 3 April, seven Ural-4320 posted on 1, 5 and 6 April, an R-149MA1 command and staff vehicle posted on 3 April and unknown Buk SAM system posted on 16 March, an R-166-0.5 signals vehicle posted on 2 April, a BMP-2(K) from 21st Motorized Rifle Brigade posted on 1 April, a 122mm BM-21 "Grad" posted on 2 April, a KamAZ-63968 "Typhoon" posted on 31 March, 122mm 2S34 "Khosta" from 21st Motorized Rifle Brigade posted ON 1 April, a Ural-4320 tanker posted ON 1 April, two KamAZ 6x6 tankers posted ON 1 April, two KamAZ 6x6 posted on 20 March, a BTR-82A(M) posted on 20 March, a KamAZ-53949 "Linza" posted on 1 April, a KamAZ 6x6 posted on 1 April, a 9S36 (for Buk-M2) posted on 1 April, a BTR-82AT from 15th Motorized Rifle Brigade posted on 1 April, 1 BTR-82A(M) posted on 1 April, a 152mm 2S19 "Msta-S" posted on 2 April and a BTR-82A(M) from 15th Motorized Rifle Brigade posted on 1 April.

Around Tereshkivka were a T-72B posted on 7 April, a T-72B3 posted on 3 April, a T-72BA from 21st Motorized Rifle Brigade posted on 2 April, a 152mm 2S19 "Msta-S" posted on 2 April and a BMO-T from 1st Mobile CBRN Protection Brigade (!) posted on 7 April.

Finally, near Kolisnyjy, just north of Pryluky were eight KamAZ 6x6 tankers posted on 7 March. This seems like a very odd group of vehicles destroyed in a very odd time and place.

8. Behind the assumed final stopping line are another fourteen vehicles, including a BTR-82A(M) at Shevchenkove posted on 14 July put clearly lost before 4 April, a BTR-82A(M) at Hrebelky posted on 5 April, an MT-LB from 6th Tank Regiment at Mokrets posted on 13 March, a BTR-82A(M) at Mokrets posted on 30 March, a T-72B from 6th Tank Regiment at Mokrets posted on 9 March, a 9Z331 TLAR (for 9K331 Tor-M1) from 288th AA Missile Regiment at Mokrets posted on 6 March, six T-72Bs from 6th Tank Regiment or 90th (Guards) Tank Division at Mokrets on 10 March and two T-72As from 6th Tank Regiment at Mokrets posted on 6 March.

Still in the area were thirteen vehicles at Bervytsya including: a MT-LB from 21st Motorized Rifle Brigade posted on 31 March, two 152mm 2S19 "Msta-S"s posted on 30 March, an 82mm 2B9 Vasilek automatic gun mortar (towed) posted on 10 April, a BTR-82A(M) posted on 2 April, two Ural-4320 posted on 2 April, three Ural-4320s posted on 11 April (but certainly lost before then), two KamAZ 6x6 tankers posted on 11 April and an unknown truck also posted on 11 April. There was also a BTR-82A(M) from 15th Motorized Rifle Brigade posted on 6 April and a Ural-4320 tanker posted on 5 April at Stara Basan.

Behind them were another 44 destroyed or captured vehicles. This included a T-72A from 6th Tank Regiment in Khvylivka posted on 2 March. On route T2515 on 13 March a KamAZ 6x6 tanker, a MTU-72 bridge layer from 90th (Guards) Tank Division, two KamAZ 6x6s with one from 90th (Guards) Tank Division and a BMP-2(K) from 6th Tank Regiment. Further east on the road posted on 17 March was a GAZ-66, a KamAZ-6350 8x8 artillery tractor and a 152mm 2A65 "Msta-B" howitzer. Further east on the road posted on 13 March was a Ural-4320 tanker and an IMR-2(M) combat engineering vehicle. All the way down the road to Ichnya posted on 7 and 12 April were three T-72B3s and a 152mm 2S19 "Msta-S". At the town of Velyka Doroha posted on 1 April were a T-72A, three T-72Bs one with 239th Tank Regiment, two KamAZ 6x6, a Ural-4320 tanker, a MT-LB

M1980 "Blade", two BTR-82A(M)s, an R-145BM1 command vehicle, a KamAZ-63968 "Typhoon", a 9A39M1-02 TEL (for Buk-M1-2), a 1V14(M) battery command and forward observer vehicle, a 1V13(M) battery fire control center, a KamAZ-53949 "Typhoon-K" and a Ural-4320. At Kalynivka were two GAZ Tigr-M posted on 20 and 30 March with one from 55th Mountain Motorized Rifle Brigade. Further east posted on 20 March were a BTR-82A(M), a BTR-80, two 9A330 Tor TLAR (for 9K330 Tor) from 288th AA Missile Regiment, three KamAZ 6x6, Ural-4320, a MT-LB and a Gaz Tigr-M.

9. The abandoned vehicles include a BMD-2 at Hostomel posted on 27 February, a BMD-2 at Hostomel from 31st Air Assault Brigade posted on 3 March, a BMD-4M at Irpin posted on 28 March, a T-72B at Stoyanka posted on 1 March, a 9A317 TELAR (for Buk-M2) at Makariv posted on 16 March, an MT-LB Ambulance at Makariv from 64th Motorized Rifle Brigade posted on 22 March, a KamAZ 6x6 at Borodyanka posted on 27 February, a BMP-2(K) at Borodyanka from 64th Motorized Rifle Brigade posted on 2 March and a BMP-1P at Borodyanka from 64th Motorized Rifle Brigade posted on 28 February.

10. Although the ones that get my attention because of other tabulations in this book include a BMD-2 at Mykolaiv posted on 6 March, a T-72B at Mokrets with 6th Tank Regiment posted on 9 March, a 9A33BM OPA-AKM TELAR at Sribne from 117th AA Missile Regiment posted on 27 February, a T-72B3 Obr. 2016 at Martynivka from 228th Motorized Rifle Regiment posted on 20 March, a T-72B3 at Ivanivka (south of Chernihiv) posted on 29 March, a GAZ Tigr-M at Rivnopillia (north of Chernihiv) posted on 24 February, a MTP-A2 recovery vehicle at Horodnya (northeast of Chernihiv) posted on 25 February, a T-72B at Shtepivka (west of Sumy) posted on 4 March, a T-72B3 Obr. 2016 at Krasnopillia (southeast of Sumy) from 1st Tank Regiment posted on 28 February, a 1V13(M) battery fire control center at Artemo-Rastivka (south of Sumy) from 4th (Guards) Tank Division posted on 28 February, a T-80U at Stanova (south of Sumy) from 4th (Guards) Tank Division posted on 28 February and a BMP-2(K) at Trostyanets (south of Sumy) from 4th (Guards) Tank Division posted on 24 March 2022. It is suspected that most of these are mechanical breakdowns and other causes. Some may be combat losses.

There is a cluster of nine abandoned vehicles and weapon systems to the north of Kharkiv. It is not sure if they are combat losses or mechanical. They include a T-72B3 at Chornohlazivka from 138th Motorized Rifle Brigade posted on 14 March, a MT-LB/K at Berzuky from 200th Motorized Rifle Brigade posted on 28 February, a 1V110 BM-21 "Grad" battery command vehicle at Prudyanka from 200th Motorized Rifle Brigade posted on 25 February, a Ural-4320 at Slatyne from 200th Motorized Rifle Brigade posted on 28 February, a KamAZ 6x6 at Slatyne from 200th Motorized Rifle Brigade posted on 5 March, two 152mm 2S3(M)s "Akatsiya" east of Bezruky from 200th Motorized Rifle Brigade posted on 19 March, a MT-LBVM/K at Ruska Lozova from 200th Motorized Rifle Brigade posted on 27 February and a 122mm BM-21 "Grad" at Ruska Lozova from 200th Motorized Rifle Brigade posted on 26 February 2022.

11. This includes eight tanks and twenty-four IFVs. From north to south and west to east these include: a BTR-MDM "Rakushka" at Prybirsk posted on 3 April, two T-80BVs at Kukhari from 69th Covering Brigade posted on 14 March, a Ural-43206 at Katyuzhanka posted on 4 April, a UAZ-469 at Katyuzhanka posted on 6 April, a PTS-2 tracked amphibious transport at Dymer posted on 31 March, a BTR-D at Lytvynivka posted on 27 July, a R-149MA1 command and staff vehicle at Demydiv posted on 7 April (total of eight vehicles, including two tanks and two IFVs).

There are thirteen vehicles (including one IFV) at Borodyanka, including a KamAZ 6x6 tanker posted on 2 April, a Ural-4320 from 78th Repair and Restoration Battalion posted on 28 February, a KamAZ 6x6 posted on 1 March, two MTO-0UB1 maintenance vehicles from 5th Tank Brigade posted on 1 March, a Ural-43206 posted on 1 March, a

Ural-4320 posted on 1 March, two Ural-43206s from 64th Motorized Rifle Brigade posted on 1 March, a Ural-4320 posted on 28 February, a KamAZ 6x6 posted on 2 April, a 9T452 transloaders for BM-27 "Uragan" MRL posted on 6 April and a BMP-2(K) from 634th Motorized Rifle Brigade posted on 2 March.

Down the route towards Makariv are twenty-two vehicles (including four tanks and two IFVs): a Ural-43206 at Nova Hreblya posted on 3 March, a T-80BVN at Nova Hreblya from 64th Motorized Rifle Brigade posted on 3 March, a T-72B at Andriivka posted on 2 April, a T-80BVM at Nalyvaikivka from 64th Motorized Rifle Brigade posted on 19 March, a BMP-2(K) at Nalyviakivka posted on 30 March, a Ural-43206 at Makariv from 37th Motorized Rifle Brigade posted on 4 April, a 122mm BM-21 "Grad" at Makariv posted on 22 March, an MT-LB M1980 "Blade" ambulance at Nebelytsya from 37th Motorized Rifle Brigade posted on 11 March, a BMP-2(K) at Sytnyaky from 37th Motorized Rifle Brigade posted on 1 March, a KrAZ-255B tanker at Kopyliv posted on 2 April, a UAZ-469 at Kopyliv posted on 2 April, a Ural-4320 at Kopyliv posted on 5 April, an M-LB ambulance at Motyzhyn posted on 28 February, a T-72B3 at Kopyliv from 37th Motorized Rifle Brigade posted on 4 March, a ZSU-23-4 Shilka at Berezivka from 5th Tank Brigade posted on 31 March, a Ural-4320 tanker at Berezivka from 5th Tank Brigade posted on 3 April, a Ural-4320 at Berezivka from 5th Tank Brigade posted on 31 March, four 122mm 2B17 Tornado-Gs at Berezivka from 5th Tank Brigade posted on 19, 20 and 31 March and a 152mm 2S3(M) "Akatsiya" at Beresivka from 5th Tank Brigade posted on 20 March.

To the west of Moshchun are a BREM-1 armored recovery vehicle posted on 30 March, a BTR-D from 331st Airborne Regiment posted on 6 April and a BMD-2 from 331st Airborne Regiment posted on 18 March.,

At Hostomel airfield are ten vehicles: two Ural-4320s posted on 28 March, two 152mm 2A65 "Msta-B" howitzers posted on 28 March, a 23mm ZU-23 posted on 2 April, a KamAZ 6x6 posted on 30 March, two Ural-4320s posted on 30 March and 6 April, a Ural Avtozaks from Rosgvardiya posted on 30 March and a KA-52 "Alligator" attack helicopter posted on 24 February (photos are provided, it does look intact).

Around Bucha and Irpin and to the south are twenty-six vehicles reported captured, including two tanks and seventeen IFVs. There are six vehicles captured that were on Buckansky Hwy and posted on 3 March: two BTR-MDs "Rakusha" from 31st Air Assault Brigade, three BMD-4Ms and a BTR-D. There was a BMD-2 at Bucha from 104th Air Assault Regiment posted on 12 March, a BMD-4M at Bucha posted on 2 March, a KamAZ with MM-501 armored cabin at Irpin with Rosgvardiya posted on 1 April, a KamAZ Avtozaks at the bridge east of Irpin from Gosgvaridiya posted on 26 February and a Ural Federal at the bridge east of Irpin from Rosgvaridiya posted on 28 February. In Bucha on Vokzalna Steet are ten vehicles mostly posted on 27 February: three BTR-Ds, three BMD-2s, one BMD-1KSh-A command and staff vehicle, one 1V119 artillery fire direction vehicle, one 9A35 Strela-10 and one 9S932-1 "Barnual-T" automated system for air defense units posted on 3 March 2022. It is not clear how these ten vehicles were captured on 27 February and if they were brought back to Ukrainian lines. Probably they were destroyed. To the south of Irpin are five more captured vehicles: a BMD-2 posted on 28 March, a BMP-2(K) posted on 268 February, a T-72B posted on 2 April, a BMD-2 posted on 29 March and a T-72B Obr. 1989 posted on 31 March.

12. This is based upon counts of vehicles on Ukr.warspotting.net. Real losses are probably higher.

Chapter 20

1. This is not well documented but clearly numbered thousands of prisoners.
2. See Colonel T.N. Dupuy, *Understanding War: History and Theory of Combat* (Paragon House Publishers, New York, 1987). The other two books have been discussed earlier.

3. The TNDM was the updated version of the combat model the QJM (Quantified Judgment Model) which Trevor Dupuy had created in the 1970s and is described in depth in his book *Numbers, Predictions and War*.

4. See the *Mystics & Statistics* blog, "A Second Independent Effort to use the QJM/TNDM to Analyze the War in Ukraine," dated 26 May 2022 at A Second Independent Effort to use the QJM/TNDM to Analyze the War in Ukraine | Mystics & Statistics (dupuyinstitute.org).

5. This assumes a wounded-to-killed ratio of 4-to-1. See discussion below for the estimate of captured and missing.

6. As reported and calculated by twitter account @HelloMrBond.

7. See Zebrodskyi, Watling, Danylyuk and Reynolds, *Preliminary Lessons in Conventional Warfighting from Russia's Invasion of Ukraine*, p. 14.

8. This was as of 0900, 30 March as reported at the time by Oryx. Oryx is a group of private researchers in Turkey and Holland who track and identify tanks lost by videos and pictures they have located. The Ukrainian Ministry of Defense was claiming as of 29 March that they had destroyed 597 tanks. See Attack On Europe: Documenting Russian Equipment Losses During The 2022 Russian Invasion Of Ukraine – Oryx (oryxspioenkop.com) and Attack On Europe: Documenting Ukrainian Equipment Losses During The 2022 Russian Invasion Of Ukraine – Oryx (oryxspioenkop.com). Also see The Russo-Ukrainian War of 2022 – Day 35 (ground actions) | Mystics & Statistics (dupuyinstitute.org).

9. See Dupuy, *Attrition*, pp. 80–1, which notes that there are 0.98 crew casualties per tank lost or 20% of the total crew. For tanks burned, it is 1.28 crew casualty per loss. For tanks that did not burn it is 0.78. This is based upon 898 tanks lost by the US First Army, June 1944–April 1945 fighting in the European Theater of Operations (ETO). Also, the Ukrainian Army captured and released records from 1st Guards Tank Army as of 15 March showed personnel losses and equipment losses by regiment. An examination of three of the tank regiments with high losses (eighteen to fourteen tanks) showed 0.58 casualties per tank lost with a wounded-to-killed ratio for those three regiments of 3.77-to-1. Pages from that report are included in the plate section. Also see Christopher A. Lawrence, "Casualty Estimates for the Russo-Ukrainian War," Mystics & Statistics, 14 December 2022 at Casualty Estimates for the Russo-Ukrainian War | Mystics & Statistics (dupuyinstitute.org).

Chapter 21

1. See Christopher A. Lawrence, "How Much is U.S. Intelligence helping Ukraine?" Mystics & Statistics, 2 April 2022 at How Much is U.S. Intelligence helping Ukraine? | Mystics & Statistics (dupuyinstitute.org).

2. See Christopher A. Lawrence, "How Much is U.S. Intelligence helping Ukraine? – part 2," *Mystics & Statistics*, 27 April 2022 at How Much is U.S. intelligence helping Ukraine? – part 2 | Mystics & Statistics (dupuyinstitute.org).

3. *Measuring the Value of Situational Awareness* (The Dupuy Institute, Annadale, VA, May 2004) at TDI – The Dupuy Institute Publications.

4. One of the offices that was supposedly advocating the RMA was the office that funded this report, The Office of Secretary of Defense (OSD) Office of Net Assessment (NA). This was run by Dr Andrew Marshall who directly requested that we do this study for them.

5. For example, in Trevor N. Dupuy's combat model the QJM, the multipliers given for being on defense (hasty) is 1.3, for defense (prepared) is 1.5 and for defense (fortified) is 1.6. See Dupuy, *Numbers, Predictions and War*, p. 230. The factors given for the defender for flat bare terrain is 1.05 for rolling bare and flat mixed terrain is 1.2, for rolling mixed terrain is 1.3, for rugged mixed terrain is 1.55 and for urban is 1.4. See Dupuy, *Numbers, Predictions and War*, p. 228. Therefore, nominally if the entire Ukrainian Army is in a hasty defense (1.3) and on rolling bare and flat mixed terrain (1.2) then the multiplier is 1.56 times 169,000

troops = 263,640, which is clearly greater than the Russian troops deployed. In the combat model, superior force value, after multipliers, does advance.

6. On 25 February, the Pentagon assessed that Russia had committed one-third of its available troops into Ukraine according to *Russia's War in Ukraine: Military and Intelligence Aspects*, p. 9.

7. Our three reports were *Measuring the Effects of Combat in Cities, Phase I* (The Dupuy Institute, McLean, VA, January 2002), *Measuring the Effects of Combat in Cities, Phase II* (The Dupuy Institute, Annandale, VA, June 2003) and *Measuring the Effect of Combat in Cities, Phase III* (The Dupuy Institute, Annandale, VA, July 2004). The revised RAND report was Todd C. Helmus and Russell W. Glenn, *Steeling the Mind: Combat Stress Reactions and Their Implications for Urban Warfare* (RAND, 2005). The core of this report is Chapter Four "Stress in the City: An Evaluation of the Risk of Combat Stress Reactions in Urban Warfare." We were given credit in a footnote in this chapter but they curiously avoided mentioning us anywhere else in the report besides the bibliography. Considering that this report was clearly created in response to and as a result of our first urban warfare report in 2002, we find this odd. Still, it was nice to have duplicate research confirm our findings.

8. *Measuring the Effects of Combat in Cities, Phase I*, p. 78. Also see Lawrence, *War by Numbers*, p. 251.

9. Or 600 dismounts. The numbers do vary depending on whether you are counting "dismounts" only or all the people in an infantry unit. It also depends on whether the brigade is counted with three or four infantry battalions. So for example, a mechanized infantry brigade with four infantry battalions on paper has almost 780 dismounts and perhaps over 1,150 total infantry. See YouTube channel "Battle Order."

10. Again, this varies, especially as Russian brigades tended to only have two deployed battalions. It would only have about 350 dismounts or around 900 infantry total.

11. They lost about 170 tanks, the majority to unmanned systems. See Dr Alexander Kott, "Karabakh War of 2020: S&T Implications," (DEVCOM Army Research Laboratory, 14 December 2020) available at www.dupuyinstitute.org/blog.

12. See Field Manual No. 3-0 (FM 3-0), *Operations* (Headquarters, Department of the Army, Washington DC, 1 October 2022), p. A-1, which lists the nine principles as Objective, Offensive, Mass, Economy of Force, Maneuver, Unity of Command, Security, Surprise and Simplicity. These are developed from the writings of J.F.C. Fuller.

13. These are drawn from The Dupuy Institute Division-Level Engagement Data Base (DLEDB). It has 191 usable engagements from the Battle of Kursk and 58 useable engagements from the 3 battles of Kharkov in 1943.

14. This is based upon a front estimated at 517km and a force of 200,000 troops. See Christopher A. Lawrence, "Length of Front Line Trace in Ukraine," *Mystics & Statistics* blog, 15 November 2022.

15. This is not meant to ignore other major conventional actions such as the India-Pakistan War of 1971, Yom Kippur War of 1973, the Iran-Iraq War of 1980–8 and the Gulf War of 1991. Still, these wars are at least thirty years in the past and do not really reflect an engagement between two roughly equivalent combatants.

16. The phrase "old lessons need to be relearned" I believe I borrowed from Dr James Storr after a meeting in Oslo in December 2022.

17. See Oryx and Dr Alexander Kott, "Karabakh War of 2020: S&T Implications" (DEVCOM Army Research Laboratory, 14 December 2020) available at www.dupuyinstitute.org/blog.

18. Including US-built Phoenix Ghost, sometimes classified as a loitering munition and the DJI Mavic 3 drone.

19. See Fact Sheet on U.S. Security Assistance for Ukraine > U.S. Department of Defense > Release.

20. See Meet the Phoenix Ghost, a secretive new drone the U.S. fast-tracked for delivery to Ukraine (yahoo.com) and Has Elusive 'Phoenix Ghost' Loitering Munition Broken Cover At Last? (forbes.com).

21. This is from Rob Lee's twitter account (@RALee85) based upon photos posted on 12 March 2022.

22. For example, Richard W. Harrison, *The Russian Way of War* (University Press of Kansas, Lawrence, KS, 2001) and David M. Glantz, *The Military Strategy of the Soviet Union: A History* (Frank Cass, Abingdon, UK, 1992).

23. See Christopher A. Lawrence, *The Battle of Prokhorovka* (Stackpole Books, Mechanicsburg, PA, 2019) and Christopher A. Lawrence, *Kursk: The Battle of Prokhorovka* (Aberdeen Books, Sheridan, CO, 2015). Also see Christopher A. Lawrence, *Aces at Kursk: The Battle for Aerial Supremacy on the Eastern Front, 1943* (Pen & Sword Books, Barnsley, UK, 2023) and Lawrence, *War by Numbers*. All these books discuss Russian combat effectiveness in 1943.

24. As noted by Dr Richard Harrison in an email dated 21 December 2022 after reviewing this write-up:

    This mania for attacking everywhere was displayed at all levels (tactical, operational and strategic) during the war [Second World War] and needlessly caused the Red Army enormous casualties.

    As to your other points, I've always considered the lack of a real NCO corps to be a major drag on the army's performance. I recall many instances of dealing with the Russian military when a minor assignment was fobbed off to a mid-level officer instead of a sergeant, as would have been the case in the U.S. Army.

    I still lay the blame on the Russians committing too few men to conquer a country of some 40 million, even if several million of those are sympathetic. This represents a colossal failure of intelligence on the Russians' part, which is all the more incredible as I'm sure the Ukrainian military was/is riddled with spies who could have reported on the Ukrainians' improvement since 2014.

25. For the DPR this includes 780 lost by the DPR by the end of March, less 4 that were clearly killed before 24 February 2022 and 212 reported killed from 1–7 April 2022.

26. In their update of 24 March 2023 they listed 13,019 deaths by date out of 18,024 deaths total. See Russia's losses in the war with Ukraine. Summary of "Mediazona" and BBC/Mediazona Figures Over Time | Mystics & Statistics (dupuyinstitute.org). This listing is regularly updated. The count here is as of 11 April 2023.

27. The wounded-to-killed ratio through the end of March was 4.55-to-1.

28. Zebrodskyi, Watling, Danylyuk and Reynolds, *Preliminary Lessons in Conventional Warfighting from Russia's Invasion of Ukraine*, p. 35.

29. Possibly a number of people will take exception to this low estimate of Russian killed. There are basically four reports of Russian losses: 1. The Russian Defense Ministry report on 25 March of 1,351 dead, 2. The First Guards Tank losses up to 15 March of 61 KIA, 3. The BBC News name count database of Russians reported killed (557 killed as of 21 March) and 4. The later BBC/Mediazona accounting (which is discussed in the text). All of these point to lower losses than many other estimates. Unfortunately, these higher estimates are not founded upon any clearly identifiable data. They may be more correct, but there is not a strong basis for accepting them as such.

30. See twitter account @RALee85 for 16 May 2022. Also see the Facebook account for the General Staff of Ukraine, which posted the six pages of the documents that were captured. The casualties are listed by name.

Chapter 22
1. See Christopher A. Lawrence, "At this point, it looks like Ukraine has been saved," *Mystics & Statistics*, dated 13 April 2022 at At this point, it looks like Ukraine has been saved | Mystics & Statistics (dupuyinstitute.org).
2. This sentence was revised slightly from the original blog post so as to read better.

Appendix I
1. There was no report for this week, but the cumulative figures in the subsequent weeks provide the figures for this week.
2. The total given in their cumulative report is 3,609. It is not clear where the one extra wounded person occurred.
3. No report for this week, but the cumulative totals indicate that unaccounted for losses were 19 killed and 195 wounded.
4. This is only a six-day period, so divided by six to get the daily total.
5. There was no report for this week. The cumulative totals for 20 October 2022 were given as 3,435 and 14.635. The cumulative totals for 11 February 2022 were given as 3,641 and 15,353. The totals for this week were calculated by subtracting the losses of 28 October–2 November 2022 from the differences between these cumulative totals.
6. This is only a six-day period.
7. This is for an eight-day period.

Appendix II
1. Sasho Todorov helped with editing this book and contributed with some of the research. During that process, he provided this write-up and the write-up in Appendix III, which were useful enough as is to include as appendices.
2. https://ukr.warspotting.net/.
3. https://geoconfirmed.azurewebsites.net/.
4. https://russian-torturers.com/en/.
5. Mykhaylo Zabrodskyi, Dr Jack Watling, Oleksandr V. Danylyuk and Nick Reynolds, *Preliminary Lessons in Conventional Warfighting from Russia's Invasion of Ukraine: February–July 2022*, Royal United Services Institute, 30 November 2022 at Preliminary Lessons in Conventional Warfighting from Russia's Invasion of Ukraine: February–July 2022 | Royal United Services Institute (rusi.org).
6. An alternate structure is provided by Seth G. Jones, "Lessons in Modern Warfare: Russia's Ill-Fated Invasion of Ukraine" (Center for Strategic & International Studies, Washington DC, June 2022) at 220601_Jones_Russia's_Ill-Fated_Invasion_0.pdf (csis-website-prod. s3.amazonaws.com), p. 2. He postulates that it consisted of four main fronts (to quote):
   • Northern Front: Russian forces pushed toward Kyiv from Belarus, led by units from the Eastern Military District, including the 29th, 35th, and 36th Combined Arms Armies.
   • Northeastern Front: Russian forces moved west toward Kyiv from Russian territory, led by units from the Central Military District, including the 41st Combined and 2nd Guards Combined Arms Armies.
   • Eastern Front: Russian forces pushed toward Kharkiv and out of the Donbas, led by units from the Western Military District, including the 1st Guards Tank Army and 20th and 6th Combined Arms Armies.
   • Southern Front: Russian forces moved from Crimea west toward Odesa, north toward Zaporizhzhia, and east toward Mariupol. They were led by units from the Southern Military District, including the 58th, 49th, and 8th Combined Arms Armies, VDV's 7th Air Assault Division, and VDV's 11th Air Assault Brigade.

The differences between these two listings are:

1. EMD is referred to as the Northern Front. It also includes 29th CAA.

2. CMD is referred to as the Northeastern Front.

3. WMD is referred to as the Eastern Front.

4. SMD is referred to as the Southern Front. The 11th Air Assault Brigade was made a guards unit in 2015.

7. These brigades are identified from north to south: 81st Air Assault, 79th Air Assault, 53rd Mechanized, 24th Mechanized, 57th Motorized, 95th Air Assault, 25th Air Assault, 30th Mechanized, 54th Mechanized, 56th Motorized and 36th Marine (plus the Azov Regiment).

Select Bibliography

Books

Carhart, Tom, West Point Warriors: Profiles of Duty, Honor, and Country in Battle (Warner Books, New York, 2002).

Dupuy, Colonel T.N., *Attrition: Forecasting Battle Casualties and Equipment Losses in Modern War* (NOVA Publications, Falls Church, VA, 1995).

Dupuy, Colonel T.N., *Numbers, Predictions and War: The Use of History to Evaluate and Predict the Outcome of Armed Conflict* (HERO Books, Fairfax, VA, 1985, originally published 1977).

Dupuy, Colonel T.N., *Understanding War: History and Theory of Combat* (Paragon House Publishers, New York, 1987).

Dupuy, Trevor N., Curt Johnson, Grace P. Hayes, *Dictionary of Military Terms: A Guide to the Language of Warfare and Military Institutions* (The H.W. Wilson Company, New York, 1986).

Glantz, David M., *The Military Strategy of the Soviet Union: A History* (Frank Cass, Abingdon, UK, 1992).

Harrison, Richard W., *The Russian Way of War* (University Press of Kansas, Lawrence, KS, 2001).

Lawrence, Christopher A., *Aces at Kursk: The Battle for Aerial Supremacy on the Eastern Front, 1943* (Pen & Sword Books, Barnsley, UK, 2023).

Lawrence, Christopher A., *War by Numbers: Understanding Conventional Combat* (Potomac Books, Lincoln, NE, 2017).

Lawrence, Christopher A., *The Battle of Prokhorovka* (Stackpole Books, Mechanicsburg, PA, 2019).

Lawrence, Christopher A., *America's Modern Wars: Understanding Iraq, Afghanistan and Vietnam* (Casemate Publishers, Philadelphia & Oxford, 2015).

Lawrence, Christopher A., *Kursk: The Battle of Prokhorovka* (Aberdeen Books, Sheridan, CO, 2015).

The Military Balance: The Annual Assessment of Global Military Capabilities and Defence Economics, 2022 (London, UK, February 2022).

Pipes, Richard, *A Concise History of the Russian Revolution* (Vintage Books, New York, 1996).

Volkogonov, Dmitri. *Stalin: Triumph and Tragedy* (Prima Publishing, Rocklin, CA, 1992).

Reports and Field Manuals

ATP 3-21.8, Infantry Platoon and Squad.

Bronk, Justin with Nick Reynolds and Jack Watling, *The Russian Air War and Ukrainian Requirements for Air Defence* (Royal United Service Institute for Defence and Security Studies (RUSI), London, 7 November 2022).

Helmus, Todd C. and Russell W. Glenn, *Steeling the Mind: Combat Stress Reactions and Their Implications for Urban Warfare* (RAND, 2005).

Karber, Dr Phillip A., "'Lessons Learned' from the Russo-Ukrainian War: Personal Observations, The Potomac Foundation, 8 July 2015 at RUS-UKR LESSONS for edit" (wordpress.com).

Measuring the Effects of Combat in Cities, Phase I (The Dupuy Institute, McLean, VA, January 2002) at TDI – The Dupuy Institute Publications.

Measuring the Effects of Combat in Cities, Phase II (The Dupuy Institute, McLean, VA, June 2003) at TDI – The Dupuy Institute Publications.

Measuring the Effects of Combat in Cities, Phase III (The Dupuy Institute, Annandale, VA, July 2004) at TDI – The Dupuy Institute Publications.

Measuring the Value of Situational Awareness (The Dupuy Institute, Annadale, VA, May 2004) at TDI – The Dupuy Institute Publications.

Field Manual No. 3-0 (FM 3-0), *Operations* (Headquarters, Department of the Army, Washington DC, 1 October 2022).

Russia's War in Ukraine: Military and Intelligence Aspects (Congressional Research Service, Washington DC, 4 September 2022).

Russia's 2022 Invasion of Ukraine: Related CRS Products (Congressional Research Service, Washington DC, 26 October 2022).

The Sustainability of the Soviet Army in Battle (Royal Military Academy, Sandhurst, September 1986).

Ukraine: Background, Conflict with Russia, and U.S. Policy (Congressional Research Service, Washington DC, 5 October 2021).

U.S. Security Assistance to Ukraine (Congressional Research Service, Washington DC, 7 December 2022).

Zebrodskyi, Mykhaylo, Jack Watling, Oleksandr V. Danylyuk and Nick Reynolds, *Preliminary Lessons in Conventional Warfighting from Russia's Invasion of Ukraine: February – July 2022* (Royal United Services Institute for Defence and Security Studies (RUSI), London, 2022).

Selected Articles and Websites

Casnova, Ika Koznarska, "Interview: Col. Nicholas Krawciw, newly nominated brigadier general," Ukrainian Weekly, Sunday, 18 December 1983.

Fox, Amos C., "The Donbas in Flames: An Operational Level Analysis of Russia's 2014–2015 Donbas Campaign," *Small War & Insurgencies*, 2022.

Jones, Seth G., "Lessons in Modern Warfare: Russia's Ill-Fated Invasion of Ukraine"(Center for Strategic & International Studies, Washington DC, June 2022) at 220601_Jones_Russia's_Ill-Fated_Invasion_0.pdf (csis-website-prod.s3.amazonaws.com).

Lawrence, Christopher A., "83,000 Russian Troops?," *Mystics & Statistics*, 13 April 2021 at 83,000 Russian Troops? | Mystics & Statistics (dupuyinstitute.org).

Lawrence, Christopher A., "Russian Invasions," *Mystics & Statistics*, 5 December 2021 at Russian Invasions | Mystics & Statistics (dupuyinstitute.org).

Lawrence, Christopher A., "So Is Russia going to actually attack Ukraine?," *Mystics & Statistics*, dated 22 January at So Is Russia going to actually attack Ukraine? | Mystics & Statistics (dupuyinstitute.org).

Lawrence, Christopher A., "The Russo-Ukrainian War of 2022 – part 1," *Mystics & Statistics*, 7 February 2022 at The Russo-Ukrainian War of 2022 – part 1 | Mystics & Statistics (dupuyinstitute.org).

Lawrence, Christopher A., "Some initial observations on the Russian Army Battalion Tactical Group (BTG) concept," *Mystics & Statistics*, 11 April 2022 at Some initial observations on the Russian Army Battalion Tactical Group (BTG) concept | Mystics & Statistics (dupuyinstitute.org). This re-posted a series of twitter posts written by Dr Shawn Woodford.

Lawrence, Christopher A., "What Makes up Combat Power?," *Mystics & Statistics*, 8 December 2017 at What Makes Up Combat Power? | Mystics & Statistics (dupuyinstitute.org).

Lawrence, Christopher A., "The Russo-Ukrainian War of 2022 – Day 6 (ground actions)," *Mystics & Statistics*, 1 March 2002 at The Russo-Ukrainian War of 2022 – Day 6 (ground actions) | Mystics & Statistics (dupuyinstitute.org).

Lawrence, Christopher A., "VVS View of Air Superiority," *Mystics & Statistics*, 16 June 2022 at VVS View of Air Superiority | Mystics & Statistics (dupuyinstitute.org). This posted an article written by William (Chip) Sayers.

Lawrence, Christopher A., "Contested Air Space over Ukraine?," *Mystics & Statistics*, 28 February 2022 at February | 2022 | Mystics & Statistics (dupuyinstitute.org).

Lawrence, Christopher A., "The Russo-Ukrainian War – Day 324," *Mystics & Statistics*, 13 January 2023 at The Russo-Ukrainian War – Day 324 | Mystics & Statistics (dupuyinstitute.org).

Lawrence, Christopher A., "The Russo-Ukrainian War of 2022 – Day 19 (ground actions)," *Mystics & Statistics*, 14 March 2022 at The Russo-Ukrainian War of 2022 – Day 19 (ground actions) | Mystics & Statistics (dupuyinstitute.org).

Lawrence, Christopher A., "Length of Front Line Trace in Ukraine," Mystics & Statistics, 15 November 2022 at Length of Front Line Trace in Ukraine | Mystics & Statistics (dupuyinstitute.org).

Lawrence, Christopher A., "A Second Independent Effort to use the QJM/TNDM to Analyze the War in Ukraine," *Mystics & Statistics*, 26 May 2022 at A Second Independent Effort to use the QJM/TNDM to Analyze the War in Ukraine | Mystics & Statistics (dupuyinstitute. org). This posted an article written by William (Chip) Sayers.

Lawrence, Christopher A., "Casualty Estimates for the Russo-Ukrainian War," *Mystics & Statistics*, 14 December 2022 at Casualty Estimates for the Russo-Ukrainian War | Mystics & Statistics (dupuyinstitute.org).

Lawrence, Christopher A., "How Much is U.S. Intelligence helping Ukraine?" *Mystics & Statistics*, 2 April 2022 at How Much is U.S. Intelligence helping Ukraine? | Mystics & Statistics (dupuyinstitute.org).

Lawrence, Christopher A., "How Much is U.S. Intelligence helping Ukraine? – part 2," *Mystics & Statistics*, 27 April 2022 at How Much is U.S. intelligence helping Ukraine? – part 2 | Mystics & Statistics (dupuyinstitute.org).

Lawrence, Christopher A., "At this point, it looks like Ukraine has been saved," Mystics & Statistics, dated 13 April 2022 at At this point, it looks like Ukraine has been saved | Mystics & Statistics (dupuyinstitute.org).

Mystics & Statistics, A blog on quantitative historical analysis hosted by The Dupuy Institute at Mystics & Statistics | A blog on quantitative historical analysis hosted by The Dupuy Institute.

Rich, Susan, "TDI Profile: Nicholas Krawciw," *International TNDM Newsletter*, Volume 2, Number 4, December 1998.

Warspotting website at Map · WarSpotting – documenting material losses in Russo-Ukrainian War.

Woodford, Dr Shawn, "The Artillery Strike That Spooked the U.S. Army," *Mystics & Statistics* blog, 29 March 2017 at The Russian Artillery Strike That Spooked The U.S. Army | Mystics & Statistics (dupuyinstitute.org).

Woodford, Shawn, "Mass Fires vs. Precision Fires on the Battlefield of Tomorrow," *Mystics & Statistics* blog, 20 July 2016 at Mass Fires vs. Precision Fires on the Battlefield of Tomorrow | Mystics & Statistics (dupuyinstitute.org).

Woodford, Shawn, "What does A2/AD look like?," *Mystics & Statistics* blog, 24 September 2016 at What does A2/AD look like? | Mystics & Statistics (dupuyinstitute.org).

Woodford, Shawn, "Betting on the Future: The Third Offset Strategy," *Mystics & Statistics* blog, 23 September 2016 at Betting On The Future: The Third Offset Strategy | Mystics & Statistics (dupuyinstitute.org).

Woodford, Shawn, "Army and Marine Corps Join Force to Define Multi-Domain Battle Concept," *Mystics & Statistics* blog, 2 February 2017 at Army And Marine Corps Join Forces To Define Multi-Domain Battle Concept | Mystics & Statistics (dupuyinstitute.org).